STUDIES IN SCRIPTURE IN EARLY JUDAISM AND CHRISTIANITY

Edited by
Craig A. Evans
Volume 23

PUBLISHED UNDER

JEWISH AND CHRISTIAN TEXTS IN
CONTEXTS AND RELATED STUDIES

Executive Editor
James H. Charlesworth

Editorial Board of Advisors
Motti Aviam, Michael Davis, Casey Elledge, Craig Evans, Loren Johns,
Amy-Jill Levine, Lee McDonald, Lidija Novakovic, Gerbern Oegema,
Henry Rietz, Brent Strawn

Volume 36

Gods, Spirits, and Worship in the Greco-Roman World and Early Christianity

Edited by
Craig A. Evans and Adam Z. Wright

t&tclark
LONDON • NEW YORK • OXFORD • NEW DELHI • SYDNEY

T&T CLARK
Bloomsbury Publishing Plc
50 Bedford Square, London, WC1B 3DP, UK
1385 Broadway, New York, NY 10018, USA
29 Earlsfort Terrace, Dublin 2, Ireland

BLOOMSBURY, T&T CLARK and the T&T Clark logo are trademarks
of Bloomsbury Publishing Plc

First published in Great Britain 2022
Paperback edition published 2023

Copyright © Craig A. Evans, Adam Z. Wright, and contributors, 2022

Craig A. Evans and Adam Z. Wright have asserted their right under the Copyright,
Designs and Patents Act, 1988, to be identified as Editors of this work.

All rights reserved. No part of this publication may be reproduced or transmitted
in any form or by any means, electronic or mechanical, including photocopying,
recording, or any information storage or retrieval system, without prior permission
in writing from the publishers.

Bloomsbury Publishing Plc does not have any control over, or responsibility for,
any third-party websites referred to or in this book. All internet addresses given in
this book were correct at the time of going to press. The author and publisher regret any
inconvenience caused if addresses have changed or sites have ceased to exist,
but can accept no responsibility for any such changes.

A catalogue record for this book is available from the British Library.

Library of Congress Cataloging-in-Publication Data
Names: Evans, Craig A, editor. | Wright, Adam Z, editor.
Title: Gods, spirits, and worship in the Greco-Roman world and early Christianity /
edited by Craig A Evans and Adam Z Wright.
Description: London ; New York : T&T Clark, 2022. |
Series: Jewish and Christian texts in contexts and related studies ; volume 23 |
Includes bibliographical references and index. | Summary: "This volume examines
how early Christians interacted with different ideas and traditions
around gods and spirits - both benevolent and malevolent - in the
Greco-Roman world"– Provided by publisher.
Identifiers: LCCN 2021037836 (print) | LCCN 2021037837 (ebook) |
ISBN 9780567703262 (hb) | ISBN 9780567703279 (epdf) |
ISBN 9780567703293 (epub)
Subjects: LCSH: Rome–Religion. | Church history–Primitive and early
church, ca. 30–600. | Christianity and other religions–Roman–History.
Classification: LCC BL803 .G64 2022 (print) |
LCC BL803 (ebook) | DDC 292–dc23
LC record available at https://lccn.loc.gov/2021037836
LC ebook record available at https://lccn.loc.gov/2021037837

ISBN: HB: 978-0-5677-0326-2
PB: 978-0-5677-0330-9
ePDF: 978-0-5677-0327-9
ePUB: 978-0-5677-0329-3

Series: Jewish and Christian Texts in Contexts and Related Studies (Volume 36),
Studies in Scripture in Early Judaism and Christianity (Volume 23)

Typeset by Newgen KnowledgeWorks Pvt. Ltd., Chennai, India

To find out more about our authors and books visit www.bloomsbury.com
and sign up for our newsletters.

For Professor Hans Dieter Betz on the occasion of his ninetieth birthday

Contents

List of Illustrations ix
Preface x
List of Abbreviations xiii

1 The Temple of Isis in the Campus Martius in Rome: Place, Space, and
   Identity in the Ancient Mediterranean World   1
   Frederick E. Brenk
2 The Myth of the Diasporic Isiac-Family as Reflected in the Epigraphical
   Evidence Connected to the Delian Sarapeia   23
   Elina Lapinoja-Pitkänen
3 Jesus, the Daimons, and the Dead   39
   Peter G. Bolt
4 Jesus and the Archetypes: A Study of the Heroic Archetype   61
   Adam Z. Wright
5 Fiery Twins: James, John, and the Sons of Zeus   73
   Jeff Pettis
6 Romulus, Roman Omens, and the Portents of the Birth and Passion of Jesus   83
   Craig A. Evans
7 Learning Rhetoric at Tarsus: The Apostle Paul and His Use of
   Aristotelian Rhetoric   123
   Alexa Wallace and Adam Z. Wright
8 Early Christian "Binding Spells"? The Formulas in 1 Cor. 12:3 Read
   against the Background of Ancient Curse Tablets   135
   Susanne Luther
9 Paul as the Originator of Women Teachers within Religious Circles   149
   Chris S. Stevens
10 The Secret of the Hidden Cross: The Form, Meaning, and Background of
   the Hellenistic Hymn Quoted in 1 Tim. 3:16   165
   Roy D. Kotansky
11 "Out with the Christians … Out with the Epicureans!" Atheism and
   Constructing the Other in Antiquity   201
   Richard A. Wright

12	Jinn and the Myth of the Shepherd *Jonathan Poletti*	217

List of Contributors 231
Index of Modern Names 233
Index of References 240

Illustrations

Figures

1.1	The Isaeum Compense by Jean Claude Golvin	2
1.2	Obelisk of Domitian in the Piazza Navona	3
1.3	Ariccia Relief, National Archaeological Museum, Rome	7
1.4	Nile Mosaic, Palestrina	9
1.5	*Isis Receives Io*, wall painting, National Archaeological Museum, Naples	11
1.6	Isiac water ceremony	14
1.7	Coin of Vespasian depicting Iseum Campense	15

Tables

2.1	The Inscriptions Mentioning the Isiac-Family or Voluntary Associations in Sarapeion A	27
2.2	The Inscriptions Mentioning the Isiac-Family or Voluntary Associations in Sarapeion B	28
2.3	The Inscriptions Mentioning the Voluntary Associations in Sarapeion C	30

Preface

The editors of *Gods, Spirits, and Worship in the Greco-Roman World and Early Christianity* are grateful to the contributors to this volume, the twenty-third in the series Studies in Scripture in Early Judaism and Christianity (SSEJC). The series was founded in the late 1980s in conjunction with a Society of Biblical Literature (SBL) program unit of the same name. We regret to note the recent passing of series co-founder James A. Sanders (1927–2020), whose keen interest in and influential contributions to the field of intertextuality, inner-biblical exegesis, and canon formation were the inspiration for the founding of both the SBL program unit and the series, of which the present collection of studies is a part. Professor Sanders, who was also founder and for many years president of the Ancient Biblical Manuscript Center in Claremont, was a highly regarded scholar of Bible and Judaica. His absence is keenly felt.

The SSEJC series is not freestanding but is published in T&T Clark's well-established biblical studies series, including the Library of New Testament Studies (LNTS), the Library of Second Temple Studies (LSTS), and the Jewish and Christian Texts (JCT). The editors are grateful to Professor James H. Charlesworth for accepting the present collection of studies in the JCT series.

The original and continuing goal of the SSEJC series is to assemble innovative studies that focus on the way Jews and Christians in late antiquity appropriated, interpreted, and presented afresh the sacred tradition of the past. As might be expected, many of the SSEJC volumes have explored the ways in which New Testament writers made use of Israel's scriptures, either specific passages or themes. But some of the volumes have also treated how Hebrew Scripture was interpreted, translated, and paraphrased in pre-Christian and non-Christian settings. Moreover, a few have focused on the physical properties and realia of the ancient texts themselves.

The present volume widens the scope of the SSEJC series by including studies that investigate non-Jewish and non-Christian sacred traditions and how these traditions bear witness to similar Jewish and Christian tendencies to appropriate and reinterpret their own sacred writings and stories. What we find is that the appropriation and reinterpretation of sacred tradition—both in written forms and in visual forms—among non-Jewish and non-Christian Greeks and Romans were similar to those activities among Jews and Christians and probably influenced how Jews and Christians understood their respective sacred traditions. We provide a few paragraphs of introduction to the studies that make up our collection.

In his fascinating and learned study Frederick Brenk examines in what ways the Isis temple in the Campus Martius in Rome served as a model and center of Isiac religion, thus promoting religious unity in the Roman Empire. Elina Lapinoja-Pitänen's study of the myth of the diasporic Isiac-family complements Brenk's study. She investigates the inscriptions mentioning the voluntary sanctuary associations devoted to the Isiac-family on Delos. She finds that these sanctuaries attracted followers from different nationalities, which made it possible to finance and build the Sarapeia. Along the way Lapinoja-Pitänen notes how some of the inscriptions offer reflections on the traditional myth of the Isiac-family, probably in an effort to make its theology more relevant and inviting for ethnicities whose respective histories did not originally include the myth of the Isiac-family.

Peter Bolt explores how the ancients, including Jesus of Nazareth and his followers, understood δαίμονες (transliterated as either "daimons" or "demons"), including their origin and activities. His fascinating and thoroughly researched study shows that most people in late antiquity, including Jews and Christians, believed that daimons were the spirits of the dead and the same as ghosts. Whereas most Jews and Christians viewed daimons as malevolent beings, non-Jews and non-Christians were open to seeing them as evil, neutral, or even positive. Adam Wright looks at the New Testament portraits of Jesus in the Greco-Roman context of ideas about heroes, or more specifically the "heroic archetype," especially with regard to the way the hero faces death and overcomes fear. He focuses on the mythological stories of Perseus, Herakles, and Theseus. Wright also observes a number of interesting correlations with *imitatio* and attempts to update tradition. Jeff Pettis explores how the twinned figures of James and John, the well-known "sons of thunder" who on one occasion, according to Synoptic tradition, threaten to call fire down from heaven, may have been viewed against a Greco-Roman religious and mythic backdrop, especially with reference to Castor and Pollux, the "sons of Zeus" or Dioscuri, as well as the backdrop of Old Testament figures such as Elijah.

Craig Evans inquires into the Roman beliefs about omens and portents, especially in reference to Romulus, legendary founder of Rome, as well as to the emperors, and how the omens and portents depicted with reference to the birth and passion of Jesus would likely have been understood by Christian and non-Christian readers alike. Alexa Wallace and Adam Wright explore what knowledge of Aristotelian rhetoric the Apostle Paul may have had, especially in light of his upbringing in the city of Tarsus. They suggest that Paul may have studied rhetoric after his conversion and after his debates with "certain Hellenistic Jews" (Acts 9:29). They further conclude that Paul may have showcased his rhetorical skills by subverting aspects of rhetoric, a strategy that was part of Aristotelian rhetoric.

Susanne Luther investigates the ways in which Paul's statement in 1 Cor. 12:3 ("no one speaking by the Spirit of God ever says 'Jesus be cursed!' and no one can say 'Jesus is Lord' except by the Holy Spirit") may have been understood against the background of late antique binding spells and curse tablets. She finds ambivalence in Paul's view of these practices, where on the one hand Paul distances himself from them and yet on occasion uses their language.

Two chapters focus on the Pastoral Epistles. Chris Stevens explores in what ways Paul promoted (or held back?) women in teaching roles. He examines Tit. 2:3-5, which he regards as understudied, and reviews some of the leading cults centered on female deities or cults, whose memberships were mostly female, such as that associated with Dionysus, as well as interesting figures such as Hypatia. He also reviews the limited roles of women in Second Temple Judaism. In light of this backdrop Stevens concludes that far from holding women back, which was all too common in late antique societies, Paul was a "radical originator of women teaching within the religious community." In the next chapter Roy Kotansky investigates the background of the Hellenistic hymn that lies behind 1 Tim. 3:16. After drawing our attention to a number of relevant artifacts and suggesting a new way to understand a difficult phrase in the verse, Kotansky concludes that this hymn is composed in such a way that it creates a visual structure whose purpose is to disguise the message of the cross, yet allow its message to be understood when recited and sung aloud.

Richard Wright explores the topic of atheism and the "other" in late antiquity. For his point of departure he appeals to Lucian of Samosata's critical biography of Alexander the charlatan and what that might tell us about how the educated in the second century might apply the labels "superstition" and "atheist." The former was used against the unlearned, the latter against intellectuals. Accordingly, Wright concludes that Christian apologists claim that pagans call them atheists (though there are no pagan texts in which this accusation is made), because this places Christians in the company of Epicureans and other philosophers and intellectuals who are labeled atheists.

Our last chapter is by Jonathan Poletti, and in some ways it is the most interesting study in this volume. Poletti exposes several myths and dubious claims that revolve around the discovery of the Dead Sea Scrolls shortly after the Second World War. What makes his chapter relevant for the present collection is the role played by superstition, including fear of jinn (evil spirits), beliefs that in the Middle East reach back to ancient times. Poletti hopes to clear up some of the confusion. Along the way he shows that modern Western scholars were just as capable of inventing fiction and legend as were the Bedouin. Readers will find especially interesting what Poletti reveals concerning the Ta'amireh tribe and the question of literacy. We suspect that many readers will be struck by how much these dubious legends resemble the tales told about the discovery of the Nag Hammadi codices in Egypt at about the same time. Perhaps the lesson we should learn is modern bias and unwarranted assumptions are not much different from those in late antiquity.

We dedicate this collection of studies to Professor Hans Dieter Betz, longtime Professor of New Testament at Claremont and Chicago, whose interest in and contributions to the Hellenistic setting of early Christianity and its sacred literature are well known. Some of the contributors to this volume had the good fortune to study with Professor Betz; all have benefited from his work. We wish him well on the occasion of his ninetieth birthday.

Abbreviations

AASOR	*The Annual of the American Schools of Oriental Research*
AB	Anchor Bible (Commentary)
ABRL	Anchor Bible Reference Library
AGJU	Arbeiten zur Geschichte des antiken Judentums und des Urchristentums
AGRW	*Associations in the Greco-Roman World: A Sourcebook*
AM	*Mitteilungen. Des Deutschen Archäologischen Instituts Athenische Abteilung*
AnBib	Analecta Biblica
ANET	J. B. Pritchard, *Ancient Near Eastern Texts Relating to the Old Testament*
ANF	*Ante-Nicene Fathers*
ANRW	*Aufstieg und Niedergang der römischen Welt*
Arch	*Archaeology*
ARW	*Archiv für Religionswissenschaft*
AthR	*Anglican Theological Review*
BA	*The Biblical Archaeologist*
BAR	*Biblical Archaeology Review*
BBR	*Bulletin for Biblical Research*
BDAG	Greek-English Lexicon of the New Testament
BECNT	Baker Exegetical Commentary on the New Testament
Bib	*Biblica*
BibInt	Biblical Interpretation Series
BIFAO	*Bulletin de l'Institut français d'archéologie orientale*
BNTC	Black's New Testament Commentaries
BR	*Biblical Research*
BRLJ	Brill Reference Library of Judaism
BTB	*Biblical Theology Bulletin*
BZNW	Beihefte zur Zeitschrift für die neutestamentliche Wissenschaft
CBQ	*Catholic Biblical Quarterly*
CeMIS	Centre for Migration and Intercultural Studies
CJ	*The Classical Journal*
DJD	Discoveries in the Judaean Desert
DSD	*Dead Sea Discoveries*
Ébib	Études Bibliques
EKKNT	Evangelisch-katholischer Kommentar zum Neuen Testament
EPRO	Études préliminaires aux religions orientales dans l'empire romain
EvQ	*Evangelical Quarterly*

FRLANT	Forschungen zur Religion und Literatur des Alten und Neuen Testaments
GMA	Roy Kotansky, *Greek Magical Amulets* (1993)
GMPT	Hans Dieter Betz (ed.), *Greek Magical Papyri in Translation* (Chicago: University of Chicago Press, 1992)
GR	*Greece and Rome*
GRBM	Greek, Roman, and Byzantine Monographs
GRBS	*Greek, Roman, and Byzantine Studies*
HFM	Historisk-filosofiske meddelelser
HNT	Handbuch zum Neuen Testament
HR	*History of Religions*
HSCP	*Harvard Studies in Classical Philology*
HTR	*Harvard Theological Review*
IBAES	Internet-Beiträge zur Ägyptologie und Sudanarchäologie
ICC	International Critical Commentary
IG XI, 4	Pierre Roussel (ed.), *Inscriptiones Deli liberae. Decreta, foedera, catalogi, dedicationes, varia* (Berlin: Georg Reimer, 1914)
IPergamon	M. Fränkel (ed.), *Die Inschriften von Pergamon*, 2 vols. (Berlin: W. Spemann, 1890–95): I. *Bis zum Ende der Königzeit* (1890); II. *Römische Zeit* (1895)
ISBE	G. W. Bromiley (ed.), *International Standard Bible Encyclopedia* (Grand Rapids: WM B. Eerdmans, 1988)
JAAR	*Journal of the American Academy of Religion*
JAOS	*Journal of the American Oriental Society*
JARCE	*Journal of the American Research Center in Egypt*
JBL	*Journal of Biblical Literature*
JCSCS	*Journal of the Canadian Society for Coptic Studies*
JCT	Jewish and Christian Texts
JETS	*Journal of the Evangelical Theological Society*
JGRChJ	*Journal of Greco-Roman Christianity and Judaism*
JNES	*Journal of Near Eastern Studies*
JQS	*Journal of Qur'anic Studies*
JRS	*Journal of Roman Studies*
JSNT	*Journal for the Study of the New Testament*
JSNTSup	Journal for the Study of the New Testament Supplements
JSOT	*Journal for the Study of the Old Testament*
JstAI	*Jerusalem Studies in Arabic and Islam*
KEK	Kritisch-exegetischer Kommentar über das Neue Testament
LCL	Loeb Classical Library
LNTS	Library of New Testament Studies
LSJ	Liddell, Scott, Jones, *A Greek-English Lexicon*
LSTS	Library of Second Temple Studies
NA^{28}	Nestle-Aland, *Novum Testamentum Graece* (28th ed.)
NHC	Nag Hammadi Codex
NHS	Nag Hammadi Studies
NIGTC	New International Greek Testament Commentary

NovT	*Novum Testamentum*
NovTSup	Novum Testamentum Supplements
NPNF²	*Nicene and Post-Nicene*, Series 2
NTAbh	Neutestamentliche Abhandlungen
NTS	*New Testament Studies*
OCP	*Orientalia Christiana Periodica*
OGIS	W. Dittenberger (ed.), *Orientis Graeci Inscriptiones Selectae* (Hildesheim: Georg Olms, 1986)
OrChrAn	*Orientalia Christiana Analecta*
PAPhs	*Proceedings of the American Philosophical Society*
PAST	Pauline Studies
PDM	Hans Dieter Betz (ed.), *Papyri Demoticae Magicae* (Chicago: The University of Chicago Press, 1992)
PEQ	*Palestine Exploration Quarterly*
PGM	K. Preisendanz and A. Henrichs (eds.), *Papyrae Graecae Magicae* (Munich: K. G. Saur, 2001)
RAC	T. Klauser et al. (eds.), *Reallexikon für Antike und Christentum* (Stuttgart: Anton Hiersemann, 1950)
RB	*Revue biblique*
REA	*Revue des études anciennes*
RevQ	*Revue de Qumrân*
RGRW	Religions in the Graeco-Roman World
RICIS	Recueil des Inscriptions concernant les Cultes Isiaques
RömMitt	*Römische Mitteilungen*
RSV	Revised Standard Version (of the Bible)
SBL	Society of Biblical Literature
SBLDS	Society of Biblical Literature Dissertation Series
SBLSP	Society of Biblical Literature Seminar Papers
SCHNT	Studia ad Corpus Hellenisticum Novi Testamenti
SEG	*Supplementum epigraphicum graecum*
SIG	W. Dittenberger (ed.), *Sylloge Inscriptionum Graecarum* (Hildesheim: Georg Olms, 1982)
SNTSMS	Society for New Testament Studies Monograph Series
SSEJC	Studies in Scripture in Early Judaism and Christianity
STDJ	Studies on the Texts of the Desert of Judah
SwJT	*Southwestern Journal of Theology*
TAPA	*Transactions of the American Philological Association*
TDNT	*Theological Dictionary of the New Testament*
THKNT	Theologischer Handkommentar zum Neuen Testament
TynBul	*Tyndale Bulletin*
VC	*Vigiliae Christianae*
VTP	Veteris Testamenti Pseudepigrapha
WBC	Word Biblical Commentary
WJA	*Würzburger Jahrbücher für die Altertumswissenschaft*
WUNT	Wissenschaftliche Untersuchungen zum Neuen Testament

ZAL	*Zeitschrift für arabische Linguistik*
ZNW	*Zeitschrift für die neutestamentliche Wissenschaft*
ZPE	*Zeitschrift für Papyrologie und Epigraphik*

1

The Temple of Isis in the Campus Martius in Rome: Place, Space, and Identity in the Ancient Mediterranean World

Frederick E. Brenk

The Temple of Isis in the Campus Martius in Rome (the Iseum Campense) raises important questions of place, space, and identity, including the place, space, and identity in Rome, in regard to Egypt and to the other Isis and Serapis shrines in the Roman world (see Figure 1.1).[1]

The temple reached out in several directions from its position in the center of Rome and in the center of the Roman Empire. Important was its relationship with Egypt, which was primarily not with contemporary Egypt but the very ancient Egypt of the pharaohs and, to a much lesser extent, Hellenistic and Roman Egypt. Another direction was its relationship with all the Isis and Serapis shrines in the Greco-Roman world with which there was a kind of spiritual rather than hierarchical communion. It thus had a very complicated identity.[2]

On the Roman side, the space of the temple, in the very center of the city, was immense, indicative of its promotion by different Imperial dynasties.[3] Katja Lembke, in her comments many years after the publication of her magisterial book on the temple, has noted how extraordinary it was.[4] Although located in the center of Rome and

---

[1] A very important meeting on the Iseum Campense in Rome took place five years ago, now published as M. J. Versluys, K. Bülow Clausen, and G. Capriotti Vittozzi, eds., *The Iseum Campense from the Roman Empire to the Modern Age: Temple—Monument*—Lieu de Mémoire, Papers of the Royal Netherlands Institute in Rome 66 (Rome: Royal Netherlands Institute and Quasar, 2018). V. Gasparini and R. Veymiers, eds., *Individuals and Materials in the Greco-Roman Cults of Isis: Agents, Images, and Practices*, RGRW 187, 2 vols. (Leiden: Brill, 2018), offers a general treatment of the Isis cult.

[2] For comments and a good, recent bibliography, see C. E. Barrett, "Egypt in Roman Visual and Material Culture," in G. Williams (ed.), *Oxford Handbooks Online* (2017), doi:10.1093/oxfordhb/9780199935390.013.18. Reconstructions of the Iseum can be found in Versluys et al., *The Isaeum Campense*, 10, and better, 80, figure 1.

[3] See S. Takács, "Cleopatra, Isis, and the Formation of Augustan Rome," in M. M. Miles (ed.), *Cleopatra: A Sphinx Revisited* (Berkeley: University of California Press, 2011), 78–95; E. Moorman, "Domitian's Remake of Augustan Rome and the Iseum Campense," in Versluys et al., *The Isaeum Campense*, 161–78; and S. Pfeiffer, "Domitian's Iseum Campense in Context," in Versluys et al., *The Isaeum Campense*, 179–94.

[4] K. Lembke, *Das Iseum Campense in Rom: Studie über den Isiskult unter Domitian*, Archäologie und Geschichte 3 (Heidelberg: Verlag Archäologie und Geschichte, 1994), 29. For her revisiting the

Figure 1.1 The Isaeum Compense by Jean Claude Golvin. Aquarelle de Jean-Claude Golvin. Musée départemental Arles Antique © Jean-Claude Golvin / Éditions Errance.

representing a foreign cult, it was of monumental size, with outstanding Egyptianizing architecture and a sculptural program which in her view was more Egyptian than Roman. One might have to qualify that statement. If one compares it with, for instance, the Temple of Isis at Philae, it really does not look at all very Egyptian, except for the obelisks it contained, of which there seem to have been several.[5] It was, in architectural jargon, "heterotopic," that is, reminiscent of other places, remaining Egyptian in many ways.[6] One can think of it as in some ways like the Obelisk of Domitian in the Piazza

issues involved, see "The Iseum Campense and Its Social, Religious and Political Impact," in Versluys et al., *The Isaeum Campense*, 29–40.

[5] See Lembke, *Das Iseum Campense*, 202–14, for the obelisks attributed to the Iseum. For Egyptian temples, see M. Minas-Nerpel, "Egyptian Temples," in C. Riggs (ed.), *The Oxford Handbook of Roman Egypt* (Oxford: Oxford University Press, 2012), 362–85.

[6] In general, for the relationship between Egypt and Rome, see L. Bricault, M. J. Versluys, and P. G. P. Meyboom, eds., *Nile into Tiber: Egypt in the Roman World*, RGRW 159 (Leiden: Brill, 2007). For the combination of Egyptian and Roman ideology, see M. J. Versluys, "Preface: A New Memphis,"

Figure 1.2 Obelisk of Domitian in the Piazza Navona. Courtesy of Ginny Evans.

Navona, which may have been located in the Iseum, combining imperial Roman ideology with an Egyptian structure and excellent hieroglyphs (see Figure 1.2).[7]

The emperors from Augustus to the Flavians somehow saw themselves as being like the ancient pharaohs, whose ideology the obelisk reflects.[8] On the other hand, some

---

in G. Capriotti Vittozzi (ed.), *La terra del Nilo sulle sponde del Tevere* (Rome: Aracne, 2013), 13–17, esp. 16–17, 115–17, 125–7, 142–4, 161–2, 165–7, and *passim* on Roman and Egyptian as somewhat indistinguishable; and M. Swetnam Burland, *Egypt in Italy: Visions of Egypt in Roman Imperial Culture* (Cambridge: Cambridge University Press, 2015), 1–17, for example, on the same subject. Illustrations of most items referred to in this article can be found in Swetnam-Burland, *Egypt in Italy*, and in Gasparini and Veymiers, *Individuals and Materials*.

[7] Lembke, "The Iseum Campense," 32–3, accepts the majority view that the obelisk stood in the center of the shrine, admitting that it cannot be proved.

[8] On this, see G. Capriotti Vittozzi, "The Flavians: Pharaonic Kingship between Egypt and Rome," in L. Bricault and M. J. Versluys (eds.), *Power, Politics, and the Cults of Isis*, RGRW 180 (Leiden: Brill, 2014), 237–59; Swetnam-Burland, *Egypt in Italy*, 65–104; F. G. Naerebout, "Statuary, Monuments, *lieu de mémoire*: The Iseum Campense, Memory and Religious Life," in Versluys et al., *The Isaeum Campense*, 41–60, esp. 50–2; and Moorman, "Domitian's Remake of Augustan Rome," 161–78.

scholars see the Flavians as imitating Augustus rather than influenced by Egypt.[9] One wonders, though, whether Domitian would have erected his obelisk in the Iseum itself and not in a large open piazza, such as Augustus chose for his, which served as the gnomon of his Solarium, the huge sundial forming a piazza south of the Ara Pacis in the Campus Martius.

The attitude toward Egypt was also rather particular. We can learn something from Plutarch's essay *On Isis and Osiris*.[10] Plutarch, arguably the greatest historian of religion of the first and early second centuries, wrote the most important ancient work we have on the cult of Isis. However, he never mentions the Iseum Campense in all his works, though he may have visited Rome three times. Nor in the essay does he mention any Isiac shrine in the Greco-Roman world. Almost all his sources are from the early Hellenistic period and to a large part go back to the Egyptian priest Manethon. In his treatise, Plutarch really tells us nothing about contemporary Isis religion. Apparently, the dedicatee, his friend Klea, a priestess of Isis and head of the cult in Chaironeia, wanted background on Egyptian Isis religion. Her request and his answer are important. He presumes to be telling Klea about real Egyptian religion. In reality, some, but not many, of the aspects of his description have been shaped by Greek influence, such as Isis's wanderings to find the body parts of Osiris, a tale which borrows aspects from the myth of Demeter in the Eleusinian mysteries. In general, his Egyptian world is like that of Herodotus, whom he never mentions in the essay.

The Isiacs in Rome wanted real Egyptian objects, priests who could read Egyptian texts, and, undoubtedly, they believed that they were practicing ancient Egyptian rites for Isis.[11] At the same time their cult appears to our eyes to be very Greco-Roman, as does much of the architecture and sculpture of the Temple. Moreover, Plutarch employs an allegorical interpretation to parts of the Isis myth, which is that of a Middle Platonist, and at one point even that of a Middle Platonist monotheist. Here he alleges that there is only one God and one providence, a God who rules the world through his subsidiary powers (*dynameis hypourgoi*; *On Isis and Osiris* 393E–394C; 378A), a phrase which seems to come right out of the mouth of Philo of Alexandria.[12] Such ideas might have been in the minds of some educated visitors to the temple.

---

[9] For example, Moorman, "Domitian's Remake of Augustan Rome"; and Pfeiffer, "Domitian's Iseaum Campense in Context," 179–94.

[10] Plutarch (c.40 CE–c.120 CE) wrote this long essay toward the end of his life. It is very important for Egyptology, since it is a description of Egyptian religion, especially as related to the cult of Isis and Osiris, and has used good Egyptian sources.

[11] Cf. Apuleius, *Metamorphoses* 11.28–30. See M. Swetnam-Burland, "Egyptian Priests in Roman Italy," in E. S. Gruen (ed.), *Cultural Identity in the Ancient Mediterranean* (Los Angeles: Getty, 2011), 336–52 (esp. 337–48); Gasparini, *Individuals and Materials*; and W. H. Keulen et al., *Apuleius Madaurensis* Metamorphoses, *Book XI: The Isis Book: Text, Introduction and Commentary*, Groningen commentaries on Apuleius (Leiden: Brill, 2015), 379.

[12] See F. E. Brenk, "'Searching for Truth?' Plutarch's *On Isis and Osiris*," in M. Erler and M. Stadler (eds.), *Platonismus und spätägyptische Religion: Plutarch und die Ägyptenrezeption in der römischen Kaiserzeit* (Berlin: University of Würzburg and De Gruyter, 2017), 55–73. See also G. E. Sterling, "When East and West Meet: Eastern Religions and Western Philosophy in Philo of Alexandria and Plutarch of Chaeronea," in G. E. Sterling, S. Pearce, and R. J. Cox (eds.), *The Studia Philonica Annual 28: Studies in Hellenistic Judaism* (Atlanta, GA: SBL, 2016), 137–50, esp. 148–50, on primitive wisdom.

The Rapport with Ancient Egypt and the Wider World

In some respects, the attitude of the Isiacs in the Iseum Campense was like that of Christians. Judging by the Greco-Roman desire to embrace religions which were considered very ancient, one might argue that Christianity would not have spread if it did not also bring with it parts of Judaism and the Old Testament. Christians were not necessarily interested in the Israel and Judaism of their time any more than the average Christian is necessarily interested in contemporary Israel and contemporary Judaism. What they learn through their sacred texts and in their liturgies is the history and Judaism of ancient Israel. Christianity has two main texts, the Old and the New Testaments, and through these they learn about Israel and Judaism, the Judaism which Christ and the Apostles knew. The attitude toward the Old Testament would correspond somewhat to the Isiacs' approach to ancient Egypt and its writings, and toward the New Testament in their perception of ancient Egyptian religion as interpreted in the Hellenistic cult of Isis and Osiris.[13]

Roman authors such as Martial, Statius, and Apuleius give some reflection of activities in the sanctuary.[14] Some visitors were simply tourists, others used the shrine as a kind of *locus amoenus*, a pleasant shady place with plants and the like, much as people today frequent elegant public galleries and palatial gardens. Still others would have simply strolled through the grounds, while many were true Isiacs who had come to worship the divinities represented there, whose shrines were in restricted areas.[15] Those missing seem to be visiting or resident Egyptians treating the temple as a home away from home. It seems to have been a cult imported by Romans, not a cult brought by Egyptians and frequented by them. We learn from Apuleius that there were Egyptian priests in the sanctuary, but he does not speak of Egyptians as such frequenting it, nor do other Roman authors.[16] In the Isis Book of Apuleius's *Metamorphoses* (11.22), at Cenchreae, the southern port of Corinth, the hero Lucius first encounters Isis. Here there is a presumably Egyptian priest, called a scribe (*grammateus*), who can read the sacred texts described (in our terms) as written in hieroglyphic and demotic. The situation here, too, was similar to that in Christianity, where only an infinitesimal percentage of the faithful, and not a much higher percentage of the priests, can read Hebrew or Aramaic, and only a somewhat higher percentage of priests can read Greek. Yet, to a large extent, the original texts are essential to their faith. Unlike modern

---

[13] On the Egyptian cult of Isis, see M. Bommas, "Isis, Osiris, and Serapis," in C. Riggs (ed.), *Oxford Handbook of Roman Egypt* (Oxford: Oxford University Press, 2012), 419–35.

[14] Martial, *Epigrams* 2.14, 8.81, 10.48 (D. R. Shackleton Bailey, *Martial, Epigrams* I–III [Cambridge, MA: Harvard University Press, 1993], 230–1, 368–71); Statius, *Silvae* 3.2.107–16 (D. R. Shackleton Bailey, *Statius Silvae* [Cambridge, MA: Harvard University Press, 2003], 196–9). Martial 2.14 refers to the thrones of the "sorrowful heifer" within the Iseum Campense, which Shackleton Bailey, at 2.14 seems to identify as Io (vol. 1, 145) but (probably correctly) as Isis later on (vol. 3, 360–1). One of the sculptures from the Iseum depicts the Hathor Cow nursing the pharaoh Haremhab (Lembke, *Das Iseum Campense*, no. 18, pl. 36).

[15] Lembke, *Das Iseum Campense*, 30.

[16] Apuleus, *Metamorphoses* (9.27–8), written in the middle of the second century, mentions the initiation into the higher rites of Osiris, the "Highest God"; see Keulen, *Apuleius, The Isis Book* ad. loc.

Christians, moreover, the Isiacs would not have had easy access to Egyptian texts through translations or to commentaries on the original texts.

The temple in Rome also had a relationship to other Isis and Serapis shrines in the Roman Empire. From the designation "*Serapaeum*" on the Forma Urbis (a colossal map of Rome carved on stone in the early third century) and from Apuleius, it is clear that the shrine was not simply of Isis, but also of Osiris.[17] The name offers a contrast with Plutarch and Apuleius, who speak of Osiris rather than of Sarapis, the Greek term, or Serapis, the Roman term for the Hellenistic reinterpretation of the ancient Egyptian god Osiris. Here again we see the tendency of Plutarch and Apuleius to think in terms of ancient Egypt rather than of Hellenistic or Roman forms of the cult. As was Rome itself in the Mediterranean world, the temple occupied a central place for all Isis and Sarapis shrines. From the remains of the Iseum Campense, there is no obvious extant representation of Greco-Roman or Egyptian Isis or Sarapis temples, for example, of Alexandria or the temple at Philae. In the Temple of Isis at Pompeii, there are representations of temples, evidently in Upper Egypt, in the large "triptychs," even if rendered in a Greco-Roman style, and these temples are not especially typical of Isis temples in the Greco-Roman world.[18] Any association between the Iseum Campense and other Greco-Roman shrines apparently was rather loose. There was no central religious authority as depicted for the nascent Christian churches in the Acts of the Apostles 15:22-29, which speaks of orders from "the apostles and presbyters in agreement with the whole church."[19] The priest in Apuleius looks upon the temple in Rome as more developed and important, and with more elevated and important initiations, but there is no evident hierarchical relationship between the Isis temple at Cenchreae, the southern port of Corinth, and that in Rome. After Lucius travels to Rome and frequents the Iseum Campense, he learns that he has been initiated into the mysteries of Isis, but not into those of Osiris (*Metamorphoses* 11.27). Presumably, these, which were a higher form of initiation, did not exist at Cenchreae.

Introducing Modifications

To manipulate the distance between Roman sensibilities and Egyptian religion, the temple made some important modifications.[20] One of them was the limitation of Egyptian gods and subordinating them to Isis. This can be seen in the Ariccia Relief,

---

[17] See, for example, Lembke, *Das Iseum Campense*.
[18] We have nothing like the Madaba map in Lebanon, with representations of other Christian churches. On the paintings, see E. Moorman, "The Temple of Isis at Pompeii," in Bricault et al., *Nile into Tiber*, 137–54, esp. 143–7.
[19] J. A. Fitzmyer, *The Acts of the Apostles: A New Translation with Introduction and Commentary*, AB 31 (New York: Doubleday, 1998), 564–5.
[20] See, for example, Lembke, *Das Isaeum Campense*, 84–103; Swetnam-Burland, "Egyptian Priests in Roman Italy;" E. Mol, "Present in Absence: The Imagination, Reconstruction, and Memory of Egypt and the Iseum Campense in Rome," in Versluys et al., *The Isaeum Campense*, 353–75; and J. Pollini, "Contact Points: The Image and Reception of Egypt and Its Gods in Rome," in J. Spier, T. F. Potts, and S. E. Cole (eds.), *Beyond the Nile: Egypt and the Classical World* (Los Angeles: J. Paul Getty Museum, 2018), 211–17.

Figure 1.3 Ariccia Relief, National Archaeological Museum, Rome, no. 77255. Courtesy of the Ministero per i Beni e le Attività Culturali-Soprintendenza Speciale per i Beni Archeologici di Roma.

dated to the late first century, in which Isis holds far and away the central place (see Figure 1.3).[21]

Isis, depicted as a Greek goddess reading a scroll, sits in a central position in an *aediculum*, a small shrine. On each side of her are two baboons flanking a statue of the dwarf god Bes, all in smaller *aedicula*. The baboon was a manifestation of Toth. The relief is broken on the left side, cutting diagonally through the last baboon on the left side. The complex of scroll and baboons has been interpreted as a representation of Isis as a symbol of writing and learning, associated with the attributes of Toth, the inventor of writing and sacred texts in the Egyptian tradition.[22]

On the right side from the viewer's perspective, we find, apart from the *aedicula* with Isis, Bes, and the baboons, an Apis Bull on a pedestal and what appears to be a small *tholos*, that is, a round temple, with a figure inside which cannot be identified. To the extreme left, we find another narrower and higher *aediculum*, with what probably would be a pharaoh rather than an Antinosiris, that is, Antinous (the beloved of Hadrian combined with Osiris rather than of Hadrian), since the relief apparently belongs to the Flavian period. On the side there is a large pillar, also in the form of a pharaoh or Antinosiris. The importance given to statues rather than live animals is important. Nonetheless, there seem to be live ibises in an apparent water channel running along the base of the relief.[23] That these are live ibises would seem to be confirmed by two

---

[21] See K. Lembke, "Ein Relief von Ariccia und seine Geschichte," *RömMitt* 101 (1994): 97–102; and "The Isaeum Campense," 34, figure 7; M. J. Versluys, "Temple—Monument—*Lieu de Mémoire*: Rethinking the Isaeum Campense," in Versluys et al., *The Isaeum Campense*, 15–28, here 22, thinks the relief may depict an idealized Isiac shrine. It could, however, be a "collage" of elements from the Iseum Campense.

[22] Capriotti Vittozzi, "The Flavians," 251–7, links these elements to Domitian.

[23] Parts of a water channel were found by Lanciani in the northern area of the shrine in 1883. See Lembke, *Das Isaeum Campense*, 239–40, no. 39, pl. 43.3.

paintings of Isiac ceremonies found at Herculaneum, in which live ibises mingle with the worshippers.[24]

In the Ariccia Relief, live birds sit on the tops of the *aedicula*, though these seem to have no particular relationship to Egyptian religion, unlike the ibises.[25] The execution of the statues in the Ariccia Relief seems to be in a Greco-Roman, not an Egyptian or Egyptianizing style, while most pillars and the *tholos* shrine are very much Greco-Roman. The presence of live ibises, however, and carved baboons certainly is not normal for a non-Isiac Greco-Roman sanctuary. It has been noted recently that only Egyptian hard stone sculptures were brought to Rome, and that the dark stones evoked the idea of Egypt, especially Alexandria.[26] Many of these objects must have been purchased and brought to Rome by the imperial administration at great cost. Yet, even the small Temple of Isis at Pompeii had at least one real Egyptian object, a stele with hieroglyphs, even though the text had nothing to do with the Isis religion.[27]

A painting of a priest in the Iseum at Pompeii suggests that small animals such as birds or snakes might have been worshipped in Isis shrines. A series of small vignettes in the portico suggests a procession, but with each officiant set in a hieratic pose before a large stele or wall. They seem to be Greco-Romans, with one or two possible exceptions, one of whom is a priest with a cobra, who could be either Egyptian or Greco-Roman. He has a shaved head and carries a cobra on a cushion.[28] Animal worship was an essential part of the ancient Egyptian religion and, thus, a link between the Iseum Campense and Egypt, but it had to be adapted. Possibly some Greeks and Romans held a theological interpretation of it, such as developed by Plutarch in his *On Isis and Osiris*.[29] Outside the ibises, there is no evidence of live animals in the Iseum Campense. Yet, a very large number of animal sculptures in Rome, many of the highest quality, have been attributed to the Iseum Campense. Some of these, such as lions, were real Egyptian statues taken from temples in Egypt.[30]

---

[24] See V. Tran tam Tinh, *Le culte des divinités orientales à Herculanum*, EPRO 17 (Leiden: Brill, 1971), 29–49, figures 40–41; Swetnam-Burland, *Egypt in Italy*, 12–14, and pl. I; and Moorman, "Ministers of Isiac Cults in Roman Wall Painting," in Gasparini and Veymiers, *Individuals and Materials*, 366–83, here 367–70, 1039, pl. 12.1 and 1040, pl. 12.2; Museo Archeologico Nazionale, Naples, MNN 8924 and 8919.

[25] Lembke, "The Iseum Campense," 33, thinks the relief depicts the central apse of the southern exedra of the shrine, with the baboons and Bes placed in the six niches of the exedra. However, the bull on a pedestal and the tholos-like shrine might be behind the Isis, Bes, and the baboons.

[26] S. W. G. Müskens, *Egypt beyond Representation: Materials and Materiality of Aegyptiaca Romana*, Archaeological Studies (Leiden: Leiden University Press, 2017), 341–64, cited by Lembke, "The Isaeum Campense," 35.

[27] For the paintings in the Temple at Pompeii, see V. Sampaolo, "VIII 7, 28, Tempio di Iside," in I. Baldassare et al. (eds.), *Pompei: pitture e mosaici* VIII. *Regio VIII–Regio IX*, Parte I (Rome: Enciclopedia Italiana, 1998), 732–849.

[28] Ibid., 762, no. 48, MNN 8875.

[29] *The E at Delphi* 393E–394C and *On Isis and Osiris* 378A. See Brenk, "Searching for Truth," 66.

[30] On the statues, esp. Egyptianizing ones, see Swetnam-Burland, *Egypt in Italy*, 18–64.

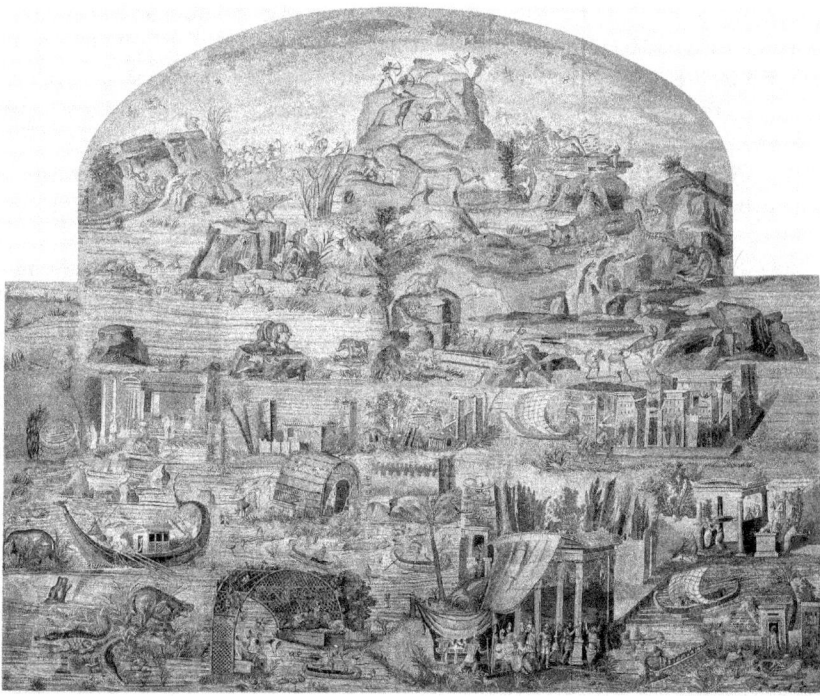

Figure 1.4 Nile Mosaic, Palestrina. Courtesy of the Museo Nazionale Prenestino.

Reconstructing the Painting Program

We can also learn a great deal, though in a hypothetical way, about the relationship of the temple with Egypt and other Isiac shrines in the Mediterranean world from another source. Hardly mentioned, if at all, by scholars is a painting program, which it certainly must have had, even though not a trace remains today. The relationship of the shrine with ancient Egypt and other Isis shrines would be clearer if, as at Pompeii and Herculaneum, some painting had been preserved. The representations in the temple at Pompeii are quite different in different rooms. Yet, most create a strong link with Egypt, and especially Upper Egypt. One can begin, however, at another place, the Sanctuary of Fortuna Primigenia constructed about 120 BCE, at Palestrina, a little over 20 miles from Rome. Here there was a huge Nile floor mosaic, mostly preserved, called the Nile Mosaic of Palestrina and of uncertain date (see Figure 1.4).[31]

As in the frescoes at Pompeii, there is a similar attachment to the Upper Nile region. As the title suggests, the mosaic represents the whole Nile, starting with Upper Egypt and the boundary with Nubia at the top and finishing at the bottom with a scene of Lower Egypt or the Delta. Most of the mosaic seems to be occupied with Upper Egypt.

---

[31] In the past it was dated to *c.* 100 BCE, but Swetnam-Burland argues that the date is uncertain (*Egypt in Italy*, 151 and note 37, and in general 151–4).

The central scene seems to be the Khoiak festival at Philae and Bigeh in Upper Egypt, when an earthen "body" of Osiris, with wheat sprouts, is taken from Philae to the nearby island of Bigeh. In the reconstructed placing of the mosaic pieces, just above a temple are Nubians hunting animals.[32] To the left of a temple, there is a sailboat, suggesting that the temple is on an island in the Nile. Immediately below the temple is a funeral procession with presumably the "body" of Osiris. In Meyboom's interpretation, the Egyptian temple on an island is the temple of Osiris at Canopus in Lower Egypt, but it seems better to identify it as the temple on Philae, near Aswan.[33]

The situation of the Iseum Campense must be reconstructed with difficulty through the Ariccia Relief, coins, and archeological remains found in different places around Rome, while the temple at Pompeii was discovered virtually intact. The paintings in the Iseum at Pompeii link the temple with both Upper and Lower Egypt as in the Palestrina mosaic. The central panels of the triptychs are exclusively on the story of the transformation of Io, who was turned by the goddess Hera into a heifer, then back into human form, while the side panels are exclusively on Upper Egypt. The main central panel of the triptychs is called "Io at Canopus," which features Isis restoring Io to human form (see Figure 1.5).[34]

A fresco in the Sacrarium has a central scene flanked by two river gods, presumably the Upper and Lower Nile, an ancient Egyptian concept of the Nile, but the major emphasis in the paintings as a whole is on Upper Egypt. Probably important for understanding the Iseum Campense is the portrayal of Egyptian scenes, including temples, in a Greco-Roman style.[35] We also find here a more ambiguous presentation of animals than in the remains of the Iseum Campense and the Ariccia Relief but with a similar reduction of the number of Egyptian gods and the dominance of Isis, as expected.[36] The Pompeian frescoes were completed during the time of Nero, though not long before the era of Domitian, to which Lembke would attribute most of the

---

[32] P. G. P. Meyboom, *The Nile Mosaic of Palestrina: Early Evidence of Egyptian Religion in Italy*, RGRW 121 (Leiden: Brill, 1995), pl. 7. See also P. H. Schrijvers, "A Literary View of the Nile Mosaic at Praeneste," in Bricault et al., *Nile into Tiber*, 223–39; M. Swetnam-Burland, "Nilotica and the Image of Egypt," in Riggs, *Oxford Handbook of Roman Egypt*, 684–97, here 685–9; and Swetnam-Burland, *Egypt in Italy*, 150–4, and pl. VIII.

[33] Meyboom, *The Nile Mosaic*, esp. 54–5, pl. 18, and 71–9. He bases his interpretation on tesserae and coins of Canopus, which like that in the mosaic have an eagle over the entrance (55 and pls. 41–2). However, on the coins, Osiris is inside the temple not outside, and the Nile Mosaic temple has four statues in front of it, not necessarily of Osiris (pl. 18). In fact, the front resembles the Temple at Luxor, which today has three of originally four colossal statues remaining in front. A relief on Hadrian's Gate at Philae depicts the tomb of Osiris on the Abaton, with a large falcon standing on the coffin surrounded by sprouting wheat (pl. 84 and appendix 8, 132–5). A relief in the eastern roof chapel of the Temple of Osiris of Hathor at Dendera depicts the boat on a stand with the coffin surmounted by a falcon for the funeral procession of Osiris-Sokaris (appendix 10, pp. 141–3, pl. 84).

[34] Ovid, *Metamorphoses* 1.736–46. Here, however, Juno, not Isis, restores Io, due to Jupiter's pleading. Nowhere is Canopus mentioned, but the transformation takes place upon her first reaching the Nile, and "now" she is worshiped by the Isiacs.

[35] An exception is, in small vignettes, the portrayal of Egyptian temples with something like horned altars at the tip, for example, Sampaolo, "Tempio di Iside," 741, no. 11, MNN 9475; and Swetnam-Burland, *Egypt in Italy*, 147–8, figure 4.3. The Egyptian temple in the Nile Mosaic has four structures, possibly pylons, with this shape (Meyboom, *The Nile Mosaic*, 27 and 30, and pl. 18).

[36] Portrayed are Isis, Osiris, Harpocrates/Horus, Nephthys, Hermanubis, Bes, Apis, and the Nile, and in the portico frescoes, the officiant wears an Anubis mask.

Figure 1.5 *Isis Receives Io*, Pompeii (VIII 7 28, sanctuary of Isis, Ekklesiasterion), wall painting, National Archaeological Museum, Naples, MNN 9558. Bibliography: *Soprintendenza Archeologica per le Province di Napoli e Caserta, Alla ricerca di Iside. Analisi, studi e restauri dell'Iseo Pompeiano nel Museo di Napoli, 1992, cat. 1.6*. Licensed under the Creative Commons Attribution-Share Alike 4.0, International license.

Iseum Campense. Thus, the time between the restoration of the temple at Pompeii after the earthquake in 62 and the completion of the Iseum of Domitian (reigning 81–96) would only have been about thirty years.

The paintings in the temple at Pompeii were very diverse and elaborate, especially in the meeting room called the Ekklesiasterion.[37] Here most of the scenes evidently

---

[37] For the paintings in the shrine, besides Sampaolo, "Tempio di Iside," see S. Adamo Muscettola, "La decorazione architettonicha e l'arredo," in S. De Caro (ed.), *Alla ricerca di Iside: Analisi, studi e restauri dell'Iseo pompeiano nel Museo di Napoli* (Rome: Arti, 1992), 63–76, which includes most of the painting and all the artifacts. See also Swetnam-Burland, *Egypt in Italy*, 105–41.

represent the Dodekaskoinos, a 125-mile stretch of the Nile south of Aswan, and with one exception, depicting island temples impossible to identify.[38] These scenes could pass for being completely Greco-Roman. The quasi-exception is the fresco called *Adoration of the Mummy*, apparently representing funeral rites on the island of Bigeh, or the Abaton ("where one cannot tread").[39] The island was immediately next to Philae and one of the places where Osiris was supposed to be buried. Here annual rites, performed during what is called the Khoiak festival, commemorated his burial. An Egyptian priest makes offerings before a mummiform coffin, under a kind of rectangular arch supported by mummiform pillars. On top of the mummy case is a large, mysterious bird with a lotus crown which could be a hawk or a non-Egyptian rendering of a phoenix.[40] The bird possibly is a manifestation of Osiris. In the background one can see a large round tomb, very much like a Roman monumental tomb. In any case, the representation is of Upper Egypt, especially the rocky part of the Nile around Philae. As such, the frescoes recall some scenes in the Nile Mosaic of Palestrina.

The scenes of the Ekklesiasterion are predominantly of Upper Egypt, since of four triptychs, eight of the side panels would be of Upper Egypt. However, the four central panels concern the myth of Io, who is liberated from her bovine form by Isis.[41] Presumably Isiacs could relate the scene to their own liberation through Isis. The four central panels with the myth of Io certainly link the temple with the Hellenistic and Greco-Roman world and possibly with Lower Egypt. The introduction of Isis into the Io myth would be a Hellenistic invention. Most notably, the son of Isis, who appears in the scene, is Harpocrates, while Hermanubis, a combination of Hermes (Mercury) and Anubis, substitutes for Anubis. Hermes also appears in another of the Io panels with Io, but in his traditional Greek form.

The Temple connects with both Upper and Lower Egypt in a room called the Sacrarium, which seems to present a more direct religious view of the religion. Here Isis is represented in a reed boat, pulling another reed boat, apparently with a box for the dismembered body parts of Osiris. The scene represents the myth behind the Greco-Roman festival called the "Finding of Osiris," possibly represented in the Ariccia Relief. In Plutarch the myth is centered around Byblos in Phoenicia and Lower Egypt.[42] Like the Nile Mosaic and the *Adoration of the Mummy*, this fresco relates to the funeral rites for Osiris. In the mythical underpinning of the ritual, the finding of the body parts of Osiris, and his resuscitation by Isis and Nephthys would be essential. In the myth as recounted by Plutarch, Isis wanders even as far as Byblos to find the remains of Osiris, and the reed boats suggest the Lower rather than the Upper Nile. In any case in the Isiac tradition at Philae, Osiris would end up on the Abaton. A scene entitled "Isis and Osiris Enthroned," most of which is missing, but of which a drawing remains, seems to represent Isis and Osiris as queen and king of the underworld, or in heaven, along

---

[38] Besides the island temple of Philae, there were two other island temples, Kalābsha and Beit (or Bayt) al-Wali, south of Philae, both of which were rescued after the building of the Aswan Dam.
[39] Sampaolo, "Tempio di Iside," 836, no. 205, MNN 8570.
[40] See Meyboom, *The Nile Mosaic*, appendix 8, 132–5, and pl. 82, and appendix 10, 141–3, and pl. 84, for similar Egyptian representations of a falcon over the body of Osiris.
[41] See Swetnam-Burland, *Egypt in Italy*, 127–35.
[42] *On Isis and Osiris* (357A–D). Byblos was possibly a virtual colony of Egypt during the Old Kingdom.

the lines of South Italian vase painting. This scene, too, could be related to the myth of the finding, burial, and resuscitation of Osiris.[43] It opens up another space, that of the other world. Another wall in the Sacrarium connects the temple to Egypt. Here we find representations of sacred animals. They are, however, painted in a rather crude, naturalistic, and non-hieratic manner.[44] This may be important, considering how the Ariccia Relief represents the baboons in shrines, along with Isis and Bes, where they could receive worship.

We can certainly imagine such paintings with their strange mixture of Greco-Roman and Egyptian elements in the Iseum Campense. One set of large paintings might have been commissioned to represent the Nile in Upper and Lower Egypt, another to represent Egyptian gods in their animal manifestations, another to represent parts of the saga of Isis and Osiris, and yet another to represent the divine pair in heavenly bliss awaiting the initiates. Less important, small scenes of the harbor at Alexandria and naval battles possibly were scattered throughout the shrine. Two paintings from Herculaneum also can add some insight into the place, space, and identity of the Iseum Campense in the Mediterranean world, since they link the temple to other Isiac shrines. The panel paintings, which came from a house, do not represent different scenes at the same shrine. In the first, called "The Rite of the Sacred Water," a priest holds a typical vessel used to hold the Nile water in his hands, with a veil covering it, much as today a priest holds a monstrance with the Eucharist (see Figure 1.6).

The priest, however, is not Egyptian, but Greco-Roman, judging by the color of his skin. A priestess stands at his right side. Both stand in front of a temple typical of Greco-Roman Isis temples, with nine or ten steps in front of them. Descending the steps on either side and in front of the temple are a group of Isiacs, possibly thirty in each group. The men seem to be on the left side, from the viewer's perspective, and women on the right, but that is not very clear. In the painting three or four Nubians are represented with bare shoulders, who perhaps could be priests, but are identified by Moorman as assistants. He believes some non-Isiacs are also in the group. Two of the Nubians seem to hold something in their hand. One of them, in front of the steps, holds a rather long rod. It is not clear if the fourth figure, who is offering sacrifice on an altar in the foreground, is Nubian or Greco-Roman, but his dress is like that of the Nubians. Two ibises walk freely in front of the altar, where a man with bare shoulders is offering a sacrifice. This is certainly a Greco-Roman temple, but it is not clear where. The large number of Nubians, ibises walking around freely, and palm trees suggest that the location is in Egypt. To the left and right of the temple are prominent palm trees. However, ibises, possibly a Nubian, and a palm tree appear in the Ariccia Relief.[45]

The second scene, called "The Rite of the Sacred Dance," is more mysterious and more Egyptian looking. The setting is similar, but the temple has only six steps leading up to it, more typical of an Isiac temple. The principal figure is a very large and athletic

---

[43] Plutarch in *On Isis and Osiris* insists that Osiris is in heaven, not in the underworld (382F–384A).
[44] Sampaolo, "Tempio di Iside," 817–18, nos. 178–9, MNN 8533; Swetnam-Burland, *Egypt in Italy*, 109–12, figure 3.4.
[45] Moorman, "Ministers of Isiac Cults in Roman Wall Painting," 367–72, 1034–6, pls. 11.2b, 11.2c, 11.2d; and 1039, pl. 12.1, MNN 8924.

Figure 1.6 Isiac water ceremony. White-robed priests of Isis perform a water ritual as chanting devotees line the steps of the goddess's temple in this wall painting from Herculaneum. Courtesy of Wiki Commons (public domain).

Nubian doing a dance at the top of the steps. A Nubian priest or servant, also at the top of the steps, seems to accompany him with a sistrum. Several other figures also seem to accompany the dance with sistra: a kneeling woman in an ecstatic pose, to the left, and another to the right, dressed as an Isiac priestess. Closer to the temple on the left is a priest or servant with bare shoulders, but it is not clear if he is a Nubian or Greco-Roman; both hold sistra. Another Nubian to the right plays a flute. Scattered around are children and possibly a man in a toga. In the middle foreground is a horned altar, with living ibises walking casually around it.[46] Whether in Egypt or outside, one can imagine similar exotic scenes in the Iseum Campense meant to connect them

---

[46] Ibid., 367–72, 1033, pl. 11.2a, and 1040, pl. 12.2, MNN 8919.

Figure 1.7 Coin of Vespasian depicting Iseum Campense.

with Egypt and with the broader world of Isis temples throughout the Mediterranean world.[47]

Further Linking with a Wider World

Another link between the Iseum Campense and this wider world is the architecture of the small temple believed to have been located at the north end of the sanctuary. Two coins representing two different structures exist. The first belongs to Vespasian and depicts a temple, with a rather exotic half-circle pediment and very prominent animals flanking it, a cobra frieze, and Isis riding the Dog Star within the pediment (see Figure 1.7).

The second coin belongs to Domitian, with a more recognizable Isis temple. The pediment is the normal triangular one. Animals, however, are very prominent, consisting of hawks at the ends of the pediment and a cobra frieze at the very top.[48] Possibly the second temple, built by Domitian after a fire, was meant to be more recognizable as an Isiac temple, making it more familiar to Isiacs from other places and connecting the temple closer to other shrines. Still, the cobra frieze makes it appear more Egyptian than most Isiac temples and links it to the previous temple.

---

[47] On this, see F. Dunand, *Le culte d'Isis dans le basin orientale de la Méditerranée*, 3 vols., EPRO 26 (Leiden: Brill, 1973); L. Bricault, *Atlas de la diffusion des cultes isiaques (IVe s. av. J.-C.–IVe s. apr. J.-C.)*.
Mémoires de l'Académie des Inscriptions et Belles-Lettres, nouvelle sërie 23 (Paris: Académie des Inscriptions et Belles-Lettres and Boccard, 2001); and M. Malaise, "La diffusion des cultes isiaques: Un problème de terminologie et de critique," in Bricault et al., *Nile into Tiber*, 20–39.

[48] See L. Bricault and R. Veymiers, "De l'Isaeum Campense comme type monétaire," in Versluys et al., *The Isaeum Campense*, 129–57, esp. 139, figure 2 and 149, figures 4 and 5; and Lembke, "The Iseum Campense," 29–40, esp. 31, figure 2, and 37, figure 12.

Two further images suggest how the Iseum Campense could have been linked to other Isis temples in the Mediterranean world. One, in the portico of the Temple of Isis at Pompeii, represents a priest or servant with bare shoulders bringing two candelabra before a statue of Harpocrates, if not Harpocrates himself. More important is the background, which shows a very large portico with pillars and in the center of the courtyard a small, rather typical Isis temple with steps in front, decorated as for a festival.[49] The small temple certainly corresponds somewhat with that on the Flavian coins of the Iseum Campense, its position in the shrine would be similar, and the portico might likewise have been similar. Finally, there is a fragment of a beautiful, extremely high-quality mosaic from the ruins of Daphne in Syria, showing an Isis priestess and a female attendant in a luxurious Isis temple.[50]

A difference between the Iseum Campense and the Pompeian temple is that Roman writers seem to connect the first with Memphis rather than with Upper Egypt. Thus, the emphasis might have been on Memphis in Lower Egypt, rather than on any temple in Upper Egypt. In the Isis Temple at Pompeii, there is little to suggest Memphis. The Apis bull, for which Memphis is famous, is represented among the animals in the Sacrarium, and there is a bull with a crown in a "peopled frieze" in the Ekklesiasterion, where it stands out by being the only one wearing a crown. One of the side panels of the triptychs in the Ekklesiasterion represents a bull grazing with cattle in a naturalistic setting on an island in the Nile. In any case, large frescoes might have been commissioned to represent temples in Lower and Upper Egypt, the Nile, Egyptian gods in their animal manifestations, parts of the saga of Isis and Osiris, a celestial scene suggesting the heavenly bliss awaiting the initiates, and the performance of certain rites in distant places. Less importantly, small scenes such as of the harbor at Alexandria or of naval battles might have been scattered throughout the shrine, as in the temple at Pompeii. Surprisingly, in the shrine at Pompeii we see no representations of the pyramids at Giza and the Sphinx, the most recognizable symbols of Egypt in the modern world.

Animal Worship as a Link with Egypt

"Animal worship" was one of the strongest elements linking the Iseum Campense with ancient Egypt, and in some way forming its identity. There can be no question that one of the most distinctive characteristics of Egyptian religion is what non-Egyptians have always called "animal worship." There is no denying that animals played a very large role there. Egypt possibly produced as many as seventy million animal mummies.[51]

---

[49] Sampaolo, "Tempio di Iside," 750–1, no. 41, MNN 8921; R. Veymiers, "Introduction: Agents, Images, Practices," in Gasparini and Veymiers, *Individuals and Materials*, vol. 1, 40–1 and vol. 2, pl. 0.17.

[50] Gasparini and Veymiers, *Individuals and Materials*, 1037, figure 11.3 (Antakaya, Hatay Arkoloji Müzesi, no. 849, region of ancient Daphne); S. A. Takács, "Pagan Cults at Antioch," in C. Kondoleon (ed.), *Antioch: The Lost Ancient City* (Princeton, NJ: Princeton University Press, 2000), 198–216 (200, figure 1).

[51] Consult the *Animal Mummy Database* (http://ancientworldonline.blogspot.com/2012/01/animal-mummy-database.html) and the *Global Egyptian Museum* (http://www.globalegyptianmuseum.org) (both online). C. Moser and J. Wright Knust, "Ritual Matters: An Introduction," in C. Moser

So what were these mummies and worship of the live animals all about? And how, in the case of the Romans, did the Iseum Campense adapt Egyptian animal worship to fit into Roman culture. Early Greek and Roman authors, with few exceptions, are very harsh toward animal worship. For example, though Augustus, when he came to Alexandria, respected Sarapis, he refused to visit the Apis bull at Memphis, because "he was accustomed to worship gods, not cattle" (Cassius Dio 51.16.3–5).[52] According to modern scholars, Greeks and Romans misunderstood Egyptian animal worship, just as people do today. An exception would be Plutarch, who in *On Isis and Osiris* argues that animal worship could be directed toward God and that the Egyptian priests probably had a belief that, if understood correctly, could be justified (*On Isis and Osiris* 382A–B). In his interpretation, animals, which were living beings, were better representations of the divine than inanimate statues: animals, which have the power of perception and feeling, and a soul, are "clearer mirrors of the divine [than statues], as instruments of the God who orders all things." The scholars who treated the problem in a congress on animal worship held in Berlin, which was published in 2013, argue that, strictly speaking, "animal worship" did not exist in Egypt, since the worship is always directed toward the god.[53] But here, like Plutarch in *On Isis and Osiris* (382A–C), we might distinguish between the elite priests with their theological speculation and the common people, who may have believed they were worshipping the animals. Worship of living animals and animal mummification did not seem to have been transferred to Isis sanctuaries in Rome, or if so, it had a very low profile. Judging by the Ariccia Relief and the two paintings from Herculaneum living ibises may have been kept in the Iseum Campense in Rome, but they may not have been "worshipped." No animal mummies seem to have been found in Rome or in Italy. Not living animals but statues of animals seem to be represented in a context of worship.

The evidence for living animal worship among the Romans is rather negative. Animal worship appears in a fresco, which contains two small *pinakes* (small insert paintings in a frame) in the Villa of Agrippa Postumus at Boscotrecase, near Pompeii,

---

and J. Wright Knust (eds.), *Ritual Matters: Material Remains and Ancient Religion*, Supplements to the Memoirs of the American Academy in Rome (Ann Arbor, MI: American Academy in Rome, 2017), 1–10, argue that the material remains always need interpretation: cf. Z. Várhelyi, "Statuary and Ritualization in Imperial Italy," in C. Moser and J. Wright Knust (eds.), *Ritual Matters: Material Remains and Ancient Religion*, Supplements to the Memoirs of the American Academy in Rome (Ann Arbor, MI: American Academy in Rome, 2017), 87–98, here 90.

[52] Cassius Dio, also known as Dio Cassius (155 CE–235 CE), held high Roman political offices. He wrote in Greek a history of Rome in eighty volumes from the mythical arrival of Aeneas in Italy until 229 CE. Most of his work only exists in fragments, but the books covering the period from 65 BCE to 12 BCE are mostly complete.

[53] Published as M. Fitzenreiter and S. Kirchner, eds., *Tierkulte im pharaonischen Ägypten und im Kulturvergleich*, IBAES IV (Berlin: IBAES, 2003). The most important contributions are D. Kessler, "Tierische Missverständnisse: Grundsätzliches zu Fragen des Tierkultes," 33–68, esp. 36–7 and 56–66; F. Feder, "Der ägyptische Tierkult nach den griechischen und römischen Autoren," 159–66; M. Fitzenreiter, "Die ägyptischen Tierkulte und die Religionsgeschichtsschreibung," 229–63; and J. F. Quack, "Die Rolle des heiligen Tieres im Buch vom Tempel," 111–24. Quack notes that Apis is made visible at every major religious celebration but that it is not clear if it is the animal or the statue (115). See also F. E. Brenk, "The Isaeum Campense and Animal Worship: Becoming Egyptian to Be Roman," in Versluys et al., *The Isaeum Campense*, 211–21, which treats Roman worship of animals in the Iseum Campense.

attributed to *c.* 12–11 BCE of the Augustan Age.[54] The one to the left represents worship of the Apis bull and to the right, of Anubis in jackal form. The figures in the left one could be an unidentified god and the crocodile god, Sobek, represented as a hybrid human/animal figure. In the one to the right, the figures seem to be Osiris and Isis worshipping Anubis in jackal form. It is also possible that the figures represent a priest and priestess in the costumes of Osiris and Isis. It is not clear whether the animals are real or statues. They are painted realistically, but the small size of the bull and the platform upon which the jackal stands suggest they are statues rather than real animals.

The animals in the Temple of Isis at Pompeii seem to be "hiding in plain sight." A very large number of animals are represented, at least forty of which might be considered sacred. Evidently the artists knew that for an "Egyptian" sanctuary they had to represent sacred animals, but at the same time they or their patrons apparently were squeamish about representing them too openly, perhaps to avoid offending Roman sensibilities. Several techniques were employed, as we have seen earlier. Some were put in a "peopled frieze," others in a kind of *lararium* setting with serpents. In the peopled frieze they appear with nonsacred or unusual sacred animals such as a horse and a goose, and a dog possibly is meant to represent the jackal Anubis. In the Sacrarium, as we have seen, the group of animals is rendered without crowns in a naturalistic setting. A small panel represents an ichneumenon (mongoose) attacking a cobra. Another technique is to represent them in far-off, exotic scenes, such as a bull on an island, ibises, and a kingfisher in Upper Egypt in the triptychs of the Ekklesiasterion. Ambiguity also comes into play as birds become somewhat unidentifiable. We find matching peacocks in place of a recognizable Egyptian phoenix. In the portico, in small vignettes, magpies and a lioness are perched on a backdrop for priests and priestesses, but the lioness is the size of a cat. In one of these vignettes, an Egyptian-looking priest carries a cobra seated on a cushion with roses. Here the cobra is clearly regarded as sacred, and the Egyptian element seems to be underscored. It might suggest, however, that the cobra was venerated by an Egyptian priest but not necessarily by Romans. A hybrid Anubis appears, but as an Isiac in a toga, wearing a jackal mask, such as described in the Isis Book of Apuleius's *Metamorphoses* (11.11). This figure, and Io in a fresco, the central panel in a triptych called "Io, Hermes, and Argo," and Io in another central panel called "Io at Canopus" are the only suggestions of a hybrid god in the temple. In the case of Io, her heifer form consists only of small horns protruding from her head. It is clear, especially from the "Io at Canopus," and the "Isis and Osiris Enthroned," that the gods in human form stand in a superior position to the animal gods. This is particularly clear from the "Io at Canopus" fresco, where a cobra is wrapped around the arm of Isis and she rests her feet on a relatively small crocodile.

There is an exception to the naturalistic presentation of animals in the Temple of Isis at Pompeii. In one of the triptych scenes, as mentioned earlier, a mysterious bird is perched on a large mummy case and sports a lotus crown.[55] There can be no mistaking, however, that this is in Upper Egypt, that the priest is Egyptian, and that the bird is

---

[54] Swetnam-Burland, *Egypt in Italy*, 53–5 and pl. II.
[55] If this was meant to be a falcon, it corresponds with the falcon above the coffin of Osiris and above the tomb on a relief in Meyboom, *The Nile Mosaic*, pl. 84 and pl. 82, respectively.

fantastic. The bird seems to be an object of worship, along with the mummified Osiris, in the mummy case. This is, however, in far-off Egypt despite a Roman-looking round tomb in the background. In any case, the paintings represent the desire of the Isiacs at Pompeii to link their religion to that Upper Egypt. At the same time, the representations seem to reveal a reluctance to depict worship of living animals on the part of Romans. Notably, no animal statue was found in the temple at Pompeii except for a panther belonging to Dionysus.

There is some other evidence for the probable reserve with which Isiacs in the temple in the Campus Martius approached animal worship. A small cameo glass vessel in the Getty Museum, dated to the early first century CE, is another rare example of the performance of animal worship.[56] One putto or cupid lays a garland on a statue of the god Toth in baboon form, while another makes an offering, as does a pharaoh in an Egyptian setting. An ibis (another form of Toth) is represented on the side of the altar. The inclusion of the pharaoh and an obelisk is a sign that this is in ancient Egypt and in Upper Egypt. The putti or cupids, who in fact are not necessarily worshipping the god, are not exactly meant to be actual human beings. Moreover, the animal represented is a statue, not a living animal, as is clear by the pedestal and less-than-life size of the animal. In the Allard Pierson Museum in Amsterdam, there is a statuette almost identical to the one portrayed on the Getty Flask. Here, as on the Getty Flask, the animal is larger in size in relation to the pedestal, but still a statue. The baboon also sports a quite large sun disk crown embellished with the image of a cobra. As with the Getty vessel, an ibis is depicted on the side of the altar.[57]

In the Iseum Campense in Rome, however, we see a difference from the Isis temple at Pompeii. Judging by the Ariccia Relief, the large number of sacred animal statues attributed to the Iseum Campense, and the explicit hieratic settings there, the reluctance toward animal worship seems to have changed. The Flavians, who openly promoted the Isis religion, seem to have had less opposition to animal worship than their predecessors. For example, Titus went to the consecration of the Apis bull in Memphis. Several of the statues from the Iseum Campense are life sized or greater and are very impressive. At a minimum they would inspire an attitude of awe in the beholder.

The Ariccia Relief helps us picture how these animals were venerated. As noted earlier, the animals were erected in *aedicula*, the equivalent of side altars in a Christian church. In a group with Isis and Bes, they obviously belong to the divine sphere, even if inferior to Isis in a larger setting, but they are not visibly inferior to Bes. Apparently in the open is a life-sized statue of the Apis bull on a pedestal. The *aediculum* in which Isis sits is larger than the others and seems to project forward, and she is flanked by two candelabra, also emphasizing her superiority to the animals and Bes. The *aediculum*

---

[56] See Swetnam-Burland, *Egypt in Italy*, 55–8 and pl. III; and K. Wight and M. Swetnam-Burland, "The Iconography of the Cameo Glass Flask at the J. Paul Getty Museum," in F. Naumann-Steckner, B. Päffgen, and R. Thomas (eds.), *Zwischen Okzident und Orient* (*Kölner Jahrbuch* 43, Berlin: Gebr. Mann, 2010), 839–46, esp. 841–4.

[57] The statuette piece, 36.3 centimeter high and 11.6 centimeter wide, is dated to 100–150 CE (Allard Pierson Museum 7946). Provenance except for "Egypt" is unknown. Thanks are due to Dr. Willem van Haarlem for this information.

of Bes is slightly behind that of Isis, but in front of those of the baboons. The Ariccia Relief also seems to portray living ibises along a water channel at the bottom but within the central scene of ecstatic worshippers. A somewhat similar relief fragment in Berlin, which disappeared during the Second World War, also represents a statue of the Apis bull on a pedestal, possibly representing the same scene as in the Ariccia Relief, since the bull and pedestal are very similar.[58] As in the Ariccia Relief, the Apis bull seems to be standing in an open space. Behind the bull is a palm tree. Importantly, the worship is not directed toward a living animal but to the statue of an animal, a difference in Egyptian religion underscored at some length in the Berlin conference on animal worship.

The number of animal statues attributed to the Iseum Campense is quite large, again projecting a link to ancient Egypt. Among the remains of the twenty-five Egyptian statues (not counting three sphinxes), nine are of animals, of which four would normally be worshipped.[59] Of the Egyptianizing statues, the percentage is higher. Of eleven statues, eight are of animals, of which five would normally be worshipped.[60] In the sixteenth century, an Apis bull was found in the Iseum Campense, but its dimensions are unknown. A relief on a granite column depicts a priest, possibly in a procession, carrying a small cow or bull (Apis?) mounted on a little platform on a handle, which he holds in his hand. The case of baboons is quite different. Three of these were discovered. Among the Egyptian statues in the Iseum Campense, two were of baboons, while there were three among the Egyptianizing ones.

Romans seemed to have relegated the practice of animal worship to statues, except for live ibises and cobras. As with the ancient Egyptians, Romans seem to have made a distinction between living animals and statues of animals. They also seem to have moved from quietly disguising worship of sacred animals to exhibiting it openly. Still, in the Iseum Campense, the figure of Isis in human form and in a central position gives her a unique status in the worship of the faithful. The depiction of a seated baboon, but with an ibis on the altar or pedestal below him, on the Getty vessel and the statuette in the Allard Pierson Museum in Amsterdam, suggests that Toth cannot be encapsulated in one animal form, that there is a distance between the god and the animal. In the

---

[58] Lembke, *Das Isaeum Campense* 24, 174–8, pls. 3.1 and 3.2; Capriotti Vittozzi, *La terra del Nilo*, 142–5, 180, figure 8.

[59] See Lembke, *Das Isaeum Campense*, 214–37: five lions (nos. 10–14, pls. 29–32); female sphinx of the eighteenth dynasty (no. 15, pl. 33.1–2); sphinx of Amasis (no. 16, pl. 34.2); reclining sphinx (no. 17, pl. 35); Hathor Cow nursing Haremhab (no. 18, pl. 36); Horus (no. 19, pl. 37.1); two baboons (nos. 20–1, pl. 37.2–3); the goddess Sekhmet (no. 22); Isis (no. 23); Isis with the child Horus (no. 24); two of a *naophoros* (no. 25, pl. 38, and no. 26); one of a *stelophoros* (no. 27, pl. 39); a fragment of a statue of Amenenhet III (no. 28, pl. 40.1); bust of Alexander or a Ptolomaic king (no. 29, pl. 40.2–3); granite head of a bald man (no. 30, pls. 41.1–2); a Ptolemaic torso (no. 31, pls. 3–4); statue base with an Egyptian inscription and part of the right foot (no. 32); statue base with two feet, one in the Egyptian style (no. 33, pl. 42.1–2); two statue fragments (one of a kneeling figure with hands on knees [no. 34] and a statue fragment with no description [no. 35]).

[60] Ibid., 238–43 (not counting two sphinxes as animals): two baboons (nos. 36, pl. 43.1–2, and no. 37); head of a baboon (no. 38); crocodile (no. 39, pl. 43.3); Apis bull (no. 40); three lions (nos. 41–3, pl. 44); sphinx of Domitian (?) (no. 44, pl. 45.1); head of a female sphinx of the eighteenth dynasty (45, pl. 34.1 [copy of sphinx no. 15]); Egyptianizing head of Domitian (?) (no. 46, pl. 45). Of these, five would be of the type normally worshipped.

case of the *Adoration of the Mummy*, if the bird represents Osiris, then it is only an animal form related to him, since his mummified body in the mummy case would be an anthropomorphic Osiris.

Conclusion

In conclusion, the Iseum Campense was closely identified with the various Imperial families, especially that of the Flavians, and the emperor essentially was the ultimate authority for all temples and religions in the Roman Empire. The Iseum Campense, a huge edifice, stood in the center of Rome and in the center of the Roman Empire. However, the emperor was basically a civil authority. There was no central religious authority as depicted for the nascent Christian churches. Yet, there was something of a spiritual bond between the various shrines of Isis and Osiris in different parts of the Roman world and Egypt, both ancient and contemporary. The Iseum Campense could symbolically reach out to Isiac shrines everywhere, and its small temple resembled that of others. A distinctive feature of Egyptian religion, animal worship was respected more so than is evident from Pompeii, even if modified in respect to the Egyptian practice. The Iseum Campense could serve as the ultimate model and center of Isiac religion, one fostered by the Roman emperors, located in the center of the power structure of the Roman world, and crossing many cultural and religious barriers. In a religious sense, for the Isiacs, as suggested by the career of Lucius in the Isis Book of Apuleius's *Metamorphoses*, all roads led to Rome. The study of the Iseum Campense, then, is truly one of "Place, Space, and Identity in the Ancient Mediterranean World."

2

The Myth of the Diasporic Isiac-Family as Reflected in the Epigraphical Evidence Connected to the Delian Sarapeia

Elina Lapinoja-Pitkänen

The aim of this chapter is to investigate the inscriptions mentioning the voluntary sanctuary associations[1] that were based in the three sanctuaries devoted to the Isiac-family on Delos (Sarapeion A, B, and C).[2] The architectural and epigraphical evidence clearly demonstrates that honoring and worshipping Egyptian gods was an important task for members of the cult of the Isiac-family on Delos. The cult had a wide appeal for the local population and already at an early stage attracted followers from different nationalities, which then facilitated the building of the Sarapeia.[3]

---

[1] The term "association" has been well established in the discussion of ancient organizations (ἔρανον, κοινὸν, collegium, etc.). See, for instance, Stephen G. Wilson, "Voluntary Associations: An Overview," in John S. Kloppenborg and Stephen G. Wilson (eds.), *Voluntary Associations in the Greco-Roman World* (London: Routledge, 1996), 1–15, here 15. The adjective "voluntary" has been added to distinguish them from institutions (state, city, or family) or institutionalized associations. To make sense of the vast amount of inscriptional material dealing with voluntary associations, researchers have created taxonomies of associations. Earlier ones were done, for instance, by Paul-François Foucart, *Des Associations Religieuses chez les Grecs: Thiases, Éranes, Orgéons: Avec le Texte des Inscriptions* (Paris: Klincksieck, 1873); and Erich Ziebarth, *Aus der antiken Schule: Sammlung Griechischer Texte auf Papyrus, Holztafeln, Ostraka* (Bonn: A. Marcus und E. Weber, 1886; rev. ed., 1910). For more contemporary taxonomies, see John S. Kloppenborg, "Collegia and Thiasoi – Issues in Function, Taxonomy and Membership," in Kloppenborg and Wilson, *Voluntary Associations in the Greco-Roman World*, 16–30, esp. 18–26; Philip A. Harland, *Associations, Synagogues, and Congregations: Claiming a Place in Ancient Mediterranean Society*, 2nd rev. ed., with links to inscriptions (Kitchener: Published by author, 2013), 25–52, available online at http://www.philipharland.com/associations/; and Richard S. Ascough, "Greco-Roman Philosophic, Religious, and Voluntary Associations," in Richard N. Longenecker (ed.), *Community Formation in the Early Church and the Church Today* (Peabody: Hendrickson, 2002), 3–24, here 1–2.

[2] What Roussel later designated Sarapeion C was excavated already by Hauvette in 1883, though the latter identified it as a sanctuary of foreign gods and not specifically a Sarapeion. See Adolf Rusch, *De Serapide et Iside in Graecia cultis* (Berlin: H. S. Herman, 1906), 40.
Sarapeion B was uncovered after completing the excavations begun by Hauvette, and Sarapeion A was discovered in 1911 and fully excavated by 1912. See Pierre Roussel, *Les Cultes égyptiens à Délos du IIIe au Ier Siècle a.v. J.-C.*, Annales de l'Est 1915 and 1916 (Paris: Berger-Levault, 1916), 12–13.

[3] The number of records pertaining to Sarapis on Delos is higher than that for any other Greek city. The earliest systematic examination of the Egyptian cults on Delos was an essay written by Pierre

Starting in the late archaic period, the Mediterranean cultural realm began experiencing marked changes in its religious atmosphere. In some sense, it was a development of the city-states' embedded religion transforming into a religion of possibilities.[4] This change in the religious atmosphere strengthened, and some would argue also created—or at the least reformed—the voluntary (religious) associations;[5] this also made it easier for foreign cults, such as the cults of the Isiac-family, to spread into traditional Greek and Roman areas. During this time, the cultural biography of Isis (and the Isiac-family) slowly morphed from that of a Nilotic Egyptian goddess toward a pan-Mediterranean one.[6] In the process of creating a Greek and Roman Isiac-family, their myth was connected to already existing bifurcated Greco-Roman mythology and transformed to better fit the Greco-Roman audience. The traditional Egyptian version of the family—including Osiris, Isis, Anubis, and Horus—was transformed to better suit the needs and already existing concepts of divinity in Greco-Roman areas. The

---

Roussel and published in 1916. He was followed, for instance, by Helmut Engelmann (*The Delian Aretalogy of Sarapis* [Leiden: Brill, 1975]) in translating, commentating on, and discussing the evidence for the worship of the Isiac-family on Delos. In addition, see, for example, Richard S. Ascough, Philip A. Harland, and John S. Kloppenborg (eds.), *AGRW* (Waco, TX: Baylor University Press, 2012). For a more comprehensive version of the categorization of associations in the Greco-Roman world, see the *AGRW* site: http://philipharland.com/greco-roman-associations/ managed by Philip A. Harland.

[4] Greg Woolf, "Isis and the Evolution of Religion," in Laurent Bricault and M. J. Versluys (eds.), *Power, Politics and the Cults of Isis: Proceedings of the Vth International Conference of Isis Studies, Boulogne-sur-Mer, October 13–15, 2011* (organized in cooperation with Jean-Louis Podvin) (Leiden: Brill, 2014), 62–92, here 63; John North, "The Development of Religious Pluralism," in J. Lieu, J. North, and T. Rajak (eds.), *The Jews among Pagans and Christians in the Roman Empire* (London: Routledge 1992), 174–93. North remarks: "Development from religion as embedded in the city-state to religion as choice of differentiated groups offering different qualities of religious doctrine, different experiences, insights or just different myths and stories to make sense of the absurdity of human experience" (178).

[5] It has been argued that this transformation was caused by a diminution of city-states' power, leading to a decline in the political, cultural, and social life of their inhabitants, which in turn acted as a stimulus boosting the development of (especially religious) voluntary associations. Kloppenborg, "Collegia and Thiasoi," 17–18. However, linking the decline of the polis and the rise of associations is not without its problems. It seems more likely that associations were alternative activities for the polis's inhabitants, based on their own cultural, social, and religious lives, rather than that of their successors. See Mogens Herman Hansen, "Introduction: The *Polis* as a Citizen-State," in Mogens Herman Hansen (ed.), *The Ancient Greek City-State: Symposium on the Occasion of the 250th Anniversary of the Royal Danish Academy of Sciences and Letters, July, 1–4 1992*, HFM 67 (Copenhagen: Royal Danish Academy of Sciences and Letters, 1993), 7–29, here 21. Furthermore, increased migration probably played a part in the development of voluntary (religious) associations; long-distance moves severed connections to one's old polis, and associations offered a way to form new social connections, both to individual inhabitants and to the polis itself.

[6] See Laurent Bricault and M. J. Versluys (eds.), *Power, Politics and the Cults of Isis: Proceedings of the Vth International Conference of Isis Studies, Boulogne-sur-Mer, October 13–15, 2011* (organized in cooperation with Jean-Louis Podvin) (Leiden: Brill, 2014), 26. The worship of the Isiac-family was divided between the continued cult in traditional areas and diasporic forms abroad. See Woolf, "Isis and the Evolution of Religion," 75.

The Myth of the Diasporic Isiac-Family

diasporic version of the Isiac-family is made up of Sarapis,[7] Isis, and Anubis, and in some cases also Harpocrates.[8]

Sarapis and the Isiac-Family on Delos

Inscription IG XI, 4 1299 and the Arrival of the Cult of Sarapis on Delos

According to the timeline of the successive sanctuaries on Delos, the beginning of the cult of Sarapis and the Isiac-family on the island was a rather modest version of man's yearning for his home country, but eventually it grew to include three individual sanctuaries and over a dozen associations worshipping Egyptian deities in Delos. An inscription (IG XI, 4 1299)[9] found in the first sanctuary (Sarapeion A) makes it possible to outline the development of the cult on Delos. The cult, or more specifically the ritual statue of Sarapis, arrived on Delos around the turn of the third and second centuries.[10] It was carried from Egypt by one Apollonius, a member of the priestly

---

[7] Sarapis was a Greco-Egyptian god who was introduced into Egyptian and Greek mythology in the third century BCE, during the Ptolemaic period. His worship might have its roots in Babylon and may have been carried from there to Egypt under the influence of Alexander's conquests. There are two version of Sarapis, Egyptian and Greco-Roman, which highlight different aspects of his character. In the Egyptian version he was a combination of features of Osiris and Apis, while outside Egypt Sarapis absorbed aspects of Osiris, Zeus, Dionysos, Helios, Hades, and Asclepius into his character, thus becoming some sort of sun god who ruled the underworld but also had healing powers. Altogether, the god Sarapis is a classic example of syncretism; see George Hart, *The Routledge Dictionary of Egyptian Gods and Goddesses*, 2nd ed. (London: Routledge, 2005), 140. Interestingly, Sarapis is a very prominent god in the Greco-Roman Isiac-family, overshadowing the others, while in the Egyptian version the gods have more equal roles.

[8] "Harpocrates" was a Greek translation of the name of the Child Horus; see Emma Swan Hall, "Harpocrates and Other Child Deities in Ancient Egyptian Sculpture," *Journal of the American Research Center in Egypt* 14 (1977): 55–8, here 55. Horus the child = Harpa-Khruti à Harpocrates. He was a god of silence and secrets, who had features of Eros incorporated into his image in some sculptures. In the context of Delos, most of the surviving inscriptions do not mention Harpocrates by name, except seven inscriptions from Sarapeion C. Interestingly, Inscription SEG 42 (1992), no. 157, from Athens also lists Harpocrates; so also RICIS 111/0102: τὸ κοινὸν τῶν διακόνων Σαράπει, Ἴσει, | Ἀνούβει, Ἁρποκράτει. See also IPergamon 336, RICIS 205/0104. Apart from these inscriptions, Harpocrates was clearly less emphasized than Horus was in the Egyptian conception.

[9] IG XI, 4 is the identifier to *Inscriptiones Graecae XI. Inscriptiones Deli*, fasc. 4, ed. Pierre Roussel (Berlin: G. Reimer, 1914), nos. 510–1349, https://inscriptions.packhum.org/book/17?location=915. The whole inscription is too long to be transcribed here, but these first ten lines cover the explanation of the cult's origin on Delos: "The priest Apollonios [II] inscribed this according to the command of the god. For our grandfather, Apollonios, an Egyptian from the priestly class, having brought his god with him from Egypt, continued serving (*therapeuōn*) his god according to ancestral custom and, it seems, lived for ninety-seven years. My father, Demetrios, followed him in serving the gods and, because of his piety, he was honoured by (10) the god with a bronze image which was set up in the temple (*naos*) of the god. He lived for sixty-one years" (*AGRW* 221 = IG XI, 4 1299). Philip A. Harland (trans.), "Story concerning a Temple for the Egyptian God Sarapis," in *AGRW* (http://philipharland.com/greco-roman-associations/221-story-concerning-a-temple-for-the-egyptian-god-sarapis/). Helmut Engelmann, for example, has also translated this inscription in his *The Delian Aretalogy of Sarapis*, but Harland's version is more accessible.

[10] Roussel, *Les Cultes Égyptiens*, 245, n. 3. For a longer discussion of the dating of the arrival of the cult of Sarapis, see Engelmann, *The Delian Aretalogy of Sarapis*, 13–14.

class who migrated, most likely on his own accord, to Delos around that time.[11] He brought a statue of the god Sarapis with him and rented a place for worship. This inscription reveals that after his death he was succeeded by his son Demetrius and his grandson Apollonius II.[12] The inscription continues, telling of a vision-dream that Apollonius II had, instructing him to buy land and build a sanctuary for Sarapis there. The inscription also includes a hymn to Sarapis composed by the poet Maiistas (lines 29–94).[13] In addition to its informative value, this inscription is an interesting description of the religious aspects of the associations devoted to Sarapis.

Delian Sarapeia

There were three different sanctuaries (Sarapeion A, B, C) devoted to Isiac-family on Delos, and they were all built along the same road in an area known as the Terrace of Foreign Gods.[14] Sanctuary A, or Sarapeion A, was built c. 215 BCE, probably next to a private building that the group had rented before they had the means to build their own meeting place.[15] The sanctuary itself was built in a shallow depression below the Inopos reservoir. It measured 302 square meters and included a small temple with a subterranean crypt which contained a spring, most likely used as a Nilometer in the purifying ritual.[16] The sanctuary included three larger rooms and a courtyard connecting these different sections.[17] Of the epigraphical and archeological evidence recovered from Sarapeion A, eight inscriptions mention the Isiac-family or voluntary associations devoted to the Isiac-family (Table 2.1).[18]

I have also included the IG XI, 4 1290 inscription in this table, even though it does not mention the Isiac-family or other Egyptian deities; however, it was devoted by an

---

[11] We do not know what made him immigrate to Delos in the first place, perhaps loss of work (a lower-level priest also had a secular profession), or he may have been an economic refugee looking for a way to make his fortune. Perhaps the fact that Delos, in addition to being a melting pot of different religions and cultures, was at that time under Ptolemaic hegemony within the Islanders' League might have made moving there easier for an Egyptian.

[12] Both Apollonius and Demetrius are theophoric names: Apollonius = Apollo-Horus, and Demetrius = Isis-Demeter. See Engelmann, *The Delian Aretalogy of Sarapis*, 11.

[13] For longer analyses of the poem of Maiistas, see Ian S. Moyer, *Egypt and the Limits of Hellenism* (Cambridge: Cambridge University Press, 2011), 179–94.

[14] That area was first excavated by Roussel in 1911 and 1912.

[15] Engelmann, *The Delian Aretalogy of Sarapis*, 13–14.

[16] Water was routed to the spring through an underwater canal from the reservoir. See B. Hudson McLean, "Voluntary Association and Churches on Delos," in Kloppenborg and Wilson, *Voluntary Associations in the Greco-Roman World*, 186–225. It is interesting how sanctuaries devoted to the diasporic adaptation of the Isiac-family still often had Nilometers, even though the connection with the Nile and the diasporic Isiac-family was clearly less emphasized than in the traditional form. For general sources on Nilometers, see, for instance, Robert A. Wild, *Water in the Cultic Worship of Isis and Sarapis* (Leiden: Brill, 1981); or Reinhold Merkelbach, *Isis regina—Zeus Sarapis: Die griechisch-ägyptische Religion nach den Quellen dargestellt*, 2nd ed. (Munich: Teubner, 2001).

[17] There were also three altars and an offertory treasury situated in the courtyard: McLean, "Voluntary Association and Churches on Delos," 205–11.

[18] For other inscriptions found in Sanctuary A, see: RICIS 202/0101, RICIS 202/0116, RICIS 202/0117, RICIS 202/0120, RICIS 202/0122, RICIS 202/0123, RICIS 202/0125, RICIS 202/0126, RICIS 202/0127, RICIS 202/0128, RICIS 202/0129, RICIS 202/0130, and RICIS 202/0131.

Table 2.1 The Inscriptions Mentioning the Isiac-Family or Voluntary Associations in Sarapeion A

Inscription	Deities Mentioned	Associations	Other
IG XI, 4 1216	Sarapis, Isis, Anubis		Mentions nineteen men and one woman
IG XI, 4 1217	Sarapis, Isis, Anubis	οἱ θεραπεύοντες	Bench
IG XI, 4 1220	Sarapis, Isis, Anubis		Also a bench, no mention of threapeuontes, but most likely connected to that association
IG XI, 4 1221	Sarapis, Isis, Anubis		A bench with dedication to: ὑπὲρ τῶν παιδίων εὐχήν
IG XI, 4 1230	Sarapis, Isis, Anubis		θεοῖς νικηφόροις
IG XI, 4 1247	Sarapis, Isis, Anubis		Bronze animal guarding cylindrical offering receptacle
IG XI, 4 1252	Sarapis, Isis		Fragmented
IG XI, 4 1290	Nike	οἱ θεραπεύοντες	
IG XI, 4 1299	Sarapis, Isis		

association worshipping the Isiac-family.[19] Sanctuary A probably accommodated the worship of Sarapis, Isis, and Anubis. The only voluntary association directly mentioned in these inscriptions is οἱ θεραπεύοντες (those who serve), but in all probability other associations would have also met in Sanctuary A.

The second sanctuary, Sarapeion B, was most likely active already by 202 BCE and was destroyed in 88 BCE.[20] It was built on a terrace of a mountain slope, on rocky and steep ground. This sanctuary was larger than Sanctuary A, measuring up to 390 square meters, and was accessed through a stairway that then opened onto a fairly large court. Immediately adjacent to the stairs was a large meeting room that had three altars on its eastern wall. The courtyard contained a small temple, a row of benches, and a slightly larger room (perhaps a shrine to a deity) that then opened onto a portico leading back to the courtyard.[21] Due the general state of disrepair of Sarapeion B, only a limited amount of archeological and epigraphical evidence is available; of these, there are five relevant inscriptions mentioning the Isiac-family and/or voluntary associations (Table 2.2).

---

[19] ὁ ἱερεὺς | Ἀπολλώνιος | καὶ οἱ συμβαλόμενοι | τῶν θεραπευτῶν || Νίκει (https://epigraphy.packhum.org/text/63775?&bookid=17&location=915). It has been suggested that the priest mentioned in this decree is Apollonios, whose grandfather was responsible for the introduction of the cult and who fought a court case against the people of Delos, when he wanted to erect Sarapeion A.

[20] Inscriptions seem to suggest that Sanctuary B might have originally been run by one man and was slowly built up to be the sanctuary of several different associations. See Engelmann, *The Delian Aretalogy of Sarapis*, 14; McLean, "Voluntary Association and Churches on Delos," 205–11. Delos was ravaged, and most of the landmarks destroyed by Menophaneses, the general of Mithridates, for it had sided with Rome in the Mithridatic war (188).

[21] McLean, "Voluntary Association and Churches on Delos," 212.

Table 2.2 The Inscriptions Mentioning the Isiac-Family or Voluntary Associations in Sarapeion B

Inscription	Deities Mentioned	Associations	Other
IG XI, 4 1223	Sarapis, Isis, Anubis, and gods sharing their temples and altars	ἐρανισταί	
IG XI, 4 1226	Sarapis, Isis, Anubis	μελ[α]νηφόρων, Σαραπιαστῶν, θεραπευταί	
IG XI, 4 1227	Sarapis, Isis, Anubis, and gods sharing their temples	δεκαδιστῶν καὶ δεκαδιστριῶν	Both male (nine names) and female (seven names) tenth-day celebrators mentioned
IG XI, 4 1228	Sarapis, Isis, Anubis	ἐνατίσται, μελανηφόρος	
IG XI, 4 1229	Isis	ἐνατίσται, μελανηφόρος	Identical with IG XI, 4 1228, except that 1229 is devoted solely to Isis

Four out of five inscriptions are dedicated to or mention Sarapis, Isis, and Anubis. Two out of these four add to the list of deities: "Gods that share their temples,"[22] and altars."[23] One (IG XI, 4 1229) out of five inscriptions mentions only the Goddess Isis, even though that inscription is identical in every other way to IG XI, 4 1228. There were probably six associations that gathered inside the walls of Sarapeion B: the contributors (ἐρανισταί), therapeuetai (θεραπευταί), sarapiasts (Σαραπιασταί),[24] tenth-day celebrators (δεκαδισταί),[25] ninth-day celebrators (ἐνατίσται), and blackwearers (μελανηφόροι).

The third and last of the Delian Sarapeia, Sarapeion C, was built before 166 BCE and had a more public character than either Sanctuary A or Sanctuary B.[26] It was built immediately adjacent to the sanctuary of the Syrian gods to the south, on a terrace surmounting the upper Inopos reservoir.[27] It was the largest of the Sarapeia and

---

[22] IG XI, 4 1227.
[23] IG XI, 4 1223.
[24] Forming the name of an association from the name of the God they worshipped was a fairly common practice in Greco-Roman culture; for example, Δημητριασταί (AGRW 159) or Ἀφροδεισιαστᾶν (IG XII, 1 962) (https://epigraphy.packhum.org/text/139514). In addition to Delos, groups addressing themselves as Sarapiasts existed mostly around Attica and the Greek islands (http://philipharland.com/greco-roman-associations/?s=sarapiast).
[25] Either separate associations for men and women or one association with both men and women members. τὸ κοινὸν τῶν δεκαδιστῶν καὶ | δεκαδιστριῶν ὧν συνήγαγεν | Ἀρίστων Σαράπιδι,Ἴσιδι, Ἀνούβιδι, | θεοῖς συννάοις. || Ἰατροκλῆς, Ἀπολλόδ[ω]ρος, Δωρίων, Γλαυκίας, | Νέων, Θεόφιλος, Ἡρακλείδης, Μένιππος Ἰατροκλ[έ]||ους, Ἡρακλείδης. Καλλώ, Εὐτυχί[ς], Φίλα, Κλέ[α], | Διάνοια, Σύνετον, Φιλοκρίτη.
[26] Roussel suggests that Sarapeion C was founded privately as a smaller complex and later enlarged and made public over time. Roussel, *Les Cultes Égyptiens*, 69.
[27] Philip Harland, trans., "Building: Sarapis Sanctuary C (ca.166–9)," AGRW, http://philipharland.com/greco-roman-associations/building-sarapis-sanctuary-c-ca-166-69-bce/.

had two main courtyards that had access to a variety of rooms and temples, such as separate temples devoted to Isis, Sarapis, Anubis, and to an unnamed deity. Most likely this temple was dedicated either to Harpocrates, since Sarapeion C is the only one with inscriptions mentioning Harpocrates, or to Hydreios, since the only inscription mentioning Hydreios was found in Sarapeion C; moreover, the temple included a massive water installation, which probably acted as the Nilometer. The sanctuary also contained several porticos.[28] Due the size of Sarapeion C, we have recovered a large amount of archeological and epigraphical evidence from the grounds, of which twenty inscriptions are relevant to the voluntary associations connected to the sanctuary (Table 2.3).

Of the Delian Sarapeia, Sarapeion C was the only one to accommodate the worship of Sarapis, Isis, Anubis, and, as the fourth part of the Isiac-family, Harpocrates. Eight out of twenty voluntary association inscriptions also mention Harpocrates.[29] Three are devoted solely to Isis and four to Sarapis, of which one is dedicated to Sarapis and Dionysos. Two (IDelos 2087–88)[30] are dedicated to Sarapis, Isis, Anubis, Harpocrates, and Hydreios. There were at least four associations meeting at Sarapeion C: the blackwearers, therapeuetai, contributors (οἱ συμβαλόμενοι), and an association named the Sarapiasts. In addition to these inscriptions, there was one well-preserved sanctuary inventory list and several more fragmentary examples recovered from Sarapeion C.[31]

This view of successive sanctuaries, where no more than two sanctuaries coexisted (Sarapeion A and Sarapeion B for a time, and then Sarapeion B and Sarapeion C for short period of time, but not A and C together), has been, and mostly still is, the leading hypothesis of how these three extraordinary sanctuaries came to be located so close together. However, Ian Moyer has raised an interesting question of whether we

---

[28] Interestingly, the fusion of Greek and Egyptian traditions in the Sarapis Sanctuary C is also present in the architectural features. It had an Egyptian-style *dromos* lined with sphinxes, but the Temple of Isis and the statue of the goddess were made in impeccably Greek style.

[29] See, for instance, IDelos 2078 = RICIS 202/0281 (116/115 BCE).
Διονύσιον Διονυσίου Σφήττιον, | ἱερέ[α γε]νόμενον, οἱ μελανηφό[ροι] | καὶ ο[ἱ] θεραπευταὶ ἀρε[τῆς ἕνεκεν καὶ] | εὐσε[β]είας καὶ ἐπιμελείας τῆς εἰς αὐ[τούς], || [Σ]αρά[π]ιδι, Ἴσιδι, Ἀνούβιδι, Ἁρποκράτει.
Those who wear black (*melanēphoroi*) and the therapeutists (*therapeutai*) set this up for Dionysios son of Dionysios from Sphettos subdivision on account of his virtue, piety, and care for them. This was dedicated to Sarapis, Isis, Anubis, and Harpocrates. Philip Harland, trans., "Honors by Melanephorians and Therapeutists for Dionysios son of Dionysios (116/115 BCE)," in *AGRW*, http://www.philipharland.com/greco-roman-associations/?p=22422.

[30] These inscriptions are extremely fragmented but seem to resemble each other. For more details of the reconstruction process, see Philip Harland, trans., "Dedication (Frag.) of Altars and a Clock for Egyptian Deities by a Melanephorian (ca. 100 BCE)," in *AGRW*, http://www.philipharland.com/greco-roman-associations/?p=22447.

[31] The best reserved is RICIS 101/0424; others: IDelos 1403 = RICIS 202/0421 (165–156 BCE); IDelos 1412 = RICIS 202/0422 (166–156 BCE); IDelos 1416 = RICIS 202/0423 (156/155 BCE); IDelos 1434 = RICIS 202/0426 (156–145 BCE); IDelos 1435 = RICIS 202/0425 (after 155 BCE); IDelos 1440 = RICIS 202/0427 (146–145 BCE); IDelos 1442 = RICIS 202/0428 (146–144 BCE); and, IDelos 1452 = RICIS 202/0433 (after 145 BCE). Philip Harland, trans., "Inventories regarding Sarapis Sanctuary C with Therapeutists and Sarapiasts (155/154 BCE)," in *AGRW*, http://philipharland.com/greco-roman-associations/inventories-of-the-sarapis-sanctuary-mentioning-therapeutists-and-sarapiasts-155154-bce/. Ascribing all of these to Sarapeion C is a bit of guesswork, but it is the most likely scenario.

Table 2.3 The Inscriptions Mentioning the Voluntary Associations in Sarapeion C

Inscription	Deities Mentioned	Associations	Other
IG XI, 4 1215	Sarapis, Isis, and θεοῖς ἐν[τεμενίοις	θερ]απευταὶ	
IG XI, 4 1224	Sarapis and Dionysos	οἱ συμβαλόμενοι	
IG XI, 4 1225	Unclear (too fragmented)	οἱ συμβαλόμενοι	
IG XI, 4 1243	Sarapis	[Σαρα]πιαστα[ὶ] οἱ σ[υμβαλόμενοι]	
IG XI, 4 1249	Unclear	μελανηφόρος	Ktesippos, melanephorians, also appears in the inventory lists from Sanctuary C
IG XI, 4 1250	Isis	μελανηφόρος	Ktesippos, melanephorians, also appears in the inventory lists from Sanctuary C
IDelos 2039	Sarapis, Isis, Anubis, and Harpocrates	μελανηφόρος, θεραπευταῖς	Fragments of a Doric architrave; Roussel made two possible reconstructions
IDelos 2075	Sarapis, Isis, and Anubis	μελανηφόρος	The synod of the blackwearers honor their benefactor
IDelos 2076	Sarapis, Isis, Anubis, and Harpocrates	μελανηφόρος	Group honoring their benefactor. The writer also mentioned: Ἡφαιστίων Μύρωνος Ἀθηναῖος ἐποίει
IDelos 2077	Sarapis, Isis, Anubis, and Harpocrates	μελανηφόρος, θεραπευταῖς	Two groups honoring their benefactor, due to his virtue and piety toward the gods and the care of the temple
IDelos 2078	Sarapis, Isis, Anubis, and Harpocrates	μελανηφόρος, θεραπευταῖς	
IDelos 2079	Isis	μελανηφόρος θεραπευταῖς	For Isis the Righteous, on behalf of the Athenians and Romans
IDelos 2080	Isis	μελανηφόρος, θεραπευταῖς	For Isis Aphrodite, on behalf of the Athenians and Romans
IDelos 2081	Sarapis, Isis, Anubis, and Harpocrates	μελανηφόρος, θεραπευταῖς	List of positions
IDelos 2085–86	Sarapis, Isis, Anubis, and Harpocrates	μελανηφόρος	An explanation of what a member of the blackwearers has done for the good of the sanctuary
IDelos 2087–88	Sarapis, Isis, Anubis, Harpocrates, and Hydreios	μελανηφόρος	Two fragmentary inscriptions that resemble each other
IDelos 2617	Sarapis	θεραπευταῖς	Six fragments of a plaque listing the names of those who contributed to the construction of a reservoir
IDelos 2618	Probably Sarapis	θεραπευταῖς	

are overly simplifying the archeological and epigraphical evidence in order to make it fit the successive sanctuaries timeline.³² He has concluded that Sarapeion C, much like Sanctuaries A and B, was active from 215 BCE at the latest. He bases his main argument on an exactly dated inscription on a silver cup dedicated by one Soteles, which was then recorded in an annual sanctuary inventory (made in 155/154 BCE).

> Another with the inscription "during the civic leadership (90) of Tlesimenos, Soteles son of Soteles, who was serving as priest of Apollo and Asklepios, dedicated this using funds from the awards," weighing 36 drachmas and 3 obols.³³

Furthermore, "archaeological estimates also put the sanctuary of Sarapeion C, though not the shrine of Sarapis itself, in the later third century."³⁴ If this is the case, it would perhaps offer an explanation of why a bronze figurine of an animal guarding a cylindrical offering receptacle was found in Sarapeion A, when it was listed in the annual inventory list found in C.³⁵ The successive timeline would argue that when the inventory list was made, around 155 BCE, temple A would have already ceased all operations and the cult would have been moved, via Sanctuary B, to Sarapeion C.³⁶ Similarly, for instance, inscriptions IG XI, 4 1307 and IG XI, 4 1215, found in Sarapeion C, have been dated to the turn of the third and second centuries BCE, the latter even to 240 BCE.³⁷

Networks of Association

Disregarding the debate over the timeline, each Sarapeion was its own representation of the cult, with its own cultic activities and ritualistic and sacrificial objects, and several sanctuary associations. These associations, for their part, had their own benefactors, gatherings, and probably also exclusive banquets for their members. Similarly, every sanctuary had its own association of the servants of the gods (θεραπευταὶ) or associations of those who serve (θεραπεύοντες),³⁸ which might have been some

---

[32] Moyer, *Egypt and the Limits of Hellenism*, 145–205.
[33] This inscription mentions who was civic leader at the time when the inscription was made. IDelos 1417, A-side line 90: ἄλλο ἐφ' οὗ ἐπιγ[ραφή· ἐ]π' ἄρ||χοντος Τλησιμένου Σωτέλης Σωτέλου ἱερατεύσας τοῦ Ἀπόλλω|νος καὶ τοῦ Ἀσκληπιοῦ ἀπὸ τῶν γερῶν. Harland, "Inventories regarding Sarapis Sanctuary C," in *Associations in the Greco-Roman World*.
[34] Moyer, *Egypt and the Limits of Hellenism*, 196, n. 172.
[35] φύλακα ἐπ' ὀ[μ]|φαλοῦ, τὸν ἐπικείμενον ἐπὶ τοῦ θησαυροῦ ἐν τῶι Σαραπιείωι, ἄστατον· | θυμιατήριον· βωμίσκον, ἐφ' οὗ ἐπιγραφή· Διόφαντος, ὁλκὴ δὲ ὡς ἡ ἐπι|γραφὴ ἄστατο. The successive timeline would argue that when the inventory was made around 155 BCE Temple A would have already ceased all operations, and the focus would have moved via Sanctuary B to Sarapeion C.
[36] However, inevitably the timeline of coexisting sanctuaries raises more questions than it provides answers. Why were there three individual sanctuaries devoted to Isiac deities on Delos?
[37] Most likely a yearly inventory list. See https://epigraphy.packhum.org/text/63792 and Harland, "Dedication (Frag.) to Sarapis and Isis by Therapeutists (ca. 240 BCE)," in *AGRW*, http://www.philipharland.com/greco-roman-associations/?p=24071.
[38] From A: IG XI, 4 1217 and IG XI, 4 1290; from B: IG XI, 4 1226; from C: IG XI, 4 1215, IDelos 2077, IDelos 2078, IDelos 2079, IDelos 2080, IDelos 2081, and IDelos 2039.

sort of sanctuary board or caretaker associations, meant to tend to everyday matters concerning their sanctuary.[39] Regardless of their possessing some level of self-reliance, epigraphical evidence suggests a fair amount of interaction between the associations— especially among the associations within an individual sanctuary. The IG XI, 4 1228 inscription mentions how ninth-day celebrator's γραμματεύς was also a μελανηφόρος:

> This was dedicated to Sarapis, Isis and Anubis by the association of ninth-day celebrators (enatistai), who are Dionysios son of Noumenios from Kassandreia (in Macedonia), the head of the society (archithiasitēs), Apollonios the secretary (grammateus) who is a member of those who wear black (melanēphoros), Mnason, Athenion, Komos, Ariston, Rhodippos, Hegias, Apollonios, Dionysios, Philostratos, Demetrios, Straton, Sosistratos, Aristoboulos, Aphrodisios, Diopeithes, Phidias, Drakon, Aischrion, Apollonios, Aphrodisios, Agathokles, Baliton, Asklepiades, Diodoros.
>
> (*In a crown:*) The association of society-members crowned Dionysios, the head of the society, because of his virtue, his piety towards the gods, and his generosity (literally: love of honor) towards the society-members.
>
> (*In another crown:*) The association of society-members crowned Apollonios the secretary who is a member of those who wear black.[40]

Similarly, votive offerings, statuettes, statues, and honorary gifts given to benefactors were often erected by several associations acting together. For instance, on Delos 2077:

> Those who wear black (*melanēphoroi*) and the therapeutists (*therapeutai*) set this up for Dionysios son of Menios from Paiania subdivision, who was priest (*hiereus*), on account of the virtue and piety which he has towards the gods and the care which he shows concerning the temple (*hieron*). This was dedicated to Sarapis, Isis, Anubis, and Harpokrates.[41]

---

[39] Ilias Arnaoutoglou argued in his recently published article ("Isiastai Sarapistai: Isiac Cult in the Easter Mediterranean," in Valentino Gasparirni and Richard Veymiers [eds.], *Individuals and Materials in the Greco-Roman Cults of Isis: Agents, Images and Practices* [Leiden: Brill, 2018]), 258–61, that one should not consider the therapeuetai groups as κοινον or associations but rather only as loosely connected groups of worshippers, since the groups lack an inner structure and offices. However, this raises the question of how such loosely connected random groups funded crowns, silver cups, or other votives?

[40] Philip Harland, trans., "Dedication to Isis by Ninth-Day Celebrators (ca. 200 BCE)," in *AGRW*, http://www.philipharland.com/greco-roman-associations/?p=7466.
Ἴσιδι | τὸ κοινὸν τῶν ἐνατιστῶν ὧν ἀρχιθιασίτης | Διονύσιος Νουμηνίου Κασσανδρεύς, γραμματεύς | Ἀπολλώνιος μελανηφόρος, Μνάσων, || Ἀθηνίων, Κῶμος, Ἀρίστων, Ῥόδιππος, | Ἡγίας, Ἀπολλώνιος, Διονύσιος, Φιλόστρατος, | Δημήτριος, Στράτων, Σωσίστρατος, | Ἀριστόβουλος, Ἀφροδίσιος, Διοπείθης, | Φιδίας, Δράκων, Αἰσχρίων, Ἀπολλώνιος, || Ἀφροδίσιος, Ἀγαθοκλῆς, | Βαλίτων, Ἀσκληπιάδης, Διόδωρος. |
In *corona laurea*: στεφανοῖ τὸ κοι|νὸν [τῷ]ν θιασιτῶν | Διονύσιον τὸν ἀρχι||θιασίτην ἀρετῆς ἕνε|κεν καὶ εὐσεβείας | τῆς εἰς τοὺς θεοὺς | καὶ φιλοτιμίας | τῆς εἰς τοὺς || θιασίτας. |
In *corona laurea*: τὸ κοινὸν | τῶν θιασι|τῶν τὸν | γραμματέα | Ἀπολλώνιον | μελανηφό|ρον.

[41] Philip Harland, trans., "Honors by Melanephorians and Therapeutists for Dionysios son of Menios (119/118 BCE)," in *AGRW*, http://www.philipharland.com/greco-roman-associations/?p=22420.

In Sarapeion C, it seems to have been fairly common for the μελανηφόρος and θεραπευταῖς to honor their benefactor(s) together.⁴² Moreover, it seems that these associations were not only dedicating offerings to and honoring the Isiac-family but also doing so for other Greco-Roman deities, which then would strengthen the networks between different associations and cults.⁴³

Inscriptions Containing Reflections of the Myth of the Isiac-Family Constructing and Reforming the Social Identity

The voluntary associations operating inside the sanctuaries, and the sanctuaries themselves, offered a communal expression of people's devotion and facilitated their search for the protection and patronage of the deities of the Isiac-family. This could be achieved, for example, through remembering and retelling the myth and through ritualistic behavior. Rituals and reminiscing about the myth created religious experiences, but they also simultaneously constructed and reshaped worshippers' identity.⁴⁴ For a group, or rather a cult in this case, to be successful—which we know the cult of the Isiac-family was in Delos—it must both entice the local population and have a wider appeal, and then be able to hold on to its members. This again calls for an efficient system of integration and the means to construct and reshape a group's social identity.⁴⁵ Once a member is part of the cult or association operating in one of the sanctuaries, he is likely to exhibit in-group favoritism and out-group discrimination. There are three characteristics that seem to matter most when creating favorable circumstances for in-group favoritism and out-group discrimination. These are: (1)

οἱ μ[ελα]νηφ[όροι κ]αὶ οἱ θερα|πευταὶ Διονύσιον Μηνίου | Παιανιέα, ἱερέα γενόμενον, | ἀρετῆς ἕνεκεν καὶ εὐσεβείας || τῆς εἰς τοὺς θεοὺς καὶ ἐπιμελεί|ας τῆς περὶ τὸ ἱερόν, Σαράπιδι, |Ἴσιδι, Ἀνούβιδι, Ἁρποκράτει. In addition to the previous, see, for example: IG XI, 4 1243 or IG XI, 4 1226.

⁴² See inscriptions: IDelos 2039, IDelos 2077, IDelos 2078, IDelos 2079, IDelos 2080, and IDelos 2081.

⁴³ See, for instance, IG XI, 4 1305 or IG XI, 4 1290.

⁴⁴ In addition to their own personal identity, which is the identity arising from one's unique characteristics, people have a social identity formed through their connection with others. According to Turner, a personal identity is composed of those primary values or identities that define us; these can be, for example, intellectual qualities and idiosyncratic tastes, that is, those things we cannot change in ourselves. In some cases, I also count religious conviction to be this type of primary value, which defines one's personal identity. See H. Tajfel and J. C. Turner, "An Integrative Theory of Intergroup Conflict," in W. G. Austin and S. Worchel (eds.), *The Social Psychology of Intergroup Relations* (Monterey, CA: Brooks/Cole, 1979), 17. For a longish discussion of the difficulty of defining personal identity, see, for example, Eric T. Olson, "Personal Identity," in Edward N. Zalta (ed.), *The Stanford Encyclopedia of Philosophy* (2017 ed.), https://plato.stanford.edu/archives/sum2 017/entries/identity–personal/. In other words, personal identity is what separates "I" from others. Alexander S. Haslam defines "social identity" thus: "Social identity is part of a person's sense of 'who they are' associated with any internalized group membership." See Alexander S. Haslam, *Psychology in Organizations: The Social Identity Approach*, 2nd ed. (London: Sage, 2004), 21.

⁴⁵ Social identity can be observed in three stages: cognitive––recognition of belonging to the group; evaluative—recognition of the value attached to the group; and emotional––attitudes group members hold toward insiders and outsiders. Tajfel and Turner, "An Integrative Theory of Intergroup Conflict," 41; Haslam, *Psychology in Organizations*, 21.

A connection between an individual's self-conception and the meaningfulness of the specific group—the more meaningful the group is for the individual's self-conception, the more he is inclined to show in-group favoritism and out-group discrimination. (2) The surrounding context matters: if the prevailing context encourages competition, groups are more likely to exhibit object and social competition.[46] This would definitely be the case if all the sanctuaries coexisted rather than succeeded one another.[47] (3) The relevance of the out-group matters.[48] In other words, when an individual is categorized or self-categorizes in terms of group membership, and defines himself through the terms of that social group, he seeks to "achieve positive self-esteem by positively differentiating their ingroup from a comparison outgroup on some valued dimension."[49] This process of positive distinctiveness, in essence, means that when individuals start to define themselves through the plural "we" rather than the singular "I," they want their "we" to be more successful and altogether better than others or "them." One way for voluntary associations and cult of Isiac-family on Delos to be successful and survive, that is, to have a stronger "we" in a religiously rich environment, is to efficiently use religious narratives and remember and retell the mythology of their deities on a day-to-day basis (this can be achieved through rituals, or, for instance, through the usage of myth-based language meant to activate a group's communal memory).[50]

Next, I will discuss three case studies, each of which represents a different type of reminiscing of the myth and mythological narratives connected to the Isiac-family and shows how these could influence the construction and maintenance of a member's identity. The first case study is not just a faint reflection of myth, but rather a long inscription retelling the mythicized history of the cult. This inscription is the aforementioned free-standing column (IG XI, 4 1299) found in Sanctuary A. It is an excellent example of a multipurpose inscription meant to both convey the cult's

---

[46] Things and situations over which groups can compete can be divided into two main categories: objective competition and social competition. Objective competition is fought over obtainable goods, such as capital, territory, or simply food. In the case of associations and congregations, members and benefactors are also subject to objective competition. Social competition focuses on intangible assets, such as honor, status, power, prestige, and so on. See M. A. Hogg and D. Abrams, *A Social Psychology of Intergroup Relations and Group Process* (London: Routledge, 1988), 50.

[47] Since there were only a limited number of wealthier members willing to act as benefactors and sponsor the daily operations of the associations, and the sanctuaries themselves. Similarly, the competition would be also over members, sanctuaries and their associations would need to have members in order to work.

[48] Tajfel and Turner, "An Integrative Theory of Intergroup Conflict," 41; Haslam, *Psychology in Organizations*, 21.

[49] Haslam, *Psychology in Organizations*, 21.

[50] Social scientific theories are useful heuristic tools that can be applied to interpret historical evidence; moreover, they are based on our minds' cognitive processes to comprehend the world around us, and the human cognition has remained virtually the same for thousands of years. Jacobus Kok, "Social Identity Complexity Theory as Heuristic Tool in New Testament Studies," *HTS Teologiese Studies/Theological Studies* 70.1 (2014): 9, Art. #2708. Petri Luomanen, Ilkka Pyysiäinen, and Risto Uro, "Introduction: Social and Cognitive Perspectives in the Study of Christian Origins and Early Judaism," in Petri Luomanen, Ilkka Pyysiäinen, and Risto Uro (eds.), *Explaining Christian Origins and Early Judaism: Contributions from Cognitive and Social Science* (Leiden: Brill, 2007), 1–33, esp. 1–29.

religious beliefs and highlight the diasporic nature of the Isiac-family;[51] and influence the social identity of members by retelling the history of the cult and emphasizing the importance of this group. The inscription mythicizes the history of their sanctuary and highlights how Sarapis, that is, the original cultic statue of Sarapis, was brought over from Egypt by the priest Apollonius.[52] He is represented as the prototypical image of a devoted cult member, one who continued to perform the rituals and serve the god according to ancestral customs and was blessed by Sarapis, for he lived a long life (ninety-seven years according to the inscription).[53] He was then succeeded by his son and grandson, in true Egyptian fashion. Retelling this history and connecting their current leader Apollonius II to the original arrival of the cult was a way to authenticate both their leader and their sanctuary's role as the genuine sanctuary and to influence their members' identity in order to create a stronger "we." In addition to highlighting the excellence of their group, this inscription constructs a clear difference between us and "the others." We are blessed by Sarapis, our sanctuary was built according to the vision from Sarapis, and our actions are pleasing to god. The others are adversaries of the god, who tried to hinder the building of the sanctuary but were not successful.[54] The construction of this certainly expensive free-standing column, in addition to building the sanctuary itself, fits well within the timeline proposed by Moyer and others, at least from the social-psychological point of view.[55] Having three similar sanctuaries nearby one another would most likely create an atmosphere of group competition, where emphasizing the excellence and authenticity of one's own sanctuary would be a classic tactic.[56]

The second example is an interesting observation connected to the difference between the Egyptian (Isis, Osiris, Horus, and Anubis) and diasporic (Isis, Sarapis, Anubis, and occasionally Harpocrates) versions of the Isiac-family. Osiris is a leading character in the Egyptian myth, whose death and reanimation forms the main thread of the story. However, in the diasporic version of the myth, and in the case of the association inscriptions from the Delian sanctuaries, the role of Osiris is rather nonexistent, with his character being effectively replaced by Sarapis. Retelling parts of the myth, and in this case substituting Osiris with Sarapis and modifying the

---

[51] This inscription effortlessly connects Sarapis and Isis together as companions: μυρία καὶ θαμβητὰ σέθεν, πολύαινε Σάραπι, ἔργα, τὰ μὲν θείας ἀνὰ τύρσιας Αἰγύπτοιο ηὔδηται, τὰ δὲ πᾶσαν ἀν' Ἑλλάδα, σεῖο θ' ὁμευνοῦ Ἴσιδος. See Engelmann, *The Delian Aretalogy of Sarapis*, 27.

[52] Strikingly he is addressed as ὁ πάππος ἡμῶν in IG XI, 4 1299, line 2.

[53] Traditionally a long life has been seen as a blessing from the gods.

[54]
> Now certain people conspired against us and the god, and sought a judgment against the temple and myself in a public trial, seeking either punishment or a fine. But the god promised me in a dream that we would win the case. Now that the proceedings have ended and we have won as is worthy of the god, we praise the gods by demonstrating appropriate gratitude. (*AGRW* 133–4)

[55] The presence of similar groups in constricted surroundings is proven to trigger group competition and out-group discrimination. Hence, highlighting the excellence, authenticity, and continuum of their own group would be important.

[56] However, it should be noted that the column would also influence groups even if the sanctuaries were consecutive, as its aretalogy is meant not only to eulogize Sarapis but also to benefit their group and sanctuary in the context of group competition.

characters of Isis and Anubis, was important in the process of assimilation of the cult through transference.[57] Those parts of the myth that would not work well in the new Greek environment were erased, while others were emphasized. However, there is one inscription that calls for more detailed attention: the inscription IDelos 2087,[58] reconstructed using the highly fragmented IDelos 2088, raises questions on the role of Osiris:

[ὁ δεῖνα Νικίου] | [— — — ρεὺς μελα]|[ν]ηφόρο[ς ὑπὲρ ἑαυτοῦ] | καὶ τῆς [γυναικὸς Πατρο]||φίλας κ[αὶ τῶν τέκνων] | Νικίου κ[αὶ Ἀπολλωνίας] | καὶ τοῦ οἰκε[ίου] Κλέωνος | τοῦ Κλέων[ο]ς, τοὺς βω|μοὺς καὶ τὸ λιθόστρωτο[ν] || καὶ τὰς σφίγγας καὶ τ[ὸ] | ὡρολόγιον Σαράπιδι, [Ἰσι]|δι, Ἀνούβιδι, Ἁρποχράτ[ει], |Ὑδρείωι ἀνέθηκ[εν] | ἐκ τῶν ἰδίων, || ἐπὶ ἱερέως Ἀρτ[εμιδώ]|ρου τοῦ Ἀπολλοδώρ[ου] | [Λ]αμπτρέ[ως, κα]νηφορού|σης Θεοφίλ[ης] τῆς Ἀρ|τεμιδώρου Λαμπτρέως || θυγατρός, ζακορεύοντος | Εὐόδου.

(On behalf of himself, his wife Patrophila, his children Nikias and Apollonia, and his relative Kleon son of Kleon, … *Name* [original emphasis] son of Nikias, a member of those who wear black (*melanēphoros*), dedicated from his own resources the altars, the mosaic, the sphinxes, and the clock to Sarapis, Isis, Anubis, Harpokrates, and Hydreios. This was done when Artemidoros son of Apollodoros from Lamptrai subdivision was priest (*hiereus*), Theophile daughter of Artemidoros from Lamptrai was basket-bearer (*kanēphoros*), and Euodos was temple-warden (*zakoros*).)[59]

This, albeit reconstructed, inscription mentions Ὑδρείωι (Hydreios), which most likely is a reference to an Osiris-Hydreios jar "Osiris-in-a-jar." This object, sometime also called an Osiris Canopus figure, was a decorated jar upon which a figurine of the head of Osiris had been placed.[60] As mentioned earlier, Sanctuary C had a fourth temple, with the water canal and the Nilometer dedicated to an unknown deity. Instead of Harpocrates, this temple could have been devoted to Osiris-Hydreios. On the level of mythology, the worship of Hydreios in the temple containing the Nilometer would indicate that worshippers, even coming to the last century BCE, were aware of the mythic narrative where Osiris was thrown into the Nile, causing it to flood.[61] If the members of Sarapeion C—more specifically the members of the μελανηφόροι association, since

---

[57] Osiris and Horus were left out and replaced in most cases. One possible reason for leaving Osiris behind might have been connected to the different concepts of the afterlife in Egyptian and Greco-Roman cultures. Since Osiris was so strongly connected to the Egyptian image of the afterlife, he had to be replaced by Sarapis, whose character was more fluid, thus offering a more identifiable deity for the Greeks and Romans.
[58] However, one has to be careful about what can be deduced based on one fragmented inscription.
[59] Harland, "Dedication (Frag.) of Altars and a Clock for Egyptian Deities by a Melanephorian (ca. 100 BCE)," in *AGRW* no. 2087, http://www.philipharland.com/greco-roman-associations/?p=22447.
[60] Wild, *Water in the Cultic Worship of Isis and Sarapis*, starting from page 113.
[61] Jaime Alvar Ezquerra and Richard Lindsay Gordon, *Romanising Oriental Gods: Myth, Salvation, and Ethics in the Cults of Cybele, Isis, and Mithras*, RGRW 165 (Leiden: Brill, 2008), 301–2, 314–16; Caitlín Barrett, *Egyptianizing Figurines from Delos: A Study in Hellenistic Religion*, Columbia Studies in the Classical Tradition 36 (Leiden: Brill, 2011), 133–6.

they are the only association mentioned in the inscription—also worshipped Osiris-Hydreios, it would distinguish the μελανηφόροι from the other associations and highlight their specialty. From a mythological point of view, connecting the worship of Hydreios or usage of the Osiris-Hydreios jar in the rituals, and association of μελανηφόροι together is a logical conclusion.

The third case study, which is clearly connected to the previous one, is an excellent example of the usage of myth-based language on a day-to-day basis. In Sanctuary C (and likely also in B) was an active association of the μελανηφόροι participating in the communal life,[62] acting as benefactors of other associations,[63] and joining in the renovations of Sanctuary C.[64] The name of this association, μελανηφόροι (the blackwearers), is a clear example of the usage of myth-based language in an everyday context. B. Hudson McLean, following, for example, Ladislav Vidman, argued that in the case of the Delian μελανηφόροι associations the color black symbolized the mourning of Isis over her murdered husband.[65] Nonetheless, the symbolism behind μελανηφόροι might be more complex, since the color black was far more multidimensional in Egyptian contexts than in Greco-Roman contexts. In Egyptian symbolism, the color black is connected with rebirth and fertility but also associated with the Nile and its yearly floods, which inundated the land with highly fertile black soil.[66] In addition, it was also the color of death and the afterlife.[67] Altogether, in Egyptian symbolism the color black was multifaceted and associated with the entire range of life, from birth to death to afterlife. In contrast, in Greco-Roman culture, the color black lacked the multidimensionality it had in Egyptian symbolism and was rather more generally associated only with death and mourning. For example, by the late third century BCE Roman magistrates began to wear a dark toga, called a *toga pulla*, to official funerary ceremonies. Whether the μελανηφόροι terminology was arising only from the Greco-Roman symbolisms of black connected with the

---

[62] Inscriptions mention μελανηφόροι in Sanctuary C: IG XI, 4 1249, IG XI, 4 1250, IDelos 2039, IDelos 2075, IDelos 2076, IDelos 2077, IDelos 2078, IDelos 2079, IDelos 2080, IDelos 2081, IDelos 2085–86, IDelos 2087–88; and from Sanctuary B: IG XI, 4 1226, IG XI, 4 1228, IG XI, 4 1229.
[63] See, for instance, inscription IG XI, 4 1226.
[64] See, for instance, inscriptions IDelos 2085 and IDelos 2086.
[65] McLean, "Voluntary Association and Churches on Delos," 211; Ladislav Vidman, *Isis Und Sarapis Bei Den Griechen Und Römern: Epigraph* (Berlin: de Gruyter, 1970).
[66] Joshua J. Mark, "Color in Ancient Egypt," *Ancient History Encyclopedia*, https://www.ancient.eu/article/999/ (last modified January 8, 2017). A key part of the character of Egyptian Isis was her connection to the Nile thus making her the black goddess.
[67] See, for example, Hart, *The Routledge Dictionary of Egyptian Gods and Goddesses*; Reginald Eldred Witt, *Isis in the Graeco-Roman World* (London: Thames and Hudson, 1971), 25–45. Besides Isis, *Blackwearer*'s mythological origin is most likely connected to Anubis, considering that he is described in some ancient text to be wearing a black cloak and his animal form had a black fur, or his skin is painted black. Nevertheless, it is most likely that wearing black stems from the mythology of Isis herself. One clue to whose mythology the "blackwearer" points comes from a text IDelos 2080, in which members are called *Blackwearers*, but Isis is the only God present: "Those who wear black (*melanēphoroi*) and the therapeutists (*therapeutai*) set this up for Gaius son of Gaius from Acharnai subdivision, priest (*hiereus*) in the year when Nausias was civic leader (*archōn*). They dedicated this to Isis Dikaiosyne ('Righteousness') on behalf of the Athenian People and the Roman People."

traditional myth (Isis mourning over her husband)[68] or from the larger contexts of Egyptian symbolism (Isis as the Nilotic goddess and ultimate mother, but also Isis mourning over Osiris) or something in between, the terminology itself still clearly arises from the mythological characterization of Isis and was also commonly used by groups other than the μελανηφόροι themselves.[69] Using myth-based language is a way to link current members to the myth and history of their goddess. It is a way to recall their shared myth and devotion on an everyday basis, crafting a commonality between members (and subgroups), but, at the same time, it also consolidates their shared history and social memory, thus creating a positive distinctiveness for the group.[70]

Conclusions

The archeological and epigraphical evidence uncovered from Delian Sarapeia proves that all the sanctuaries were devoted to the diasporic modification of the Isiac-family. Sarapeion A and Sarapeion B facilitated the worship of Sarapis, Isis, and Anubis, while some of the inscriptions found in Sarapeion C were also dedicated to the fourth deity of the diasporic Isiac-family—Harpocrates. Each sanctuary was its own representation of the cult, with its own cultic activities and ritualistic and sacrificial objects and with several sanctuary associations. These associations, for their part, had their own benefactors, gatherings, and exclusive banquets for their members. Interestingly, some of the inscriptions also seem to offer reflections of the traditional myth of the Isiac-family, like in the case of Hydreios, which could indicate that even if the sanctuaries themselves were devoted to the diasporic version of the family, the traditional Isiac-family was not completely erased. Remembering and retelling the myth, connected to either the traditional or the diasporic version of the Isiac-family, by using specific language is also a way to diversify and strengthen a group's social identity and social memory. Inscriptions prove that associations used myth-based language to remember and retell the mythological narratives in order to not only express their religious devotion and seek patronage of their deities but also reinforce their identity.

---

[68] If this was the case, then it is an interesting amalgamation of Greco-Roman symbolism and traditional mythology of Isiac-family. Since in the Diasporic version, Isis is paired with Sarapis, and the narrative of the death of her husband is not included to the mythical diasporic narratives.
[69] The influential individuals such as Ktesippos son of Ktesippos of Chios proudly proclaimed the performance of the duty of μελανηφόροι.
[70] One of the definitions of social memory is the idea that this memory is never an actual representation of history or the past but rather a modification to fit the needs of the present day. See Ritva Williams, "BTB Readers' Guide: Social Memory," *BTB* 41 (2011): 189–200. According to van Eck, "Social identity is constructed by the remembering and retelling (configuration) of narratives from the past, and the present is reframed (refiguration) by telling the narrative through memory." Ernest van Eck, "Social Memory and Identity: Luke 19:12b–24 and 27," *Biblical Theology Bulletin* 41.4 (2011): 201–12.

3

Jesus, the Daimons, and the Dead[1]

Peter G. Bolt

Although it would be a rare reader today who would equate the "demons" "exorcised" by Jesus with ghosts, that is, spirits of deceased human beings who still exert an influence upon the living, many ancient readers of the Gospels would have done so automatically. The first part of this chapter will show that many people in the Greco-Roman world would simply assume the connection between daimons and the spirits of the dead.[2] The second part then asks what they would have made of Mark's exorcism scenes, with this connection as part of their repertoire.

Daimons and the Dead in the Greco-Roman World

In order to demonstrate how the daimons were connected with the dead, this section consists of a vocabulary study of the δαίμων/δαιμόνιον family of words. Although this

---

[1] This chapter is a slightly expanded version of that in A. N. S. Lane, ed., *The Unseen World: Christian Reflections on Angels, Demons and the Heavenly Realm* (Carlisle: Paternoster, 1996), 75–102. The original essay was written while preparing material for my doctorate, since published as *Jesus' Defeat of Death: Persuading Mark's Early Readers*, SNTSMS 125 (Cambridge: Cambridge University Press, 2003). The following abbreviations have been used: *ANET* = J. B. Pritchard, *Ancient Near Eastern Texts Relating to the Old Testament* (Princeton, NJ: University Press, 1969³); *DT* = A. Audollent, *Defixionum Tabellae* (Paris: A. Fontemoing, 1904); *DTA* = R. Wunsch, *Defixionum Tabellae Atticae*, IG III App. (Berlin: G. Reimerum, 1897); *GMA* = R. Kotansky, *Greek Magical Amulets: The Inscribed Gold, Silver, Copper, and Bronze Lamellae*; Part 1: *Published Texts of Known Provenance*, Papyrologica Coloniensia 22/1 (Opladen: Westdeutscher, 1994); *GMPT* = H. D. Betz, ed., *The Greek Magical Papyri in Translation, including the Demotic Spells* (Chicago: University of Chicago Press, 1986²); Isbell = C. D. Isbell, ed., *Corpus of the Aramaic Incantation Bowls*, SBLDS 17 (Missoula, MT: Scholars, 1975); LSSupp = F. Sokolowski, *Lois sacrées des cités grecques, Supplément* (Paris: De Boccard, 1962); *PGM* = K. Preisendanz and A. Henrichs, *Papyrae Graecae Magicae: Die griechischen Zauberpapyri*, 2 vols. (Stuttgart: Teubner, 1972, 1973); *PDM* = H. D. Betz, as above, Demotic Spells; SGD = D. R. Jordan, "A Survey of Greek Defixiones Not Included in the Special Corpora," *GRBS* 26 (1985): 151–97; SuppMag = R. W. Daniel and F. Maltomini, *Supplementum magicum*, Papyrologica Coloniensia 16 (Opladen: Westdeutscher, 1990–2). In collections, the number of the text is given in bold to distinguish from page numbers.

[2] Surveys of biblical daimonology have regularly noticed the connection, even if only to deny it: for example, W. Foerster, "δαίμων κτλ.," in G. Kittel (ed.), *TDNT* (Grand Rapids, MI: Eerdmans, 1964), II.6; G. H. Twelftree, "Demon, Devil, Satan," in J. B. Green and S. McKnight (eds.), *Dictionary of Jesus and the Gospels* (Leicester: IVP, 1992), 164; J. J. Rousseau and R. Arav, "Exorcism," in *Jesus and His World: An Archaeological and Cultural Dictionary* (Minneapolis, MN: Fortress, 1995), 88.

approach may have its weaknesses,³ it is more than sufficient to establish the point at hand.⁴ In an attempt to allow the meaning of the terms to emerge from the discussion of the usage, I have adopted the practice of simply referring to the word group using the transliteration "daimons," rather than the much more metaphysically loaded "demons." The link between the daimons and the dead is a persistent feature of the literary sources.⁵

Metaphysical confusion surrounding the daimonic is not only a part of the modern world, but it exists in the literature of the ancient world as well.

> More and more the word [i.e., daimon] came to mean lesser spirits and spirits intermediate between men and ... the gods. However, it was not certain that they were not simply the spirits of deceased men or men about to be incarnated,

---

³ For example, (1) the evidence for Greco-Roman daimonology may be more extensive than simply this one word study. Nevertheless, the word study is certainly a grand opening to the field. (2) Like the LXX and Josephus, the Gospel accounts prefer δαιμόνιον to what some have suggested is the more loaded term, δαίμων. However, a survey of the terms outside the Bible suggests that the terms are very closely related, often synonymous. This observation gains support from the variants on the five occurrences of δαίμων in the NT MSS (Mt. 8:31, cf. Mk 5:12; Lk. 8:29; Rev. 16:14, 18:2) and also from the Fathers' common use of δαίμων when explaining Gospel passages which use δαιμόνιον. (3) It has been argued that Mark's preference is against the δαιμ- vocabulary, in favor of "unclean spirit." However, this appears to be an overstatement of the evidence. Mark uses δαιμονίζεσθαι (1:32; 5:15, 16, 18) always as a substantive participle and in his narration; δαιμόνιον four times in summaries (1:34, 34, 39; 6:13) and twice in his narration (3:15; 7:30; [16:9]), as well as four times in the mouths of others (3:22; 7:26, 29; 9:38; [16:17]). On the other hand, πνεῦμα ἀκάθαρτον appears as part of Mark's narration six times (1:23, 26; 5:2, 13; 6:7; 7:25) and only once in his summaries (3:11), as well as being thrice in the mouths of others (1:27; 3:30; 5:8). In chapter 9 he also refers to πνεῦμα ἄλαλον (9:17, 20, 25; [καὶ κωφόν] 9:25). His usage of the δαιμ- group is sufficiently frequent and intertwined with "unclean spirit" to ensure that his Greco-Roman readers would refer both to the same beings. This justifies my blurring of the categories for the sake of the argument. The expression "unclean spirit/daimon" is extremely rare outside the Gospels: twice in the LXX (Zech. 13:2; 1 Macc. 1:48 א) but once in the Greek intertestamental material (TBenj 5:2). An Ethiopic equivalent once in *Jub.* 10:1, and a Hebrew equivalent twice at Qumran (1QS 4.21-22; 11Q5[11QPsᵃ] 19.13-15), and occasionally in the Rabbis, where it is clearly associated with magic. It is nonexistent in the Greek materials not dependent on the biblical writings, although it approximates the Pythagorean notion of "unclean souls," which were apparently related to daimons and heroes (D.L. 8.31-32); cf. Plutarch, *De gen.* 591C, where the unclean souls are not accepted in the upper regions. If readers made such an association, the case argued here would be strengthened.

⁴ Casting the net more widely simply strengthens the case. Note, for example, the Egyptian charm for an exorcism against a headache, c. 1250–1100 BCE, which calls upon the gods/spirits "to remove that enemy, dead man or dead woman, adversary male or female which is in the face of N, born of M" (BMPap. 10685C). The Semitic context provides many examples of ghosts operating in ways that require "exorcism"; cf. R. C. Thompson, *Semitic Magic: Its Origins and Development* (New York: Ktav, 1908; repr. 1971), 2–38; and *The Devils and Evil Spirits of Babylonia: Being Babylonian and Assyrian Incantations against the Demons, Ghouls, Vampires, Hobgoblins, Ghosts, and Kindred Evil Spirits, Which Attack Mankind*; vol. 1: *Evil Spirits* (London: Luzac, 1903); and J. A. Scurlock, *Magical Means of Dealing with Ghosts in Ancient Mesopotamia* (unpublished PhD dissertation, University of Chicago, 1988). In addition, three of the later Aramaic Incantation Bowls also include an invocation to a "ghost," שלניחא, Isbell **12**.2, **13**.4, **19**.7.

⁵ It can be detected elsewhere, for example, in the *nekromanteia* and *nekyomanteia*, places where one could consult the soul of the dead man found throughout Greece and referred to in grave inscriptions; F. E. Brenk, "In the Light of the Moon: Demonology in the Early Imperial Period," in W. Haase (ed.), *ANRW* II.16.3 (Berlin: de Gruyter, 1986), 2071, 2143.

and thus enormous confusion as to their existence, role, and origin was to be found.[6]

Of course, as we shall see in this chapter, the two are not necessarily strict alternatives, for the intermediate spirits could well have originated from deceased humans. But clearly part of the "confusion" detected here is due to the daimons' link with the spirits of the dead. There is no hint of this link in Homer[7] (pre-700 BCE), but he uses "daimon" sparingly anyway, prompting the suggestion that beliefs regarding daimons belong to the uneducated lower classes, the educated upper class preferring the anthropomorphic gods.[8] Hesiod (pre-700 BCE) argues that when the men of the golden age died, they were transformed to become watchers over humanity (*Op.*, 121-6),[9] called "pure *daimons* dwelling upon the earth" (τοὶ δαίμονες ἁγνοὶ ἐπιχθόνιοι).[10] They "roam everywhere over the earth, clothed in mist and keep watch on judgements and cruel deeds, givers of wealth." Since this passage from Hesiod becomes the point of departure for later discussions, it is worth noting that, even at this early stage, daimons are clearly intermediate spirits who are spirits of the departed, albeit the "departed golden race."

As well as bearing witness to the emergence of the term "daimon" being applied to various named gods and being associated with *tyche* (fate, fortune),[11] and fostering the idea of *daimones* as *alastores* or avenging spirits,[12] Greek tragedy (early fifth century BCE +) contains several references to them as spirits of the departed.[13] As for the New Comedy (last quarter fourth century to the death of Philemon 264/3), Menander[14] has the notion that each man is guided by a daimon, whether good or evil, which may perhaps be an adaptation of an earlier belief.[15] If so, it should be recognized that this concept logically precedes the daimon as the spirit of the departed. It is, for example,

---

[6] Ibid., 2068–9. M. Smith, "The Occult in Josephus," in L. H. Feldman and G. Hata (eds.), *Josephus, Judaism and Christianity* (Leiden: Brill, 1987), 240–1, detects a similar confusion in Josephus.
[7] Brenk, "Light," 2075. Neither are they a class of spirits.
[8] So Chantraine, reported in ibid., 2081.
[9] *Opera et Dies*. Loeb edition: H. G. Evelyn-White, *Hesiod. The Homeric Hymns and Homerica* (LCL; Cambridge, MA: Harvard University Press, 1914; repr. 1982).
[10] In Plato, *Crat.* 398A, MSS BT read ὑποχθόνιοι, "under the earth," against vulg. ἐπιχθόνιοι.
[11] Brenk, "Light," 2082–3. Consistently in Sophocles; occasionally attested in the inscriptional evidence (2143).
[12] For example, Aeschylus, *Pers.* 354.
[13] Ibid., 620ff. Atossa's libations are to "summon up the *daimon* of Dareios" (τόν τε δαίμονα Δαραῖον ἀνακαλεῖσθε), "the glorious *daimon*" (δαίμονα μεγαυχῆ, 642), who is a "soul from below" (ἔνερθεν ψυχήν, 630)—and, as someone murdered by his relatives, was a good candidate to become a ghost; cf. Aesch., *Cho.* 125, where Electra, invoking her father, tells Hermes: "summon for me the *daimons* beneath the earth" (κηρύξας τοὺς γῆς ἔνερθε δαίμονας). In Eur., *Alc.* 1003, the chorus says of Alcestis: "now she is a blessed *daimon*" (νῦν δ' ἐστὶ μάκαιρα δαίμων), and Hercules, victorious over Death, says, "I closed in conflict, with the Lord of *daimons*" (μάχην συνάψας δαιμόνων τῷ κυρίῳ, 1140; cf. 843–4).
[14] "By every man at birth a δαίμων stands, A guide of virtue for life's mysteries"; cited in Plutarch, *De tranquillitate animi* 474B. Plutarch disagrees in favor of Empedocles' notion that there are two forces mingled within each person.
[15] Brenk, "Light," 2084, who, on the basis of Phokylides in Clement, *Strom.* 5.14.127, suggests that Menander may have had a dualistic notion; contrast previous note.

the necessary presupposition of the hero-cult that it is the daimon by which a person lived, which is still active once they die.[16]

Although the picture becomes increasingly complex when we come to the philosophical literature, given the various elaborations of the daimons' role as intermediate beings, the link with the spirits of the dead is still present. Plato (429–347 BCE) certainly used daimon of divinity and fate and regarded the daimons as intermediate beings. He especially promoted the concept of the personal daimon that controls the fate of each individual.[17] Plato's elaboration of the daimons as intermediate beings, although based on earlier hints,[18] was still fairly innovative.[19] Since a distinction between a person's postmortem soul and their personal daimon can be detected at a number of points in his writing, the two are not always identical for Plato. But the two views are by no means in opposition, for, as noted earlier, this concept is logically prior to daimons as the spirits of the dead. Alongside his generally more elaborate daimonology, Plato still allows Socrates to conclude that Hesiod

> and all the other poets are right, who say that when a good man dies he has a great portion and honour among the dead, and becomes a *daimon*, … And so I assert that every good man, whether living or dead, is *daimonic* (δαιμόνιον), and rightly called a *daimon* (δαίμονα). (Plato, *Crat.*, 398B–C)

Here the personal daimon appears to be derived from the older understanding of the daimon as the spirit of the (heroic?) dead.[20]

While continuing the idea of daimons as intermediate beings, both Xenocrates (head of the Academy, 339–314 BCE) and the greatly influential Posidonius (*c*. 135–51/50 BCE) called the souls of the departed δαίμονες. A previous incarnation is implied by Xenocrates' notion of a "survival":[21]

> εἰσὶ γάρ, ὡς ἐν ἀνθρώποις, καὶ δαίμοσιν ἀρετῆς διαφοραί, καὶ τοῦ παθητικοῦ τοῖς μὲν ἀσθενὲς καὶ ἀμαυρὸν ἔτι λείψανον ὥσπερ περίττωμα, τοῖς δὲ πολὺ καὶ δυσκατάσβεστον ἔνεστιν. (Plutarch, *De def. orac.* 417B)

---

[16] See further, Peter G. Bolt, "Mk 16:1–8: The Empty Tomb of a Hero?," *TynBul* 47 (1996): 27–37.

[17] For example, *Tim.* 90A–C. Cf. the famous δαιμόνιον, which guided Socrates' destiny.

[18] Plutarch (Cleombrotus) dates the theory to Hesiod's fourfold distinction of beings; *Op.* 121-6 (*De def. orac.* 415B).

[19] Cf. Bravo's comment on *Symp.* 202D–203A: "la théorie du démonique esquissée dans ce passage ne correspond nullement aux croyances ni aux pratiques normales du temps de Platon ou d'époques plus anciennes"; B. Bravo, "Une Tablette Magique D'Olbia Pontique, les Morts, les Héros et les Démons," *Poikilia: Études offertes à Jean-Pierre Vernant* (Paris: EHESS, 1987), 208.

[20] H. D. Betz, "The Delphic Maxim 'Know Yourself' in the Greek Magical Papyri," *HR* 21 (1981): 158: "the older concept of the soul as *daimon* (δαίμων or δαιμόνιον) had become highly important in the Socratic and Platonic traditions of thought, especially because of its connection with the so-called *daimonion* of Socrates." He points out that later Philosophy discussed whether this daimon was to be simply identified with the self and the soul. Cf. *Phaedo* 107D–108B; *Resp.* 469A, cf. 427B, 540C; *Leg.* 717B–718A.

[21] "Daraus folgt doch wohl, daß die Dämonen einst Menschenseelen waren; den ein λείψανον kann das Unvernünftige nur aus dem irdischen Leben der Seele sein"; R. Heinze, *Xenocrates: Darstellung der Lehre und Sammlung der Fragmente* (Leipzig: Teubner, 1892; repr. Hildesheim: Georg Olms 1965), 83.

(For, as among men, so also among the *daimons*, there are different degrees of excellence, and in regard to the things of the passions, in some there is a weak and shadowy remainder, the dregs, as it were, but in others this is excessive and hard to extinguish.)

Although the Stoics in general avoided the δαιμ- vocabulary, Posidonius apparently taught that

εἰ οὖν διαμένουσιν αἱ ψυχαί, δαίμοσιν αἱ αὐταὶ γίνονται. (Sextus Empiricus Loeb III.I.74)[22]

(If then souls persist, the same souls become *daimons*.)

In addition, according to Diogenes Laertius, the Stoics (Posidonius?), with evident reliance upon Hesiod,

φασὶ δ᾽ εἶναι καί τινας δαίμονας ἀνθρώπων συμπάθειαν ἔχοντας, ἐπόπτας τῶν ἀνθρωπείων πραγμάτων· καὶ ἥρωας τὰς ὑπολελειμμένας τῶν σπουδαίων ψυχάς. (Diogenes Laertius, 7.151)

(hold that there are *daimons* who are in sympathy with mankind and watch over human affairs. They believe too in heroes, that is, the souls of the righteous that have survived their bodies.)

Evidence from Plutarch (50–120+ CE) indicates that such ideas persisted in philosophical circles into and beyond the time of the NT period. During the extended discussion of daimonological views in *De defectu oraculorum*, it is clear that the same connection is still known and debated.

For example, Ammonius believed Hesiod to have made the connection when he asks, "Do you think that the *daimons* are something other than *souls* that make their rounds [οἴει ἕτερόν τι τοὺς δαίμονας ἢ ψυχὰς ὄντας περιπολεῖν], according to Hesiod, in mist apparelled" (431B). Although inserting a Platonic touch,[23] Lamprias' reply indicates that Ammonius agrees with Hesiod's conception in this regard (431E): "if the souls which have been severed from a body, or have had no part with one at all, are *daimons* according to you and the divine Hesiod." Both Hesiod and Ammonius evidently believe that at least some of the daimons are those of the deceased. Lamprias is also happy to indulge this opinion, as long as he can argue that any power the soul possesses after death, it also possesses before death, even if in much diminished form due to being blinded by its combination with the mortal (431E ff.).[24]

---

[22] Ibid., 98. Heinze comments: "d.h. nicht: 'so werden sie den Dämonen gleich'—denn dann müßte die Existenz von Dämonen schon bewiesen sein—sondern: 'so werden sie das, was man gemeinhin unter Dämonen versteht.' Danach sind also die Dämonen des Posidonius, wie die des Xenokrates, abgeschiedene Seelen."

[23] Cf. (1) the phrase "or have had no part with one at all," alluding to pre-incarnate souls; and (2) the notion of the personal daimon.

[24] The idea that the incarnated soul is the weaker can be contrasted with Homer's view that "the shades" were of much diminished power in comparison with that possessed in mortal life (*Il.* 23:103–104; *Od.* 11.475–76). G. J. Riley, *Resurrection Reconsidered: Thomas and John in Controversy*

Later in the same essay, "which goes so much into this *daimon* lore,"[25] Cleombrotus first commends "those who place the race of *daimons* midway between gods and men" (οἱ τὸ τῶν δαιμόνων γένος ἐν μέσῳ θέντες θεῶν καὶ ἀνθρώπων) (415A), before suggesting various possibilities for the origin of this idea: perhaps Zoroastrian or Thracian (Orphic) or Egyptian or Phrygian. In justifying the latter two, he states that this can be inferred from the mystery initiation rites of both lands (ταῖς ἑκατέρωθι τελεταῖς), since they exhibit "many things mortal and mournful being mixed" (ἀναμεμειγμένα πολλὰ θνητὰ καὶ πένθιμα). This evidently assumes that the daimons are in some way connected with "things mortal and mournful,"[26] and since it is the observable evidence upon which his case for daimons is built, this connection appears to be obvious to all those involved in the conversation.

In summing up his discussion of *De defectu oraculorum*, Brenk states:

> [Plutarch's] speakers refuse to abandon the contention that *daimones* are really the souls of the departed. Two strands then clearly emerge, *daimones* as independent spirits, and as the souls of the departed, and it is fair to say that the strands could never be completely unraveled once they had become entangled.[27]

Although these strands should not be so opposed as to make them completely distinct, both are clearly present. Just as surely as the daimons are beings between the mortal and the immortal, so too are they connected with the souls of the dead.

Plutarch's other writings further illustrate this connection, despite it being somewhat peripheral to his own more elaborate Platonic daimonology. In *Symp*. III.7 (655E) he alludes to the custom "amongst us" (παρ' ἡμῖν) of sacrificing to Agathos Daimon, which was a chthonic spirit and guardian of the house, perhaps originally a ghost. Elsewhere, he reports the visit of Euthynoüs to a ψυχομαντεῖον (a place where the dead are conjured up) and the appearance of a young man who said, "I am the ghost of your son" (δαίμων τοῦ υἱέος σου) (*Cons. Ad Apoll*. 109C–D). When a plague raged among the Romans, it was averted when Apollo gave an oracle instructing them to appease the wrath of Saturn and "the spirits of those who had perished unlawfully" (τοὺς δαίμονας τῶν ἀνόμως ἀπολομένων) (*Parall. Graec. et Rom*. 308A), such people being prime candidates for becoming ghosts.[28] The Romans' ancestral spirits, the Lares, are called "*daimons* of punishment like the Furies" (ἐρινυώδεις τινές εἰσι καὶ ποίνιμοι δαίμονες) (*Quaest. Rom*. §51, 277A). One of the Sayings of the Spartans (236D) tells of a person who passed a grave-mound at night: "A certain *daimon* having become visible [φαντασιωθεὶς δαιμόνιόν τι], he ran at it with his spear

---

(Minneapolis, MN: Fortress, 1995), 56, detects increasing substantiality in the shades by the second Nekyia, *Od*. 24.15–204, and into the Aeneid. This can also be detected in the curse tablets; see later in the chapter.

[25] Brenk, "Light," 2082.
[26] Ibid., 2123–4; Plutarch insists that the mysteries show the true nature of daimons.
[27] Ibid., 2082. Cleombrotus probably represents the views Plutarch is opposing (2122).
[28] Those who died a violent (βιαιοθάνατοι) or sudden or early death (ἄωροι) were especially likely to become ghosts. The spirits of such people are regularly invoked in the magical material.

saying: 'Whither shall you flee me, soul who is about to die twice [πῇ με φεύγεις, δὶς ἀποθανουμένη ψυχή]?'"[29]

The interplay between souls and daimons is even present in the essays containing fairly elaborate daimonology. The vision of *De facie* (944C) pictures the largest hollow on the moon, "Hecate's Recess," "where the souls suffer and exact penalties for whatever they have endured or committed after having already become *daimons*" (ὅπου καὶ δίκας διδόασιν αἱ ψυχαὶ καὶ λαμβάνουσιν ὧν ἂν ἤδη γεγενημέναι δαίμονες ἢ πάθωσιν ἢ δράσωσι). The next section explains that the daimons (οἱ δαίμονες) do not stay forever on the moon but are assigned various roles in regard to oracles and the mysteries, and as punishers and saviors. If these acts are not performed properly, "they are cast out upon earth again confined in human bodies." In the vision of the other world provided by *De gen.* (591C), the moon is said to be "belonging to terrestrial *daimons*" (δαιμόνων ἐπιχθονίων οὖσα) (cf. Hesiod, *Op.*, 121-6). Timarchus sees stars, but his guide replies, "Without knowing it, you see the *daimons* themselves" (αὐτοὺς τοὺς δαίμονας ὁρῶν ἀγνοεῖς) (591D). He then explains the relationship between the soul and the body, saying that the part submerged in the body is called the soul (ψυχή), whereas the part left free from corruption is called the understanding (νοῦς), by "those who take it to be within themselves, … but those who conceive the matter rightly call it a *daimon*, as being external" (591E).[30] The discussion clearly links the souls with the daimons: whereas the stars that are extinguished are souls which sink back to the body, the stars that are lighted are souls that "float back from the body after death"; and the ones that move on high are "the *daimons* of men said to possess understanding" (591F). The same essay (593DE), after recalling Hesiod that δαίμονές εἰσιν ἀνθρώπων ἐπιμελεῖς, draws an analogy between a retired athlete who still encourages those in training and "those who are done with the contests of life, and who, from prowess of soul, have become *daimons*" (οἱ πεπαυμένοι τῶν περὶ τὸν βίον ἀγώνων δι' ἀρετὴν ψυχῆς γενόμενοι δαίμονες).[31] The analogy "indicates once more that for Plutarch *daimones* seem primarily to be former souls."[32]

One of the parallels between the lives of Brutus and Dion was that both saw a phantom which told of their coming death (*Dion* 2). The phantom φάσμα—also called τὸ δαιμόνιον (12)—appearing to Brutus (*Caes.* 49.11), has all the signs of being a ghost. It is heralded by a noise, and when Brutus looks toward the lamp which was going out,[33] "he saw a fearful vision of a man of unnatural size and harsh aspect." The phantom tells

---

[29] The Spartan no doubt simply intended to get rid of the ghost; for dying twice in Plutarch's more Platonic thought; cf. "As to the death we die, one death reduces man from three factors [i.e., body, soul, mind] to two and another reduces him from two to one [i.e., mind]" (*De facie* 943A). Cf. Plato's "mortal soul" (*Tim.* 42D, 61C, 69C-D).

[30] Cf. Plato, *Tim.* 90A: "As regards the lordly kind of our soul, … we declare that God has given to each of us, as his *daimon*, that kind of soul which is housed in the top of our body and which raises us … up from earth towards our kindred in the heaven."

[31] Cf. *De I et O*, 360EF.

[32] Brenk, "Light," 2124.

[33] This is the moment when such a fearful vision would be expected; cf. the Britons' saying (Plutarch, *De def. orac.* 419F): "as a lamp when it is being lighted has no terrors, but when it goes out is distressing to many, so." The editor refers to a saying by Lucretius, "a smouldering lamp may cause apoplexy." In the Magical Papyri, lamps are often used in conjuring spirits.

Brutus that he is his δαίμων κακός (evil daimon; cf. *Brut.* 36–7). Although he usually assigns such stories to superstition, because of the standing of these two men, Plutarch complains:

> οὐκ οἶδα μὴ τῶν πάνυ παλαιῶν τὸν ἀτοπώτατον ἀναγκασθῶμεν προσδέχεσθαι λόγον, ὡς τὰ φαῦλα δαιμόνια καὶ βάσκανα, προσφθονοῦντα τοῖς ἀγαθοῖς ἀνδράσι καὶ ταῖς πράξεσιν ἐνιστάμενα, ταραχὰς καὶ φόβους ἐπάγει, σείοντα καὶ σφάλλοντα τὴν ἀρετήν, ὡς μὴ διαμείναντες ἄπτωτες ἐν τῷ καλῷ καὶ ἀκέραιοι βελτίονος ἐκείνων μοίρας μετὰ τὴν τελευτὴν τύχωσιν. (*Dion* 2)
>
> (I do not know but we shall be compelled to accept that most extraordinary doctrine of the oldest times, that mean and malignant *daimons*, in envy of good men and opposition to their deeds, try to confound and terrify them, causing their virtue to rock and totter, in order that they may not continue erect and inviolate in the path of honour and so attain a better portion after death than themselves [the daimons].)

In the assumption that the daimons are similar to those who will die, and that those who will die will be like the daimons, Plutarch implies fairly clearly that the daimons are spirits of the dead and vice versa. This text not only provides the modus operandi of these spirits, that is, terrifying and confounding good men, but it also explains the rationale for this behavior in terms of the afterlife. These spirits of the dead seek to ruin the performance of the living so that their postmortem lot is worse than that of the spirits themselves. In other words, in the opinion of the ancients—an opinion which, on the basis of the experience of Dion and Brutus, Plutarch, albeit tentatively,[34] commends to his contemporaries—not only are the daimons spirits in the afterlife who are malevolently active in this world but this activity is also directed toward the fate of others in the afterlife who are themselves potential daimons.

Plutarch is immensely important as a source for ancient daimonological views[35] and has played such a key role in daimonological studies that it is perhaps true to say that modern studies have not progressed beyond his own presentation.[36] It is significant for the purposes of my argument, therefore, that alongside the presence of the daimons as intermediate beings, his writings also illustrate the connection between the daimons and the spirits of the dead,[37] which may, in fact, be his most basic belief.[38]

---

[34] Brenk, "Light," 2128–9, suggests that he critiques this view (from Chrysippos); cf. *Brut.* 37, but the language seems to indicate a tentative suggestion.

[35] From him "much of literary demonology in the early Imperial period has to be drawn"; Brenk, "Light," 2082.

[36] J. Z. Smith, "Towards Interpreting Demonic Powers in Historic and Roman Antiquity," in W. Haase (ed.), *ANRW* II.16.1 (Berlin: de Gruyter, 1978), 436, finds this remarkable.

[37] Other texts may also be relevant: for example, in *Cam.* 21.2, are the men opting to join the departed spirits by staying in the city? Or texts with potential magical allusions, which therefore suggest that the daimon referred to is a spirit of the dead (*Crass.* 22.4; *Pub.* 13.4, cf. curse tablets against charioteers?).

[38] Brenk, "Light," 2125: "most important of all for Plutarch's general conception or tendency in his writing is the understanding of *daimones* as former souls"; cf. 2124, 2127–6.

To sum up the discussion thus far: it can be argued that the continued presence of the connection between the daimons and the dead in the philosophical literature, alongside the more elaborate, emergent daimonology, may indicate that "even these circles had to orientate themselves by popular ideas," despite combating or seeking to move beyond them.³⁹

Evidently, these popular ideas were persistent and strong, especially for the person who was, in Deissmann's phrase, "a mere loafer at the docks, leading a vegetable existence, … with no religion except for a belief in daemons!"⁴⁰ The connection is particularly clear in magical practice, where the attempt to enlist the aid of infernal daimons is clearly an attempt to utilize the powers of the dead.

Using bizarre imagery, Morton Smith points out that

> the intellectuals, the authors and readers of literary and scientific texts, are a tiny upper class, the thin, brilliant skin of a soap bubble filled with smoke. … The surface of the soap bubble reflects the brilliant scene of the Roman Empire—consuls, armies and client kings, cities, temples, and theaters. Through these reflections we catch only glimpses of the dark cloud behind them.⁴¹

The dark cloud to which he refers is the realm of the occult. Despite the fact that the occult, "although popular, is not fashionable in [modern] academic, rationalistic circles … the ancient world lies mostly in that twilight zone of popular beliefs."

In this realm, two types of magic can be distinguished: the spiritistic and the natural, although

> "natural magic" shows no explicit connection with spirits, ghosts, demons, or gods … in the case of the spiritistic type of magic, the ghosts of the dead are called up by the necromancer to give oracles or to discover hidden treasures. They are also sent to enter into the bodies of men, to afflict them with diseases and to cure them; and in many other ways they are forced to do the will of the magician, whose spells and incantations are held to be powerful enough to control the will of such spirits.⁴²

Although regarded suspiciously at official levels, such magic was widespread in the ancient world at more private—or even underground—levels of society.⁴³ It could be

---

³⁹ Foerster, "δαίμων," 1; cf. 3–6.
⁴⁰ A. Deissmann, *Light from the Ancient East: The New Testament Illustrated by Recently Discovered Texts of the Graeco-Roman World* (London: Hodder & Stoughton, 1927), 247.
⁴¹ Smith, "Occult," 236.
⁴² E. Langton, *Good and Evil Spirits: A Study of the Jewish and Christian Doctrine, Its Origin and Development* (London: SPCK, 1942), 42, in reverse.
⁴³ R. M. Ogilvie, *The Romans and Their Gods* (London: Chatto & Windus, 1969), 105. For sanctions against magic, see C. R. I. Phillips, "*Nullum Crimen sine Lege*: Socioreligious Sanctions on Magic," in C. A. Faraone and D. Obbink (eds.), *Magika Hiera: Ancient Greek Magic & Religion* (Oxford: Oxford University Press, 1991), 262–76.

innocuous, or positive (as in desperate attempts to ward off disease), but it could also be malevolent[44] (as epitomized by the curse tablets).

The Magical sources illustrate spiritistic magic at work. Although the Magical Papyri are mostly later than the NT period,[45] they are nevertheless useful for comparative purposes, since it is highly probable that they represent collections of much earlier material,[46] and magical practices were conservative,[47] or even reactionary.[48] The curse tablets provide further support that some of the practices in the Magical Papyri are much older than the papyri themselves.[49] For my purposes, the dating question is not crucial, since the testimony of the papyri and the curse tablets combine to show that the connection between the daimons and the dead was made across the several centuries on either side of the NT period.

The connection with the dead is often reinforced by the context of usage. Many of the papyrus spells were used in connection with graves and corpses, and several have been found in graves, even in the mouth of a mummy (*PGM* XIXa). Most of the curse tablets come from graves;[50] some from other places connected with the underworld, such as chthonic sanctuaries or wells and other bodies of water.[51] This is not simply because such places were convenient "openings" to the underworld deities, with the

---

[44] Such magic was a socially unacceptable means to protecting or procuring socially acceptable ends (e.g., success in family, business); cf. H. S. Versnel, "Beyond Cursing: The Appeal to Justice in Judicial Prayers," in Faraone and Obbink, *Magika Hiera*, 62–3.

[45] At least four are earlier: a curse (*PGM* XL, fourth century BCE [*GMPT*: fourth century CE sic!]); a charm against headache/inflammation (*PGM* XX, second/first century BCE) and two love charms (PMonGr inv 216 = *GMPT* CXVII, first century BCE; SuppMag **72** = *GMPT* CXXII, Augustan). W. Brashear, "The Greek Magical Papyri: An Introduction and Survey; Annotated Bibliography (1928–1994)," in W. Haase (ed.), *ANRW* II.18.5 (Berlin: de Gruyter, 1995), 3491–92, lists others assigned to the first century, but this dating is not without dispute: XVI (Jordan, see later: second/third century CE); CXI (*GMPT*: third/fourth century CE); XV? (*GMPT*: third century CE); XXXa, XXXIb, and XXXIa are oracular questions and so can be excluded (so *GMPT*).

[46] Many extant spells are exemplars into which the magician would insert the client's name. Evidence such as the presence of spelling blunders indicates that the recipes were not well understood by the practitioners; the style of script can indicate a spell was professionally produced. Acts 19:19 indicates that there was a large market for magic books in the NT period.

[47] Cf. the curse tablets provide evidence across a millennium. The "confession inscriptions" also provide an analogy: "the dated confession inscriptions themselves prove precisely how persistently a religious practice can be maintained over two centuries, even to details of wording"; Versnel, "Cursing," 76. It is also relevant that magical assumptions and practices seem to be fairly uniform across cultures and over large time spans.

[48] Although certainty is impossible, due to varying potential durability of different materials, the continued practice of writing on lead even when other mediums were available may be an example; retrograde writing may be another, becoming "'petrified' in the ritual and henceforth assum[ing] greater significance"; C. A. Faraone, "The Agonistic Context of Early Greek Binding Spells," in Faraone and Obbink, *Magika Hiera*, 7–8; and perhaps even the use of foreign words as if their efficacy depended upon their non-translation.

[49] "Detailed instructions for the manufacture and burial of *defixiones* are preserved in the magical handbooks of the third and fourth centuries A.D. and seem to be in general agreement with the archaeological evidence for the earlier periods, e.g., *PGM* V.304; VII.394, 417; IX; XXXVI.1–35, 231; LVIII"; Faraone, "Agonistic," 22 n. 5.

[50] SGD **1** and **2** were actually placed in the right hand of the deceased.

[51] Only later tablets originate in wells; see D. R. Jordan, "Two Inscribed Lead Tablets from a Well in the Athenian Kerameikos," *AM* 95 (1980): 231–2.

corpse being used like a "pillar-box,"[52] but, insofar as these spells are "letters," many are addressed to the corpse,[53] either in an attempt to enlist help in gaining the power of an underworld god or, more importantly for my purposes, to enlist the ghost itself.

Many of the spells in the Magical Papyri show us that the daimons manipulated by the magician were patently connected to the spirits of the dead. The invocation of the daimons in the dark (οἱ ἐν τῷ σκότει δαίμονες; *PGM* XXXVI.138), or those "beneath the earth" (δαίμονες οἱ ὑπὸ τὸν χθόνον; 146), can be compared with the notion that it is the dead who are away from the light.[54] These "daimons of men who once gazed on the light" (δαίμονες ἀνθρώπων οἱ πρὶν φάος εἰσορόωντες)[55] are those who dwell "in the region of the corpses" (νεκύων ἐπὶ χῶρον) (*PGM* IV.446 = 1968, cf. VIII.81).

It is from this region that the spells often seek to enlist an "attendant" (πάρεδρος) (*PGM* I.1 and 42) or an "assistant" (παραστάτης) (*PGM* IV.1849–50). According to "a tested spell for invisibility" (fourth/fifth century CE), after "taking an eye of an ape or of a corpse that has died a violent death" (λαβὼν πιθήκου ὀφθαλμὸν ἢ νέκυος βιοθανάτου) (*PGM* I.248), the user is to say, "Rise up, infernal *daimon*" (ἀνάστηθι, δαίμων καταχθόνιε) (253). The use of the corpse of one killed violently makes it clear that the magician is conjuring the spirit of this dead person, the "*daimon* below the ground."

In "Nephotes to Psammetichos, an invocation to Typhon/Helios" (*PGM* IV.245–7), we read that at Typhon's name the ground, "the depths of the sea, Hades, Heaven, the sun, the moon, the visible chorus of stars, the whole universe all tremble, the name which when it is uttered forcibly brings gods and *daimons* to it" (θεοὺς καὶ δαίμονας ἐπ' αὐτὸ βίᾳ φέρει). Having used the invocation "whomever you called will appear, god or dead man [ὃν φωνεῖς, θεος ἢ νέκυς], and he will give an answer" (249).

The use of an assistant daimon who is the spirit of a dead person is especially clear in the love charms, as exemplified by the "Wondrous Spell for binding a lover" (*PGM* IV.296–466).[56] Two figures are made, inscribed, and pierced, a similar procedure to that used in the curse tablets.[57] The tablet is tied to the figures, and they are all placed beside the grave of one who has died untimely or violently as the sun sets (332–3; cf. 435). The spell is written and then recited. Alongside the chthonic gods, the binding spell is entrusted to the chthonic daimons (δαίμοσι καταχθονίοις),[58] to men and

---

[52] R. Garland, *The Greek Way of Death* (London: Duckworth, 1985), 6, 86, following D. C. Kurtz and J. Boardman, *Greek Burial Customs* (London: Thames & Hudson, 1971), 217.

[53] Cf. Faraone, "Agonistic," 4; Jordan, "Kerameikos," 234.

[54] "To see the light" is a standard Homeric image for being alive (*Il.* 18.61; *Od.* 4.540 etc.). This was imitated by the later poets, for whom, conversely, to leave the sun's light meant to die (Hes., *Op.* 155, cf. *Theog.* 669; *Hymn to Demeter* 35). A departed soul could be called back into the light (Aesch., *Pers.* 630; cf. Ps.-Phoc. 100–101). Cf. the darkness of the underworld in the series of curse tablets in D. R. Jordan, "Defixiones from a Well Near the Southwest Corner of the Athenian Agora," *Hesperia* 54 (1985): 205–55.

[55] Cf. Preisendanz, vol. II, p. 239, 9; PGM [I.317], IV.444 = 1965.

[56] For a parallel text, see SuppMag **49** (third/fourth century CE).

[57] An almost identical figure with a lead tablet has been found in Egypt. See S. Kambitsis, "Une nouvelle tablette magique d'Égypte, Musée du Louvre, Inv. E 27145, 3ᵉ / 4ᵉ siècle," *BIFAO* 76 (1976): 213–23. For photograph, see J. Gager, ed., *Curse Tablets and Binding Spells from the Ancient World* (Oxford: University Press, 1992), 98.

[58] This phrase is also found in DTA **99** (third century BCE).

women who have died untimely deaths, to youths and maidens (ἀώροις τε |καὶ ἀώραις, μέλλαξί τε καὶ παρθένοις) to lend their aid. It then adjures all the daimons in this place (πάντας δαίμονας |τούς ἐν τῷ τόπῳ τούτῳ), that is, the cemetery, to come to the aid of this daimon (τῷ δαί |μονι τούτῳ), that is, the particular corpse in the grave, for the magician's use. He then calls upon the daimon of the corpse: "Arouse yourself, whoever you may be, whether male or female" (ἀνέγειρέ μοισαυτόν, ὅςτις ποτ' εἶ, |εἴτε ἄρρην, εἴτε θῆλυς). Later, the spell reminds the daimons of the great name by which they tremble, and once again the daimon of the corpse is invoked, this time with the special term νεκύδαιμον or "corpse daimon" (361, 368, 396–7). This ghost is told: "Rouse only yourself from the repose which holds you, whoever you are, whether male or female, and go" (ἔγειρον μόνον[59] ςεαυτόν ἀπὸ τῆς ἐχούςης |ςε ἀναπαύςεως, ὅςτις ποτὲ εἶ, εἴτε ἄρρης, εἴτε θῆ|λυς, καὶ ὕπαγε) (369–70).

As in several other charms, Helios is invoked—the one who not only rules heaven and earth but also "Chaos and Hades, where Men's *daimons* dwell who once gazed on the light"—because the magician wishes him to bring up the daimon he wants to use, the one from the grave:[60] "Hear, blessed one, for I call you who rule Heaven and earth, and even now I beg you, blessed one, Unfailing one, the master of the world, If you go to the depths of earth and search The regions of the dead, send this *daimon* [δαίμονα τοῦτον]" (*PGM* IV.442-8). This daimon of the corpse, once delivered, will then be sent to the woman the man wishes to draw to him: "Be kind to me, forefather, scion of The world, self-gendered, fire-bringer, aglow Like gold, shining on mortals, master of The world, / *daimon* of restless fire, unfailing, With gold disk, sending earth pure light in beams. Send the *daimon*, whomever I have requested, to her, NN" (458–62).[61]

Another love/fetching charm (SuppMag **44**) confirms the connection from the opposite direction when it assigns to a soul the role accorded elsewhere to a daimon: the woman is fetched "by means of the soul of the one who died prematurely" (διὰ | τῆς ψυχῆς τοῦ ἀώ[[ο]]ρου) (l.13).[62]

Addressing the ghost of the corpse is such a standard feature of the magical procedure that, in time, the practice generated a special word. Many later spells are addressed to a νεκύδαιμον (*PGM* IV.361, 368, 397, 2031, 2060; V.334; XII.494, plural: [ν]εκυδαίμω[α]ς, <κατὰ> νεκύ[ων]; XIXa.15, also called κύριε δαῖμον, 151; SuppMag **49**;[63] cf. IV.1474–5: τὰ εἴδωλα τῶν μεκύων). Of special interest in this regard

---

[59] This appears to be an indication of the fear in which these spells were used: he does not want the daimon to bring any "uninvited guests," who may not, perhaps, be as containable! Cf. the protective measures recommended in the spells.

[60] Such Helios invocations assume the ancient view of the Sun's nocturnal journey through the underworld, known both in Semitic culture (cf. the Hittite Prayer of Kantuzilis: "O Sun God, when thou goes down to the nether world [to be] with him, forget not to speak with that patron god of mine and apprise him of Kantuzilis' plight" [*ANET* 400–1, ll.1–5]) and Greek (*Od.* 10.190–91). Cf. the prominent role played by the Sun god in Mesopotamian ghost incantations (Scurlock, *Magical Means*, 179–80, 264–5, 305, 328, etc.).

[61] The drawing spell of King Pituos' has similar features (*PGM* IV.1968–70). For other love charms employing the spirits of the dead, cf. *PGM* IV.1390–98; XV; XIXa; SuppMag **49, 50, 51, 45**, and so on.

[62] The charm ends with a command in the plural (ἄξατε), which "may be directed to the individual ἄωρος [one who died early] whose soul is mentioned in line 14 as well as to the other νεκυδαίμονες in the same cemetery"; R. Daniel, "Two Love Charms," *ZPE* 19 (1975): 264.

[63] D. R. Jordan, "A Love Charm with Verses," *ZPE* 72 (1988): 245–59.

is *PGM* XVI, because it was originally assigned by handwriting to the first century CE, even though more recent estimates place it more probably in the second or third.[64] This papyrus contains a love charm repeated nine times virtually word for word, apart from the different magical names and gods inserted, the ghost of the corpse being invoked at least eight times (1, 9, 17–18, 25, 34, 43, 54, 61, ?67, ?73).

Peculiar to magical texts, the word underlines what is the practice of other spells. They are addressing the spirit of the dead: "O corpse-*daimon*" or, better, "O ghost."[65] Archeological discoveries have yielded some sixteen hundred curse tablets, or *defixiones*, which "became popular in the fifth century BCE and continued in use in Mediterranean lands until at least the sixth century of our era." They not only "provide our best continuous evidence for the practice of magic in the millennium from classical times to the close of antiquity"[66] but also confirm that the daimons were connected to the dead.

The use of such tablets for cursing enemies, part of the malevolent magic mentioned in the literary sources (e.g., Plato, *Resp.* 364B), is attested for in the first century. A Flavian inscription from Tuder may thank one Iuppiter O. M. for bringing to light a buried *defixio*, which cursed a number of *decuriones* (CIL 11.4639), although this is not the only reading.

> If *defixia* simply means "attached" and if *monumentis* refers to a public monument, the result would be a public act rather than an instance of a *defixio*.[67] But if *defixia* is used in a technical sense, that is, in preparing a curse tablet, and if *monumentis* refers to tombs, we would have a clear reference to a *defixio*.[68]

In an earlier and more famous example, *defixiones* discovered in the walls and floors of the house of Germanicus in Syrian Antioch associated with his supposedly unnatural death in 19 CE brought terror to the masses and led to the execution of a scapegoat:[69]

> And it is a fact that explorations in the floor and walls brought to light the remains of human bodies, spells, curses, leaden tablets engraved with the name Germanicus, charred and blood-smeared ashes, and others of the implements of witchcraft by which it is believed the living soul can be devoted to the powers of the grave. (Tacitus, *Ann.* 2.69)

Thus, as with the magic in the papyri, Tacitus knows that these tablets were used in the attempt to enlist the forces of the dead to the malevolent purposes of the magician (or his client).

---

[64] D. R. Jordan, "A New Reading of a Papyrus Love Charm in the Louvre," *ZPE* 74 (1988): 232–3, who provides a number of improvements on *PGM*.
[65] Jordan, "Love Charm," translates both νεκύδαιμον and δαίμον "ghost" in SuppMag **49**.
[66] For this paragraph, SGD **151**, updating the number of defixiones from 1100.
[67] This argument reflects that of D. R. Jordan, who does not think curse tablets were involved (*per litt.* 2/4/96).
[68] Gager, *Curse Tablets*, 135, who takes it in the latter sense, as does Versnel, "Cursing," 63.
[69] Cf. the bronze tablet, inscribed in Greek, discovered in a tomb, which was reported to be associated with Caesar's death, Suetonius, *Julius* 81.

In the earlier tablets, the corpse is not regarded as a power at all, but its very inertness is the key to the efficacy of the curses. A change occurs, however, in about the fourth century BCE, and the dead becomes a power to be invoked.[70] About this time also the spirit of the dead begins to be called δαίμων: *DTA* **102** (fourth century BCE) is an epistle sent to a corpse, called a [δ]αίμων;[71] and in *DTA* **99** (third century BCE) the δαίμων χθόνιος is, once again, properly regarded as the spirit νεκύδαιμον,[72] the daimon(s) of this place,[73] those buried here,[74] or even "*daimons*, those roaming about in this place,"[75] that is, the grave or cemetery. Although occasionally the νεκύδαιμον is given a name,[76] that is, that of the corpse, more frequently it is addressed as the daimon "whoever you are," that is, the anonymous corpse.[77]

In sum, the curse tablets provide evidence that the spirits of the dead were evoked as powers since the fourth century BCE, and at that time they were also called "daimons." Both the curse tablets and the papyri show that this belief in the daimons as the dead eventually became enshrined in magical vocabulary with the term νεκύδαιμον. It is amid this progression—which amounts to a strengthening of the same belief—that the Gospel writers spoke of Jesus casting out daimons. But before coming to the Gospel material, it is worth observing that the same connection is found in writings which are culturally akin to them.

Daimons and the Dead in Hellenistic Jewish Literature

The connection between the daimons and the dead, as well as its exploitation in magical practices, can be discerned in the LXX, Pseudo-Phocylides, Philo and Josephus, as well as in the Pseudepigrapha.

In the LXX, the δαιμ- group associates idolatry with the worship of daimons[78] and is closely linked with the dead and with magic.[79] Reflecting as it does necromantic practices, that is, calling on the dead to aid the living, Isaiah 65 (esp. vv. 3, 11) illustrates all three features in the one passage.

---

[70] For this paragraph, see Bravo, "Tablette."
[71] Ibid., 203: "Le démon, ici, est évidemment le démon du mort aupres duquel l'auteur va déposer sa tablette."
[72] DT **234, 235, 237, 239, 240, 242**—all first century CE (Audollent); SGD **152, 153, 160, 162**; BM 1878.10–19.2; see D. R. Jordan, "Inscribed Lead Tablets from the Games in the Sanctuary of Poseidon," *Hesperia* 63 (1994): 123 n.22; SuppMag **42.11–12**; SuppMag **46**.
[73] DT **22, 38** (= SuppMag **54**), **198**; cf. **234**.
[74] DT **25, 25, 26, 29, 30, 31**, [**32, 33**], **34, 35, 271**; SuppMag **45**.
[75] DT **38** (= SuppMag **54**) ll. 35–36: δ[αί|μο]νες οἱ ἐν τῷ τόπω τού[τω.] φοιτῶντες …
[76] SuppMag **37, 47, 50**; PGM XXXII and, for the formulary allowing such insertions, IV.2180.
[77] DT **234, 235, 237, 238, 239, 240, 242**, [**249**]—all first century CE (Audollent); Jordan, "Agora," **12**.
[78] Deut. 32:17; Isa. 65:3, 11 (S δαίμων; A B δαιμονίῳ; לַבֵּן); Ψ 96 (95):5; 106 (105): 37.
[79] All usages in Tobit (3:8, 17; 6:7, 7, 13, 14, 15, 17; 8:3) refer to the daimon Asmodeus, whose sole function is to kill, and whose "exorcism" is achieved by magical means. Isa. 13:21; 34:14; Bar. 4:7, 35 (cf. Rev. 18:2) all use the topos of a destroyed city being filled with daimons/ghosts; and Ψ 91 (90): 6 (Sm δαιμονιώδης) appropriated by magical texts for centuries. More generally, prohibitions against magical practices indicate that these were also part of things Canaanite, as was human sacrifice (which can be detected behind the texts in previous note). Thus idolatry, magic, and daimons/ghosts can all be connected.

The Sentences of Pseudo-Phocylides (30 BCE–40 CE), which show a knowledge of magic,[80] probably assumes this connection when it warns:

Μὴ τύμβον φθιμένων ἀνορύξῃς μηδ᾿ ἀθέατα δείξῃς ἠελίῳ καὶ δαιμόνιον χόλον ὄρσῃς. (Ps.-Phoc. 100–101)

(Do not dig up the grave of the deceased, neither expose | to the sun what may not be seen, lest you stir up the *daimonic* anger.)

Although, for the sake of his Hellenistic audience, Philo equates the angelic beings of the Jewish literature with the daimons (as intermediate beings) of the Greek literature, the very fact that the daimons are also placed upon his continuum of souls indicates that they are related (*Somn.* 1.135–41; *Gig.* 6–12), if not explicitly equated (*Gig.* 16) to souls.

The connection between daimons and the dead emerges very clearly when Philo reports that Caius murdered his father-in-law "after dismissing all thought of his dead wife's *daimons*" (πολλὰ χαίρειν φράσας τοῖς δαίμοσι τῆς ἀποθανούσης γυναικός). This incidental reference (*Legat.* 65) shows that the connection existed in Rome in 39–40 CE and, given the lack of either critique or explanation, that it was part of the repertoire of both author and audience.

Several passages in Josephus assume the connection between the daimons and the dead.[81] To provide but one example, Josephus says that, despite its tendency to kill the one attempting to pluck it,[82] the plant rue possesses one highly prized virtue:

τὰ γὰρ καλούμενα δαιμόνια, ταῦτα δὲ πονηρῶν ἐστιν ἀνθρώπων πνεύματα τοῖς ζῶσιν εἰσδυόμενα καὶ κτείνοντα τοὺς βοηθείας μὴ τυγχάνοντας, αὕτη ταχέως ἐξελαύνει, κἂν προσενεχθῇ μόνον τοῖς νοσοῦσι. (*J.W.* 7.185; cf. *Ant.* 8.45–49)

(For the so-called *daimons*—in other words, the spirits of wicked men which enter the living and kill them unless aid is forthcoming—are promptly expelled by this root, if merely applied to the patients.)

Here the daimons are defined in terms of the ghosts of the wicked, bent on human destruction.

The connection between idolatry, daimons, and the dead, already noted in the Septuagint (earlier), is also found in several pseudepigraphal texts. The Greek text of *1 En.* 99:7 speaks of the idolater worshipping "phantoms and *daimons* and abominations and evil spirits" (λατρεύ[οντες φαν]τάσμασιν καὶ δαιμονίοι[ς καὶ βδελύγ]μασιν καὶ πνεύμασιν πονη[ροῖς),[83] and *1 En.* 19:1 speaks of the Watchers leading others astray

---

[80] §149 explicitly refers to magic; but magical practices may also lie behind §§100–102 (rather than grave-robbery for medical dissection) and §150, despite the fact that this has apparently not been canvassed previously; cf. P. W. van der Horst, *The Sentences of Pseudo-Phocylides*, VTP 4 (Leiden: Brill, 1978).

[81] The daimonic powers of the dead worked on the side of justice (*J.W.* 1.82, 84; *Ant.* 13.314, 317, 415–16, etc.); as vengeful ghosts (*J.W.* 1.599, 607; cf. *Ant.* 17.1) or spirits of the blessed dead (*J.W.* 6.47).

[82] There were protective spells against the dangers of picking plants; cf. *PGM* IV.286–95.

[83] Nickelsburg's translation takes the Greek text into account: "worship phantoms and demons and abominations and evil spirits" (G. W. E. Nickelsburg, *1 Enoch*, Hermeneia [Minneapolis,

"to sacrifice to the *daimons*" (ἐπιθύειν τοῖς δαιμονίοις), which is the language of the Septuagint (Deut. 32:17; Ps. 105[ET: 106]:37; cf. 1 Cor. 10:20). Noting the connection between demons and idolatry in these two passages, *Jub.* 22:16-23, and elsewhere (Deut. 32:17; Gal. 4:8; 1 Cor. 10:20-22; Rev. 9:20; cf. *T. Job* 3:3-4), Nickelsburg posits a common and long tradition which "might justify translating φαντάσμασιν [in *1 En.* 99:7] as 'phantoms' or 'ghosts' rather than simply 'apparitions.'"[84]

The same threefold connection appears in denunciations of idolatry in the Sibylline Oracles, such as when Rome, after a prediction of her fall, is asked what god will save her, since those she worshipped were "demons without life, images of the worn-out dead" (δαίμονας ἀψύχους, νεκύων εἴδωλα καμόντων) (*Sib. Or.* 8.47). Another lengthy denunciation speaks of the idolators "with the smell of sacrifice filling the feast, as if for their own corpses" (θοίνη κνισσοῦντες, ὡς τοῖς ἰδίοις νεκύεσσιν), while they "pour out blood to *daimons*" (δαίμοσιν αἷμα χέουσιν), "doing [such things] to *daimonic* corpses, as to heavenly beings" (δαίμοσι ποιήσουσι νεκροῖς, ὡς οὐρανίοισιν) (8.384, 386, 393). Another fragment indicts them saying, "You have made your sacrifices to the *daimons* in Hades" (δαίμοσι τὰς θυσίας ἐποιήσατε τοῖσιν ἐν Ἄιδη) (21.22 [frag. 1.22]), locating the daimons in the realm of the dead. Similarly, in an obscure fragment of the Apocalypse of Adam, the connection between the daimons and the dead is nevertheless clear, in the reference to "daimons passing through in their tombs" (διέρχονται δαίμονες ἐν τοῖς μνήμασιν) (Apoc. Adam 1:4).[85]

To sum up this section: it would be too much to claim that all people everywhere automatically connected the daimonic with the dead. In philosophical circles more elaborate daimonologies had emerged and were emerging in which the daimonic spirits were intermediate beings. However, it is clear that at the more popular level, as represented by the magical world, daimons were persistently identified with ghosts and that this also protrudes into the literary sources, both Greco-Roman and Hellenistic-Jewish. Since the early readers of Mark were most probably closer to the world of magic than they were to the world of the philosophers, the next section of this chapter asks how such an identification would affect the hearing of Mark's four exorcisms.[86]

MN: Fortress, 2001]; cf. M. A. Knibb, *The Ethiopic Book of Enoch: A New Edition in the Light of the Aramaic Dead Sea Fragments* [Oxford: Clarendon, 1978], 2.233): "And they worship stone, and *some* (15r, c10) carve images of gold and of silver and of wood and of clay, and *some, with no knowledge,* worship unclean spirits and demons and every (kind of) error, but no help will be obtained from them"; and Isaac: "(And those) who worship stones, and those who carve images of gold and of silver and of wood and of clay, and those who worship evil spirits and demons, and all kinds of idols not according to knowledge, they shall get no manner of help in them"; in J. H. Charlesworth, *The Old Testament Pseudepigrapha* (New York: Doubleday, 1983), vol. 1.

[84] Nickelsburg, *1 Enoch*, 492.

[85] Access from *Accordance*. For text, see M. R. James, "A Fragment of the Apocalypse of Adam in Greek," in *Apocrypha Anecdota II*, Texts and Studies 2.3 (Cambridge: Cambridge University Press, 1893), 138–45; G. J. Reinink, "Das Problem des Ursprung des Testamentes Adams," OrChrAn 197 (1972): 387–99; S. E. Robinson, *The Testament of Adam: An Examination of the Syriac and Greek Traditions*, SBLDS 52 (Chico, CA: Scholars, 1982).

[86] The connection is also relevant for other portions of Mark, such as the summaries (1:32-34, 39; 3:11, 15, 22–23, 30; 6:7; 9:38), the charge made against Jesus (3:22-30), and the death of the Baptist (6:14-29). The latter two passages, and those in the following material, are dealt with more fully in Bolt, *Jesus' Defeat of Death*.

Hearing Jesus's Exorcisms from This Point of View

The involvement of ghosts in exorcisms is well attested from Ancient Egypt, Ancient Babylon and Assyria, and in the second-century Greek writers Lucian (*Philops.* 16)[87] and Philostratus (*Vit. Apoll.* 3.38, 4.20). Later readers apparently read Gospel exorcism accounts from this point of view, despite the Fathers' objections,[88] and perhaps this would have been automatic for many of Mark's earlier readers as well. What would such a reading be like?

If we are inquiring into the nature of the beings which control the man in the Capernaum synagogue (Mk 1:21-28), then there is not much to go on in the story. Evidently they perceived their battle with Jesus to be a struggle to the death, for they asked whether Jesus had come to destroy them (v. 24). Although there is nothing in the account itself which specifically links the "unclean spirits" with ghosts,[89] there are several links with the world of magic (the naming, the binding, the violence, and the noise on exit; vv. 24–25). Since it assumed the connection, readers familiar with magic would recognize that Jesus was being engaged by departed spirits, after the fashion of a magical encounter. The story ends having firmly established Jesus's authority over the spirits (v. 27).

What difference would it make if the hearer of this story automatically made the connection? The important thing for Mark's narrative is the spirits' question, "Have you come to destroy us?" (v. 24). If Jesus does destroy the daimons, what would result? The hostility of ghosts to humans, whether or not those ghosts had been set upon the victim by some magician (or his client), could have many and varied unpleasant effects on ordinary life.[90] The daimons' question raises the possibility that

---

[87] W. D. Smith, "So-Called Possession in Pre-Christian Greece," *TAPA* 96 (1965): 403–26, claims this as the first exorcism in Greek literature. However, a fragment of a fifth-century BCE mime may allude to an exorcism; cf. D. L. Page, *Select Papyri III*, LCL (London: Heinemann, 1941; repr. 1970), 73.

[88] For example, Chrysostom, *Hom. on Matthew* 28 3; *2 Hom. on Lazarus* 6.235.6. The critique of the daimon/ghost connection is at least as early as Tatian 16.1. P. Brown, "Sorcery, Demons and the Rise of Christianity," in M. Douglas (ed.), *Witchcraft: Confessions & Accusations* (London: Tavistock, 1970), 32, summarizes:

> Where the teachings of the Fathers of the Church clash with popular belief, it is invariably in the direction of denying the human links involved in sorcery (they will deny, for instance, that it is the souls of the dead that are the agents of misfortune), in order to emphasize [sic] the purely demonic nature of the misfortunes that might afflict their congregations.

Their successful campaign may be a major reason for the virtual elimination of the daimon/ghost connection from later discussion.

[89] Equally, there is nothing to connect it with the usual "cosmic dualism" hypothesis. Persian dualism would be rather passé for a Greco-Roman reader; cf. Brenk, "Light," 2092.

[90] The widespread fear of ghosts can be variously illustrated, not least by the fact that both Greece and Rome had at least one annual festival for getting rid of them (Anthesteria; Lemuria); and cf. those in Cyrene (LSSupp **115**) and Selinous, discussed in M. H. Jameson, D. R. Jordan, and R. D. Kotansky, *A Lex Sacra from Selinous*, GRBM 11 (Durham, NC: Duke University, 1993). Certain features of Attic law can also be explained in terms of the fear of ghosts; L. R. Farnell, *The Higher Aspects of Greek Religion* (Chicago: Ares, 1977), 89. The impact of magic upon practically every aspect of ordinary life also provides testimony to the fear of ghosts in which people must have lived; cf. the philosophers' need to speak against δεισιδαιμονία (superstition), for example, Philo, *Gig.* 16; Plut., *De superstitione*.

Jesus had come to destroy these beings. If so, he would also end their manipulation by magicians and the resulting evil effects, thus breaking the fear of such influences and effects by which large segments of the populace were held. The question raises the exciting possibility that Jesus was about to unlock the stranglehold of the dead on the living.[91]

The Gerasene daimoniac constitutes the exorcism of all exorcisms in the Gospel of Mark (Mk 5:1-20). Here there are specific links between this man's daimons and the dead. The man is located in the tombs, which were widely recognized as the haunts of daimons, not surprisingly given the discussion so far. The connection with the dead is strengthened by the links with Isaiah 65, where people sit in the tombs for necromantic purposes; and perhaps also by the man's great strength. Perhaps I can take further comfort from the fact that at least one commentator has recognized that the daimons possessing this man are the spirits of the dead—even speculating that they are the ghosts of those who fell in battle with the Romans![92]

Not surprisingly, there are a number of features reminiscent of magical practice in this story as well: the great cry (Mk 5:7); the use of ὀρκίζω (v. 7)[93]—although here it is used in reverse; μή με βασανίσῃς, the word used in magical texts;[94] the request for the name (v. 9).[95] These features combine to make the story a clash between two great powers. The man who could not be bound (v. 4) attempts to bind Jesus (v. 7)—as if Jesus is the superior daimon and the daimon is the magician![96] Nevertheless, Jesus gains mastery over him and his spirits instead.

Why do the daimons request that Jesus not send them "out of the region" (ἔξω τῆς χώρας; v. 10)? Demonic fear is a feature of the magical spells—in fact, its modus operandi. But if their fear is simply of being sent outside the region of the Gerasenes (cf. v. 1), or even the region of the tombs, it seems difficult to account for. Instead, they are probably referring to an underworld space. As we saw earlier, in the spells invoking Helios, the region of the dead is the realm in which the daimons are recruited by Helios on his nightly underworld journey, to be released by him for the use of the necromancer in the upper world.[97] This fear may be illustrated by the threat of a silver phylaktery to remove them from this region, which allows the possibility of continued

---

[91] Although an actual destruction of the daimons would be no problem for the philosophically minded, for whom their mortality was one of the characteristics which differentiated them from the immortal gods (Plutarch, *De def. orac.* 418E), a destruction of the daimons' influence in this world best fits the NT material.

[92] G. Theissen, *The Miracle Stories of the Early Christian Tradition* (Philadelphia, PA: Fortress, 1983), 89 n. 21; 255 n. 58.

[93] This word and its compounds are extremely common in the magical texts; cf. Acts 19:13.

[94] S. Eitrem, *Some Notes on the Demonology of the New Testament* (Osloae: Universitetsforlaget, 1966), 24–5. See Versnel, "Cursing," 73, for the requests for the gods to use such juridicial torture. The love charms request that the victim be tortured by their thoughts of the interested party; for example, *DT* **242, 271**.

[95] Cf. *PGM* XIII, where the god will refuse to listen if you do not know the names.

[96] The concern to bind people and spirits is also an obvious hallmark of magical practice.

[97] Cf. also the *defixio* SEG **803** (third century CE) which asks Helios to send "the wailing of the violently killed" upon an opponent, presumably by bringing their daimons up with him.

traffic with the world above, to regions "below the springs and the abyss."[98] Does the fear of such nether regions lie behind their question?[99]

To our reader who connects daimons with the departed spirits, this man from the tombs is literally filled with a legion of the dead. The clash with Jesus shows that Jesus can control such hordes, cast them out, and even banish them from the region which allows them to exert an influence in the upper world. These spirits of death were bent on destruction (cf. Josephus, *J.W.* 7.185; Philostratus, *Vit. Apoll.* 3.38), but Jesus, acting as a superior spirit, certainly sent them back to their proper domain and perhaps even "destroyed" them.

In the previous incident narrated by Mark, several questions had been raised which received no answer, and so they function as guides to the reading of what follows. The disciples had asked, "Don't you care that we are perishing?" (4:38) and "Who then is this that even the winds and waves obey him?" (4:41).[100] The questions begin to find answers in Gerasa, where Jesus demonstrates not only that he does care for one who is perishing under the evil and destructive influence of the world of the dead but also that he is the one who can liberate people from such beings. The story is cast as a contest between Jesus and the power(s) of death. The man leaves the tombs and once again enters ordinary life. The "dead" had come to life again.

The exorcism of the Syro-Phonecian woman's daughter (Mk 7:24-30) does not tell us anything extra about the daimon's metaphysics. In the flow of the story, however, it reinforces the fact that Jesus can deal with such spirits. The new twist here is that he does so even for a Greek.

When it comes to the boy at the base of the mountain suffering from a killing spirit (Mk 9:14-29), many such boys were used in magical divination to channel the spirits of the dead.[101] The destructive nature of the afflicting spirit is evident (Mk 9:22), as would be expected if it were a vengeful ghost. Jesus has no doubt about his ability to deal with such a spirit and commands it to come out and never to enter again (v. 25). This latter prohibition is also found in magical materials,[102] as is the discussion of "kinds" of daimon (v. 29).[103]

---

[98] *GMA* 52; cf. D. R. Jordan, "A New Reading of a Phylactery from Beirut," *ZPE* 88 (1991): 61–9. See also *PGM* IV.1247–48, where the daimons are bound with fetters and delivered into "the black chaos in perdition" (εἰc τὸ μέλαν χάοc ἐν ταῖc ἀπωλείαιc).

[99] This is how Luke takes the reference (8:31); cf. Mt. 8:29, for the fear of torture before the appointed time—perhaps when they are sent into the Abyss (cf. 25:41)?

[100] Jesus's question regarding the disciples' (lack of) faith also guides the following stories (v. 40).

[101] For the use of boys in magic, cf. *PGM* V.1–53, 370–446; cf. VII.664–85, 348–58, 540–78; XIII.749–59; LXII.24–46; also frequently in *PDM*. Cf. Plutarch, *De def. orac.* 418B. The story itself is similar to *Vit. Apoll.* 3.38. See further, T. Hopfner, "Die Kindermedien in den griechisch-ägyptischen Zauberpapyri," in *Receuil d'études dédiées à la mémoire de N. P. Kondakov* (Prague: Seminarium Kondakovianum, 1926), 65–74.

[102] The forbidding of return is "no superfluous addition"; cf. Eitrem, *Notes*, 33; *Ant.* 7.2.5; 8.45–9; *Vit. Apoll.* 4.20, and, by implication, *PGM* IV.1254, 3015: "Consistent with this prevention, according to old Assyrian magic, a good *daimon* had to take the place left vacant by the evil one who is driven out."

[103] *PGM* IV.3040 asks for the identification of the kind of daimon and 3080 promises deliverance from whatever kind; cf. V.165. For one unmoved by prayer, see IV.1786.

Jesus apparently knows his spirits, and his exorcism is so powerful that he appears to kill the boy (v. 26).[104] The initial shock (perhaps he has come to destroy the daimons, but in the process does he destroy their victims too?) reinforces the ultimate lesson, for when he raises the boy, as if from the dead (v. 27), someone who regarded daimons as ghosts would see a powerful demonstration that Jesus's dealings with the powers of the dead issued in "resurrection life" for their victims.

For the person who viewed the daimons as ghosts of the dead, Jesus's exorcisms would be seen as an assault upon the world of the dead, and even upon death itself. Later sources reveal that Jesus was mistaken for a magician,[105] that is, as someone who manipulated the spirits of the dead. This probably began within Jesus's lifetime. This may have been the assumption behind the use of Jesus's name by the unknown exorcist (Mk 9:38), as later by the Jewish exorcists in Ephesus (Acts 19:13-17) and possibly also Simon the sorcerer from Samaria (Acts 8:9-24, noting v. 12 for "the name"), and even later by some of the magicians of the Magical Papyri. But Jesus also faced this charge explicitly during his ministry, when the Pharisees accused him of manipulating the daimons through the prince of daimons (Mk 3:22). It is highly likely that when Herod explained Jesus's activity by the speculation that John had been raised, he was also thinking of Jesus using John's ghost to produce miraculous results.[106] As both an ἀκέφαλος, "beheaded one," and a βιαιοθάνατος, "one who was killed violently," John would have a very powerful ghost (cf. Lucian, *Philops*. 9).

But Jesus was also different from other magicians. In Mark's story, among other things, he was cast as a superior spirit (5:1-20); rumored to be a ghost-manipulator (6:14-16); and even mistaken for a ghost himself (6:49).[107] The end of the story presents him as a crucified man, that is, one with the potential to be a very powerful spirit indeed.

The daimons were scared that he had come to destroy them. He was able to destroy the legion of ghosts in Gerasa, as well as to liberate the young Greek girl and the boy at the foot of the mountain in a lasting way. All this raises the following question for our reader: Did he simply have the power to manipulate the world of the dead, like any other magician? Or had he begun an assault on the dead in order to break the stranglehold that the dead held on the living?

By the end of the story, Mark's readers are left gazing upon the empty tomb of a man who had been crucified and hearing the declaration that he had risen. Apparently

---

[104] Chrysostom mentions the slaying of boys in connection with magic (see n. 88 earlier), and Simon Magus claims to have used such a boy in *Clementine Recognitions* II.13, 15. Is this practice behind PGM IV.2647 and Ps.-Phoc. 150 (given 149)? Clearchus tells of Aristotle's encounter with a magician who could draw out the soul of a sleeping boy to leave his body like that of a corpse; see the discussion in H. Lewy, "Aristotle and the Jewish Sage According to Clearchus of Soli," *HTR* 31 (1938): 208–9. For a discussion of "ritual murder," cf. A. Henrichs, *Die Phoinikika des Lollianos: Fragmente eines neuen griechischen Romans*, Papyrologische Texte und Abhandlungen 14 (Bonn: Habelt, 1972), 31–7.

[105] Cf. M. Smith, *Jesus the Magician* (London: Victor Golancz, 1978), chapter 4.

[106] C. H. Kraeling, "Was Jesus Accused of Necromancy?," *JBL* 59 (1940): 147–57; Smith, *Magician*, 33–4.

[107] Interestingly, φάντασμα (phantom) becomes δαιμόνιον in the Syriac Sinaiticus.

Jesus's assault on the dead was complete,[108] and the dead would no longer hold sway over life because a far greater spirit was now alive in their world.[109] Mark's story holds promise that his readers could look at their world with new eyes and face it with less fear, because a man who had been crucified had risen from the dead.[110]

---

[108] In this case, his exorcisms would have an integral, qualitative connection with the resurrection from the dead, not merely an indirect connection through some abstract concept of divine power or rule.

[109] Cf. Lk. 24:39; cf. C. F. Evans, *Saint Luke* (London: SCM, 1990), 919. Ignatius's loose rendering (*Smyrn* 3.2) has: "I am not a bodiless *daimon*" (οὐκ εἰμὶ δαιμόνιον ἀσώματον); as did the *Preaching of Peter* (cf. Origen, *de Princ*. i. prol. 8).

[110] Although my focus has been on Mark, the connection between daimons and the dead has further implications for the reading of the other Gospels and, indeed, for the daimonology of the NT. For my further work in this area since the original publication of this chapter, see "Life, Death, and the Afterlife in the Greco-Roman World," in R. N. Longenecker (ed.), *Life in the Face of Death: The Resurrection Message of the New Testament*, McMaster New Testament Studies 3 (Grand Rapids, MI: Eerdmans, 1998), 51–79; Bolt, "Towards a Biblical Theology of the Defeat of the Evil Powers"; and, with D. S. West, "Christ's Victory over the Powers and Pastoral Practice," in P. G. Bolt (ed.), *Christ's Victory over Evil: Biblical Theology and Pastoral Ministry* (Leicester: IVP, 2009), 35–81, 210–32; and various essays in P. G. Bolt and S. Beekmann, *Silencing Satan: A Handbook of Biblical Demonology* (Eugene, OR: Wipf and Stock, 2012).

4

Jesus and the Archetypes: A Study of the Heroic Archetype

Adam Z. Wright

The first-century Gospels appear within a world setting that was rich with story and, in particular, with mythology. These stories and myths covered a variety of topics and introduced a plethora of characters. The purpose of this chapter is to examine mythology and in particular how the heroes of mythology are introduced with regard to their purpose. More specifically, the hero of ancient myth follows a particular pattern that can be discerned, and this pattern can be found in most, if not all, ancient Mediterranean cultures. It is termed an archetype precisely because of its prevalence, and the archetype appears as a result of a shared preoccupation with fear, especially the fear of death. Examining the archetypes in this way will tell us why many characters appear the way they do and why, psychologically speaking, these characters continue to appeal to us centuries—and millennia—later.

The question about how relevant a study of the archetypes is fits within a greater discussion of intertextuality,[1] which becomes an important topic within biblical studies for a number of reasons: to determine genre, influence from other texts, the function of the text, potential communication with other texts, to name a few. Typically, we consider intertextuality in three different ways. The first is imitation (Latin: *imitatio*), which posits that the author of a text consciously refers to another text. A rather obvious example of this is found in a direct quotation where a Gospel writer directly quotes the words of a Hebrew text. This is done by way of what I have called an "Alexandrian Signpost," such as in the example, "You have heard it said (Ἠκούσατε ὅτι ἐρρέθη)."[2] Other ways that imitation occurs are in the form of allusion and metaphor, both of which are more precarious. For example, an allusion to another text can be rather subjective, meaning that an author may have intended a link but the reader is unable to notice it. Alternatively, a certain reader can perceive an allusion that was neither intended by the author nor recognized by other readers. Metaphor talks of one subject by way of another, which leaves some level of interpretation for the reader. This,

---

[1] There are a large number of studies that discuss intertextuality; however, I draw the reader's attention to one in particular: Stanley E. Porter, *Hearing the Old Testament in the New Testament* (Grand Rapids, MI: Eerdmans, 2006).

[2] See Adam Z. Wright, "Detecting Allusions in the Pauline Corpus: A Method," in Stanley E. Porter and David I. Yoon (eds.), *Paul and Gnosis*, Pauline Studies 9 (Leiden: Brill, 2016), 59–79.

again, may result in a number of competing interpretations—though not necessarily invalid—and ones that the author did not intend.

The second way that intertextuality is considered is by way of subversion (Latin: *aemulatio*), which showcases the ways in which a character imitates another yet represents different values. This has been noted in a variety of studies that consider how the earliest Christians compared Jesus to Caesar as the Son of God, both of whose coming was considered to be "good news."[3] This subversion then prompts the reader to make comparisons between the characters in question and arrive at certain conclusions based on those comparisons.

What imitation and subversion have in common is a method for comparison that one might reasonably employ with regard to several texts from a common time and place, or that have a common literary ancestral origin. This is certainly true of the early Christian scriptures and those of the Old Testament. This could also be true of Greco-Roman literature, whose relationship with early Christianity could be considered rather unsavory in theological terms, but whose proximity of culture and context cannot be denied. But what neither imitation nor subversion can truly address is how and why two texts, written outside of cultural proximity, can have significant overlap. Such questions give rise to the concept of a shared literary heritage and, if true, a heritage that would be very difficult to trace with accuracy. This problem raises the third way that intertextuality can be considered: an examination of archetypes. Archetypes address a fundamental question that goes beyond issues of temporality and proximity, which is a certain psychological experience that all of humanity shares.

In what follows, I will discuss fear as this common experience and showcase how the heroic archetype is formulated as a response to it. This archetype can be found in a variety of cultures throughout the ancient Mediterranean, and I will showcase how certain heroes from the Greco-Roman literary tradition function in the same manner as those from the Judeo-Christian literary tradition.

Fear as the Basis of Archetypal Representation

A theory of archetypes is based on the idea that writers, despite their contextual and temporal distances, can produce similar themes in their characters and stories.[4] What is more, the archetypal idea should be pervasive enough that any reader, regardless of context, can perceive and understand the archetype in a meaningful way. As Jung put it,[5]

---

[3] See Craig A. Evans, "Mark's Incipit and the Priene Calendar Inscription: From Jewish Gospel to Greco-Roman Gospel," *JGRChJ* 1 (2000): 67–81.

[4] As Campbell says: "The hero, therefore, is the man or woman who has been able to battle past his personal and local historical limitations to the generally valid, normally human forms." See Joseph Campbell, *The Hero with a Thousand Faces* (Novato, CA: New World Library, 2008), 14.

[5] In terms of archetypal theory, it is difficult to progress here without referencing Jungian psychoanalytic theory. Jung often mentions the archetypes during his discussions of symbology in myth, and his theories are largely based on his observations of what he calls a "collective unconscious." He developed this theory based on the number of similarities he found in the dreams of his many patients. These patients came to him from a variety of contexts, cultures, and regions of

From the unconscious there emanate determining influences which, independently of tradition, guarantee in every single individual a similarity and even a sameness of experience, and also of the way it is represented imaginatively. One of the main proofs of this is the almost universal parallelism between mythological motifs, which, on account of their quality as primordial images, I have called *archetypes*.[6]

This means that something truly archetypal must be internal, as opposed to an external source of motivation and, as stated, the internal, psychological motivation for archetypal representation is a preoccupation with the fear. This is not to say that other emotions are not present in a discussion about archetypal patterns, but I argue here that the fear—particularly a contention with fear—provides the basis for archetypal expression.[7]

Fear can be categorized into two tiers: the first being death and the second being those things that lead to death, such as falling, suffocation, pain, isolation, sudden movements (becoming prey), the unknown/abnormal, incapacitation, or disease.[8] The reason why death occupies the first tier is because it is unavoidable. According to Becker, "The idea of death haunts the human animal like nothing else; it is the mainspring of human activity—activity designed to avoid the fatality of death, to overcome it by denying it in some way that it is the final destination for man."[9] Following this logic, Hinton argues that death is the perceived separation from everything we love and from everything that gives our lives meaning, and perhaps even calls into question the purpose of life itself.[10] Feder argues that separation and pain are synonymous with death,[11] and Gordon notes that the death of a loved one is one of the most emotionally painful experiences that a human can have.[12] It appears that the fear of death is so prevalent that psychologists have begun to use the term "fear anxiety" to describe the neuroses associated with thinking about death.[13]

the world, so it begs the question as to why similarities could be found at all. In addition, Jung began to notice a number of similarities between the religious symbology found in a variety of ancient cultures. While I will not defend his theory in entirety here, I would be remiss not to mention it with reference to this study.

[6] Carl Jung, *The Archetypes and the Collective Unconscious*, vol. 9 (Princeton, NJ: Princeton University Press, 1969), 58; original emphasis.

[7] This could call into question such emotions as love, especially with regard to 1 Jn 4:18, "There is no fear in love. But perfect love drives out fear, because fear has to do with punishment. The one who fears is not made perfect in love." Such a verse might suggest that love is a more powerful psychological expression than fear, but I maintain that, in order for one to experience love as described in this verse, one must first be well acquainted with its opposite: fear of isolation.

[8] See also James George Frazer, *The Fear of the Dead in Primitive Religion* (New York: Biblo & Tannen, 1966), 10–11.

[9] Ernest Becker, *The Denial of Death* (New York: Free Press, 1973), ix.

[10] John Hinton, "The Physical and Mental Distress of the Dying," *Quarterly Journal of Medicine* 32 (1967): 1–21. See also C. C. Moore and J. B. Williamson, "The Universal Fear of Death and the Cultural Response," in Clifton D. Bryant (ed.), *Handbook of Death and Dying*, 2 vols. (London: Sage, 2003), 1:3–13.

[11] Samuel Feder, "Attitudes of Patients with Advanced Malignancy," in Edwin S. Shneidman (ed.), *Death: Current Perspectives* (Palo Alto, CA: Mayfield, 1976), 430–7.

[12] For a complete discussion, see Rosemary Gordon, *Dying and Creating: A Search for Meaning* (London: Karnac, 2000).

[13] Richard Shultz, "Death Anxiety: Intuitive and Empirical Perspectives," in Larry A. Busen (ed.), *Death and Dying: Theory/Research/Practice* (Dubuque, IA: William C. Brown, 1979), 66–87.

What these studies indicate is that all of our fears stem from our anticipation of death or the experience of death itself. This has led humanity to devise the means by which they can avoid premature death, or the second-tier fears—the things that lead to death. Not only this, but such observations promote the idea that humanity has always understood death, and the things that lead to it, as a "deviation" from ordered life and health. This meant that, for ancient cultures, the things mentioned here disturbed normal human experience and deserved an explanation.[14]

Cosmology as the Beginnings of Archetypal Expression

Such explanations have often come in the form of religious practice and belief, particularly that outside phenomena, such as the gods, spirits of the dead, or demons had become angry and inflicted the living with chaotic trouble. Such a belief is reflected in various near-Eastern cultures and their cosmologies, such as Egyptian, Mesopotamian, Indian, Jewish, and Greco-Roman; namely, that the world is an ordered place that was established by a deity and such order is sometimes disrupted by chaotic forces.[15]

For example, the Mesopotamians understood Chaos as a formless material that was ruled by the chaotic dragon Tiamat. It was then Marduk, a hero of the gods, who defeated Tiamat and crafted the earth out of the dragon's body.[16] The Vedic Indians likewise understood the world to have begun in a struggle between the hero-god Indra and the arch-demon Vritra, who is portrayed as a snake (*ahi*) or as a boar who dwells on the boarders of darkness. Indra defeats Vritra and begins to form the cosmos, dividing the *sat* from the *asat*, or the existent from the nonexistent.

Other traditions about the creation of the cosmos have less to do with battle and rather showcase the power of a god who creates with word and action. The Egyptians believed that the cosmos was shaped from formless, chaotic material into an ordered world.[17] The chaos was called Nun, and the sun-god Ra (though some argue that it was instead Ptah) rose to bring order to Nun.[18] This process conceptualized order as *ma'at* (base) and became the basis of Egyptian civility. Greek tradition exhibits this pattern with the creation of certain elements, or places, through the work of the god *Eros*: the sky (Uranus), the waters (Pontus), the earth (Gaia), Tartarus (the antithesis of Gaia),

---

[14] For a complete discussion of this idea, see Bronislaw Malinowski, *Magic, Science and Religion and Other Essays* (Boston: Beacon, 1948).

[15] This movement from Chaos to Order is important for discerning fear. If the first- and second-tier fears are synonymous with Chaos, it then means that Order represents a state where fear is quelled. It makes sense then why monsters and demons occupy the position of gatekeeper, so to speak, to Order. It is also why monsters, especially in the example of Marduk, or demons, in the case of Jesus, are to be defeated so that fear, or Chaos, is quelled.

[16] To see a number of competing theories and interpretations, see Norman Cohn, *Cosmos, Chaos, and the World to Come: The Ancient Roots of Apocalyptic Faith* (London: Yale University Press, 1993), 31–45.

[17] Ibid., 5.

[18] Ibid., 6–7.

and the darkness (Nyx/Erebus).[19] Jewish tradition, at least in Genesis 1, describes how Yahweh creates Order from the formless deep (Hebrew: תֹהוּ) through speech alone.[20]

The Archetype of the Hero as Tradition

From these few examples, we can gather that certain Mediterranean cultures understood the creation of the world as a formation of Order from Chaos. As such, the heroes of a culture's mythology follow in this tradition of creating Order from Chaos. It is important to note the creation myths here because they form the foundation upon which later mythological stories are built. Thus, the hero seeks to reestablish Order from Chaos as an imitation of the very act of creation, and this reestablishment is understood as a connection with the divine. This is precisely why the hero who acts out the archetype of the hero is usually semidivine, and the hero is then symbolically connected with his or her creator god by means of imitation.[21] This is also why the genealogies of past generations of heroes who embody this archetype are important: the act of reestablishing Order from impending Chaos is a tradition that links the hero's actions to their lineage and therefore to the divine.[22]

Creating Order can take a variety of forms which are expressed symbolically through story and religious practice. Such story and practice are then meant to organize and inspire the people who read them or partake in them, making the gods and heroes a means of orienting oneself toward the highest virtues within society and away from chaotic fear—the first- and second-tiered fears.[23]

The archetype of the hero represents the psychological struggle that humans engage in against their fears. This is why the hero is often juxtaposed with some form of monster or immense task, both symbolic representations of fear itself. The hero may also find themselves in battle against a foe or even at war with themselves.[24] Regardless of the

---

[19] Creation, as such, is noted by Ovid: "Before there was earth or sea or the sky that covers everything, all nature was the same the wide world across. It was that which we call *Chaos*; a raw confused mass, nothing but inert matter, badly combined discordant atoms of things, all mixed up in the same place" (*Metamorphoses* 1.5-9).

[20] We are told, however, in Ps. 74:13-17 that Yahweh divided the waters and defeated the Leviathan before he set the boundaries of the created world. It is possible that the Leviathan could have been interpreted in the same way as the Mesopotamian Tiamat.

[21] One may think here of the many semidivine or divine heroes: Achilles, Aeneas, Bellerophon, Castor and Pollux, Dionysus, Herakles, Odysseus, Peleus, Perseus, Theseus, and Jesus.

[22] This could be why Matthew and Luke link Jesus to both Adam, the son of God, and King David, the kingly representation of God to Israel. This is also why the Roman Imperial Cult became important, namely, that the emperor (Augustus) established peaceful order in the world and was understood as divine as a result.

[23] One may think of Aristotle who described the purpose of tragic drama as purging oneself of fear and pity (*Poetics*, 1449b). There is considerable debate with regard to what Aristotle meant by "purge." However, when considered in light of how one purges their fear through exposure to its symbolic representation, purging of fear is related to the result that one achieves by engaging with the symbolic on a psychological level. As for pity, it is possible that one could take the Chaotic position, so to speak, and empathize with Achilles instead of Hector, for example. This kind of interpretation speaks to the nature of humanity in that we can both embody Order and Chaos.

[24] The most obvious examples are found in the tragedy of Sophocles' *Oedipus the King* and *Ajax*.

plot, the hero advances himself or herself against the most fearful of things which, as mentioned earlier, can include: death, falling, suffocation, pain, isolation, sudden movements (becoming prey), the unknown/abnormal, incapacitation, or disease. This process is an attempt to alleviate fear and promote psychological wellness within an individual in the form of hope, and the hero thus displays the ideal traits that the audience of myth should emulate.

The Archetype of Hero in Greco-Roman Literature: Three Heroes

There are many examples of the hero archetype found throughout the Greco-Roman literary traditions, and this section will discuss three: Perseus, Herakles, and Theseus. Most of these heroes have a divine origin and strive against some form of Chaos—a result of their own behavior or because of something present in their context—to achieve Order. As Matyszak puts it, "Heroic feats usually ended with a monster dead, and the earth that bit more orderly and safer for humanity."[25] As mentioned, the archetype describes the psychological process of contesting with fear, and the audience is drawn into the same process thereby making their own lives more orderly.

There is also a set of criteria with regard to the hero's quest that is typological. In order to be recognized as a heroic myth, so to speak, the myth must showcase the following: the hero must be divine or of royal birth; the hero is separated from society by their call; the hero encounters Chaos (symbolic fear) and overcomes it by establishing Order;[26] the hero then returns to their people and imbues upon them some blessing that was gained throughout their journey.[27] In each of the examples listed in this chapter, the hero displays this archetypal cycle of the hero.

The first example of the hero archetype is found in Perseus, who was the son of Zeus and a hero of pre-Homeric Greece.[28] He was born of Zeus and Danaë and despised by his grandfather, Acrisius. Reluctant to kill his daughter and grandchild directly, Acrisius placed Danaë and Perseus in a wooden box and set them adrift on the sea, hoping that they would die in the waves instead. They survived, however, and were taken to safety by a fisherman named Dictys. Dictys had a brother named Polydectes who despised Perseus because he wanted to marry Danaë and Perseus blocked his right to do so. As a result, Polydectes arranged to marry another

---

[25] Philip Matyszak, *The Greek and Roman Myths: A Guide to the Classical Stories* (New York: Thames and Hudson, 2010), 126.
[26] Since the hero symbolically confronts chaos and overcomes it, a hero's actions are linguistically described as a metaphorical journey, such as crossing over, entering, descending, exploring, rising, or ascending. The metaphor of a journey thus becomes symbolic for the transition, or reorientation, of an individual from chaos into order, a process that begins with addressing, or confronting, the chaotic element in their psyches.
[27] Such a cycle is also noted by Campbell who points to verisimilitude in the Greco-Roman myths of Prometheus, Jason, and Aeneas, as well as the Indian myth of the Buddha. See Campbell, *Hero*, 23–7.
[28] A version of the story of Perseus can be found in Pseudo-Apollodorus, *The Library* 2.4.1–5.

woman, Hippodamia, and invited the local young men to the celebration. Each brought with him a gift, but Perseus, because he was poor, had none. Mocked by Polydectes, Perseus promised that he would bring a gift greater than the others: the Medusa's head.

And so, Perseus embarked on his journey to slay the Medusa. The Medusa was a once-beautiful maiden who was turned into a monster by Athena, her hair a collection of serpents and her gaze one that turned a person to stone. Perseus was helpless against the monster except for the gifts granted to him by Athena and Hermes: winged sandals for quick travel, a sword, a bronze shield, and a helmet that made him invisible. Cleverly making use of the gifts, he removed the Medusa's head and escaped. On his return to Polydectes, he encountered a young woman named Andromeda left chained on a beach to be consumed by a great sea monster. At this moment, the sea monster approached Andromeda to consume her, but Perseus made use of Medusa's head and turned the sea serpent to stone. Taking Andromeda with him, Perseus returned to Polydectes and turned him and his cohort to stone, thus saving his mother, Danaë, from his advances for good.

The Medusa here represents a collection of fears, such as the fear of the abnormal, incapacitation, pain, becoming prey—all of which lead to death. Not only this, but Perseus twice escapes the ill intentions of certain men who want to kill him, against whom he gets his revenge: Acrisius and Polydectes.[29]

Another example is found in Herakles, another son of Zeus and descendent of Perseus.[30] The stories of Herakles were very popular in the Greco-Roman world, and he became an object of worship in many places.[31] He was miraculously conceived of divine origin and was twin to a brother named Iphicles. Hera was enraged at Zeus' infidelity, and she swore to have her revenge on the child. To do so, she sent two serpents into the twins' cradle, but the plan was foiled because the infant Herakles overpowered and killed the serpents, having been found laughing as he held their lifeless bodies.

As he grew, Herakles could not avoid Hera's hatred. He was driven mad to such an extent that he murdered his own family. To purify himself,[32] he completed twelve labors, many of which included defeating some kind of monster: the Nemean Lion, the Hydra, the Ceryneian Hind, the Erymanthian Boar, the Stymphalian Birds, and the Cretan Bull. He also accomplished a number of tasks that ordinary mortals could

---

[29] Acrisius is later killed inadvertently by Perseus as fulfillment of a prophecy that he would be killed by his grandson, and this is why Acrisius first wanted to banish Perseus. Sometime after he defeated the Medusa, Perseus went to compete in a certain athletic competition where he threw the discus and struck an unsuspecting Acrisius.

[30] For the story of Herakles, see Pseudo-Apollodorus, *Library* 2.4.8–2.7.7.

[31] According to Ovid: "The tales of might Herakles have filled the world, and overcome Juno's hatred" (*Metamorphoses*, 9.140). The image of Herakles was even painted on the shields of the Theban hoplites since he was supposedly born in Thebes (Matyszak, *Myths*, 149).

[32] A murderer, whether human or god, had to undergo a ritual of purification, which could include exile. When this had been completed, the guilty party would have to sacrifice a goat or a ram as atonement for the blood of the victim. See Northrup Frye and Jay MacPherson, *Biblical and Classical Myths: The Mythological Framework of Western Culture* (Toronto: University of Toronto Press, 2004), n. 4, 423.

not: cleaning the Augean Stables, collecting the Mares of Diomedes, capturing the Girdle of the Amazon Queen, stealing the Cattle of Geryon, gathering the Apples of Hesperides, and capturing Cerberus. Some traditions describe Herakles as the founder the Olympic Games, having established Priam as king of Troy, taking part in the battles between the gods and giants, and uniting a large portion of Greece through successful warfare.[33] He later died having been poisoned by his wife Deianeira. However, before he died, he made a pyre and, while it was burning, it is said that a cloud passed over Herakles, and a clap of thunder could be heard as lightning carried him to heaven. Thereafter, he obtained immortality and made peace with Hera, marrying her daughter Hebe and having two children.[34]

The journeys and feats of Herakles are marked with many victorious battles, yet he was consistently plagued by Hera's judgment. However, despite certain challenges from Hera or his own levels of impurity, he was deemed worthy of immortality by Zeus. The purpose of the myth is, therefore, to showcase how a child of Zeus is given certain status by establishing Order as his father did. As with Perseus, Order came about through reorienting himself after having gone mad, the defeat of certain monsters, and the defeat of enemies who represented disunity in Greece.

Theseus was the hero of Athens who created Order much in the same ways that his forbearers did.[35] He was part divine as the son of Poseidon and Aethra, and he held Herakles as a model for his behavior and future feats of bravery. His most famous feat, however, was the slaying of the Minotaur in Crete, which led to the salvation of many Athenian youths who were ritualistically sacrificed to the bull.

Yet, before he accomplished victory in Crete, Theseus won several battles against notoriously dangerous villains. The first was against Corynetes, who would murder travelers with his club. Theseus was able to procure the club and do the same to Corynetes. The second was Sinis, nicknamed the "Pine-bender" for his ability to bend pine trees to the ground, to which he attached his victims. Theseus was able to overcome him and do the same to Sinis. The third was Sciron, who would trick travelers into washing his feet only to kick them off the cliff to be eaten by a large turtle. Like those before, Theseus tricked his opponent, and Sciron was eaten by the turtle. Last, Theseus overcame Procrustes, who invited strangers to stay at his home where he would violently manipulate their bodies to fit a particular bed. Once again, Theseus did the same to Procrustes and ended his violent reputation.

Sometime later, after his victories in Athens, word arrived from Crete to have fourteen youths sent for sacrifice to the Minotaur. Theseus went along as one of the fourteen and overheard Minos, the king of Crete, boasting that he was a son of Zeus. Minos raised his hands to the sky and prayed to Zeus, who answered with a roll of thunder. Minos returned the challenge to Theseus by throwing a golden signet ring into the sea and asking Theseus to retrieve it. Theseus did so with the help of

---

[33] See Matyszak, *Myths*, 158; Pseudo-Apollodorus, *Library* 2.6.1–2.7.7.

[34] As MacPherson puts it: "To end his suffering, he asked his friends and servants to build him a great pyre on Mount Oeta and place him on it: there among the flames his mortal part was burned away, while his immortal part was carried up to Olympus in the chariot of Zeus" (MacPherson, *Biblical and Classical Myths*, 325–6).

[35] For the story of Theseus, see Pseudo-Apollodorus, *Library*, 3.16.1–*Epitome* 1.23.

Amphitrite, the wife of Poseidon, who commanded a school of dolphins to help retrieve the ring.

Having arrived in Crete, Theseus gains the affection and help of Ariadne, the daughter of Minos, who gave him thread and a sword to help him navigate the labyrinth and slay the Minotaur. He then found his way back out of the labyrinth and escaped Crete with the rest of the Athenian cohort and Ariadne.

Apollodorus tells us that Theseus won many battles after his escape from Crete, defeating many enemies and even descending to Hades where he was saved by Herakles. Theseus did not live much longer, however, as he was thrown off a cliff into the sea by Lycomedes, king of Scyros, and died.[36]

Like Perseus and Herakles before him, Theseus is heroic because he was able to bring some level of Order to the chaotic elements that caused grief for his people. Each of the villains represent the fear of death and the fear of becoming prey. Likewise, the Minotaur represents the fear of death and becoming prey, but also the fear of the abnormal and unexpected. The labyrinth itself represents the fear of isolation as well as the fear of the unknown, both of which Theseus was able to overcome with the keen insight and help of Ariadne.

Jesus: The Complete Vision of the Hero Archetype

It has been argued that literary depictions of archetypes are a means by which a society, community, or nation copes with, or alleviates, its fear. However, archetypes are fascinating because they appear in a variety of literary contexts, even literary contexts that are temporally and contextually quite different. This tells us something important about fear, namely, that every human faces it regardless of their time or context. I designated fear into a two-tiered structure: the first tier being death, and the second being those things that lead to death such as falling, suffocation, pain, isolation, sudden movements (becoming prey), the unknown/abnormal, incapacitation, or disease. These fears are sometimes symbolized as monsters, such as the Minotaur or the Medusa as in the earlier examples. However, fears can also take the form of corrupted governments or religious systems, perhaps even the evils that lie within one's own psyche.[37] The archetype of the hero then becomes the literary expression of facing these fears, and it becomes a model or source of inspiration for readers. In this regard, Jesus is depicted as the hero. In what follows, I will discuss just how Jesus follows the pattern of the hero as a divine hero who challenges the systems that are considered chaotic in order to establish Order.

---

[36] See Pseudo-Apollodorus, *Library*, Epilogue 1.24.
[37] This is certainly true within the *Antigone* in which Antigone faces the pressures of what she believes is a corrupted government. It is also true in the *Bacchae* in which Dionysus returns to Thebes to restore certain religious rites that have been forbidden by a corrupted government leader. As for one's own corruption, this concept can be found in the *Oedipus Rex* in which Oedipus must confront his own corruption to save his people.

What Is in a Name? Jesus as the Heroic Son of God

Jesus as the Son of God is attested at the beginning of each Synoptic Gospel (Mt. 1:1; Mk 1:1; Lk. 1:35).[38] We are also told that Jesus is born of Mary yet conceived by the Holy Spirit (Mt. 1:18; Lk. 1:35). From this, we are to understand that Jesus is divine, an aspect that fits within the aforementioned heroic traditions of the Greeks. It also alerts an ancient reader to a particular status, and therefore a role, that Jesus will fulfill: the creation of Order from Chaos. As mentioned, this role fulfills the heroic mandate that is linked with cosmology: Yahweh ordered the world from Chaos through speech (Genesis 1).[39] As such, a hero follows in the pattern of creating Order from Chaos, and it is through enacting this pattern that they are considered to be a son of god.[40] This means that Jesus will use speech to create Order through his ministry, and the reason for why Jesus accomplishes his duty through nonviolent means.

This is an interesting point to consider in light of one of the most obvious allusions to Hebrew Scripture. Jesus (Greek: Ἰησοῦς) is given the same name as the hero that led the Israelites into the Promised Land, Joshua (Greek: Ἰησοῦς; Hebrew: יהושע). The Hebrew name means "God is salvation" and applies to Joshua in the sense that he led God's people into the land promised to them, a memorial to how Yahweh had saved them from the tyranny of Egypt (Josh. 1:6). The story of Joshua is similar to the Greek tradition in that it is laden with physical violence, yet it is quite distinct from the story of Jesus in this regard. However, one could consider the story of Joshua similar to that of Jesus in a metaphorical sense: the physical violence with which the Promised Land was taken is thus symbolic of how one should deal with the sin in their own life, namely, that truthful speech is the necessary tool to dismantle a corrupted ethical system.[41] As such, truthful speech is understood as a form of metaphorical violence, and it is through *this* kind of violence that Jesus—as the Son of God—begins to challenge a corrupted system that was perpetrated by the religious elite.[42]

---

[38] With regard to Mark's incipit, I include the epithets with consideration of the textual issues. See my arguments in Adam Z. Wright, "Recognizing Jesus: A Study of Recognition Scenes in Mark's Gospel," *JGRChJ* 10 (2014): 174–93.

[39] This appears differently from other cosmological traditions in which the creator god battles against a personified form of Chaos—as in the Mesopotamian story of Marduk battling against Tiamat. However, Yahweh contends with no one, and the creation of Order can be seen as a nonhostile action.

[40] As can be expected, Jesus is twice addressed as the Son of God by a heavenly voice—supposedly that of Yahweh—that confers the epithet upon him (Mt. 3:17, 17:5; Mk 1:13, 9:7; Lk. 3:22, 9:35). One may also think of the Jewish kings of the past who were anointed and considered to be sons of God due to their role as establishing God's order among his people (Ps. 2:7).

[41] I direct the reader toward the Sermon on the Mount in Matthew 5–7, in which Jesus delineates the external from the internal with regard to how one should focus their attention. In particular, see Mt. 5:21-26, 27-30; 7:1-12.

[42] This is a marked change, or consideration, in the ancient world which addresses how one should live well. In other words, for Jesus, eliminating outside influences—especially through violence—is not the way to create true Order. Instead, one should reorganize their own motivations (Mt. 15:18). This marks the effort to reestablish how Yahweh had ordered things in Eden, a time before sin had corrupted humanity's experience; a chaotic experience epitomized by murder after expulsion from Eden (Genesis 4).

In addition to the religious elite, Jesus is confronted by other forms of chaos which draw attention to the role of the heroic Son of God. At the outset of his ministry, Jesus is confronted by Satan in the wilderness, who attempts to dissuade him from his goal of instituting the Kingdom of God or Heaven (Mk 1:12-13; Mt. 4:1-11; Lk. 4:1-13). Geographically, the wilderness occupies the "outside" and most removed place from the Temple, and the Synoptic tradition provides a clear parallel between Jesus and Israel's wanderings before they enter the Promised Land. This is an important observation because the hero's journey can be understood as a metaphorical journey from Chaos to Order or, symbolized a different way, from the outside to the inside. This is why Jesus's ministry, much like Israel's establishment, must start in the wilderness and not in Jerusalem itself. In this sense, Jesus meets with personified Chaos who acts as a gatekeeper, so to speak, into the realms of Order where Jesus intends to go.[43] At any rate, Jesus is presented a choice: to establish a kingdom based on being a hero (Son of God; see Mt. 4:3, 6; Lk. 4:3, 9) or achieve the Kingdom through voluntary suffering.[44]

This leads us to a discussion of how the crucifixion and subsequent resurrection fit within the narrative of the hero. The resurrection marks Jesus's confrontation with the first-tier fear: death. In this sense, the resurrection removes the finality of death, lessening its distress. Not only this, but Jesus's resurrection marks a model for the believer, namely, that achieving the Kingdom would include voluntary suffering as the model for the purging of certain elements within a person's psyche. This is precisely why Paul regards the resurrection of first importance to the Christian faith (1 Cor. 15:3, 14). Quelling the fear of death was perhaps the final step in the creation of Order, an undoing of the effects of sin in Genesis 3, and essential for creating the mindset of the believer who seeks to move themselves consistently from Chaos into Order (Rom. 12:2; 2 Cor. 4:16).

Another way that Jesus creates Order comes in the form of his healing miracles. Sickness and disease are synonymous with sin throughout Jewish tradition (Jn 9:2).[45]

---

[43] The wilderness is therefore understood as a place where demons dwell, perhaps why the young man overcome by Legion in Mark 5 lives among the impure regions of the dead—"impure" being another typology for Chaos. This is also why, when he begins to exorcise certain demons, Jesus is addressed as the Son of God—though rather ironically and perhaps as a means to mock him.

[44] An important point should be made here about the nature of heroic suffering as it relates to establishing Order from Chaos. To achieve the Kingdom means to suffer voluntarily and not to posit oneself in a position of power—something that Satan himself represents here. There are many cases of heroic suffering throughout the Greco-Roman world, typically in tragedy, that are attempts to orient the audience toward willful action. This action could be psychological—as opposed to political or action through violence—and functions as a call to action against a corrupt institution that disallows psychological process, as I think it is within the Gospels. In other words, a position of power, such as the one Satan represents, is one that does not promote willful suffering to achieve Order. Instead, such a position looks to avoid willful suffering by consolidating power. So much could be said of Rome, and it is of little surprise that Jesus is often compared to Caesar. So much could also be said of the temple establishment that, by the time of Jesus, had allied itself with Rome and had instituted a corrupted taxation system with its *Publicani*. It is against Rome and the corrupted temple system that Jesus is pitted; again, why so much of the Gospel story showcases the conflict between Jesus and the religious elite.

[45] The idea that sickness and death are a deviation from wholeness, and therefore holiness, is attested in the work of Douglas and her consideration of the Levitical laws. See Mary Douglas, *Purity and Danger: An Analysis of the Concepts of Pollution and Taboo* (London: Ark Paperbacks, 1984), 41–57, especially 53.

This was first established in the Torah, in which a large number of regulations are put in place to help one avoid certain impurities related to sickness and sin. Douglas, following closely with the work of Smith, notes that "taboos, usually inspired by fear, were used as precautions against malignant spirits, and were common to all primitive peoples and often took the form of rules of uncleanness."[46] From this quotation, it appears that the taboos that appear around sickness—and, by extension, demonic possession—give rise to a level of fear, both first- and second-tier fears. It then comes as little surprise that Jesus appears as a healer extraordinaire, whose powers are unmatched.

The miracles are not done for the miracles' sake, and they are conducted because Jesus is reinstating wholeness, which is synonymous with Order. These, along with the exorcisms, remove the second-tier fears, especially fear of disease or isolation. When Jesus conducts a miracle, he quells the fear linked with the ailment and removes the taboo associated with it. Healing meant that a person would be reintegrated into society or metaphorically brought from the chaotic outside and back into the ordered realm of society. It also meant that the regulations by which a person was condemned were rendered obsolete in the sense that they no longer applied. This is certainly true of the man who begged Jesus to make him clean (Mk 1:40; Lk. 5:12) or the woman who touched Jesus's garment (Mt. 9:20-22; Mk 5:25-34; Lk. 8:43-48). In this regard, people understood Jesus as *the* gateway to order, perhaps why Jesus referred to himself as such in Jn 10:9, which meant that salvation was synonymous with Order, even psychologically so.

Conclusions

This chapter has argued that the archetype of the hero, as expressed in the mythological stories of Perseus, Herakles, Theseus, and also in the stories of Jesus, showcase a contention with fear. I have divided fear into two tiers: the first being death, and the second containing those things that lead directly to death. The hero contends with certain things which are symbolic of fear—monsters, demons, or enemies—and defeats them as an attempt to create Order from the Chaos that these opponents represent. These stories are meant to orient the audience and have a direct impact on their psychological processes as they relate to fear. Jesus, as the greatest of the archetypes, showcases how he confronts, and defeats, not one particular fear but each of them. This is represented in the exorcisms, the healing miracles, and the resurrection from the dead. As such, Jesus fits within an archetypical heroic tradition that an ancient reader would have understood and appreciated.

---

[46] See ibid., 142.

5

Fiery Twins: James, John, and the Sons of Zeus

Jeff Pettis

This chapter aims toward a critical understanding and interpretation of the twinned figures James and John as presented in the Synoptic Gospels and in the context of Greco-Roman mythology.[1] It is divided into four parts. The first part, "Naming in Mk 3:13-19," examines Mk 3:13-19 as the earliest Synoptic text which speaks directly of Jesus identifying the disciples James and John as Boanerges, the sons of thunder, whose father is Zeus. The second part, "Lk. 9:51-56 and Fire from Heaven," examines Lk. 9:51-56, a detailed account of James and John who desire to speak down fire from heaven. Then, "Elijah (2 Kgs 1:10, 12) and the Transfiguration in Mk 9:2-8" examines parallel canonical material—specifically Elijah's bringing down fire from heaven (2 Kgs 1:10-12) as well as Jesus's Transfiguration (Mk 9:2-8). Building off of the first three sections, the fourth section then considers two specific themes—conflict and rising—which occur within these texts and elsewhere in the Synoptic writings. A summary statement and discussion on further directions of investigation conclude the study.

Naming in Mk 3:13-19

In Mk 3:13-19 Jesus ascends, ἀναβαίνει, onto a high mountain, and it is from this rare place that he is said to have "made [ἐποίησεν] twelve." This includes James the son of Zebedee and John his brother.[2] The brothers appear together in Synoptic Gospel texts and are given no distinctions to separate them one from the other. In other words, they appear as twins.[3] Of the pair, James is always referenced first. At least eight references

---

[1] The present study is an expanded version of a paper presented in the "Mysticism, Esotericism, and Gnosticism in Antiquity Group" at the 2018 annual meeting of the Society of Biblical Literature held in Denver, Colorado.

[2] The mother may have been Salome (cf. Mk 15:40; cf. Mt. 27:56). The Zebedee family may have been well-off financially. The author of Mark (1:20) says that the father Zebedee had hired servants for fishing, while the author of Luke (5:1-11) speaks of two fishing boats being used by Peter, James, and John. Note that James (Greek: *Iakobos*) son of Zebedee is often referred to as "John the Greater" to distinguish him from John son of Alphaeus (James the Less) listed in the New Testament as one of the twelve disciples, and James the brother of Jesus (James the Just).

[3] See Dennis R. MacDonald, *The Homeric Epics and the Gospel of Mark* (New Haven: Yale University Press, 2000), 24. As MacDonald points out, James and John even speak in unison in their request to sit with Jesus in glory (Mk 10:35-40) (see 26).

to James and John occur in the Gospel of Mark, five in the Gospel of Luke, and three in the Gospel of Matthew.

In Mk 3:17 Jesus surnames (ἐπέθηκεν) the twin brothers "Boanerges" (Βοανηργές).[4] The author of Mark translates the Aramaic surname Boanerges to mean "sons of thunder" (υἱοὶ βροντῆς). The language makes a direct connection between James and John and the sons of the Greco-Roman deity Zeus, perceived to be the God of thunder and lightning. The title Boanerges is specific to the Gospel of Mark and does not occur elsewhere in the New Testament, including the calling accounts Lk. 6:12-16 ("James and John") and Mt. 10:1-4 ("James and John sons of Zebedee"). The precise meaning and spelling of the title Boanerges is uncertain and has a history of critical discussion.[5] The Hebrew for Beaneries, *bene rages*, may translate as "wrath," with the meaning "hot-tempered."[6]

The authors of the Gospel of Matthew and the Gospel of Luke ignore by omission Mark's reference to Jesus naming James and John Boanerges, "sons of thunder" (Mk 3:17). However, Lk. 9:51-56 present a detailed account of James and John in light of the sons of Zeus in reference to fire from heaven:

> When the days drew near for him to be received up, he set his face to go to Jerusalem. And he sent messengers ahead of him, who went and entered a village of the Samaritans, to make ready for him; but the people would not receive him, because his face was set toward Jerusalem. And when his disciples James and John saw it, they said, "Lord, do you want us to bid fire come down from heaven and consume them?" But he turned and rebuked them. And they went on to another village.

As with Mk 3:13-19, James and John in Lk. 9:51-56 appear in direct relation to Jesus. In this case, story narrative occurs with the anticipation of Jesus being "ascended" (*analempseos*; Lk. 9:51)—something which will take place in Acts 1:6-11. With both texts there occurs a clear sense of intentionality on the part of Jesus. In Mk 3:13-19 Jesus's main purpose of ascent is to select the twelve disciples. For Luke the purpose is going to Jerusalem. He "set his face to go [αὐτὸς τὸ πρόσωπον ἐστήρισεν τοῦ πορεύεσθαι] to Jerusalem" (Lk. 9:51). This course of travel will take the group through Samaritan territory.[7]

It is precisely because of this alignment toward Jerusalem and subsequent intended travel through the Samaritan village that the Samaritans do not receive Jesus in 9:53 (οὐκ ἐδέξαντο αὐτόν). The Samaritan rejection draws a marked response from James and John in Lk. 9:54. The immediacy of their response suggests hostility on the part of

---

[4] Also Simon receives a surname, "Peter" (3:16). These three surnamed disciples will appear together in other narrative texts, including Mk 9:2-8, the Transfiguration; and 14:32-41, Gethsemane.

[5] F. Danker, *A Greek-English Lexicon of the New Testament and Other Early Christian Literature*, 3rd ed. (Chicago: University of Chicago Press, 2000), 179–80.

[6] Ibid., 791–2.

[7] Three times the author makes specific reference to Jesus's *prosopon* (face; Lk. 9:51, 52, 53), a detail that occurs also with Jesus's transfiguration (Lk. 9:29; "the appearance [τὸ εἶδος] of his face [προσώπου] was altered [ἕτερον]"). See also Mt. 17:6.

the twins. (Do they have a temper?) The text also tells of the allegiance of James and John to Jesus, whom they address as κύριε (9:54b). The twins want to act out against the Samaritans on his behalf but only with Jesus's approval: "Lord, do you desire." Do the twins therefore serve in some capacity as guardians—ones who "are seeing" (ἰδόντες; 9:54), looking out for their master? As such, they may take on a protective role as Jesus's personal disciples.

Lk. 9:51-56 and Fire from Heaven

The author of the Gospel of Luke details what appears to be the "said" capacities of the twins. First, they have the ability to exact direct influence over the immediate world through spoken word (κύριε, θέλεις εἴπωμεν [Lord do you desire that we should speak]). Second, through spoken word they have access to fire and the ability to bring it down (καταβῆναι) from heaven. In the case of the Samaritan rejection of Jesus, the twins' inquiry to bring down fire from heaven is for the express purpose *analosai autous* (to destroy them), that is, the Samaritan village. Compare the mythological background of the Dioscuri sons of Zeus who are known to have sacked the cities Aphidna and Las.[8]

As with Mk 3:13-19, therefore, James and John in Lk. 9:52-56 appear together in a context of verticality—here the anticipation of Jesus's ascent. Their appearance occurs amid a course of travel moving directly to Jerusalem. They encounter conflict along the way. The Samaritans will not receive Jesus. In response the twins make known their intention to use their powers of word and fire as punishment against the Samaritans. At the same time, James and John are presented as recognizing and showing obedience to Jesus as a central authority figure and who refuses their impulse. The text shows the twins as being watchful guardians, having supernatural capacities over the immediate world, and are somewhat hostile on behalf of Jesus their leader and hero.

Elijah (2 Kgs 1:10, 12) and the Transfiguration in Mk 9:2-8

The notion of fire coming down from heaven for specifically destructive purposes occurs also with the prophet Elijah in 2 Kgs 1:10, 12. The event is mediated through an angel of the Lord who tells Elijah to meet the corrupt king Ahaziah's captain and his fifty troops. According to the text, Elijah is sitting on top of a hill from which he declares: "If I am a man of God, let fire come down from heaven and consume you and your fifty." Immediately fire came down from heaven and consumed the captain and his fifty (2 Kgs 1:10b). Fire from heaven with lethal consequences through Elijah's mediation occurs a second time to another captain and fifty troops of Ahaziah. But Elijah answered them, "If I am a man of God, let fire come down from heaven

---

[8] MacDonald, *The Homeric Epics and the Gospel of Mark*, 30.

and consume you and your fifty." The fire of God then came down from heaven and consumed him and his fifty (2 Kgs 1:12b).

In contrast to the destructive force of fire mediated through the prophet Elijah, 1 Kgs 18:37-39 relates an account where divine fire falls and consumes the altar sacrifice made by Elijah. The event takes place on Mount Carmel. It occurs as a means to establish the superiority of YHWH over the 450 prophets of Baal.[9] The author notes that the people seeing the event "fall on their faces" in reverence, saying: "The Lord, he is God; the Lord, he is God" (1 Kgs 18:39). Compare Lev. 9:22-24, where fire from heaven consumes a sacrifice to the divine at the altar with Aaron and Moses, causing the onlookers to fall on their faces.[10]

In the accounts of the Transfiguration of Jesus in the Synoptic Gospels, the prophet Elijah appears with Moses and Jesus before James, John, and Peter on a high mountain (Mk 9:2-8; Mt. 17:1-8; Lk. 9:28-36). The author of Mark says that the divine figures Moses and Elijah were "talking together" (συλλαλοῦντες) to Jesus (Mk 9:4). The experience includes a theophanic claiming of Jesus's sonship,[11] and in Mt. 17:6 the three disciples fall on their faces in awe when they hear it. All three synoptic texts make it clear that in the absence of Elijah and Moses, James and John with Peter see only Jesus who stands as the central figure.

Thus the Transfiguration scene occurs, it would seem, as a noticeable religio-spiritual gathering. It brings multiple figures together in one place, a high mountain alone and as part of the manifest divinity of Jesus. All of the figures—Jesus, Moses, Elijah, Peter, James and John—within the larger Judeo-Christian narrative history have some level of connection with fire and with sacrifice, and are in this way rooted in Judaic cultic frame by the synoptic authors. The event occurs in a context of intentionality and immediacy of Jesus's forthcoming execution as well as his glorification.

Themes: Conflict and Rising

Two overarching themes come forth in the consideration of James and John in the texts examined here and in other texts to be considered in what follows. First James and John (and Elijah) appear in a context of religio-spiritual conflict. As precursor, Elijah acts according to divine command against Ahaziah king of Judah who introduces offensive forms of worship. James and John respond to conflict with the Samaritans and their rejection of Jesus as Jesus sets his face to Jerusalem the place of his execution. On the mountain the twins with Peter are given new names, an act

---

[9] "'Answer me, O Lord, answer me, that this people may know that thou, O Lord, art God, and that thou hast turned their hearts back.' Then the fire of the Lord fell, and consumed the burnt offering, and the wood, and the stones, and the dust, and licked up the water that was in the trench" (1 Kgs 18:37-39).

[10] Aaron "comes down" making offerings. He joins Moses and both go into the tent of meeting. Upon coming out of the tent they bless the people. The glory of the Lord appears, "and fire [from heaven] came forth from before the Lord and consumed the burnt offering and the fat upon the altar." According to the text, the people who saw it shouted and fell on their faces (Lev. 9:24).

[11] According to Mt. 17:6, when the three disciples heard this, they fell on their faces (ἔπεσαν ἐπὶ πρόσωπον αὐτῶν) and were filled with awe.

with apocalyptic meaning (see Rev. 22:4: "they shall see his face, and his name shall be on their foreheads").[12] In Mk 1:29-30 James and John with Andrew and Simon are with Jesus who heals Simon's mother-in-law of fever ("being fiery")—a scene that takes place still resonant with Jesus's public fight with the unclean spirit(s) (Mk 1:21-28). The Transfiguration account anticipates Jesus's death, articulated in Mk 8:31: "And he began to teach them that the Son of man must suffer many things, and be rejected." This notion of "opposition" seems choreographed in Mk 13:1-9, as Jesus with the twins sits on the Mount of Olives "opposite" (κατέναντι) the temple and speaks of the chaos of forthcoming destruction as well as suffering of the twins, Peter, and Andrew.[13] In Mk 10:38-39, as the disciples and Jesus are going up to the temple, Jesus is clear to say that he himself and James and John will "drink the cup." In Mk 5:35-43 James and John along with Peter enter the house of Jarius amid tumult and ridicule to heal the daughter of Darius who is "sleeping."[14] In Mk 14:32-42 Jesus enters the Garden of Gethsemane with James and John: "And he took with him Peter and James and John, and began to be greatly distressed and troubled. And he said to them, 'My soul is very sorrowful, even to death.'"

I argue then that New Testament authors present James and John in relation to immediate and anticipated life–death conflict rooted in Jewish-Christian apocalyptic and blood sacrifice. In the various narrative presentations the twins appear close to the heat of the flames both on earth and in heaven. At the same time, although they are close to and seem, at least according to Lk. 9:52-56, to have direct access to these flames, they are kept at a respectful distance. Jesus disallows the request of the twins to destroy the Samaritans. He pushes them away from drinking "his cup" of sacrificial blood. They are rendered speechless by seeing Jesus transfigure and told to listen as opposed to building three tents (Mk 9:5-7). He keeps them at a distance in the garden—"Sit here, while I pray" (Mk 14:32-42). James and John are presented as involved and near to events, but never fully so. Rather they question Jesus about the signs of the end, they make requests to sit at his right and left when he comes into glory, and they are presented as ones who "see," that is, bear witness to Jesus changing shape on a mountain, bring a girl back to life in a house, the Samaritan rejection of Jesus, his sorrow in the Garden of Gethsemane, Jesus's words of doom on the mount. They are granted an insider relationship with Jesus who separates them from the rest of the group and brings them with him up the mountain, into the house, into the garden.

Yet, authors seem intent on establishing limitations to this insider orientation, and it is very much the case that, identified and presented in direct relationship to Jesus,

---

[12] See Ched Myers and O. M. Hendricks, Jr., *Binding the Strong Man: A Political Reading of Mark's Story of Jesus* (Maryknoll, NY: Orbis Books, 1988; repr. 2008), 162. See also Rev. 3:12: "He who conquers, I will make him a pillar in the temple of my God; never shall he go out of it, and I will write on him the name of my God, and the name of the city of my God, the new Jerusalem which comes down from my God out of heaven, and my own new name."

[13] But take heed to yourselves; for they will deliver you up to councils; and you will be beaten in synagogues; and you will stand before governors and kings for my sake, to bear testimony before them (Mk 10.9).

[14] "When they came to the house of the ruler of the synagogue, he saw a tumult, and people weeping and wailing loudly. And when he had entered, he said to them, 'Why do you make a tumult and weep? The child is not dead but sleeping.' And they laughed at him" (Mk 14:38-40).

James and John the twins are not given full authority, nor have full understanding which is at all equal to Jesus himself. Ultimately, they will remain removed from the reality of the cross, being replaced by two thieves who instead will flank Jesus on the cross, one on the right and one on the left (Mk 15:27). On the contrary, James and John seem cast in an almost reckless light, impulsive after the manner of Peter with whom they are often joined, asking untimely questions, falling asleep rather than being attentive, wanting to act out with fire, and demanding of Jesus the best seats in the house. In all of this there is something entertaining, even endearing about these fiery twins, who seem to be only wanting the right thing. That right thing, as I read the texts, is that their hero be taken seriously and the meaning of his teachings realized in the context of their immediate world history.

Authors cast James and John in the context of conflict and also present the twins in relation to the higher, spiritual realm. In Mk 3:13-19 it is on a mountain that the twins are selected along with the other disciples of Jesus. In Lk. 9:52-56 the response of James and John against the Samaritans occurs in the context of Jesus's anticipated ascension. Upon the mountain James and John with Peter see Jesus transfigured like lightening (ἐξαστράπτων; Lk. 9:28-29).[15] The author of Mark emphasizes that they ascend to a "high" mountain (ὄρος ὑψηλόν) set apart (Mk 9:2). In Mk 10:32-45 Jesus and the disciples are "traveling up" (ἀναβαίνοντες) to Jerusalem when he speaks of his coming execution and James and John make their request to him. It is on the Mount of Olives that James and John with Peter and Andrew hear Jesus speak of world destruction (Mk 13:1-37). Consider also the identification of Elijah their prototype as one who "sits on the mount" as an agent of divine fire (2 Kgs 1:9) and is taken into the heavens on a chariot of fire (2 Kgs 2:11-12).[16]

It would seem then that James and John connect not only with conflict and social and religious breakdown in the earth realm, but with spirituality and flight in the higher realm. Like Elijah, the twins set apart are at home, vigilant, and present in the rarified place of ascents, mountain tops, locations of resurrection, and glorification. It then follows that Jesus calls the twins Boanerges, also called the Dioscuri, Castor and Pollux the "sons of Zeus" who fly through the air as fiery agents to guard and protect human endeavor. The sons of Zeus also have the power of fire from heaven as "glorious … deliverers of humans," as told in the ancient Homeric Hymn 33.[17] In a storm they manifest like spirits round the vertical mast of a ship—also known as St. Elmo's Fire.[18] In Acts 28:11 Paul speaks of traveling to Rome on a ship "with the Twin Brothers as

---

[15] Compare the angel which descends from heaven to Jesus's tomb. "His appearance was like lightning, and his raiment white as snow" (Mt. 28:3). Origen of Alexandria argues that the disciples on that mountain are deemed worthy to see it. "But it seems to me, that those who are led up by Jesus into the high mountain, and are deemed worthy of beholding His transfiguration apart, are not without purpose led up six days after the discourses previously spoken." Origen of Alexandria, *Commentary on the Gospel of Matthew* 12:36. See also Jeff Pettis, "Transfiguration," in John A. McGuckin (ed.), *The Westminster Handbook to Origen of Alexandria* (Louisville, KY: WJKP, 2004), 204–5.

[16] "And as they still went on and talked, behold, a chariot of fire and horses of fire separated the two of them. And Elijah went up by a whirlwind into heaven. And Elisha saw it and he cried, 'My father, my father! The chariots of Israel and its horsemen!' And he saw him no more" (2 Kgs 2:11-12).

[17] MacDonald, *The Homeric Epics and the Gospel of Mark*, 26.

[18] Ibid.

figurehead" (παρασήμῳ Διοσκούροις). The images probably appeared on either side of the ship's prow to assure safe journey.

Further Considerations

This examination is a beginning step toward a deeper understanding of the extent to which the authors of the Gospel of Mark and of Luke present James and John in relation to both ancient Jewish thought as well Greco-Roman myth and mythology. More work needs to be done in order to bring to light the influences around the notion of twinship and the figures James and John in the New Testament. For example, it would be unlikely that the author of the Gospel of Mark was unaware of narrative traditions relating to the Maccabean Wars. This might include the 2 Macc. 10:29-30 account of five men on horses with golden bridles.[19] Two of these men ride in lead position. They shoot arrows and lightning against the enemy to protect Maccabeus who is between them. According to the Greek text, the group of men "appear" (ἐφάνησαν) as if manifested from a higher realm. The imagery is noticeably Dioscuric. The text also says that the enemy becomes "confounded with blindness" (2 Macc. 10:30). Rendel Harris observes that causing blindness is one of the punishments common to Castor and Pollux.[20]

Consider also 2 Macc. 3:25 where two young men appear before the Syrian enemy Heliodorus who is intent on desecrating the Jewish Temple. They are noticeable in strength and appearance and flank Heliodorus as they inflict injury upon him and "scourged him continuously, inflicting many blows on him" (2 Macc. 3:26).[21] They appear "notable in strength, excellent in beauty, and comely in apparel." The story replicates the Roman imagery of Castor and Pollux powerfully mounted on white steeds.[22] According to Harris, the Dioscuri imagery in 2 Maccabees is evidence that in the time of the Maccabean Wars the Dioscuri have not yet been replaced by holy

---

[19]
> But when the battle waxed strong, there appeared unto the enemies from heaven five comely men upon horses, with bridles of gold, and two of them led the Jews, and took Maccabeus betwixt them, and covered him on every side weapons, and kept him safe, but shot arrows and lightnings against the enemies: so that being confounded with blindness, and full of trouble, they were killed. (2 Macc. 10:29-30)

[20] Rendel Harris, *Boanerges* (Cambridge: Cambridge University Press, 1913), 290.

[21]
> While they were calling upon the Almighty Lord that he would keep what had been entrusted safe and secure for those who had entrusted it, Heliodorus went on with what had been decided. But when he arrived at the treasury with his bodyguard, then and there the Sovereign of spirits and of all authority caused so great a manifestation that all who had been so bold as to accompany him were astounded by the power of God, and became faint with terror. For there appeared to them a magnificently caparisoned horse, with a rider of frightening mien, and it rushed furiously at Heliodorus and struck at him with its front hoofs. Its rider was seen to have armor and weapons of gold. Two young men also appeared to him, remarkably strong, gloriously beautiful and splendidly dressed, who stood on each side of him and scourged him continuously, inflicting many blows on him. (2 Macc. 3:22-26)

[22] Harris, *Boanerges*, 189.

angels.²³ Harris argues that the author of 2 Maccabees wrote close to the time of early Christianity: "So we have brought Dioscurism into Palestinian history at a time which nearly coincides with the time of production of the Gospels."²⁴

There is also the need for further investigation into the Greco-Roman myth and mythology around twinship. In the chapter I bring to light this phenomenon as it appears through the Dioscuri traditions. However, the significance of twins is quite present and substantial within the larger ancient world. Further investigation will include a detailed examination of the seventh-century BCE Hymn to the Dioscuri. It will also examine the various uses and manifestations of twinship mythology in various representations, geographies, and cultures. What are the different ways in which twinship is understood in antiquity? As Rendel Harris notes of the ancient world: "Every place has twins amongst its heroes and demigods but every place appears to name them differently."²⁵ The aim will be to gain a better sense of the prevalence of twins as heroes and demigods in the time and context of the early church.

Conclusions

The themes of flight and ascent on the one hand and the immediacy of Judeo-Christian apocalyptic rooted in religio-social conflict on the other constitute and bear forth from the ancient mythopoeic material of fiery twins and heroes. The authors of Luke and Mark draw from and negotiate this material with an intentionality to establish Jesus as the ultimate authority, the Son of Man rooted in the cultic fire and deluge to be soon realized as understood by early Christian groups. As such, these texts are telling of a rhetoric of degrees of divinity perceived and apportioned by early Christian writers. The twins James and John have heavenly identification as well as inner access to Jesus their teacher. Along with Jesus they are presented thus as ones caught up in that apocalyptic fever with its pithy yearning spoken through vision and prediction.²⁶ However, neither they nor, it follows, the heavenly twins of Zeus are presented as being on a level equal to Jesus. Rather, they appear with constancy, their presence as if to frame their hero, one on the left, one on the right, not unlike the boys of Zeus who mirror each other in ancient imagery, flank sides of ships, and frame gates of travel. One can only wonder if somewhere in the background Mark has in mind the figures of burning seraphim framing the throne of the Lord of hosts, as relayed in Isa. 6.1-6.²⁷

---

[23] Ibid., 290.
[24] Ibid., 290.
[25] Ibid., 304.
[26] They become "christianized," according MacDonald, *The Homeric Epics and the Gospel of Mark*, 25.
[27]
> In the year that King Uzziah died I saw the Lord sitting upon a throne, high and lifted up; and his train filled the temple. Above him stood the seraphim; each had six wings: with two he covered his face, and with two he covered his feet, and with two he flew. And one called to another and said: "Holy, holy, holy is the Lord of hosts; the whole earth is full of his glory." And the foundations of the thresholds shook at the voice of him who called, and the house was filled with smoke. And I said: "Woe is me! For I am lost; for I am a man of unclean lips, and I dwell in the midst of a people of unclean lips; for my eyes have seen the King, the Lord

Ultimately, it is Jesus alone, transfigured, who will stand before the twin disciples (and Peter) on the mountain, his clothing, as the author Luke notes, "white as lightening" (Lk. 9:29). Even Moses and the fiery prophet Elijah on the mountain with Jesus are unequal to Jesus: "And suddenly looking around they [the disciples] no longer saw any one with them but Jesus only" (Mk 9:8).

> of hosts!" Then flew one of the seraphim to me, having in his hand a burning coal which he had taken with tongs from the altar. (Isa. 6.1-6)

6

Romulus, Roman Omens, and the Portents of the Birth and Passion of Jesus

Craig A. Evans

In one of his letters, Paul remarks that "Jews demand signs [σημεῖα] and Greeks seek wisdom" (1 Cor. 1:22). The apostle could have added, "and Romans seek omens and portents." Indeed, the Romans were keenly interested in omens, portents, ancient prophecies—anything and everything that might provide clues to the future, counsel in making personal decisions, and guidance in persuading the public in political affairs.[1] Omens, especially those linked to stories about Romulus, were especially important for establishing the credentials of Roman emperors.

In New Testament literature we find reference to "signs," as we should expect (especially so in the public activities of Jesus as recounted in the Gospel of John), but we also encounter in the Gospels and Acts what apparently were thought of as omens and portents, though the traditional vocabulary, as we shall see, is used sparingly. We find a number of these examples in the Passion narratives.

In what follows I will look at (1) how Greeks and especially Romans understood omens, portents, and prophecies; (2) the omens that are said to have taken place at the birth of Jesus; and (3) the omens that are said to have taken place during the Passion of Jesus.

Omens, Portents, and Prophecies among Greeks and Romans

The role of omens and portents reaches back to the very beginnings of Greek culture.[2] Indications of things to come could be recognized in a dream (ὄνειρος, ὄναρ), in

---

[1] Omens and portents historically played an important role in Roman politics, such as who should hold office. See J. North, "Diviners and Divination at Rome," in M. Beard and J. North (eds.), *Pagan Priests: Religion and Power in the Ancient World* (Ithaca, NY: Cornell University Press, 1990), 51–71; C. G. Brown, "Caesar's and Cicero's Attitudes towards Divination and the Transformation of Political Ideology in the Crisis of the Republic," in U. Berner and I. Tanaseanu-Döbler (eds.), *Religion und Kritik in der Antike* (Berlin: LIT-Verlag, 2009), 61–70. Julius Caesar was suspected of manipulating an attempt at divination, in order to secure a favorable omen (cf. Suetonius, *Divus Julius* 79).

[2] A. J. Podlecki, "Omens in the *Odyssey*," *GR* 14 (1967): 12–23.

prophecy (προφητεία), in a word or sound (φήμη), in an oracle (λόγιον, χρησμός), in an augury (οἰώνισμα, οἰώνισις), in divination (μαντεία, μαντική, θειασμός), and in a variety of signs (σημεῖον, σύμβολος, σύμβολον), visions (ὅραμα, ὅρασις, ὄψις), apparitions (φάσμα), wonders (θαυμαστός, τέρας), omens (οἰώνισμα, οἰωνός, κληδών), and acts of nature.³ Some of this vocabulary overlaps in nuance and usage, of course. "Signs and wonders" (σημεῖα καὶ τέρατα) are often paired. Most of these nouns have corresponding cognate verbs, and most of this vocabulary has Latin equivalents (*augurium, auguratio, auspicium, divinatio, monstrum, omen, oraculum, ostentum, portentum, praesagium, prodigium, signum, vaticinatio,* etc.).⁴

These Greek and Latin lists do not exhaust the terminology. There are professional titles and offices also, such as priest, seer, soothsayer, astrologer, and diviner (*argeus*, ἀστρολόγος, *astrologus, augur, conjector,* ἐπιθειάζων, *flamen, haruspex,* ἱερεύς, μάντεις, *mathematicus, pontifex, sacerdos*). They practiced augury (often by examining entrails of birds and animals) and interpreted prophecies (written or oral), omens, signs, and so on. Of great interest were certain types of birds (esp. eagles and owls), birds in general (οἰωνίσματα),⁵ and celestial phenomena, such as lightning, thunder, wind, eclipses, stars, and comets. All were thought to have meaning.⁶ Greco-Roman ideas about omens and portents are deeply rooted in older Chaldean beliefs and practices.⁷

In the Homeric literature lightning, earthquakes, and other acts of nature were often seen as a sign (orig. σῆμα, pl. σήματα), as seen in the *Iliad*, for example, when lightning occurs at the outset of the campaign against Troy (*Iliad* 2.353). Thunder too was seen as an important omen (*Iliad* 8.170-1). The behavior of birds was studied with great interest. In some cases it was believed that Zeus himself sent the bird or birds (*Iliad* 13.821-3).⁸ Lightning and a lobeless liver convince the leaders of a Spartan expedition to disband (Xenophon, *Hellenica* 4.7.4-7).

Gregory Vlastos remarks that

> such things as the causes of winds, rain, lightning and thunder, rivers, meteorites, eclipses, earthquakes, plagues—were matters of vivid religious import to their contemporaries. Lightning, thunder, a storm, an earthquake were "signs from

---

³ Verbs include θειάζειν, θεσπίζειν, μαντεύεσθαι, οἰωνίζεσθαι, and χρησμολογεῖν, among others.
⁴ Verbs include *augurium capere, divinare, praesagire,* and, *praedicere,* among others.
⁵ Rome's leadership was reluctant to send a military force either "because Heaven opposed their expedition by means of auspices [δι' οἰωνῶν], Sibylline oracles, or some traditional religious scruple" (Dionysius of Halicarnassus, *Antiquitates romanae* 8.373); translation based on E. Cary, *Dionysius of Halicarnassus: Roman Antiquities V Books VIII-IX.24*, LCL 372 (London: Heinemann, 1945), 111. What Cary translates as "of auspices" is literally "of birds," that is, birds of omen.
⁶ R. Bloch, *Les prodiges dans l'Antiquité classique: Grèce, Étruie et Rome* (Paris: Presses Universitaires de France, 1963); B. MacBain, *Prodigy and Expiation: A Study in Religion and Politics in Republican Rome*, Collection Latomus 177 (Bruxelles: Latomus, 1982).
⁷ H. Lewy, *Chaldaean Oracles and Theurgy: Mysticism, Magic and Platonish in the Later Roman Empire*, 3rd ed., ed. M. Tardieu; Collection des Études Augustiniennes 77 (Turnhout: Brepols, 2011); P. Ripat, "Roman Omens, Roman Audiences, and Roman History," *GR* 53 (2006): 155-74.
⁸ On birds and augury, see C. B. Gulick, "Omens and Augury in Plautus," *HSCP* 7 (1896): 235-47; Podlecki, "Omens in the *Odyssey*," 17; S. J. Green, "Malevolent Gods and Promethean Birds: Contesting Augury in Augustus's Rome," *Transactions of the American Philological Association* 139 (2009): 147-67.

Zeus" (διοσημίαι) that could stop a meeting of the Law Courts or of the Assembly; religious feeling for an eclipse could overrule military intelligence to cause the greatest disaster ever suffered by Athenian arms. (Cf. Thucydides, *Historiae* 7.50.4).[9]

The dark fears of Alexander the Great (356–323 BCE) near the end of his life reflect the superstitions of his time. We are told that Alexander heard about or personally observed a number of omens as he approached Babylon, especially after the death of his close friend Hephaestion: a lion was kicked to death by a donkey, a mysterious youth was seen seated on the king's throne, seers began issuing warnings, and so forth (Plutarch, *Alexander* 73–4).

Alexander no longer trusted his friends and was convinced that he no longer enjoyed the favor of the gods. According to Plutarch:

> Alexander, then, since he had now become sensitive to indications of the divine will and perturbed and apprehensive in his mind, converted every unusual and strange occurrence, were it never so insignificant, into a prodigy and portent [τέρας ἐποιεῖτο καὶ σημεῖον]; and sacrificers, purifiers, and diviners [θυομένων καὶ καθαιρόντων καὶ μαντευόντων] filled his palace. So, you see, while it is a dire thing to be incredulous towards indications of the divine will and to have contempt for them, superstition [δεισιδαιμονία] is likewise a dire thing, which, after the manner of water ever seeking the lower levels, filled with folly the Alexander who now had become a prey to his fears. Notwithstanding, in consequence of oracular responses [χρησμῶν] ... he laid aside his grief and once again engaged in sacrifices and bouts of drinking.[10] (Plutarch, *Alexander* 75.1–2)

Plutarch's comments about the need to find balance between disbelief and contempt on the one hand and fearful superstition on the other hand reflect the main point of his treatise *De superstitione* (*Moralia* 164E–171F). Although the authorship of the treatise is somewhat in doubt,[11] its tone and the position that it takes on the relevant issues are overall consistent with the views Plutarch expresses elsewhere.

---

[9] G. Vlastos, "Theology and Philosophy in Early Greek Thought," *Philosophical Quarterly* 2.7 (1952): 97–123 (97). The passage from Thucydides reads:

> All was at last ready, and they were on the point of sailing away, when an eclipse of the moon, which was then at the full, took place. Most of the Athenians, deeply impressed by this occurrence, now urged the generals to wait; and Nicias, who was somewhat over-addicted to divination [θειασμῷ] and practices of that kind, refused from that moment even to take the question of departure into consideration, until they had waited the thrice nine days prescribed by the soothsayers [ὡς οἱ μάντεις ἐξηγοῦντο]. (Trans. R. Crawley, *History of the Peloponnesian War* [London: J. M. Dent, 1910], 512)

The decision not to withdraw proved disastrous.

[10] Trans. based on B. Perrin, *Plutarch, Lives: Demosthenes and Cicero, Alexander and Caesar*, LCL 99 (London: Heinemann, 1919), 431, 433.

[11] See the discussion of this point in M. Smith, "De Superstitione (Moralia 164E–171F)," in H. D. Betz (ed.), *Plutarch's Theological Writings and Early Christian Literature*, SCHNT 3 (Leiden: Brill, 1975), 1–35. The Greek title of the treatise is Περὶ δεισιδαιμονίας. In *Moralia* 164E and 165B Plutarch argues that ignorance of the gods produces atheism in the tough-minded, but in the soft-headed

The word δεισιδαιμονία, which is translated earlier as "superstition," is ambiguous. It can be negative, in the sense that one is too occupied with matters of divinities and spirits. But δεισιδαιμονία can also simply mean that one has interest in spiritual matters.[12] This is probably the nuance in Acts 17:22-23, where Paul addresses the Athenians: "Men of Athens, I perceive that in every way you are very religious [δεισιδαιμονεστέρους]. For as I passed along, and observed the objects of your worship." Here δεισιδαιμονεστέρους, the comparative adjective of the noun δεισιδαιμονία, seems to be more or less neutral, referring to an interest in divinity without necessarily implying an unhealthy fear.[13] There is no hint in the Acts narrative that anyone was offended by Paul's comment or that Paul himself thought his comment was in any way derogatory. Of course, the fact that an image is set up with an inscription that reads Ἀγνώστῳ θεῷ (To an Unknown God; v. 23) may suggest at least some fear on the part of the Athenians, that is, the fear of overlooking and therefore offending a divinity. In short, δεισιδαιμονία is "religion" (or *religio*), as in Polybius (cf. *Historiae* 6.56.6) and Strabo (cf. *Geographica* 1.2.8).[14]

We might briefly consider what Plutarch thinks about portents and omens. In the aforementioned tractate on δεισιδαιμονία he discounts troubling dreams (*Moralia* 165E-F; though see 941F, where Plutarch seems more open to their meaning and value). Plutarch believes that the gods exist, but that they are hardly concerned with human affairs. Therefore fearing them or placating them is foolish and misguided. In this regard Plutarch is very much an Epicurean. Fear of the gods leads to magic and invoking foreign names and barbarous words (166A-B). Hades is regarded as an illusion (167A).

In his treatise *De genio Socratis* (*Moralia* 575A-598F) Plutarch expresses the view that omens and divination (μαντεύματα) are of minimal value, perhaps even of no value at all (577D, 580A-B, 582B). Gods may give signs (σημεῖα), but most people fail to understand them and so resort to divination (μαντική), which is hopelessly subjective (593C-D). But Plutarch does concede that lightning without thunder, on the right side, can be a good sign (σημεῖον καλόν) and so might provide guidance (594E). When it comes to omens and portents, whatever one's views, discretion (εὐλάβεια) is well advised (586F).

When it came to omens, most Romans were not as moderate and thoughtful as Plutarch. Indeed, Romans were every bit as superstitious as the Greeks, perhaps more

---

it produces fear (cf. 167D-E). Neither is good. Of the two, Plutarch opines, atheism is the most harmful (167A-B).

[12] Gulick, "Omens and Augury in Plautus," 238; F. Solmsen, "Cicero on Religio and Superstitutio," *Classical Weekly* 37 (1944): 159-60; R. C. Ross, "Superstitio," *CJ* 64 (1969): 354-8; M. Smith, "Superstitio," in K. H. Richards (ed.), *Society of Biblical Literature 1981 Seminar Papers*, SBLSP 20 (Chico, CA: Scholars, 1981), 349-55. Ross traces the history of the use of the word *superstitio*. Gulick notes that a person believed to possess clairvoyant powers was regarded as *superstitiosus*.

[13] J. A. Fitzmyer, *The Acts of the Apostles*, AB 31 (New York: Doubleday, 1998), 606: δεισιδαιμονία basically means "reverence for deities."

[14] Although at one time δεισιδαιμονία and *religio* were distinguished, Cicero informs us (*De natura deorum* 2.71). Smith ("De Superstitione," 3) suggests that Plutarch thinks of δεισιδαιμονία as involving matters that one should "handle with care" (as in *Moralia* 586F, which will be mentioned shortly).

so. This is seen throughout Rome's history. For example, when Hannibal's army invaded Italy and approached Rome, everyone in the city was filled with dread. Polybius tells us:

> All the oracles [πάντα ... λόγια] that had ever been delivered to them were in men's mouths, every temple and every house was full of signs and prodigies [σημείων δὲ καὶ τεράτων], so that vows, sacrifices, supplicatory processions and litanies pervaded the city. For in seasons of danger the Romans are much given to propitiating both gods and men, and there is nothing at such times in rites of the kind that they regard as unbecoming or beneath their dignity.[15] (*Historiae* 3.112.8–9)

In essence Polybius is saying that in times of crisis the Romans will do anything; no rite is too ridiculous, no omen, however odd, is to be discounted.

Judging by the historians and biographers, the emperors of Rome seem to have been as superstitious as anyone. Even the historians themselves, who customarily write with restraint, provide numerous accounts of omens, portents, and prophecies that in one way or another presaged the accession, success, failure, or demise of all Roman emperors and hopefuls. The survey that follows should provide a context in which the omens and portents described in the Gospel Infancy and Passion narratives can be better appreciated.

Julius Caesar (100–44 BCE):[16] Neither Plutarch nor Suetonius provides us with stories of prodigies at the birth or during the early childhood of Julius Caesar.[17] Both do tell us of Sulla's prediction that Caesar will someday impact Rome, even beyond the condemned Marius, declared an enemy of the state. According to Suetonius, Sulla "cried, either by divine inspiration [*divinitus*] or a shrewd forecast: 'Have your way and take him; only bear in mind that the man you are so eager to save will one day deal the death blow to the cause of the aristocracy ... for in this Caesar there is more than one Marius'" (*Divus Julius* 1.3; cf. Plutarch, *Caesar* 1.2). During his prime the up and coming Julius Caesar had a startling dream. The "soothsayers [*conjectores*] inspired him with high hopes by their interpretation ... that he was destined to rule the world"[18] (Suetonius, *Divus Julius* 7.2). Caesar's claims to have descended from kings on his mother's side and from Venus on his father's side (6.1), both of which apparently were taken very seriously (cf. Marcus Velleius Paterculus, *Historiae* 2.41.1: "tracing his descent from Venus ... a claim conceded by all investigators of antiquity [*inter omnis antiquitatis studiosos*]"), only added to prophetic expectations.[19]

---

[15] Translated and adapted from W. R. Paton, *Polybius: The Histories II*, LCL 137 (London: Heinemann, 1922), 279.

[16] A. Goldsworthy, *Caesar: Life of a Colossus* (London: Weidenfeld & Nicolson, 2006); J. Osgood, *Caesar's Legacy: Civil War and the Emergence of the Roman Empire* (Cambridge: Cambridge University Press, 2006).

[17] Suetonius may have recounted events relating to Caesar's birth and childhood, but the beginning of *Divus Julius* is lost. The same may be the case with respect to Plutarch's biography.

[18] Trans. J. C. Rolfe, *Suetonius*, vol. I, LCL 31, rev. ed. (Cambridge, MA: Harvard University Press, 1998), 43. The *conjector* was an interpreter of dreams.

[19] All of this may strike us moderns as strange and improbable, but as Keith Hopkins reminds us, "We should be careful not to suppress what Romans thought was happening." See K. Hopkins, *Conquerors and Slaves* (Cambridge: Cambridge University Press, 1978), 233. In most cases what the people of

The assassination of Caesar was preceded by numerous omens and strange sightings, or so it was widely reported and believed. Suetonius says that "Caesar's approaching murder was foretold to him by unmistakable signs [*prodigiis denuntiata*]" (*Divus Julius* 81.1). Under Caesar's authority some old tombs were being cleared away for the building of new houses. During this work a bronze tablet was uncovered bearing a Greek inscription that read: "Whenever the bones of Capys shall be moved, it will come to pass that a son of Ilium shall be slain at the hands of his kindred, and presently avenged at heavy cost to Italy" (81.1).[20] Suetonius tells us that "the soothsayer [*haruspex*] Spurinna warned (Caesar) to beware danger" (81.2) and that Caesar himself dreamed "that he was flying above the clouds and … clasping the hand of Jupiter" (81.3).[21] After Caesar's assassination and during the games that his heir Augustus held in honor of his *apotheōsis*, a "comet [*stella*] shone for seven successive days, rising about the eleventh hour and was believed to be the soul of Caesar" (88.1).[22] Vergil claims the sun darkened following Caesar's death (*Georgica* 1.467-8; cf. Pliny, *Naturalis historia* 2.30.97; Plutarch, *Caesar* 69.4).

Plutarch says people reported that "amazing signs and apparitions [σημεῖα θαυμαστὰ καὶ φάσματα] were seen," such as "lights in the heavens, crashing sounds borne all about by night, and birds of omen [ὄρνιθας] coming down into the forum." Strabo, Plutarch adds, "says that multitudes of men all on fire were seen rushing up, and a soldier's slave threw from his hand a copious flame … and that when Caesar himself was sacrificing, the heart of the victim was not to be found" (*Caesar* 63.1-2; cf. Suetonius, *Divus Julius* 81.4). Plutarch reports further that people claimed a certain "seer [μάντις] warned Caesar to be on guard against a great peril on the day of the month of March, which the Romans call the Ides" (*Caesar* 63.3).

Plutarch tells of Caesar's wife's dream, in which she either holds her murdered husband in her arms or an ornament given to Caesar by the senate is torn down (*Caesar* 63.5-6; cf. Suetonius, *Divus Julius* 81.3; Paterculus, *Historiae* 2.57.1-2). Calpurnia his wife begged Caesar "to enquire by other modes of divination [διὰ μαντικῆς] and by sacrifices concerning the future" (Plutarch, *Caesar* 63.6). Caesar did so, for "never before had he perceived in Calpurnia any womanish superstition [δεισιδαιμονία]." Calpurnia's reference to "other modes of divination" meant that Caesar should not rely on her dream alone. The "seers [οἱ μάντεις] also, after many sacrifices, told him that the omens were unfavorable" (63.7). One Cinna, a friend of Caesar, also dreamed and had a "strange vision [ὄψιν … ἄτοπον]" (68.2).[23]

---

late antiquity report is what they truly believed has occurred, which includes the conviction that the omens are real, that they truly indicate the insights, if not the will of the gods. Even the idea that one was sired by a god—as bizarre as it might sound to us today—was in the thinking of late antique Romans very much a possibility. Indeed, such belief had a great deal of explanatory power when it came to people of remarkable abilities and achievements.

[20] Rolfe, *Suetonius*, vol. I, 137.
[21] Caesar supposedly knew his death was near but did not try to avoid it. See Ripat, "Roman Omens," 166-73.
[22] Rolfe, *Suetonius*, vol. I, 147. During the reign of Commodus (180-92 CE) we are told that prodigies (*prodigia*) took place, including the appearance of a comet (*stella*) and fire in the heavens (Aelius Lampridius, *Commodus Antoninus* 16.1-2).
[23] For additional references to omens surrounding the death of Caesar, see Cassius Dio, *Historia Romana* 44.18.1-4; Appian, *Bella civilia* 2.115-16.

Marcus Antonius (83–30 BCE):[24] Most of our biographical information about Marcus Antonius, or Antony, comes from Plutarch, though Suetonius and other historians refer to Julius Caesar's younger associate in their respective histories and biographies of Caesar and Octavian. There are a few references to signs and omens relating to Antony that are worth mentioning. In a dispute with Julius Caesar over an appointment, Antony shouted that "the omens were opposed [τοὺς οἰωνοὺς ἐναντιοῦσθαι]." Influenced by this opinion, Caesar yielded to Antony (Plutarch, *Antonius* 11.3). Whether there were any omens or, if so, how seriously Antony took them is not clear. Evidently Caesar did.

After Caesar's assassination and his becoming personally acquainted with Octavian, Antony "saw a strange vision [ὄψιν εἶδεν ἄτοπον]," in which he saw his right hand struck by lightning (16.4). The vision, along with rumors, convinced Antony that Octavian was plotting against him. Later still, an Egyptian seer (μαντικός), one of those who "cast nativities" (τῶν τὰς γενέσεις ἐπισκοπούντων),[25] warned Antony that his fortune was dimmed by Octavian's (33.2).[26] Prior to leading his army into battle Antony observed various rituals, including wearing a wreath from a sacred olive tree and, "in obedience to a certain oracle [κατά τι λόγιον]," filling a vessel with water from a certain spring and carrying it with him (34.1).

Antony's acts of vengeance against enemies prompted one Varro, as he was about to die, to prophesy the death of the tyrant (Paterculus, *Historiae* 2.71.2). A number of signs (σημεῖα) preceded the war between Octavian and Antony. Not one was favorable. These included earthquakes, the destruction of a building by lightning, a sweating statue, storms, collapsing monuments, and birds of omen (Plutarch, *Antonius* 60.2–3). All of these omens were fulfilled, it was believed, in Octavian's victory over Antony.

Octavian/Augustus (63 BCE–14 CE):[27] After Augustus became emperor it was remembered that a few months before his birth "a portent was generally observed at Rome" to the effect that one would be born who would become king of the Romans. The senate, we are told, "decreed that no male child born that year should be reared" (Suetonius, *Divus Augustus* 94.3). Atia, the mother of Augustus, had a strange dream shortly before she conceived. The dream, accompanied by serpentine marks on her body, convinced her that her son was actually conceived by Apollo (94.4). On the very day of the emperor's birth, so goes the story, lightning struck a wall, which brought to mind an old prophecy that someone from the town would one day rule the world. At long last the omen (*ostentum*) that foretold (*portendisse*) the rule of Augustus was

---

[24] The latter part of Antony's career, including his downfall, is inextricably intertwined with the final years of Cleopatra. See A. Goldsworthy, *Antony and Cleopatra* (London: Yale University Press, 2010); P. de Ruggiero, *Mark Antony: A Plain Blunt Man* (Barnsley: Pen and Sword Military, 2013).

[25] To "cast nativity" is to observe (hence the use of the verb ἐπισκοποῦν, "to observe" or "examine") and interpret the positions of heavenly bodies at the time of someone's birth. From these observations and interpretations the seer can forecast one's destiny.

[26] The Egyptian seer told Antony that his "guardian genius" (δαίμων) shrank in fear when in the presence of Octavian.

[27] For recent and very readable biographies, see A. Everitt, *Augustus: The Life of Rome's First Emperor* (New York: Random House, 2006); A. Goldsworthy, *Augustus: From Revolutionary to Emperor* (London: Weidenfeld & Nicolson, 2014).

fulfilled (94.2). Other omens, including one reminiscent of an omen accompanying the birth of Alexander the Great, preceded or attended the birth of Augustus (94.5-6).

Frogs, birds, and other creatures reacted to the youthful Augustus (94.7). Quintus Catulus, who dedicated the Capitol, dreamed that a lad sat in the lap of the statue of Jupiter. When Catulus attempted to remove the boy, a voice cautioned him declaring that the lad was to be Rome's savior (94.8-9). Even Julius Caesar perceived an omen that convinced him that his young relative would someday succeed him (94.11). It was also said that the emperor's nursery in his grandfather's country house was in some sense possessed or sacred, for to enter this room safely (and people rarely entered it) required purification (*religio*). Those "who approach it without ceremony are seized with shuddering and terror." One man who dared to sleep in this room, having observed no rites of purification, was found the next morning thrown out "by a mysterious force," half-dead, along with his bedclothes (Suetonius, *Divus Augustus* 6).

Hearing of his great-uncle's assassination, Augustus hurried to Rome. When he entered the city, people "saw above his head the orb of the sun with a circle about it, colored like the rainbow, seeming thereby to place a crown upon the head of one destined soon to greatness" (Paterculus, *Historiae* 2.59.6). Augustus claimed that he had escaped capture at the hands of Cassius, one of Caesar's assassins, because of the dream (*onar*) of a friend (Plutarch, *Antonius* 22.2).

As emperor, Augustus erected a temple in honor of Apollo on a spot on the Palatine where "the soothsayers [*haruspices*] declared that the god had shown his desire by striking it with lightning" (Suetonius, *Divus Augustus* 29.3). Near the beginning of his absolute rule, the year that he assumed the office of *pontifex maximus*, Augustus "collected whatever prophetic writings of Greek or Latin origin were in circulation anonymously or under the names of authors of little repute, and burned more than two thousand of them, retaining only the Sibylline books and making a choice even among those" (31.1).

The destruction of prophetic books, including some of the Sibylline books suspected of being of recent and pseudonymous authorship, was to prevent soothsayers from interpreting these books and uttering prophecies about the fate of Augustus. Omens could scarcely be outlawed or destroyed, but books, whose ambiguous prophecies sometimes led to panic or plots, could be destroyed. We are told elsewhere that Augustus respected ancient rites, even foreign ones, but held in contempt those that were not ancient or well established. Apparently the emperor regarded Jewish religion—officially recognized by Rome—as insufficiently ancient, for he commended his grandson Gaius for not praying at the temple in Jerusalem when he had the opportunity to do so (93).

It was dreams that above all else influenced Augustus. He took seriously his own dreams and those of others that seemed to relate to him (91.1). There were seasons in his life when his dreams were especially frequent, often leading Augustus to take various actions (91.2). Numerous omens attended the emperor's battles (95-6). As he prepared to engage Antony at Actium, he met a wagon driver whose name was Eutychcus (fortunate) and whose donkey was called Nikōn (victory). After his victory over Antony at Actium, Augustus set up bronze images of the driver and his donkey (96.2; cf. Plutarch, *Antonius* 55.3).

Several omens and portents gave warning of the approaching death of Augustus (Suetonius, *Divus Augustus* 97.1: *evidentissimis ostentis praecognita est*, "were known in advance by unmistakable signs"). A bird flies overhead, lightning strikes and melts the first letter of CAESARE on one of the emperor's statues, indicating that he had only one hundred days to live. (The letter destroyed was the letter C, which as a number has the value of "100.") Augustus tried everything to avert his fate, even fleeing the city; but he became ill nonetheless (97.3). Not long afterward he suddenly died (99.1–2).

Tiberius (42 BCE–37 CE): Suetonius reports that Tiberius possessed "strong and unwavering confidence in his destiny, which he had conceived from his early years because of omens and predictions [*ostentis et praedictionibus*]" (*Tiberius* 14.1). During her pregnancy Livia, the mother of Tiberius and future wife of Augustus, tried "to divine by various omens whether she would bring forth a male." Her experiments convinced her that she would have a son and that he was destined for greatness. When Tiberius was an infant, "the astrologer [*mathematicus*] Scribonius promised him an illustrious career and even that one day he would be king" (14.2). When on campaign as a military commander, altars suddenly gleamed with fire as he passed by. Shortly before his recall to Rome, an eagle, "a bird never before seen in Rhodes, perched upon the roof of his house" (14.3–4). Other omens were observed and recalled. Tiberius explained to his troops that whenever his reading light flickered and went out, it was a positive omen (*ostentum*) and had been such in his family's history (19).

As emperor, Tiberius had a premonition that his reputation would someday suffer. Accordingly, he refused the honorary title "Father of his Country," lest it be revoked later to his shame (67.1–4). Although not overly pious (he was "neglectful of the gods"), he was superstitious, was "addicted to astrology [*addictus mathematicae*]," and fearing thunder and lightning he would wear a laurel wreath to avoid being struck (69). A number of omens took place at the end of his life: on his last birthday Tiberius dreamt that a statue of Apollo, which the emperor had set up in the Temple of Augustus, spoke to him that he would not live long enough to dedicate it; days before his death the lighthouse at Capreae, the emperor's island retreat, was toppled by an earthquake; and fire suddenly blazed up from cold ashes in the hearth (74). Word of the emperor's death led to shouts of joy, including the insulting ditty, "Tiberius to the Tiber!" (75.1).

Gaius Caligula (12–41 CE): As a young man Caligula was appointed augur, later pontiff (Suetonius, *Caligula* 12.1). Few omens are mentioned with respect to his birth and life, but much is said of his death:

> (Caligula's) approaching murder was foretold by many prodigies [*multa prodigia*]. The statue of Jupiter at Olympia, which he had ordered to be taken to pieces and moved to Rome, suddenly uttered such a peal of laughter that the scaffoldings collapsed and the workmen took to their heels; and at once a man called Assius turned up, who declared that he had been bidden in a dream to sacrifice a bull to Jupiter. The Capitol at Capua was struck by lightning … the soothsayer [*mathematicus*] Sulla too, when Gaius consulted him about his horoscope, declared that inevitable death was close at hand. … The day before he was killed he dreamed that he stood in heaven beside the throne of Jupiter and that the god struck him with the toe of his right foot and hurled him to earth. (57.1–3).[28]

---

[28] Translated and adapted from Rolfe, *Suetonius*, vol. I, 501, 503.

Suetonius brings his biography of Caligula to a close noting that some "things which had happened on that very day shortly before he was killed were also regarded as portents [*prodigiorum*]" (57.3).²⁹ These included a number of odd coincidences, including Caligula's being splattered with blood during a sacrifice (57.4). On signal a number of assassins struck down the hated emperor (58.2–3). His body was hastily and partially cremated and then buried without ceremony in gardens that belonged to the Lamian family. The gardens, we are told, were thereafter disturbed by ghosts (*umbris inquietatos*) and that not a night passed without some terror (*terrore*) making an appearance (59).

Claudius (10 BCE–54 CE): No omen hinted at the future greatness of Claudius until the reign of his nephew Caligula. Then, while Claudius was walking through the forum, "an eagle flying by lit upon his shoulder"³⁰ (Suetonius, *Divus Claudius* 7), signifying his future rule. When he became emperor, Claudius "scrupulously observed the custom of having the praetor call an assembly and proclaim a holiday, whenever there was an earthquake in the city; as well as that of offering up a supplication whenever a bird of ill-omen was seen on the Capitol" (22).³¹ The death of Claudius was preceded by various omens (*praesagia*), including the "rise of a long-haired star [*crinitae stellae*], commonly called a comet [*cometen*]; the striking of his father Drusus' tomb by lightning; and the fact that many magistrates of all ranks died that year" (46). Dio Cassius refers to a "thunder-bolt that fell upon the standards of the Praetorians, and the opening of its own accord of the temple of Jupiter Victor" (*Historia Romana* 61.35.1).³²

Nero (37–68 CE): A number of omens or utterances thought to be omens attended the birth of Nero Claudius Caesar and his subsequent purification (Suetonius, *Nero* 6.1–2; Tacitus, *Annales* 11.11). Dio Cassius relates that at the birth of Nero, just before dawn, "rays of light not cast by any visible beam of the sun enveloped him" (*Historia Romana* 61.36.2).³³ An astrologer (τις ἀστρολόγος) studied the stars and deduced that someday Nero would rule and also murder his mother (ibid.). Not long after Seneca was appointed as Nero's tutor he had a dream that presaged Nero's future cruelty (Suetonius, *Nero* 7.1).

In 59 Nero had his mother Agrippina murdered, evidently in fulfillment of the aforementioned prophecy. In Tacitus the prophecy is given by several astrologers (*Chaldaci*) who had warned that should her son Nero reign, she would be slain. "Let him slay, so that he might reign," she is remembered to have replied (Tacitus, *Annales* 14.9; cf. Dio Cassius, *Historia Romana* 61.36.2).³⁴ The following year a "long-haired star" (*stella crinita*), that is, a comet, appeared on successive nights, "a thing which is commonly believed to portend the death of great rulers" (Suetonius, *Nero* 36.1; cf.

---

²⁹ Ibid.
³⁰ Trans. J. C. Rolfe, *Suetonius*, vol. II, LCL 38, rev. ed. (Cambridge, MA: Harvard University Press, 1997), 15.
³¹ Ibid., 45.
³² Translated and adapted from E. Cary, *Dio Cassius* VIII: *Roman History Books 61–70*, LCL176 (Cambridge, MA: Harvard University Press, 1925), 33.
³³ Translated and adapted from ibid., 35.
³⁴ We are told that Agrippina later regretted uttering these rash words. After murdering his mother, Nero found it necessary to employ *magi* to summon her ghost, which had been haunting him, and seek forgiveness (Suetonius, *Nero* 34.4).

Tacitus, *Annales* 14.22: "which portends [*portendat*] change in regents"). An astrologer (*astrologus*) informed Nero that the way to nullify such omens (*ostenta*) and so avoid his fate was through the deaths of some distinguished men. Hearing this, Nero had several men assassinated (Suetonius, *Nero* 36.1–2).

Later, astrologers (*mathematici*) predicted that Nero would one day be repudiated (40.2). Tacitus (*Annales* 15.47) tells of reports of omens that foretold disasters to come. These omens included numerous lightning flashes, a comet ("a phenomenon to which Nero always made atonement in noble blood"; cf. Suetonius, *Nero* 36.2), two-headed embryos (human or animal), and a calf whose head was attached to a leg, all of which were interpreted by the soothsayers (*haruspicum*) as portending the coming of a new ruler.[35]

Near the end of his life Nero "was frightened by manifest portents from dreams [*portentis somniorum*], auspices [*auspicorum*], and omens [*ominum*], both old and new" (46.1; cf. Tacitus, *Annales* 16.14). Some of his dreams were nightmares. Strange and unexpected things occurred. In panic, Nero fled the city but was startled by an earthquake, a flash of lightning, and shouts of soldiers in the distance prophesying his end and the success of Galba (Suetonius, *Nero* 48.2).

A few months before his death, Nero "attended an inspection of victims, but could not get a favorable omen" (56). With the death of Nero, the Julio-Claudian line of Caesars came to an end. The demise of the family was signified by one final omen: the death of the laurel trees that over the years the family had planted. The "whole grove died," says Suetonius, "from the root up [*silva omnis exaruit radicitus*]." Not long after, the "Temple of the Caesars was struck by lightning, the heads fell from all the statues at the same time, and his sceptre, too, was dashed from the hand of Augustus" (Suetonius, *Galba* 1).[36] Even the reports and rumors of "false Neros" who would soon return to Rome and reign were viewed as portents, or at least as suggestive of uncertainties regarding the hated emperor's death.[37]

Galba (3 BCE–69 CE): Servius Sulpicius Galba (or Lucius Livius Galba Ocella) was born into a wealthy family and served with distinction in the Roman army and later as governor in Spain. In the turmoil following the rebellion of Julius Vindex in Gaul and Nero's suicide Galba gained the support of the Praetorian Guard and was proclaimed emperor in June 68.[38]

Omens were part of Galba's life and accession to the throne. It was recalled that as a lad, he was presented to Augustus, who said to him in Greek: "You too, child, will have a nibble at this power of ours" (Suetonius, *Galba* 4.1). On one occasion an eagle snatched the intestines of a victim sacrificed by Galba's grandfather (4.2). Some interpreted this as an omen that the family would achieve greatness, to which a skeptic retorted, "When a mule has a foal." Years later, when Galba began his march for Rome,

---

[35] J. H. W. G. Liebeschuetz, *Continuity and Change in Roman Religion* (Oxford: Oxford University Press, 1979), 155–66; D. Sansone, "Nero's Final Hours," *Illinois Classical Studies* 18 (1993): 179–89.
[36] Sansone, "Nero's Final Hours," 181, 183.
[37] Ibid., 186.
[38] G. E. F. Chilver, "The Army in Politics, A.D. 68–70," *JRS* 47 (1957): 29–35. Chilver's study applies to the whole of the chaotic period, not only to Galba and his brief reign.

to seize power, it was reported that a mule had a foal, a report which horrified some but greatly encouraged the soon-to-be emperor (4.3).

Plutarch reports "soothsayers and Chaldeans" (μάντεις καὶ Χαλδαῖοι) assured Galba that he would survive Nero and that Otho would serve him (Plutarch, *Galba* 23.4). After arriving in Spain, Galba offered up sacrifice. During the ceremony a young man's hair suddenly turned white, suggesting a transition in government. Other omens occurred (Suetonius, *Galba* 8.2). When Vindex rebelled in Gaul, Galba was encouraged by additional "favorable auspices and omens" (*auspiciis et ominibus*). These included a prophecy (*vaticinatione*), which a priest later found hidden in his temple, "the very same prediction" spoken by an inspired person two centuries earlier, to the effect that "one day there would come forth from Spain the ruler and lord of the world" (9.2). Preparing for war a ring was found, bearing a precious stone engraved with Victory: "Immediately afterwards a ship from Alexandria loaded with arms arrived ... without a pilot, without a single sailor or passenger, removing all doubt in anyone's mind that the war was just and holy and undertaken with the approval of the gods" (9.4).

Suetonius tells his readers that "many prodigies in rapid succession [*magna et assidua monstra*] from the very beginning of his reign had foretold [*portenderant*] Galba's end exactly as it happened" (18.1). These included the following: an ox that was being sacrificed suddenly broke loose and charged Galba's chariot splattering the emperor with blood; a guard hastening to Galba almost accidentally pierced him with his lance; when he finally entered Rome and then the palace, earthquakes occurred that made a strange sound; Galba was haunted by dreams, and odd things happened when he offered sacrifice (18.1–3). A soothsayer (*haruspex*) warned him of danger, saying assassins were near (19.1; cf. Plutarch, *Galba* 24.2–3: "treachery hung over the emperor's head"). He was right, for not long after, Galba was struck down (Suetonius, *Nero* 19.2–20.2). He died in his seventy-third year (23), as had been hinted at in a prophecy years earlier, which Nero had misunderstood (40.3).

Otho (32–69 CE): Marcus Salvius Otho was on friendly terms with Nero and later supported Galba in his bid for the throne. Disappointed with Galba, in January 69 he conspired with the Praetorian Guard and overthrew him. Otho wanted to present himself as the proper heir of Nero, but the legions of the Rhine backed Vitellius.[39] Otho's aspirations for rule were inspired by a forecast by an astrologer (*mathematicus*) named Seleucus (Suetonius, *Otho* 4.1). Plutarch says there "were many reports of signs and apparitions [σημείων δὲ καὶ φαντασμάτων], most of which were of uncertain and dubious origin" (Plutarch, *Otho* 4.4). These included the dropping of the reins of Victory in the chariot in the Capitol, a statue of Gaius Caesar that turned to face the east, and a strange shift in the current of the Tiber River (4.4–5; on the shift in the statue, see Suetonius, *Vespasian* 5.7). At Regium Lepidum (between Modena and Parma) a strange, long-resident bird disappeared (Tacitus, *Historiae* 2.50.2).[40]

---

[39] For history of this year, see K. Wellesley, *The Long Year, AD 69* (London: Elek, 1975).
[40] M. G. Morgan, "Two Omens in Tacitus' 'Histories' (2, 50, 2 and 1, 62, 2–3)," *Rheinisches Museum für Philologie* NF 136 (1993): 321–9, here 321–4.

The soothsayer (this time called a *haruspex*) continued to encourage Otho with various predictions (*praedicta*) and warnings (Suetonius, *Otho* 6.1–2). Not long after, Otho was plagued with nightmares, including hauntings of Galba's ghost (7.2: *manes Galbae*). He hastily prepared, "without any regard even for the omens [*religionum*]," to meet the approaching Vitellius (8.3). Otho was defeated and in April 69 he committed suicide (9.3).

Vitellius (15–9 CE): Aulus Vitellius was the son of the influential Lucius Vitellius and was on friendly terms with the emperors Caligula, Claudius, and Nero. Galba appointed him governor of lower Germania in 68, which positioned him for his later move against Otho in the spring of 69. Vitellius was proclaimed emperor by his troops in January 69 and then became emperor in fact when Otho committed suicide a few months later. In December 69 Vitellius was overthrown, dragged through the streets of Rome, and finally put to death.

It was the parents of Vitellius who feared for their son, because of his horoscope:

> His parents were so aghast at his horoscope as announced by the astrologers [*praedictam a mathematicis*] that his father tried his utmost, while he lived, to prevent the assignment of any province to his son; and when he was sent to the legions and hailed as emperor, his mother immediately mourned over him as lost. (Suetonius, *Vitellius* 3.2)

When hailed as emperor, the dining room caught fire from the stove and many interpreted the event as an evil omen. Vitellius, however, joked, saying it was a good sign, for "to us light is given!" (8.2). When he began his march against Otho, "an eagle suddenly flew towards them … and after hovering about the standards, slowly preceded their line of march" (9.1; cf. Tacitus, *Historiae* 1.62.2–3).[41] This was widely regarded as a good omen. But when the equestrian statues, which were being set up, suddenly collapsed, this was widely regarded as a bad omen (Suetonius, *Vitellius* 10). Vitellius himself clung to an oracle (*oraculum*) that had "prophesied [*vaticinante*] that he would rule securely and for a long time, but only if he should survive a parent" (14.5). For this reason, it was believed, he had caused the death of his mother, by denying her food during an illness. Vitellius was slain by one Antonius Primus, a man from Gaul, in fulfillment, it was believed, of a prophecy that the short-lived emperor "was destined to fall into the power of some man of Gaul" (18).

In light of the frivolous and subjective nature of many of the "omens" relating to Vitellius, perhaps I should for a moment interrupt my review of the emperors in order to call attention to the skepticism expressed in Cicero's treatise *De divinatione* ("On Divination"). Cicero (106–43 BCE) warns against the tendency seen in some people who view almost everything that occurs as an omen. He reminds his readers of the story circulating about Marcus Licinius Crassus (d. 53 BCE). As he prepared to depart with his army for Syria, a fig seller repeatedly cried out, *Cavneas*! ("Cavnean figs!"). Because the cry *cavneas* could be heard as *cave ne eas*, "Beware, don't go," some believed that

---

[41] Ibid., 324–8.

the fig seller's words were an omen of warning. This belief was confirmed when it was later learned that Crassus fell into a trap and was killed. Cicero saw in this event no more than coincidence. He comments, "If we are going to accept chance utterances of this kind as omens, we had better look out when we stumble, or break a shoe-string, or sneeze!" (Cicero, *De divinatione* 2.40; cf. Pliny, *Historia naturalis* 15.83). It is unlikely, however, that the average Roman of that period would have agreed with him. In the minds of many the fig seller's words were indeed ominous and the death of Crassus constituted proof of that assumption. I now continue with my review.

Vespasian (9–79 CE): Titus Flavius Vespasianus came from a modest family, which did not achieve senatorial rank until the rule of Julio-Claudian emperors. Vespasian served in the military with distinction (summed up in Suetonius, *Divus Vespasianus* 4.1–2) and gained his greatest honor and eventually the throne thanks to the Jewish rebellion of 66–70 CE.[42] His political rise was foretold by many omens (*ostenta*), even if not recognized until much later (cf. Tacitus, *Historiae* 1.10, 2.1).[43]

One omen involved an old, sacred oak tree on the Flavian family estate. On three occasions, when Vespasia (Vespasian's grandmother) gave birth, the old tree "suddenly put forth a branch from its trunk, obvious indications of the destiny of each child" (*Divus Vespanianus* 5.2). The omen was interpreted to signify that a grandson would someday rule the world. (The omen may have been interpreted as a parallel of the omen of the Julio-Claudian grove.) During Vespasian's youth, when he was eating breakfast, "a stray dog brought in a human hand from the cross-roads and dropped it under the table" (5.4). On yet another occasion, when Vespasian was dining, "an ox that was ploughing shook off its yoke, burst into the dining room, and after scattering the servants, fell at the very feet of Vespasian as he reclined at table, and bowed its neck" (5.4).

While in Judea, Vespasian "consulted the oracle (*oraculum*) of the god of Carmel [*Carmeli dei*]." He was told that "whatever he planned or wished, however great it might be, would come to pass" (5.6; cf. Tacitus, *Historiae* 2.78.3).[44] It was in Judea, of course, that Vespasian encountered Josephus, who foretold that the general would someday be emperor (*Divus Vespasianus* 5.7; cf. 4.5). "Omens [*praesagia*] were also reported in Rome," Suetonius relates. "Nero in his latter days was admonished in a dream to take the sacred chariot of Jupiter … from its shrine to the house of Vespasian"

---

[42] B. Levick, *The Emperor Vespasian*, rev. ed. (London: Taylor and Francis, 2005).

[43] R. Lattimore, "Portents and Prophecies in Connection with the Emperor Vespasian," *CJ* 29 (1934): 441–9. Lattimore notes that in sheer number, the omens related to Vespasian were second only to Augustus himself (443).

[44] According to Tacitus, at Mount Carmel Vespasian was advised by a priest named Basilides. There is no mention of a "god of Carmel." One wonders if there is confusion between the priest of Carmel named Basilides and the mysterious appearance in the temple of Serapis of Vespasian's old servant named Basilides. Tacitus says that "old omens" (*vetera omina*) were recalled by Vespasian (*Historiae* 2.78.2). A number of studies have investigated the Basilides tradition: K. Scott, "The Rôle of Basilides in the Events of A.D. 69," *JRS* 24 (1934): 138–40; M. G. Morgan, "Vespasian and the Omens in *Histories* 2.78," *Phoenix* 50 (1996): 41–55; D. Wardle, "Suetonius on *Vespasianus Religiosus* in AD 69–70: Signs and Times," *Zeitschrift für klassische Philologie* 140 (2012): 184–201. Scott argues that the Basilides mentioned in *OGIS* 665 (col. iii, line 36) is this person and that the Basilides of Mount Carmel in Israel and the Basilides of the Serapis Temple in Alexandria are one and the same.

(5.7). A statue of divus Augustus turned of its own accord to the east; two eagles fought; when one was victorious, a third eagle arrived and drove off the victor (5.7).

When he was acclaimed emperor, Vespasian relocated to Egypt and there "entered the temple of Serapis alone, to consult the auspices as to the duration of his power." While in the temple his servant, whose name coincidentally was Basilides ("kingly" or "royal") and who could hardly walk, mysteriously appeared and offered Vespasian "sacred boughs, garlands, and loaves" (7.1). Shortly thereafter a report came that Vitellius had been slain. Seated on the tribunal, Vespasian was prevailed upon to touch the eyes of a blind man and to touch the leg of a lame man; both were healed.[45] "At the same time, by the direction of certain soothsayers [*vaticinantium*], some vases of antique workmanship were dug up in a consecrated spot at Tegea in Arcadia and on them was an image very like Vespasian" (7.2–3). Vespasian's faith in his horoscope never wavered; he was confident that he would be succeeded by his sons and that the Flavian dynasty, as indicated by a dream, would endure for at least twenty-seven years (25). And so it happened.

Notwithstanding the favorable omens, Vespasian and his supporters worked hard at propaganda that supported his credentials.[46] Omens—recalled from long ago or recently reported—were circulated. The decision to build right away the *Templum Pacis* (temple of peace) was part of this effort.[47] The ostensible purpose of the temple was to celebrate the victory over Israel, which to some extent it was; but the real purpose was to elevate the Flavians in the eyes of the Roman elite. So also the minting of the *Judaea Capta* (Judea captured) coins from the gold of the Jewish temple.[48]

Omens portended the death of Vespasian. "Signs [σημεῖα] had occurred," says Cassius Dio, "indicating his approaching end, such as the comet star [ἀστὴρ ὁ κομήτης] which was visible for a long time and the opening of (the door of) the mausoleum of Augustus of its own accord" (*Historia Romana* 66.1). Vespasian did not think the omen of the comet, known as the "long-haired star" (as seen in examples earlier), related to him. "This is an omen [προσημαίνει], not for me," said the emperor, "but for the

---

[45] See A. D. Nock, "Deification and Julian," *JRS* 47 (1957): 115–23, here 118 = *Essays on Religion and the Ancient World* (Oxford: Clarendon Press, 1972), 2.833–46, here 838; D. L. Tiede, *The Charismatic Figure as Miracle-Worker*, SBLDS 1 (Missoula, MT: Scholars, 1972), 91–3; T. S. Luke, "A Healing Touch for Empire: Vespasian's Wonders in Domitianic Rome," *GR* 57 (2010): 77–106. Tiede notes that the healings in Egypt gave Vespasian the credentials he needed, while Luke says healing the two men in Alexandria was a sign that Vespasian was the new Serapis.

[46] A. Ferrill, "Otho, Vitellius, and the Propaganda of Vespasian," *CJ* 60 (1965): 267–9. Ferrill notes that Vespasian and supporters created the illusion that the would-be emperor had Otho's endorsement. Ferrill also underscores how important omens were for establishing Vespasian's legitimacy.

[47] C. F. Noreña, "Medium and Message in Vespasian's Templum Pacis," *Memoirs of the American Academy in Rome* 48 (2003): 25–43; R. Taraporewalla, "The Templum Pacis: Construction of Memory under Vespasian," *Acta Classica* 53 (2010): 145–63.

[48] C. H. V. Sutherland, "Roman Imperial Coins in the Oxford Collection. (II) Vespasian to Domitian," *Numismatic Chronicle and Journal of the Royal Numismatic Society* Fifth Series 20 (1940): 255–64; B. W. Jones, "Some Thoughts on the Propaganda of Vespasian and Domitian," *CJ* 66 (1971): 251; D. Barag, "The Palestinian 'Judaea Capta' Coins of Vespasian and Titus and the Era on the Coins of Agrippa II Minted under the Flavians," *Numismatic Chronicle* Seventh Series 18 (1978): 14–23 + plates 3–5. In his brief note, Jones comments: "It is obvious ... that the coins minted under the Flavians were meant to establish the emperor's image."

Parthian king; for he has long hair, whereas I am bald" (66.2). This time Vespasian was wrong.

Besides the Greco-Roman historians and biographers Josephus also refers to several omens and portents that preceded Vespasian's acclamation as emperor. At the beginning of *Judean War* Joseph informs his readers that he will narrate Vespasian's advance toward Jerusalem, which was "diverted by the call to imperial dignity," a call preceded by "portents that came to him concerning this [τά τε γενόμενα περὶ ταύτης αὐτῷ σημεῖα]" (*J.W.* 1.23). True to his promise these portents, as well as his prophecy, are recalled when Vespasian is acclaimed:

> Among many other omens [τά τε ἄλλα σημεῖα πολλά], which had everywhere foreshadowed [προφαίνοντα] his imperial honors, he recalled the words of Josephus, who had ventured, even in Nero's lifetime, to address him as emperor. ... Then he (Vespasian) referred to his predictions [τὰς μαντείας] ... which time and the event had proved to be divine [θείας] ... "one who foretold [προθεσπίσαντα] my elevation to power and was a minister of the voice of God [τῆς τοῦ θεοῦ φωνῆς]." (4.624–5)

Josephus is well known, of course, for his reinterpretation of the "ambiguous oracle [χρησμὸς ἀμφίβολος]" (probably Num. 24:17, "a star goes forth from Jacob"), which he applies to Vespasian (*J.W.* 6.312–15). Although it is disputed, I believe the oracle became a topic of Jewish speculation because of the comet that appeared in the sky and resembled a sword (6.289–91). In the Greco-Roman world the "long-haired stars" (Latin: *crinitae stellar*) or comets (*cometen*/κομῆται) were often interpreted as signifying the death of a ruler and/or the advent of a new ruler (Suetonius, *Divus Claudius* 46; Tacitus, *Annales* 14.22; Dio Cassius, *Historia Romana* 64.8.1). Josephus tells his readers (who were first and foremost members and supporters of the Flavian family) that the oracle, though Jewish, was fulfilled in Vespasian because he was proclaimed emperor "on Jewish soil" (*J.W.* 6.313).[49]

Some of the omens and portents described in the Greek and Roman biographies and histories are attested in early Christian history and writings. One immediately thinks of the death of Herod Agrippa I, as recounted in Acts and in Josephus. The account in Acts is the briefer and simpler of the two. We are told that Agrippa "put on his royal robes" and addressed the people, who shouted, "The voice of a god [θεοῦ φωνή], and not of a man!" Acts reports, almost laconically, "Immediately an angel of the Lord smote him, because he (Agrippa) did not give God the glory; and he was eaten by worms and died" (Acts 12:21-23).

---

[49] I argue for this interpretation in C. A. Evans, "The Star of Balaam and the Prophecy of Josephus concerning Vespasian," in J. J. Collins and A. Geyser-Fouché (eds.), *Scribal Practice, Text, and Canon in the Dead Sea Scrolls: Essays in Memory of Peter W. Flint*, STDJ 130 (Leiden: Brill, 2019), 297–333. Shortly after his capture, Josephus utters his prophecy to Vespasian and Titus: "You imagine, Vespasian, that in the person of Josephus you have taken a mere captive ... You will be Caesar, Vespasian, you will be emperor, you and your son here" (*J.W.* 3.400–2). The Greek text is corrupt, but the meaning seems clear enough. For a suggested emendation, see R. Merkelbach, "Des Josephus Prophezeiung für Vespasian," *Rheinisches Museum für Philologie* NF 122 (1979): 361.

Josephus describes the apparel of Agrippa in much greater detail, noting that the robe was "a garment made wholly of silver, and of a texture truly wonderful" and that people were almost terrified to look upon him in the reflection of the sun's rays (*Ant.* 19.343–4). Agrippa's flatterers raised their voices, addressing him as a god (θεὸν προσαγορεύοντες): "May you be propitious to us and if we have hitherto feared you as a man, yet henceforth we agree that you are more than mortal in your being" (19.345).[50] Josephus comments, "The king did not rebuke them nor did he reject their flattery as impious. But shortly thereafter he looked up and saw an owl perched on a rope over his head. At once, recognizing this as a harbinger of woes just as it had once been of good tidings, he felt a stab of pain" (19.346). Josephus has recalled the owl that Agrippa had observed not many years before when he was in prison. A fellow prisoner interpreted the owl as an omen of Agrippa's imminent release but that when he should see it again, it meant "death in five days" (18.195–202). We are told, true to the prophecy, that after suffering with great abdominal pain for five days Agrippa died (19.350).

The owl as omen, either for good or ill, is very much at home in Roman beliefs regarding bird omens. The reference in Acts to Agrippa's being "eaten by worms" would have in itself been viewed as a very negative sign. That it was a judgment from God is made quite clear in Acts and in *Jewish Antiquities*. In the former, the author tells us that an "angel of the Lord" struck Agrippa. In the latter, Agrippa himself acknowledges his blasphemy and the blasphemy of his flatterers.

Jewish readers of Acts and perhaps also of *Antiquities* would have been reminded of the death of the impious Antiochus IV Epiphanes (d. 164 BCE), whose pogroms against the Jewish people included defilement of the Jewish temple. After threatening the Jewish people,[51] the Seleucid king is "seized with a pain in his bowels for which there was no relief ... the ungodly man's body swarmed with worms," and so on (2 Macc. 9:5-9). A number of commentators suspect an allusion to the worm of Isa. 66:24 ("their worm shall not die, their fire shall not be quenched").[52] Gonzalo Aranda Pérez, for example, says "this form of death is a foretaste of the later destiny of Antiochus" and then references Isa. 66:24.[53] Not all agree, but the repeated references to the "stench" (ὀσμή; vv. 9, 10, 12) of the king's decaying flesh and to "revulsion" (βαρύνεσθαι), along with reference to the worms, make us think of the corpses of the wicked, which in Isa. 66:24 the righteous view and find "abhorrent" (דראון). The miserable description of the king's condition does seem intended to bring to mind his gruesome postmortem destiny, as Aranda Pérez suggested.

---

[50] Note too that whereas in Acts the people shout that Agrippa spoke with the "voice of a god," in Josephus the people actually identify Agrippa as a god. Perhaps I am overinterpreting here, but Josephus may have heightened the blasphemy of the episode for the benefit of his elite Roman readers. He has, moreover, underscored from a Jewish point of view the blasphemy of what the flatterers said by placing on the lips of Agrippa an explicit acknowledgment of guilt.

[51] Antiochus states: "I will make Jerusalem a cemetery of Jews!" (2 Macc. 9:4).

[52] N. J. McEleney, "1–2 Maccabees," in R. E. Brown et al. (eds.), *The New Jerome Biblical Commentary* (Englewood Cliffs, NJ: Prentice Hall, 1990), 444; R. Doran, "2 Maccabees," in M. Goodman (ed.), *The Apocrypha*, The Oxford Bible Commentary (Oxford: Oxford University Press, 2001), 175.

[53] G. Aranda Pérez, "2 Maccabees," in W. R. Farmer et al. (eds.), *The International Bible Commentary: A Catholic and Ecumenical Commentary for the Twenty-First Century* (Collegeville, PA: Liturgical, 1998), 747.

And finally, Herod the Great suffered a similar fate. As he neared death, the king was afflicted with gangrene and worms in his privates (*J.W.* 1.656). Other rulers and people of power—women as well as men—suffered painful, wormy deaths for having offended the gods through acts of cruelty, excessive violence, or hybris,[54] as in the case of Agrippa.

Omens at the Birth of Jesus

There are relatively few omens, strictly speaking, in the birth narratives of the Gospels of Matthew and Luke, but there are several features that nevertheless would have been viewed by Jew and Gentile alike as presaging Jesus's greatness. Commentators rightly call attention to approximate parallels with stories told about the birth of Octavian, who later will become Emperor Augustus.[55] Suetonius, writing a few decades after the evangelists Matthew and Luke, remarks in reference to Octavian that "it will not be out of place to add an account of the omens which occurred before he was born, on the very day of his birth, and afterwards, from which it was possible to anticipate and perceive his future greatness" (*Divus Augustus* 94.1).[56] The evangelists could have said the same in reference to Jesus of Nazareth. In fact, that is what Matthew and Luke have done; they have added an account of the strange and marvelous events that took place before the birth of Jesus, the day of his birth, and the time that followed.

In Matthew, Mary is found to be with child before the consummation of her marriage to Joseph (Mt. 1:18). An angel of the Lord appears to Joseph in a dream (ἄγγελος κυρίου κατ' ὄναρ ἐφάνη αὐτῷ), informing him that her pregnancy is of the Holy Spirit (1:20). Joseph is told that Mary will bear a son, who will be called Jesus, because (playing on the meaning of *Jesus*, or Yeshuʻa, "the Lord saves") "he will save his people from their sins" (1:21). This dream is not called an omen or sign, but this is how it would have been understood by Jews, Greeks, and Romans in late antiquity. What Joseph is told fulfills an ancient prophecy (1:22-23; i.e., Isa. 7:14).

Mary's unexpected pregnancy is not called a miracle or omen as such, but that is how it would have been viewed, at least by those who took the story seriously. We think of Julius Caesar's dream, interpreted by some to the effect that he would one day rule the world (Suetonius, *Divus Julius* 7.2). Caesar also claimed that he descended from the goddess Venus on his father's side (6.1; Marcus Velleius Paterculus, *Historiae* 2.41.1). In

---

[54] For more examples of agonizing deaths involving worms, see W. Nestle, "Legenden vom Tod der Gottesverächter," *ARW* 33 (1936): 246–69; T. W. Africa, "Worms and the Death of Kings: A Cautionary Note on Disease and History," *Classical Antiquity* 1 (1982): 1–17; D. R. Schwartz, *2 Maccabees*, Commentaries on Early Jewish Literature (Berlin: de Gruyter, 2008), 357. I explore the worm tradition of Isa. 66:24 and its influence on ideas about hell in C. A. Evans, "The Fiery Origins of Gehenna in Isaiah, Enoch, Jesus, and Beyond," in C. A. Evans, P. T. Sloan, and B. LePort (eds.), *Visions and Violence in the Pseudepigrapha*, JCT 34, SSEJC 22 (London: T&T Clark, 2022), 141–70, esp. 151–52.

[55] C. H. Talbert, *Reading Luke: A Literary and Theological Commentary on the Third Gospel*, Reading the New Testament (New York: Crossroad, 1982), 16–17. Talbert succinctly sums up the components in the respective Infancy narratives of Octavian and Jesus.

[56] Translation based on Rolfe, *Suetonius*, vol. I, 287.

the second century CE the adventurer and trickster Alexander of Abonoteichus claimed that his father was none other than Zeus (*apud* Lucian, *Alexander pseudomantis* 7). For Matthew, of course, Mary's miraculous conception fulfills Jewish Scripture, not pagan mythology.

Magi come to Jerusalem seeking the one "born king of the Jews," for they "have seen his star" and so "have come to worship him" (Mt. 2:1-2). Those familiar with Israel's ancient Scriptures would probably think of Balaam's mysterious oracle about the star that will go forth from Jacob (Num. 24:17), an oracle that in Jewish and Christian traditions alike was understood in messianic terms. Prophecies and omens about stars, signifying the fall and rise of kings and kingdoms, were not limited to Jewish tradition but reached back to the Ancient Near East and by the time of Augustus and Jesus were widespread in the Roman world (e.g., Suetonius, *Divus Vespasianus* 4.5: "There had spread all over the Orient an old and established belief that it was fated at that time for men coming from Judea to rule the world").[57]

It is interesting, too, to note that the magi of Matthew do not utter prophecies or offer counsel (which often happens in the stories about the Roman emperors). No *haruspex* (dream interpreter) explains anything to Joseph or Mary. In seeing the star, the magi deduce (how, we are not sure) that the "king of the Jews" has been born (Mt. 2:2), but when they see the holy family we are only told that they rejoiced and offered gifts (2:10-11). The magi are then warned in a dream to return home by a different route (2:12).

Earlier we looked at examples in which the appearance of a star was interpreted as an omen portending the death of various Roman emperors. In Matthew the star portends the birth of a new king of the Jews, to be sure, but from a Roman point of view the star portended the imminent death of the reigning king. Apparently that is how Herod the Great perceived it. We should assume that however knowledgeable of Jewish Scripture and interpretation Herod might have been, his understanding of the world, which would have included the meaning of omens, would have been very Roman. The birth of Jesus and the accompanying star constituted a serious threat from his point of view, for these events implied that Herod will soon die, that his dynasty will come to an end. Long-tailed stars or comets, says astrologer Claudius Ptolemy, means a king or a prince "will die" (*Centiloquy* §100; cf. *Sib. Or.* 3:334-6). Herod probably understood the star the same way, so it was no wonder that in Matthew's narrative world the aging, fearful monarch desired to kill the infant Jesus in a desperate bid to cancel the omen and hopefully prolong his life. (Recall that the parents of Vitellius

---

[57] J. W. van Henten, "The World Leader from the Land of the Jews: Josephus, *Jewish War* 6.300–315; Tacitus, *Histories* 5.13; and Suetonius, *Vespasian* 4.5," in P. Barthel and G. van Kooten (eds.), *The Star of Bethlehem and the Magi: Interdisciplinary Perspectives from Experts on the Ancient Near East, the Greco-Roman World, and Modern Astronomy* (Leiden: Brill, 2015), 361–86; Helen R. Jacobus, "Balaam's 'Star Oracle' (Num 24:15–9)," in Barthel and van Kooten, *The Star of Bethlehem and the Magi*, 399–429; and H. I. Newman, "Stars of the Messiah," in M. Kister et al. (eds.), *Tradition, Transmission, and Transformation from Second Temple Literature through Judaism and Christianity in Late Antiquity: Proceedings of the Thirteenth International Symposium of the Orion Center for the Study of the Dead Sea Scrolls and Associated Literature* (Leiden: Brill, 2015), 272–303.

attempt to avert the omen regarding their son—Suetonius, *Vitellius* 3.2; hoping to avert negative omens Nero has several prominent men murdered—*Nero* 36.2).

Like the magi, Joseph is also warned in a dream to flee to Egypt (Mt. 2:13). After Herod dies, "an angel of the Lord appeared in a dream to Joseph in Egypt," commanding him to return to the land of Israel (2:19-20). Joseph is again warned in a dream to relocate to Galilee, in the village of Nazareth (2:22-23). Six times in the Gospel of Matthew people are instructed or warned in dreams. Four times Joseph is warned. The magi were warned once and the wife of Pontius Pilate the governor will also be warned regarding Jesus (27:19). As we have seen earlier, dreams were commonplace in the stories of Rome's emperors (Julius Caesar's dream, in Suetonius, *Divus Julius* 81.3; his wife's dream, in Plutarch, *Caesar* 63.5-6; the dream of Octavian's mother regarding his birth, in Suetonius, *Divus Augustus* 94.4, etc.). In the Jewish world, of course, dreams involving men named Joseph are not unknown (Joseph in Genesis 40-41; Josephus in *J.W.* 3.351-3).[58]

Herod attempts to nullify the omen of the star and birth of the infant in Bethlehem by slaughtering all recently born youths. Commentators rightly point out the potential parallel in the story of Octavian (Augustus), in which it was remembered that a "portent" had been observed in Rome, which was interpreted as signifying that a woman was about to give birth to a man who would rule over Rome as a king. The senate decreed that "no male child born that year should be raised" (Suetonius, *Divus Augustus* 94.3). It is likely that many readers of the Gospel of Matthew would have been aware that Herod and Augustus had been friends and had been mutually supportive. The approximate parallel between the threatened infancy of Octavian and the threatened infancy of Jesus, at the hands of Herod, would have been appreciated by many. And as just mentioned earlier, Nero attempted to nullify omens (*ostenta*) portending his death by assassinating several distinguished men (Suetonius, *Nero* 36.1-2).

Notwithstanding a number of parallels, the "omens" of the Matthean Infancy narrative are really not omens, so far as the evangelist is concerned. Rather, they are fulfillments of scriptural prophecies. Citing Scripture as fulfilled five times in the Infancy narrative (Mt. 1:22-23; 2:5-6, 15, 17-18, 23) serves an apologetic in a Jewish setting, to be sure, but it also underscores the point that pivotal moments in the early life of Jesus were not indicated by omens that could mean almost anything and apply to almost anyone; rather, these pivotal moments were indicated and clarified by ancient prophecies, whose meanings situated Jesus firmly in the story of Israel.

The tenor of the Infancy narrative in the Gospel of Luke is quite different, but there are features that would have impressed readers in the Roman Empire. While serving in the temple in Jerusalem Zechariah the priest sees an angel, which speaks with him and assures him that despite his and his wife's advanced age they will have a son who will play an important role in Israel's redemption (Lk. 1:8-20). When Zechariah emerged from the temple, unable to speak, the people assume that he had seen a vision (1:21-23). As promised, Zechariah's wife Elizabeth conceives (1:24-25). An angel then

---

[58] Josephus took great interest in the dream stories of Joseph, son of Jacob, recounting them at length (*Ant.* 2.11-86). See the major study of Josephus and dreams in R. K. Gnuse, *Dreams and Dream Reports in the Writings of Josephus: A Traditio-Historical Analysis*, AGJU 36 (Leiden: Brill, 1996).

appears to Mary of Nazareth, informing her that she too will give birth to a child who "will be great and will be called the Son of the Most High," who will sit on "the throne of his father David" and "reign over the house of Jacob forever" (1:26-33). Soon after, Mary meets her kinswoman Elizabeth and the infant in her womb leaps for joy (1:39-41). When Elizabeth gives birth, Zechariah regains his ability to speak and declares that the child's name will be John (1:57-66). Most inhabitants of the Roman Empire would view these unusual events as omens.

Luke's Infancy narrative is rich with supernatural occurrences, but none of these unusual events should be regarded as omens, in need of interpretation. The angel who appears time and again speaks plainly and what he announces comes to pass. The angel also utters prophecies, which are reiterated in poetic songs by the human participants in the drama. Even as the angel told Zechariah that his son "will turn many of the sons of Israel to the Lord their God" and will "go before him in the spirit and power of Elijah" (1:16-17), so it will happen later in the narrative (3:1-20). When John is born, Zechariah is filled with the Holy Spirit and utters a prophetic word of praise in which, among other things, he speaks of Israel's salvation (1:67-79). In response to what the angel has told her and after meeting her kinswoman Elizabeth, Mary utters her prophetic word of praise, the Magnificat, in which God's mercy toward Israel is recalled (1:46-55).

Jewish readers and hearers of Luke's Infancy narrative would have been reminded of Israel's ancient stories, in which angels appear to patriarchs and matriarchs, providing instruction and uttering prophecies (e.g., Gen. 16:7, 19:15, 21:17, 22:11-15, 32:1). Non-Jewish readers and hearers would appreciate the appearance of angelic beings and prophetic utterances, though they would view them through the Greco-Roman literary and popular lenses of ἄγγελοι and δαίμονες who conveyed to humans divine knowledge and spiritual insight. In Greco-Roman literature the gods Hermes and Iris were angels, or messengers, par excellence.[59]

The next major section of Luke's Infancy narrative (i.e., chapter 2) is introduced with a reference to an imperial command: "A decree went out from Caesar Augustus that all the world should be enrolled" (Lk. 2:1). This "Caesar" is Octavian, of course, the first emperor to be called Augustus, who has ruled the Roman Empire absolutely for some twenty-five years and will rule it for another fifteen years or more. Given the approximate parallels with the omens and prodigies told about Octavian, one must wonder if by mentioning Caesar, the evangelist has invited his readers to compare Jesus with Emperor Augustus. After Jesus is born, an angel announces the good news to shepherds (2:8-20).

---

[59] For example, according to Plato, Hermes is both messenger (ἄγγελος) and interpreter (*Cratylus* 407E). In the *Iliad* Iris is referred to the "messenger from Zeus" (Homer, *Iliad* 2.786-7; cf. 3.121). Achilles asks Iris, "'Goddess Iris [Ἴρι θεά], who of the gods sent you as a messenger [ἄγγελον] to me?' And to him again spoke wind-footed, swift Iris: 'Hera sent me forth, the glorious wife of Zeus'" (18.182). A number of Greek and Latin inscriptions make reference to angels, sometimes identifying them with the gods or even "most high god" (e.g., *AE* 106; *CIL* XIV 24). See F. Cumont, "Les Anges du Paganisme," *Révue de l'histoire des religions* 72 (1915): 159–82; F. Sokolowski, "Sur le Culte d'Angelos dans le Paganisme Grec et Romain," *HTR* 53 (1960): 225–9; R. Cline, *Ancient Angels: Conceptualizing Angeloi in the Roman Empire*, RGRW 182 (Leiden: Brill, 2011). *Angeloi* and *daimones*—both good and bad—make frequent appearances in magical texts.

The angel of the Lord tells the shepherds: "I bring you good news of a great joy [εὐαγγελίζομαι ὑμῖν χαρὰν μεγάλην] which will come to all the people; for to you is born [ἐτέχθη] this day in the city of David a Savior [σωτήρ], who is Christ the Lord" (Lk. 2:10-11). The language of this announcement echoes the language used to celebrate the birth of Caesar Augustus. In a series of inscriptions set up just a few years before the birth of Jesus we read:

> Providence ... has given us Augustus, whom she filled with virtue that he might benefit humankind, sending him as a savior [σωτῆρα], both for us and our descendants, that he might end war and arrange all things, and ... by his appearance, surpassing all benefactors [εὐεργέτας] ... and since the birth of the god [ἡ γενέθλιος τοῦ θεοῦ] Augustus was on account of him the beginning of the good news for the world [ἦρξεν δὲ τῶι κόσμωι τῶν δι' αὐτὸν εὐαγγελίων]. (*OGIS* 458, 9 BCE)[60]

Augustus here is not only called "savior" (σωτήρ) and "god" (θεός), he is also called "benefactor" (εὐεργέτης).[61] It is interesting to note that among the New Testament Gospels only Luke uses the words "benefactor," "benefaction" (εὐεργεσία), and "to do good" (εὐεργετεῖν). Jesus instructs his disciples: "The kings of the Gentiles exercise lordship over them; and those in authority over them are called benefactors [εὐεργέται]. But not so with you; rather let the greatest among you become as the youngest, and the leader as one who serves" (Lk. 22:25-26). In the book of Acts Peter refers to an act of benefaction (εὐεργεσία) and Jesus is said to have gone about Israel "doing good and healing all [εὐεργετῶν καὶ ἰώμενος πάντας] that were oppressed by the devil" (Acts 4:9, 10:38). In other words, Jesus really was a benefactor.

The other significant overlap of ideas in the imperial birthday proclamation and the Christian proclamation revolves around the language of "good news." In Christian circles this was usually expressed in the singular (εὐαγγέλιον), and in non-Christian usage it was usually expressed in the plural (εὐαγγέλια).[62] The idea of good news, as clearly expressed in the birthday inscription in honor of Augustus, became a commonplace in the Roman cult of the divine emperor (which was a development of the idea in earlier Hellenism). But the idea was well established in Jewish Scripture and

---

[60] The inscription is composite, made up mostly of the inscription from Priene. For Greek text, see W. Dittenberger, ed., *Orientis Graeci Inscriptiones Selectae: Supplementum Sylloges Inscriptionum Graecarum*, 2 vols. (Leipzig: S. Hirzel, 1903–5), 2:51–2. For bibliography, translation, and notes, see F. W. Danker, *Benefactor: Epigraphic Study of a Graeco-Roman and New Testament Semantic Field* (St. Louis, MO: Clayton, 1982), 215–22. At the beginning of the first column the inscription references "the birthday of most divine Caesar" (ἡ τοῦ θειοτάτου Καίσαρος γενέθλιος ἡμέρα).

[61] Augustus is often called "son of god" (υἱὸς θεοῦ/*divi filius*), which becomes standard language in the cult of the emperor (e.g., *IGR* I 901, IV 309; *ILS* 107, 113; P.Ryl 601; P.Oslo 26; et al.). In another inscription, Augustus is described as "the Benefactor and Savior [τὸν εὐεργέτην καὶ σωτῆρα] of the entire world" (*IGR* III 719).

[62] An example of the plural is found in LXX 2 Sam. 4:10: "he was as one bringing good news [εὐαγγελιζόμενος] ... I ought to have given a reward for good new [εὐαγγέλια]." Biblical literature normally uses the verb form. Josephus twice uses εὐαγγέλια in reference to Vespasian, when he was proclaimed emperor (*J.W.* 4.618, 656: "Vespasian was greeted by the good news [εὐαγγέλια] from Rome and by embassies of congratulation from every quarter of the world, now his own").

tradition as well. Nowhere was the hope of "good news" more emphatically expressed than in the second half of Isaiah (40:9, 52:7, 61:1). In Isaiah, especially as the prophetic book came to expression in Aramaic, the good news is associated with the kingdom of God and the reign of the Messiah, the Lord's Anointed.[63]

Although the language of good news, either expressed with noun or with verb, does not appear in Matthew's Infancy narrative, the story of the magi, who bring with them "gold and frankincense and myrrh" (χρυσὸν καὶ λίβανον καὶ σμύρναν) (Mt. 2:11), seems to echo Isa. 60:5-6, a passage that does make reference to good news. The parallels with Isaiah 60 appear to be more than mere coincidence. The most relevant part of the passage reads: "And there shall come to you herds of camels, and the camels of Madiam and Gaiphar shall cover you. All those from Saba shall come, bringing gold, and they shall bring frankincense [φέροντες χρυσίον καὶ λίβανον οἴσουσιν] and announce the good news of the salvation of the Lord [τὸ σωτήριον κυρίου εὐαγγελιοῦνται]" (LXX Isa. 60:5d-6; cf. Ps. 72:10-11). If the Matthean evangelist was aware of the parallel, then perhaps he intended a Solomonic typology (cf. 1 Kgs 10:1-2, 25, where the Queen of Sheba brings gifts, including frankincense, to Solomon).[64]

And finally, the Infancy narrative in Luke includes a story of the youthful Jesus who stays behind in the temple precincts that he might engage scholars (Lk. 2:40-52). As noted earlier, similar stories are told of the youthful Octavian, whose behavior was thought to adumbrate future greatness. Luke concludes the story of the "Finding" with the summarizing words: "And Jesus increased in wisdom and in stature, and in favor with God and man" (2:52). This summary intentionally echoes what is said of the youthful Samuel, who was raised in the house of God: "Now the boy Samuel continued to grow both in stature and in favor with the Lord and with men" (1 Sam. 2:26). This Samuel would years later anoint David as Israel's king. This same David, of course, became the progenitor of Israel's Messiah. We again see in the Gospel tradition the bringing together of language and imagery that recall both Jewish and biblical tradition on the one hand and Greco-Roman tradition on the other.

Passion Omens

The public activities of Jesus were marked by healing, which in both Jewish and Greco-Roman thinking potentially supported claims of a divine destiny. Two events in the pre-Passion narrative that would have stood out as omens were the drowning of the

---

[63] The good news, "Your God reigns" in Hebrew Isa. 52:7 becomes "the kingdom of your God has been revealed" in the Aramaic. The "Lord will reign" in Hebrew Mic. 4:7 and "O tower of the flock" in Hebrew Mic. 4:8 become "the kingdom of the Lord shall be revealed" and "O Messiah of Israel," respectively, in Aramaic. There are additional examples in the Aramaic.

[64] D. C. Allison Jr. and W. D. Davies, *A Critical and Exegetical Commentary on the Gospel according to Saint Matthew. Volume I: Introduction and Commentary on Matthew I–VII*, ICC (Edinburgh: T & T Clark, 1988), 250–1; R. T. France, *The Gospel of Matthew*, NICNT (Grand Rapids, MI: Eerdmans, 2007), 76: "The reader who knows the OT stories cannot fail to be reminded of the visit of the Queen of Sheba with her gifts of 'gold and great quantity of spices.'" See also D. A. Hagner, *Matthew 1–13*, WBC 33A (Dallas, TX: Word, 1993), 31. Hagner comments that these Old Testament "passages are saying in part the same thing that Matthew says."

pigs and the cursing of the fig tree, the only supernatural events inaugurated by Jesus that resulted in harm.

On the east side of the Sea of Galilee Jesus encounters a demonized man who lived among the tombs and terrorized the locals (Mk 5:1-20). Although until now no one has been able to control this wretched man ("the chains he wrenched apart, and the fetters he broke in pieces"; 5:4), when he meets Jesus he falls at his feet and begs for mercy: "I adjure you by God, do not torment me" (5:7). Jesus asks his name and the man says, "My name is Legion [λεγιὼν ὄνομά μοι]; for we are many" (5:9). The evil and violent host asks to be sent into a nearby herd of swine and Jesus permits it, with the result that the swine stampede and plunge into the lake and drown (5:12-13).

Most agree that the name "Legion" and the presence of the swine would bring to mind for most readers the Roman Legion X Fretensis, known for its mascot the boar's head.[65] Fretensis was one of the first legions to arrive in Israel in response to the Jewish revolt in 66 CE (Josephus, *J.W.* 5.69, 135). Although stationed in Syria to the north prior to the revolt, we should not assume that Galileans in the time of Jesus, almost forty years earlier, did not know of this legion and its symbolism, including its mascot. It is simplistic and unwarranted to date the writing and circulation of the Gospel of Mark to a time no earlier than after the arrival of Legio X in Judea in 66.[66]

Although there is nothing explicitly anti-Roman or anti-Gentile in the story of the healing of the demonized man in the region east of the Sea of Galilee, readers and hearers of this story would likely infer from it Jesus's power over Rome. In the destruction of a legion of evil spirits, ironically embodied within swine—the very mascot of a well-known and nearby Roman legion—late antique readers and hearers would probably conclude that Jesus possessed an authority that could rival the authority of Caesar himself.[67]

The second pre-Passion omen involves the fig tree. Finding no fruit on the tree, Jesus says, "May no one ever eat fruit from you again" (Mk 11:14). The following morning the disciples "saw the fig tree withered away to its roots" (11:20-21). This description of the tree, literally "withered from its roots" (ἐξηραμμένην ἐκ ῥιζῶν), recalls what Suetonius said of the Julio-Claudian grove of trees—that with the death of Nero, "the whole grove died from the root up [*exaruit radicitus*]" (Suetonius, *Galba* 1). In the case of the imperial family, the death of the trees signified the end of a dynasty. In the case

---

[65] E. Dabrowa, *Legio X Fretensis: A Prosopographical Study of its Officers (I–III c. A.D.)*, Historia Einzelschriften 66 (Stuttgart: Franz Steiner, 1993).

[66] Officers and smaller units attached to Legio X Fretensis moved about in the region as early as 18 CE and so would have been known before the outbreak of the revolt. In a Greek inscription dating before 65, found a century ago in excavations at Ascalon, southern Judea, the people of Ascalon express appreciation for one Aulus Instuleius Tenax, a centurion of Legio X Fretensis (cf. *CIIP* III 2335). This Tenax is later transferred to Legio XII Fulminata and mentioned in an inscription in Memnon, Egypt, that dates to 65 (*CIL* III 30 = *ILS* 8759a). This is why the otherwise undated Ascalon inscription must have been inscribed a few years prior to 65 CE. The inscriptions and chronology are discussed in Dabrowa, *Legio X Fretensis*, 89. The archeological evidence of Legio X's presence in and around Jerusalem from the time of the revolt and after is extensive.

[67] J. L. P. Wolmarans, "Who Asked Jesus to Leave the Territory of Gerasa (Mark 5:17)?" *Neot* 28 (1994): 87–92, plausibly suggests that it was the owners of the herd of swine, contracted to provide the Roman army with meat, who requested Jesus to leave their region. If he is correct, a Roman legion has been harmed materially, not merely symbolically.

of Jesus, however, the death of the fruitless fig tree signified the approaching end of the priestly establishment that opposed him. It did not signify the end of Jesus.

The Passion narratives contain a number of omens that inhabitants of late antique Rome would have appreciated, especially in reference to great men. This belief is expressed in reference to an eclipse that occurred as Pelopidas prepared his army for battle: "The sun was eclipsed and the city was dark [σκότος] in the daytime … for it was supposed to be a great sign from heaven with regard to a conspicuous man" (Plutarch, *Pelopidas* 31.2-3).[68] All three of the Synoptic Gospels speak of darkness while Jesus was on the cross: "Now from the sixth hour there was darkness [σκότος] over all the land [ἐπὶ πᾶσαν τὴν γῆν] until the ninth hour" (Mt. 27:45; cf. Mk 15:33; Lk. 23:44-45a).[69] Plutarch tells us that after the death of Julius Caesar, the sun's rays were dim. "For during all that year its orb rose pale and without radiance, while the heat that came down from it was slight and ineffectual, so that the air in its circulation was dark and heavy owing to the feebleness of the warmth that penetrated it" (*Caesar* 69.3-4).[70] Diogenes Laertius says that when the philosopher Carneades died, "the moon is said to have been eclipsed … the brightest luminary in heaven next to the sun thereby gave token of her sympathy" (*Vita Philosophorum* 4.64).[71]

Darkness over the land as an omen either in anticipation of death or after death has occurred was a belief that reached back to ancient times. Legend had it that "there was a total eclipse of the sun and a general darkness [σκότος] as in the night covered the earth [τὴν γῆν]" when the mother of Romulus was violated and "that at his death the same thing happened" (Dionysius of Halicarnassus, *Antiquitates romanae* 2.56.6; Cicero, *De republica* 6.22; Ovid, *Fasti* 2.493; Plutarch, *Romulus* 27.6).[72]

As already noted, the sun grew dark when Julius Caesar died (Vergil, *Georgica* 1.467-8). Late antique Jewish ideas about darkness were similar. The ninth plague against Egypt was darkness. Exodus says that "there was a thick darkness [σκότος γνόφος][73] in all the land [ἐπὶ πᾶσαν γῆν] of Egypt three days," though the Israelites had light (Exod. 10:21-23).[74] Some of the language and ideas about darkness and solar eclipses are reflected in Philo's retelling of the ninth plague. He says that "a plague arose greater than all that had gone before; for, in bright daylight, darkness was suddenly

---

[68] Translation based on B. Perrin, *Plutarch, Lives: Agesilaus and Pompey, Pelopidas and Marcellus*, LCL 87 (London: Heinemann, 1917), 421. As it turned out, the eclipse was not a positive omen, for Pelopidas was shortly thereafter killed in battle. Note, too, that this eclipse was called ἐξ οὐρανοῦ … σημεῖον ("a sign from heaven") as in Mk 8:11 (σημεῖον ἀπὸ τοῦ οὐρανοῦ).

[69] Luke adds, apparently by way of explanation, "while the sun's light failed." The fourth Gospel says nothing about darkness. The Synoptic tradition of darkness is embellished in the second-century narratives found in the *Gospel of Peter* (5:15, 18) and *Acts of Pilate* (11:1-2).

[70] Translation from Perrin, *Plutarch Lives: Demosthenes and Cicero*, 607.

[71] R. D. Hicks, *Diogenes Laertius I*, LCL 184 (London: Heinemann, 1925), 441.

[72] Translation based on E. Cary, *Dionysius of Halicarnassus: Roman Antiquities I: Books I–II*, LCL 319 (London: Heinemann, 1937), 475.

[73] Lit. "a dark darkness."

[74] Mk 15:33 reads ἐφ' ὅλην τὴν γῆν ("upon the whole land"; followed in Lk. 23:44), which in Mt 27:45 reads, ἐπὶ πᾶσαν τὴν γῆν ("upon all the land") perhaps as an intentional echo of OG Exod. 10:22.

overspread [ἐξαπιναίως ἀναχεῖται σκότος], possibly because there was an eclipse of the sun more completely than the ordinary" (*De vita Mosis* 1.123).[75]

According to the Synoptic tradition, when Jesus dies, the "curtain of the temple was torn in two, from top to bottom" (Mt. 27:51a; cf. Mk 15:38; Lk. 23:45). Matthew adds that "the earth shook, and the rocks were split" (27:51b); so also on Sunday, the day of the resurrection, "there was a great earthquake" (28:2). As already mentioned, damage to buildings, statues, and other structures is another omen or indicator of the presence of a deity. Similarly when Jesus dies, the curtain of the Jerusalem temple was torn. (Which curtain is in view and how it could be seen from Golgotha is debated.[76]) In Jewish tradition the story of the tearing of the temple curtain seems to be unique.[77] The portents described in Josephus (*J.W.* 6.293–6), in the apocryphal life of Habakkuk (*Vita Prophetarum* 12:12), and in Tacitus (*Historiae* 5.13) say nothing about the curtain.[78] In later Christian tradition the temple building itself is damaged (*Gospel of the Nazarenes*, apud Jerome, *Epistula* 120 [*ad Hedibian*]).[79]

As we have seen, earthquakes, strikes of lightning, and damaged buildings were also seen as omens in the Greco-Roman world (e.g., Plutarch, *Antonius* 60.2; Suetonius, *Tiberius* 74; *Galba* 18.2). Herodotus remarks that there had been such a long run of bad luck in Greece, "it was no marvel that there should be an earthquake [κινηθῆναι] in Delos when there had been none before" (*Historiae* 6.98.3; cf. Thucydides, *Historiae* 3.89.1–2, σεισμῶν δὲ γενομένων πολλῶν … τῶν σεισμῶν κατεχόντων, "many earthquakes occurring … earthquakes kept happening").[80]

More importantly, earthquakes were often linked to theophanies. This is seen in Old Testament and Ancient Near Eastern literatures (Exod. 19:18: When Yahweh descended on Sinai "the whole mountain quaked greatly"; 1 Kgs 19:11-12; Job 9:6;

---

[75] Translation from F. H. Colson, *Philo VI*, LCL 289 (London: Heinemann, 1935), 339. In Lk. 23:45 the darkness is said to have been due to "the sun's light having failed" (ἐκλιπόντος), that is, having been eclipsed. Both Philo and the evangelist Luke are attempting to explain the darkness.

[76] It was probably the inner curtain (cf. LXX Exod. 27:16). It is described in Josephus, *J.W.* 5.207–212. I hardly think it is necessary to conclude that the evangelists thought Golgotha was located on the Mount of Olives; *pace* H. M. Jackson, "The Death of Jesus in Mark and the Miracle from the Cross," *NTS* 33 (1987): 16–37, here 24–5.

[77] The apparent exceptions in *T. Levi* 10:3 and *Vita Prophetarum* 12:12a are probably Christian glosses. On the meaning of the *velum scissum* (the torn curtain) in the Synoptic Gospels, see D. M. Gurtner, *The Torn Veil: Matthew's Exposition of the Death of Jesus*, SNTSMS 139 (Cambridge: Cambridge University Press, 2007). Gurtner argues plausibly that the torn curtain is the inner curtain of the temple (not the outer curtain) and that its tearing signifies God's relocation from the sanctuary to his Son Jesus. For Matthew, this is the significance of the prophecy fulfilled in Jesus ("the Lord saves"): Immanuel, "God with us" (Mt. 1:23).

[78] Josephus refers to the eastern gate found open morning after morning, which frightens the priests, while Tacitus speaks of "gates." *Vita Prophetarum* says, "The capitals of the two pillars will be taken away" (12:12). The omens against the temple, especially those in reference to the gate(s), appear in later rabbinic literature (e.g., *y. Sota* 6.3; *b. Yoma* 39b).

[79] Jerome writes: "But in the Gospel that is written in Hebrew characters we read not that the curtain of the temple was torn, but that the lintel of the temple of wondrous size collapsed." This tradition is repeated elsewhere in Jerome and in other Christian writings.

[80] Translation from K. Clarke, *Shaping the Geography of Empire: Man and Nature in Herodotus' Histories* (Oxford: Oxford University Press, 2018), 268. Herodotus literally says "a shaking" or "a movement."

Pss. 18:7, 77:18, 97:4; Isa. 6:4, 24:20; Joel 3:16; Hag. 2:6).[81] It is also seen in the classic tradition, as in the appearance of Apollo (e.g., Callimachus, *Hymnus in Apollinem* 1, "How the shrine shakes [ἐσείσατο]!"), the appearance of Dionysus (e.g., Euripides, *Bacchae* 585-93, "Shake [σεῖε] the world's floor, you spirit of earthquake!"), the appearance of Mars (e.g., Publius Papinius Statius, *Thebais* 7.65, "the earth quakes [*tremit*]" at the approach of the god), and the appearance of Asclepius (e.g., Ovid, *Metamorphoses* 15.671–2, "at his coming the statue, altars, doors, the marble pavement and gilded roof, all rocked"). It is in response to the darkness, the shout of Jesus, and the tearing of the temple curtain that the Roman centurion exclaims, ἀληθῶς οὗτος ὁ ἄνθρωπος υἱὸς θεοῦ ἦν ("Truly this man was son of god," Mk 15:39). The centurion's anarthrous υἱὸς θεοῦ is the equivalent of the Latin *filius dei* or (more usually) *divi filius*, the language used in reference to the Roman emperor (e.g., BGU 628; SB 401). The epiphanic qualities of the risen Jesus are exaggerated in second-century literature (e.g., *Descensus Christi ad Inferos* 5:1).

The Matthean evangelist adds two conspicuous omens, one ordinary and the other extraordinary. The ordinary omen is the report of Pilate's wife's dream. She warns her husband: "Have nothing to do with that righteous man, for I have suffered much over him today in a dream" (27:19). Pilate's wife sent word of her dream to her husband, when he had sat down on the judgment seat (ἐπὶ τοῦ βήματος). Many readers will be reminded of Julius Caesar's wife's dream (Plutarch, *Caesar* 63.5-6; cf. Suetonius, *Divus Julius* 81.3; Paterculus, *Historiae* 2.57.1-2) and her urging her husband to seek divine guidance (Plutarch, *Caesar* 63.6). In the context of Matthew's Gospel, where God has previously warned Joseph and the magi through dreams, Pilate's wife's dream would be understood as a message from God and therefore a divine witness that Jesus was indeed "righteous" and not deserving of condemnation. Alas, for Caesar and Pilate; neither heeded the warnings of their wives' dreams. For Caesar this meant assassination; for Pilate it meant an ignominious suicide.[82]

Matthew also relates an extraordinary omen. Matthew, and Matthew alone, narrates the story of the saints who are raised up when Jesus dies:

> And behold, the curtain of the temple was torn in two, from top to bottom; and the earth shook, and the rocks were split; [52] the tombs also were opened, and many bodies of the saints who had fallen asleep were raised, [53] and coming out of the tombs after his resurrection they went into the holy city and appeared to many. [54]

---

[81] In a Sumerian hymn, King Shulgi declares, "On that day, the storm howled, the tempest swirled, Northwind (and) Southwind roared eagerly, Lightning devoured in heaven alongside the seven winds, The deafening storm made the earth tremble" (*Hymn of Shulgi* 62-5). Translation from J. B. Pritchard, *Ancient Near Eastern Texts Relating to the Old Testament* (Princeton, NJ: Princeton University Press, 1969), 586.

[82] Eusebius reports that not long after his removal from office Pilate committed suicide (*Historia ecclesiastica* 2.7.1). In Byzantine and Medieval apocrypha (e.g., *Cura sanitatis Tiberii*, *Mors Pilati*, and *Vindicta Salvatoris*) the suicide of Pilate is described in lurid and fantastic terms. According to *Mors Pilati*, demons haunt the corpse of Pilate and terrify people. One thinks of the hasty burial of the assassinated Caligula in the gardens of the Lamian family, after which they were haunted by ghosts and fearsome apparitions (Suetonius, *Caligula* 59). On the traditions of Pilate's suicide, see T. Grüll, "The Legendary Fate of Pontius Pilate," *Classica et Mediaevalia* 61 (2010): 151-76.

When the centurion and those who were with him, keeping watch over Jesus, saw the earthquake and what took place, they were filled with awe, and said, "Truly this was the Son of God!" (Mt. 27:51-54)

Matthew has inserted vv. 51b–53 into the material he finds in Mark (i.e., between verses 38 and 39 in Mark 15). The earthquake explains the tearing of the curtain (which appears in Mark but without explanation). The earthquake also splits rocks and breaks open tombs, thus allowing "many bodies" (πολλὰ σώματα) of dead "holy ones" (ἁγίων), or saints, to arise and exit their tombs. This of course creates a theological problem, for the resurrection of Jesus constitutes the "first fruits of those who have fallen asleep" (cf. 1 Cor. 15:20, 23; Col. 1:18, "firstborn from the dead"). Jesus dies on Friday and is raised on Sunday; but the dead saints are raised *on Friday*, thus in a sense making *them not Jesus* the first fruits of those who have fallen asleep. The evangelist or a later copyist tries to remedy the problem by adding at the beginning of Mt. 27:53 the qualifying phrase, μετὰ τὴν ἔγερσιν αὐτοῦ, "after his resurrection."[83] But this gloss really does not solve the problem, for saints were still raised up *before* Jesus, whenever they exit their tombs. The gloss, moreover, creates a new problem, for we are to imagine the raised saints loitering in their tombs from Friday afternoon until Sunday morning when they finally emerge.

Although it is debated, Mt. 27:52-53 as a whole may represent an early gloss that attempts to narrate the Harrowing of Hades, in which Jesus rescues the righteous dead.[84] This idea is probably expressed in 1 Peter: "For Christ also died for sins ... that he might bring us to God, being put to death in the flesh but made alive in the spirit; 19 in which he went and preached to the spirits in prison" (3:18-19; cf. 4:6 "the gospel was preached even to the dead, that though judged in the flesh like men, they might live in the spirit like God"). Several early Christian texts appear to presuppose the tradition (e.g., Eph. 4:8-10: "In saying, 'He ascended,' what does it mean but that he had also descended into the lower parts of the earth?"; *Gos. Pet.* 10:41: "Have you preached to them that sleep?"; *Mart. Asc. Isa.* 9:17: "Many of the righteous will ascend with him"; *Odes* 42:10-20, esp. v. 11: "Sheol saw me and was shattered, and Death ejected me and many with me"; *Acts of Thomas* 10: "who went down even to Hades; who also, having opened the doors, brought out from there those who had been shut in for many ages in the treasuries of darkness, and showed them the way that leads up on high"; 32: where

---

[83] For example, W. C. Allen, *A Critical and Exegetical Commentary on the Gospel according to St. Matthew*, ICC (Edinburgh: T & T Clark, 1907), 296 (added by the evangelist); E. Klostermann, *Das Matthäusevangelium*, HNT 4, 4th ed. (Tübingen: Mohr [Siebeck], 1971), 225 (a later scribal gloss inspired by 1 Cor. 15:20; Col. 1:18). Several recent commentaries and studies have taken one or other of these positions.

[84] For two competent studies that argue against seeing Mt. 27:53a as gloss or an interpolation, or the whole of 27:52-53 as an interpolation, see C. L. Quarles, "Μετὰ τὴν ἔγερσιν αὐτοῦ: A Scribal Interpolation in Matthew 27:53?" *TC: A Journal of Biblical Textual Criticism* (2015): 1–15; "Matthew 27:51–53: Meaning, Genre Intertextuality, Theology, and Reception History," *JETS* 59 (2016): 271–86. In agreement with Quarles, I concede that there is virtually no early manuscript evidence in support of proposed glosses or interpolations. However, it should be noted that Mt. 27:51b-53 does not appear in the *Gospel of Peter* (mid-second century), which otherwise relies heavily on Matthean material in its distinctive Passion narrative.

Satan says: "I am he who inhabits and hold the abyss of Tartarus, but the Son of God has wronged me against my will and selected his own out of me"; 156: "gathered all").[85]

Matthew's καὶ ἡ γῆ ἐσείσθη καὶ αἱ πέτραι ἐσχίσθησαν ("and the earth shook, and the rocks split": v. 51b), was probably an original part of Matthew, for the Matthean centurion "saw the earthquake" (τὸν σεισμόν: v. 54) and the evangelist will again introduce an earthquake Sunday morning: καὶ ἰδοὺ σεισμὸς ἐγένετο μέγας ("and there was a great earthquake": 28:2a). The earthquake of 27:51b includes splitting rocks, which for the evangelist may have been intended as an allusion to the eschatological scenario depicted in Zechariah 14, when on the Day of the Lord the feet of the Lord "shall stand on the Mount Olives, which lies before Jerusalem on the east; and the Mount of Olives shall be split in two [σχισθήσεται] from east to west ... Then the Lord your God will come, and all the holy ones [πάντες οἱ ἅγιοι] with him" (Zech. 14:4-5).[86]

The Matthean detail of the spitting of the rocks also facilitated the opening of rock-cut tombs that encircle Jerusalem to the north, east, and south. All of these tombs were sealed with stone doors, most of which were square shaped though about 10 percent were round. In Matthew's earthquake some of these tombs are broken open, which then allows the bodies of the holy dead to be raised up and appear to the living. In my opinion, this gloss, made up of vv. 52–53, originated as an embellishment of Sunday's earthquake and resurrection of Jesus. Motivated by the doctrine of the Harrowing of Hades the embellishment probably was intended as a graphic illustration of Jesus as "firstborn of the dead" or "first fruits of those who have fallen asleep." However, the scribe who added it to the Matthean text inserted it *at the wrong place*. (This could have happened easily had the gloss first appeared in the margin of a manuscript and only later was inserted into the text proper. When first added to the margin, it was intended to supplement the earthquake of 28:2 [σεισμὸς ἐγένετο μέγας], not the earthquake of 27:51 [ἡ γῆ ἐσείσθη].) A later scribe added it to Friday's earthquake story, rather than to Sunday's earthquake story, thus creating the problem that the subsequent gloss in v. 53, "after his resurrection," attempted to correct. (This gloss, too, probably initially appeared in the margin and then later was inserted into the text itself.)

---

[85] For literature that treats the Harrowing of Hades, see R. E. Brown, *The Death of the Messiah: From Gethsemane to the Grave—A Commentary on the Passion Narratives in the Four Gospels*, 2 vols. (New York: Doubleday, 1994), 2:1127-9; J. A. Trumbower, "Jesus' Descent to the Underworld," in *Rescue for the Dead: The Posthumous Salvation of Non-Christians in Early Christianity*, Oxford Studies in Historical Theology (Oxford: Oxford University Press, 2001), 91–108; D. C. Allison, "'After His Resurrection' (Matt 27, 53) and the *descens ad inferos*," in P. Lampe (ed.), *Neutestamentliche Exegese im Dialog: Hermeneutik - Wirkungsgeschichte - Matthäusevangelium. Festschrift für Ulrich Luz zum 70. Geburtstag* (Neukirchen-Vluyn: Neukirchener, 2008), 335–54; G. Frank, "Christ's Descent to the Underworld in Ancient Ritual and Legend," in R. J. Daly (ed.), *Apocalyptic Thought in Early Christianity*, Holy Cross Studies in Patristic Theology and History (Grand Rapids, MI: Baker Academic, 2009), 211–26. For a recent study of the origin and development of the *descensus* tradition, see J. H. Charlesworth, "Exploring the Origins of the *descensus ad inferos*," in A. J. Avery-Peck, C. A. Evans, and J. Neusner (eds.), *Earliest Christianity within the Boundaries of Judaism: Essays in Honor of Bruce Chilton*, BRLJ 49 (Leiden: Brill, 2016), 372–95. The translation of *Odes of Solomon* 42 is from p. 379. The translations of *Acts of Thomas* 10, 32 are from J. K. Elliott, *The Apocryphal New Testament: A Collection of Apocryphal Christian Literature in an English Translation Based on M. R. James* (Oxford: Clarendon, 1993), 451, 460.

[86] An allusion to Zech. 14:4-5 is widely recognized among commentators. See, among others, U. Luz, *Matthew 21–28*, Hermeneia (Minneapolis, MN: Fortress, 2005), 566–7.

In its earliest form, the tradition of the Harrowing of Hades was wholly positive, in that Jesus descends into the nether world, proclaims the good news of his victory over sin and death, and then brings up with himself the righteous. In later popular tradition, as we find it in *Descensus Christi ad Inferos*, which at some point becomes part of the *Acts of Pilate/Gospel of Nicodemus* cycle, the harrowing becomes combative and violent. In short, it becomes a warlike victory over evil, personified as the beings Satan and Hades, the god of death. This is clearly expressed in *Descensus Christi ad Inferos*, where after hearing Christ shouting and beating down the gates, a fearful and enraged Hades rebukes Satan for his folly in crucifying Jesus, "so that he should come here and strip us naked? Turn and see that not one dead man is left in me [οὐδεὶς νεκρὸς ἐν ἐμοὶ κατελείφθη] … How did you contrive to bring down such a man into this darkness, through whom you have been deprived of all who have died since the beginning?" (7:1).[87] Jesus has rescued the righteous dead and now—as illustrated in the gloss we find in Matthew 27—they have emerged from their tombs and have shown themselves to many.

The Passion narrative abruptly ends Sunday morning, with the startling discovery and announcements of the empty tomb, the presence of mysterious figures, and the appearances of the resurrected Jesus (Mt. 16:1-8, 28:1-8; Lk. 24:1-10). Mark's account is simplest (not least because it is the briefest). The evangelist states only that the women "saw a young man sitting on the right side dressed in a white robe" (16:5). In Luke the "young man" of Mark's account becomes "two men … in dazzling apparel" (24:4). But in Matthew he is described as "an angel of the Lord," whose "appearance was like lightning, and his raiment white as snow" (28:2-4). The guards—presumably Roman (cf. Mt. 27:62-66)—are terrified and "became like dead men" (28:4). In the *Gospel of Peter* two towering angels emerge from the tomb assisting the risen Jesus (10:39-40).

The confusion over the discovery of the empty tomb and the presence of heavenly personages is ended when the risen Jesus appears to his followers and provides them with new purpose. In Mark this is only implied, in that the young man tells the frightened women that Jesus will "go before" his disciples in Galilee (Mk 16:7). In the other Gospels the risen Jesus will himself instruct his disciples, sending them into the world to proclaim the good news (Mt. 28:16-20; Lk. 24:44-49; Jn 20:11-29; Acts 1:3-8). The disciples recognize the divinity of Jesus (Jn 20:28: "My lord and my God!") and worship him (Mt. 28:9). According to the Gospel of Luke, Jesus bids his disciples farewell and ascends into heaven (Lk. 24:50-53; cf. Acts 1:9-11).

Greco-Roman myths and traditions are rife with accounts of strange events at the deaths of great figures. Many of these stories related to Rome's legendary founder and first king Romulus, also known as Quirinus. Many of the omens and strange features that are part of the Romulus legends find approximate parallels in the New Testament Gospel accounts of the transfiguration, resurrection, commission, and ascension of Jesus. I will focus on the Romulus legend, for it becomes the template against which subsequent ideas and testimonials regarding *apotheōsis* (turning into a god) were measured.

---

[87] Translation based on Elliott, *The Apocryphal New Testament*, 188–9. For additional sources that express ideas about the *descensus*, see Charlesworth, "Exploring the Origins," 382–5.

One of the oldest Latin authors that we know of who wrote of the legend of Romulus and the founding of Rome was Quintus Ennius (c. 239–c. 169 BCE). The legend is recounted in the first two books of his fifteen-book *Annales*, of which only fragments remain, thanks to numerous quotations found in the writings of later authors. A few of these quotations are germane to our present interests. Varro (116–27 BCE), author of *De lingua Latina*, of which books 5–10 are partly extant, apparently quotes a line from *Annales* book I, when he says, "One there will be whom you will raise up to the blue precincts of heaven [*in caerula caeli templa*]" (Ennius, *Annales* frag. 64, *apud* Varro, *De lingua Latina* 7.6; quoted without *templa* in Ovid, *Metamorphoses* 14.814; *Fasti* 2.487).[88] The reference is to the *apotheōsis* and ascension of Romulus, the only son of Mars to be so honored. From *Annales* book II, Cicero (106–43 BCE) quotes Ennius for an illustration of how people respond to the death of a just king: "They talked thus among themselves: 'O Romulus, divine Romulus [*Romule die*], what a guardian of your country did the gods beget in you! O father and begetter, O blood sprung from the gods [*dis*]!'" (Ennius, *Annales* frag. 118, *apud* Cicero, *De republica* 1.41.61).[89] Cicero appeals to Ennius once more: "What do they say next [with respect to Romulus]? 'You it was who brought us forth into the world of light [*luminis oras*]'" (Ennius, *Annales* frags. 119–20, *apud* Cicero, *De republica* 1.41.61).[90] Nonius Marcellus (early fourth century CE) quotes from Ennius in his massive compilation of teachings: "You I worship [*veneror*], Father Quirinus; and you, Hora, consort of Quirinus" (Ennius, *Annales* frag. 116, *apud* Nonius Marcellus, *De compendiosa doctrina* 120.1).[91] In his commentary on Vergil's *Aeneid*, Servius (fourth century CE) discusses the meaning of *aevum* (eternity) and appeals to what Ennius says in his *Annales*: "Romulus lives for eternity [*aevum*] in heaven with the gods [*in caelo cum dis*] that gave him birth" (Ennius, *Annales* frags. 114–15, *apud* Servius, *Ad Virgilii Aeneidem commentarii* 6.763).[92]

The Romulus legend plays an especially important role in the works of Vergil (c. 70–19 BCE), a role very much in service of Augustan propaganda. Marianne Palmer

---

[88] Translation based on E. H. Warmington, *Remains of Old Latin* I: *Ennius and Caecilius*, LCL 294 (Cambridge MA: Harvard University Press, 1935), 23. Warmington acknowledges that the attribution is not certain. For text and translation of Varro, see also R. G. Kent, *Varro on the Latin Language* I. Books V–VII, LCL 333 (London: Heinemann, 1937), 272–3. For text and translation of Ovid's *Metamorphoses*, see also F. J. Miller, *Ovid: Metamorphoses* II. Books IX–XV, LCL 43 (London: Heinemann, 1916), 358–9. For text and translation of Ovid's *Fasti*, see J. G. Frazer, *Ovid's Fasti*, LCL 253 (London: Heinemann, 1931), 92–3.

[89] Translation based on Warmington, *Remains*, 41. For text of Ennius, *Annales* frag. 118, in Cicero's *De republica* 1.41.61, see M. N. Bouillet, *M. T. Ciceronis part tertia* V (Paris: Lemaire, 1831), 197.

[90] Translation based on Warmington, *Remains*, 41. For text of Ennius, *Annales* frags. 119–20 in Cicero's *De republica* 1.41.61, see G. H. Poyser, *Cicero De Re Publica* (Cambridge: Cambridge University Press, 1948), 53.

[91] Translation based on Warmington, *Remains*, 39. For text of Nonius Marcellus's *De compendiosa doctrina* 120.1, see W. M. Lindsay, *Nonii Marcelli De compendiosa doctrina* I (Leipzig: Teubner, 1903), 172.

[92] Translation based on Warmington, *Remains*, 39. The text of Ennius, *Annales* frags. 114–15 in Servius, *Virgilii Aeneidem commentarii* will be found in *Vergilius cum comentatiis quinque videlicet Servii* (Venice: Bartholomaeus de Zanis, 1493). Latin text and commentary on Vergil, *Aeneid* 6.763 and the quotation of Ennius, *Annales* frags. 114–15 will be found on both sides of folio 239. See also H. A. Lion, *Commentarii in Virgilium Serviani*, 2 vols. (Göttingen: Vandenhoeck & Ruprecht, 1826), 1:402. Servius comments that "*Aevum* properly means 'eternity' [*aeternitas*], which comes to no one but gods [*deos*]." He then cites the line from Ennius, *Annales*.

Bonz has rightly stated that the purpose of the *Aeneid* was "to define Rome's moral and religious values and to inspire its people with a patriotic vision of a world whose eschatological fulfillment was embodied in the Augustan identification with the return to the Golden Age."[93] To do this, Vergil weaves the legend of Romulus, founder of Rome, into the tapestry of his epic. In *Georgica* Romulus is recalled as Rome's original protector, a role that now has fallen to Augustus: "Gods of my country [*di patrii*], Heroes of the land, you Romulus, and you Vesta, our mother, who guard Tuscan Tiber and the Palatine of Rome" (*Georgica* 1.498–499).[94] A few lines later we hear how the gods have grudgingly given Caesar to Rome, complaining that the great man is preoccupied with triumphs (1.503–504). The implication is that Caesar exalts and protects Rome in the same way that Romulus did long ago. Similar themes appear in the *Aeneid*. Vergil reminds his readers of the legend of Romulus raised by the she-wolf (*Aeneid* 1.275–277) and then a few lines later he brings Caesar into the poetic narrative (1.286–289). Comparison with Romulus is again implied. Like Romulus of old, Augustus is a savior, a deity who "shall also be invoked in vows [*vocabitur hic quoque votis*]" (1.290). Much later in the *Aeneid* Romulus reappears (6.777–789), which again facilitates reference to Caesar, destined to appear on earth, we are told, as "Augustus Caesar, son of a god [*divi genus*], who shall again set up the Golden Age" (6.789–792).[95]

We find much better preserved traditions concerning Romulus in three contemporaneous writers. Dionysius of Halicarnassus (*c.* 60 BCE–10 CE) recounts the confusion surrounding the disappearance of Romulus:

> While the Romans were yet in doubt whether divine providence or human treachery had been the cause of his disappearance [τὸν ἀφανισμὸν αὐτοῦ], a certain man, named [Proculus] Julius ... arrived in the Forum and said that, as he was coming in from the country, he saw Romulus departing from the city ... as he drew near to him, he heard him say these words, "Julius, announce [ἄγγελλε] to the Romans from me, that the genius to whom I was allotted at my birth is conducting me to the gods [εἰς θεούς], now that I have finished my mortal life [τὸν θνητὸν ἐκπληρώσαντα αἰῶνα], and that I am Quirinus." (*Antiquitates romanae* 2.63.2–4)[96]

The story of the man's strange encounter with Romulus—known as Quirinus after his deification—is a staple in the myth.

According to Livy (59 BCE–17 CE), while Romulus was reviewing his army, "suddenly a storm came up, with loud claps of thunder, and enveloped him in a cloud so thick as to hide him from the sight of the assembly; and from that moment Romulus was no more on earth" (Livy, *Ab urbe condita* 1.16.1). It was asserted that "he had been caught up [*raptum*] on high in the blast ... they all with one accord hailed Romulus as a god

---

[93] M. P. Bonz, *The Past as Legacy: Luke-Acts and Ancient Epic* (Minneapolis, MN: Fortress, 2000), 38.
[94] Translation based on H. R. Fairclough, *Virgil: Ecologues, Georgics, Aeneid 1–6*, LCL 63 (London: Heinemann, 1978), 115.
[95] Translation based on ibid., 561.
[96] Translation based on E. Cary, *Dionysius of Halicarnassus: Roman Antiquities I. Books I–II*, LCL 319 (London: Heinemann, 1937), 495.

and a god's son [*deum deo natum*] ... and with prayers besought his favor" (1.16.2-3). The aforementioned Proculus Julius testified: "Romulus descended suddenly from the sky at dawn this morning and appeared to me. ... 'Go [*abi*],' he said, 'and announce [*nuntia*] to the Romans the will of Heaven that my Rome shall be the capital of the world'" (1.16.6-7).[97]

In *Fasti* Ovid (43 BCE-17 CE) declares of Romulus that "the warlike god won his place among the stars" (2.478); and that "the sun vanished and rising clouds obscured the heaven, and there fell a heavy shower of rain in torrents. Then it thundered, then the sky was riven by shooting flames" (2.493-495).[98] Ovid also tells of the man's encounter with the newly minted god:

> But Julius Proculus was coming from Alba Longa; the moon was shining, and there was no need of a torch, when of a sudden the hedges on his left shook and trembled ... Romulus, fair of aspect, in stature more than human, and clad in a goodly robe, stood there in the middle of the road and said, "Forbid the Quirites to mourn, let them not profane my divinity by their tears. Bid the pious throng bring incense and propitiate the new Quirinus, ..." So he ordered, and from the other's eyes he vanished into thin air [*evanuit auras*]. (2.505-509)

Proculus did as he was told. He summoned the people and testified to what he had seen and heard, instructing the people of Rome, with the result that "temples were built to the god [*deo*]" (2.511).[99]

Ovid has more to say in *Metamorphoses* about the *apotheōsis* of Romulus. He tells us that Mars, father of Romulus, informed the heavenly council that it is time "to take him from earth and set him in the heavens [*inponere caelo*]" (*Metamorphoses* 14.811). In agreement Zeus then

> filled the earth with thunder and lightning. Gradivus knew this for the assured sign of the translation which had been promised him ... he mounted his chariot drawn by steeds ... Gliding downward through the air, he halted on the summit of the wooded Palatine. There ... he caught him up from the earth. His mortal part dissolved into thin air ... And now a fair form clothes him, worthier of the high couches of the gods ... clad in the sacred robe. (14.811-828)[100]

According to Plutarch (before 50-after 120 CE), at death "Romulus disappeared suddenly [Ῥωμύλου δὲ ἄφνω μεταλλάξαντος], and no portion of his body or fragment of his clothing remained to be seen [ὤφθη] ... strange and unaccountable disorders with incredible changes filled the air; the light of the sun failed ... with awful peals of thunder" (*Romulus* 27.5-6). Hearing these reports and believing them, the multitude

---

[97] Translations based on B. O. Foster, *Livy* I. Books I and II, LCL 114 (London: Heinemann, 1919), 57, 59.
[98] Translations based on Frazer, *Ovid's Fasti*, 91, 93.
[99] Translations based on ibid., 93, 95.
[100] Translations based on Miller, *Ovid: Metamorphoses* II, 359.

rejoiced and "departed worshipping [προσκυνοῦντας] him with good hopes of his favor" (27.8).[101]

Plutarch also gives an account of the meeting of Julius and Romulus: A man,

> Julius Proculus by name, went into the Forum and solemnly swore by the most sacred emblems before all the people that, as he was travelling on the road, he had seen Romulus coming to meet him, fair and stately to the eye as never before, and arrayed in bright and shining armor. He himself, then, frighted at the sight ... Romulus replied, "It was the pleasure of the gods, O Proculus, from whom I came, that I should be with mankind only a short time, and that after founding a city destined to be the greatest on earth for empire and glory, I should dwell again in heaven. So farewell, and tell the Romans .... And I Quirinus will be your propitious deity [εὐμενὴς ἔσομαι δαίμων]." These things seemed to the Romans to be believable [ταῦτα πιστὰ μὲν εἶναι ... ἐδόκει]. (*Romulus* 28.1–3)[102]

The principal elements in the various versions of the strange disappearance, *apotheōsis*, post-*apotheōsis* appearances, and the commission that Romulus gave to Julius Proculus for the people of Rome are remarkably consistent. Greeks and Romans sometimes found parallels between the accounts of the *apotheōsis* of the emperors and those of mortals (such as Romulus, Asclepius, and others). One might say that in a sense the *apotheōsis* of Romulus and what that signified for Rome became paradigmatic, especially in the age of the emperors. Omens and strange events that could be seen as parallels with the story of Romulus potentially provided compelling endorsement of one's claim of imperial power and subsequent hopes for postmortem deification.

The connection between the *apotheōses* of Romulus and other famous men in Greco-Roman history on the one hand and contemporary emperors on the other was not lost of Justin Martyr (*c.* 100–160 CE). In his *First Apology* he makes this very point in noting the parallels between Greco-Roman stories of *apotheōsis* and what Christians believe about the resurrection and ascension of Jesus:

> When we say that ... after his crucifixion, death, and resurrection he went up to heaven, we introduce nothing stranger than those you call the sons of Zeus [υἱοὺς τῷ Διΐ]. For you know how many sons of Zeus [υἱοὺς τοῦ Διός] are said by the writers you hold in honor to have gone up to heaven [ἀνεληλυθέναι εἰς οὐρανόν]—Asclepius, who was also a healer, after being struck by lightning, Dionysius after being torn apart, Heracles after giving himself to the fire to escape from pain, the Dioscuri begotten of Leda, and Perseus begotten of Danae. What do we say about Ariadne and those said, like her, to have been set among the stars [κατηστερίσθαι]? And what do we say about your deceased emperors [τοὺς ἀποθνῄσκοντας παρ' ὑμῖν αὐτοκράτορας]? If you deem them worthy to be made into gods [ἀπαθανατίζεσθαι ἀξιοῦτε] you also bring forward someone who swears

---

[101] Translations based on B. Perrin, *Plutarch, Lives: Theseus and Romulus, Lycurgus and Numa, Solon and Publicola*, LCL 46 (London: Heinemann, 1914), 175, 177.

[102] Translation based on ibid., 177, 179.

that he has seen the cremated Caesar going up to heaven from the pyre [ἐκ τῆς πυρᾶς ἀνερχόμενον εἰς τὸν οὐρανὸν τὸν κατακαέντα Καίσαρα]. (*1 Apologia* 21.1–3)[103]

Justin Martyr is familiar with the stories that have been reviewed earlier. He specifically references the *apotheōses* of Asclepius, Dionysius, Heracles, the Dioscuri, and Perseus. Justin does not mention Romulus by name, but he surely knew of the myth.[104] More to Justin's point is Roman belief and practice concerning the deceased emperors. Some are deemed worthy "to be made into gods," or, more literally, "to be made immortal." The verb ἀπαθανατίζεσθαι means "to aim at immortality" (LSJ), or in the passive as we find it here, "to be made immortal." In this context it is the equivalent of ἀποθεοῦν (to deify; LSJ), from which the noun ἀποθέωσις, *apotheōsis*, is derived. It is interesting to note, too, that Justin does not call these deified figures "sons of God" (υἱοὶ τοῦ θεοῦ); rather, he calls them "sons of Zeus" (υἱοὶ τοῦ Διός), clearly identifying them with what is from his point of view a pagan deity, not with the Judeo-Christian God, which in Justin's mind is not only the true God but the *only* God. Calling these figures "sons of Zeus" was likely a conscious decision on Justin's part.

In Justin's time seven emperors had been deified—Augustus, Claudius, Vespasian, Titus, Nerva, Trajan, and Hadrian— and seven were not—Tiberius, Caligula, Nero, Galba, Otho, Vitellius, and Domitian. In the case of an emperor deemed worthy of such honor, says Justin, "you also bring forward someone who swears that he has seen the cremated Caesar going up to heaven from the pyre." One of the most notable examples in this case involved the assassinated Julius Caesar. A star, or comet (*stella*), was seen "for seven successive days, rising about the eleventh hour and was believed to be the soul of Caesar, who had been taken to heaven [*in caelum recepti*]" (Suetonius, *Divus Julius* 88.1). The template for being "set among the stars" (κατηστερίσθαι) was, of course, Romulus, who "won his place among the stars" (Ovid, *Fasti* 2.478). In the case of Romulus, we have the oft-told story of Julius Proculus who met Rome's hero on the road and provided the citizens of Rome with a solemn account of his experience, which many found credible.

There are several features in the Easter narratives—more if we include the Mount of Transfiguration—that correspond with the death and *apotheōsis* traditions related to Romulus, other deities, and the emperors: There is mystery surrounding the death of Jesus, including strange and frightening signs such as darkness and an earthquake. The tomb of Jesus is found empty; he seemingly has disappeared, even as Romulus seemingly vanished. Heavenly figures are present at the tomb. The risen Jesus meets some of his followers, who bear witness to these encounters. His body is transformed, even as the body of Romulus is transformed. Jesus speaks of ascension to his Father in heaven (Jn 20:17), and then he is seen ascending into heaven (in Lk. 24:50-51;

---

[103] Translation based on D. Minns and P. Parvis, *Justin, Philosopher and and Martyr: Apologies*, Oxford Early Christian Texts (Oxford: Oxford University Press, 2009), 133, 135.

[104] The Romulus myth is mentioned in Theophilus, Justin's contemporary: "Rome, founded by Romulus, the alleged child [ὑπὸ Ῥωμύλου τοῦ παιδὸς ἱστορουμένου] of Mars and Ilia" (*Ad Autolycum* 3.27). Tertullian mentions it also (*Ad nationes* 3.2.9).

Acts 1:9-11), even as Romulus ascended. Like Romulus, when Jesus ascends, he is enveloped in a cloud (Acts 1:9). Two men on the road to Emmaus meet the risen Jesus (Lk. 24:13-27), even as Julius Proculus meets Romulus on the road. The risen Jesus mysteriously appears to his disciples who are hiding in a room, whose doors are locked (Jn 20:19-23, 26-29). On a mountain top the risen Jesus commissions his followers (Mt. 28:16-20), even as Romulus gave instruction on the Palatine Hill in Rome.[105] The disciples believe in Jesus and even worship him (Mt. 28:9, 17; Jn 20:28-29), as Romulus is believed and worshipped. A martyred disciple (Stephen) sees Jesus "standing at the right hand" (Acts 7:55-56). An angry Saul of Tarsus sees the risen Jesus in a bright light from heaven (Acts 9:3-8).

Outside of the Gospel narratives we find significant parallels. In language that the people of Rome would have appreciated, even if they had found it scandalous, Paul, in his letter to the Christians of Rome, declares that Jesus was "designated Son of God in power according to the Spirit of holiness by his resurrection from the dead, Jesus Christ our Lord" (τοῦ ὁρισθέντος υἱοῦ θεοῦ ἐν δυνάμει κατὰ πνεῦμα ἁγιωσύνης ἐξ ἀναστάσεως νεκρῶν, Ἰησοῦ Χριστοῦ τοῦ κυρίου ἡμῶν; Rom. 1:4). Many Romans would have interpreted such a bold statement in terms of *apotheōsis*. When Paul assures Christians in Thessalonikē that Jesus will come (παρουσία/*adventus*) from heaven (1 Thess. 1:10, 4:15) and the living will be "caught up" or *raptured* (1 Thess. 4:16-17; cf. Livy, *Ab urbe condita* 1.16.3, "he had been caught up [*raptum*] on high in the blast"),[106] he has again used language that the people of the Roman Empire would associate with the translation of a hero from earth to heaven.

One curious feature in the Resurrection and Ascension narratives is the nonappearance of a star. A star plays a role in Matthew's Infancy narrative, which presupposes Western as well as Eastern expectations, but there is no mention of a star or comet or any celestial phenomena in the several New Testament accounts of the death, burial, resurrection, and ascension of Jesus. Jesus's person is transformed (Lk. 24:15-16, 31; Jn 20:14-16),[107] amazingly so if we view the Transfiguration as a misplaced

---

[105] Compare Romulus's command *abi ... nuntia* ("go, announce"; Livy, *Ab urbe condita* 1.16.7) with Jesus's command πορευθέντες ... μαθητεύσατε ("go, instruct"; Mt. 28:19).

[106] In Greek the word is ἁρπαγησόμεθα ("we shall be caught up"). In the Latin it is translated as *rapiemur*.

[107] The description of Jesus's face and clothing (Mk 9:3, στίλβοντα λευκὰ λίαν, "glistening, intensely white"; Mt. 17:2, ἔλαμψεν τὸ πρόσωπον αὐτοῦ ὡς ὁ ἥλιος, "his face shone like the sun"; λευκὰ ὡς τὸ φῶς, "white as light"; Lk. 9:29, λευκὸς ἐξαστράπτων, "dazzling white") corresponds in important ways with the descriptions of the transformed Romulus/Quirinus. But the Transfiguration story itself reflects the imagery and language of the stories of Moses on Mount Sinai (esp. Exodus 24; cf. Exod. 34:29, where it is said in reference to Moses that "the skin of his face shone because he had been talking with God"; and in the Targum, "the splendor of the glory of his face had increased"). Even Luke's description of the "two men" at the tomb (Lk. 24:4)—who are surely angels—as dressed "in dazzling apparel" (ἐν ἐσθῆτι ἀστραπτούσῃ), that is, "in lightning-like apparel," reflects biblical language as much as Greco-Roman language. One thinks of the angel described in Daniel: "And his body was like tharsis, and his face like an appearance of lightning [ὅρασις ἀστραπῆς], and his eyes like torches of fire [λαμπάδες πυρός], and his arms and feet like dazzling bronze [χαλκὸς ἐξαστράπτων], and the sound of his talking like the sound of a throng" (LXX Dan. 10:6). In the book of Revelation John the seer says,

I saw seven golden lampstands, and in the midst of the lampstands one like a son of man, clothed with a long robe and with a golden girdle round his breast; his head and his hair were

resurrection story (Mt. 17:1-8; Mk 9:2-8; Lk. 9:28-36).[108] But even here, apart from the appearance of a cloud and a voice from heaven, there are no celestial phenomena. At the baptism a dove descends upon Jesus as he emerges from the water and a voice calls out, identifying him as God's Son (Mt. 3:13-17; Mk 1:9-11; Lk. 3:21-22; Jn 1:29-34). The appearance of a bird would evoke ideas of omen in the minds of Jews (Josephus, *Ant.* 18.195, 19.346), as well as Greeks and Romans.

Notwithstanding the nonappearance of stars or other forms of celestial phenomena at the time of Jesus's translation, the appearances of stars or comets did call for comment in Christentum in later centuries. The venerable Bede speaks of comets that appeared over the skies of Europe in the seventh and eighth centuries:

> The 678th year of the Lord's incarnation, which is the 8th year of the reign of King Egfrid, there appeared in the month of August a star which is called a comet [*stella quae dicitur cometa*]; which continued three months, rising in the morning hours and giving forth as it were a high pillar of glittering flame [*excelsam radiantis flammae quasi columnam praeferens*]. In that year a dissension arose between King Egfrid and the most reverend Bishop Wilfrid.[109]

> The 729th year of the Lord's incarnation there appeared two comets [*cometae duae*] about the sun and struck great terror into the beholders thereof. For one went before the sun at its rising in the morning; the other followed the setting of the sun in the evening, both presaging as it were terrible destruction to the east as well as the west … they appeared in the month of January, and continued about two weeks. At that time the Saracens, like a very sore plague, wasted France with pitiful destruction, and themselves not long after were justly punished in the same country for their unbelief.[110]

Bede (and probably many in Europe) believed that these comets were linked in some way to events on earth. In the case of the first appearance, the comet seems to have been understood as a reflection (or presage?) of the conflict between King Egfrid and Bishop Wilfrid. The two comets that appeared a generation later were understood to foreshadow the coming Muslim invasion of France. Both of these testimonials broadly reflect the much older notions that comets were omens of death of kings, regime change, war, major upheavals, and the like. None of these comets, however,

---

white as white wool, white as snow [λευκαὶ ὡς ἔριον λευκὸν ὡς χιών]; his eyes were like a flame of fire [οἱ ὀφθαλμοὶ αὐτοῦ ὡς φλὸξ πυρός], his feet were like burnished bronze [ὅμοιοι χαλκολιβάνῳ], refined as in a furnace, and his voice was like the sound of many waters … and his face was like the sun shining in full strength [ἡ ὄψις αὐτοῦ ὡς ὁ ἥλιος φαίνει ἐν τῇ δυνάμει αὐτοῦ]. (Rev. 1:12-16)

We have here some of the language of LXX Dan. 7:9-10, 10:6.

[108] As argued by C. E. Carlston, "Transfiguration and Resurrection," *JBL* 80 (1961): 233–40. But I have my doubts. For arguments against the suggestion, see R. H. Stein, "Is the Transfiguration (Mark 9:2–8) a Misplaced Resurrection Account?" *JBL* (1976): 79–96.

[109] For Latin text and English translation, see J. E. King, *Baedae Opera Historica* II, LCL 248 (Cambridge, MA: Harvard University Press, 1930), 68–71.

[110] Bede refers to the Muslim invasion of Europe, as well as to the 732 defeat of the Islamic armies at Tours (France). For Latin text and English translation, see ibid., 366–9.

was linked to the translation of Jesus or to his intercessory role in heaven. Thus it seems to hold true that the star/comet omen, so popular in Greco-Roman tradition in stories of *apotheōsis* and heavenly translation, did not find a place in the Christian stories of the death, resurrection, and ascension of Jesus. Thanks to Num. 24:17, which in Jewish circles was understood as a messianic prophecy, the star played a role in the Matthean Infancy narrative. But it played no role in the death, resurrection, and ascension of Jesus.

Concluding Comments

Christian proclamation of the death, resurrection, and ascension of Jesus was colored and enriched with themes and vocabulary from Israel's sacred Scriptures, as we would expect, but it was also colored by the popular beliefs and stories about heroes who were translated into heaven as gods.[111] The greatest of these figures was Romulus, the legendary founder of the city of Rome, which by the time of Augustus and Jesus had become a mighty empire. It is not surprising that Rome's greatest personalities, especially the emperors, sought after "equality with god" (τὸ εἶναι ἴσα θεῷ, as Paul puts it in Phil. 2:6).[112] To do so, the promotion of propaganda before ascending to imperial honors, during the reign itself, and then after death was essential. Eyewitness testimonials of omens—whether "recalled" from long ago, or more recently witnessed at the time of or shortly after death—were necessary to assure the desired result. Omens that brought to mind the ancient and revered stories of Romulus were prized above all.[113]

In a recent study Wendy Cotter has argued persuasively that the principal backdrop to Matthew's version of the Resurrection narrative is the story of Romulus.[114] "Once it is seen how easily Matthew has placed Jesus in the same category as the most exalted emperors and rulers, we see how the listeners understand the worldwide and eternal significance of the kind of power that Jesus holds."[115]

---

[111] The imagery Christians used for describing aspects of Christology was also colored by Greco-Roman ideas. For a learned discussion of this important aspect of the discussion, see M. D. Litwa, *IESUS DEUS: The Early Christian Depiction of Jesus as a Mediterranean God* (Minneapolis, MN: Fortress, 2014).

[112] The idea and language of "equality with god" is authentically Greco-Roman. In one text we read that Herakles "was honored as equal with the gods [ἴσα θεοῖς]" (Ps.-Plato, *Axiochus* 364A). In an inscription to Ptolemy I, king of Egypt, we read: "to all who have honored the svior Ptolemy with honors equal to gods [ἰσοθέοις]" (*SIG* 390.27). In a letter, Germanicus, son of Emperor Tiberius, complains of excessive acclamations that "are for the gods" (ἰσοθέους; *Select Papyri* no. 211 [19 CE]).

[113] For further discussion of the Romulus tradition, see D. Porte, "Romulus-Quirinus, prince et dieu, dieu des princes. Etude sur le personnage de Quirinus et sur son évolution, des origines à Auguste," in W. Haase (ed.), *Religion (Heidentum: Römische Götterkulte, orientalische Kulte in der römischen Welt)* (Berlin: de Gruyter, 1981), 300–42.

[114] W. Cotter, "Greco-Roman Apotheosis Traditions and the Resurrection Appearances in Matthew," in D. E. Aune (ed.), *The Gospel of Matthew in Current Study: Studies in Memory of William G. Thompson, S.J.* (Grand Rapids, MI: Eerdmans, 2001), 127–53.

[115] Ibid., 152.

The four evangelists drew upon some of the Roman omen traditions, especially those linked to Romulus. But the Jewish traditions and the sacred Scriptures out of which these traditions grew retained hermeneutical and theological priority.[116] The incipient apologetic of the four evangelists adumbrated the more complex and elaborate apologetic of Christian writers such as Justin in the second century and Tertullian and Clement of Alexandria in the third century, who tried to show how Jesus matched or surpassed the virtues of the Greco-Roman heroes and gods. It was not all apologetic, of course; it was also evangelism.

The Jesus movement of the first century was primarily preoccupied with a skeptical synagogue, which remained unconvinced that the crucified miracle worker from Galilee really was the Messiah. To persuade the synagogue, appeal was made to Israel's sacred Scriptures. The Jesus movement of the second and third centuries was primarily preoccupied with a skeptical Roman Empire that compared the supposed virtues of a Jewish Savior against the well-established and trusted ancient traditions of the Greco-Roman gods and heroes. For the Christian movement to make any progress in an environment like this, it was necessary to show that the benefactions of the "good news" of Jesus and his community far outweighed the supposed benefactions of the good news of Caesar, who represented and in some sense embodied the glory and virtues of the Greco-Roman heroes and gods. Proof of Caesar's success in his vital role as Rome's *pontifex maximus* (the great priest) was his postmortem translation to heaven, ratified on earth by his official enrolment in the Roman pantheon. The omens that were usually cited, which provided justification for deification, were often like those that had become part of the Romulus story. It was in this context that the followers of Jesus proclaimed their good news in hopes of evangelizing both synagogue and empire.[117]

---

[116] Which Cotter (ibid., 153) rightly acknowledges.
[117] See F. G. Downing, "A Rival to Romulus," in *Doing Things with Words in the First Christian Century*, LNTS 200 (London: Bloomsbury T&T Clark, 2000), 133–51. There are distinctive features in Luke's Resurrection narrative that reflect aspects of Romulan and related tradition. See S. Matthews, "Elijah, Ezekiel, and Romulus: Luke's Flesh and Bones (Luke 24:39) in Light of Ancient Narratives of Ascent, Resurrection, and Apotheosis," in G. J. Brooke and A. Feldman (eds.), *On Prophets, Warriors, and Kings: Former Prophets through the Eyes of Their Interpreters*, BZNW 470 (Berlin: de Gruyter, 2016), 161–82; I. Muñoz Gallarte, "Luke 24 Reconsidered: The Figure of the Ghost in Post-Classical Greek Literature," *NovT* 59 (2017): 131–46. On the Judaic antecedents of early Christian understandings of the resurrection and ascension of Jesus, see R. D. Aus, *The Death, Burial, and Resurrection of Jesus, and the Death, Burial, and Translation of Moses in Judaic Tradition*, Studies in Judaism (Lanham, MD: University Press of America, 2008).

7

Learning Rhetoric at Tarsus: The Apostle Paul and His Use of Aristotelian Rhetoric

Alexa Wallace and Adam Z. Wright

Introduction

Many new questions and considerations about Paul's education and use of rhetoric have arisen in recent years, and with good reason.[1] Paul was certainly Jewish and yet had close connections with Greek and Roman thought.[2] How did each of these things affect how he spoke? Was he equally affected by all three? Asked a different way, are there moments at which Paul's adherence to traditional Jewish modes of teaching gives way to Greek or Roman forms of rhetoric? Or did Paul forgo his Jewish traditions and completely adopt Greco-Roman philosophical thought? And are such distinctions even necessary for determining what he said in his letters? This is certainly a complex set of questions, and as Porter states, "The framing of the question [of ethnicity] exposes the fact that the distinctions themselves involve a complex of ethnic, social, and cultural designations."[3]

The purpose of this chapter is to examine how, and in what ways, Paul's rhetoric may have been informed by Greek rhetorical models. This kind of study typically begins with the question of Paul's education, with significant focus on Paul's early life in Tarsus. However, what is often overlooked within these studies is that Paul returned to Tarsus after his conversion to Christianity (Acts 9:28-30). One cannot be certain just

---

[1] Some more notable volumes and essays include: Michael Wade Martin and Mikeal C. Parsons, *Ancient Rhetoric and the New Testament: The Influence of Elementary Greek Composition* (Waco, TX: Baylor University Press, 2018); Stanley E. Porter and Bryan R. Dyer, "Oral Texts? A Reassessment of the Oral and Rhetorical Nature of Paul's Letters in Light of Recent Studies," *JETS* 55 (2012): 323–41; Ben Witherington III, *New Testament Rhetoric: An Introductory Guide to the Art of Persuasion in and of the New Testament* (Eugene, OR: Cascade, 2009); *What's in the Word: Rethinking the Socio-Rhetorical Character of the New Testament* (Waco, TX: Baylor University Press, 2009); Duane F. Watson, *The Rhetoric of the New Testament: A Bibliographic Survey* (Leiden: Brill, 2006); Stanley E. Porter, *Handbook of Classical Rhetoric in the Hellenistic Period, 330 B.C.–A.D. 400* (Leiden: Brill, 1997).

[2] For an excellent survey of Roman citizenship and the criteria surrounding it, see Sean Adams, "Roman Citizenship and Understanding Acts 22:22–29," in Stanley E. Porter (ed.), *Paul: Jew, Greek, and Roman*, PAST 5 (Leiden: Brill, 2008), 309–26.

[3] Stanley E. Porter, "Paul as Jew, Greek, and Roman: An Introduction," in Porter, *Paul: Jew, Greek, and Roman*, 1.

how long Paul stayed in Tarsus, but the timing of his return there is conspicuous: after a negative interaction with certain Hellenistic Jews in Jerusalem. What is even more conspicuous is that Paul is summoned—some time later—from Tarsus to begin preaching to the Greeks in Antioch (Acts 11:19-26). Is it possible that, having spent considerable time in Tarsus honing his rhetorical skills, Paul found a way to convince the Greeks of the resurrected Jesus? And, if so, would these skills have placed him in a position of incredible influence, so much so that he was chosen first to help preach in Antioch and then to travel throughout Asia Minor and Greece as the "Apostle to the Gentiles" (Acts 9:15, 22:21; Rom. 1:14-15, 15:18-21; Gal. 1:15-16, 2:9; Eph. 3:7-9)?

Given that Tarsus was a center for education in the ancient world, it should come as no surprise that Paul returned there from Jerusalem for the purpose of bettering his rhetorical skills. But exactly what did Paul learn about Greek rhetoric and how did such knowledge aid him in his interactions and preaching style? Paul's letters exhibit an awareness of certain categories of rhetoric, especially Aristotelian ones: Ethos, Pathos, and Logos. Though we have no writings from his pre-Christian days with which to compare his letters, we must consider his negative interactions with the Hellenistic Jews in Jerusalem as evidence that Paul was perhaps not as well versed in Greek rhetoric as was needed to appease them. However, what convinces us that Paul did, in fact, know about these categories of rhetoric is that he subverts them at times. This may be why many do not view Paul's knowledge of these categories as sufficient to explain what we see in his letters, but it is our view that Paul could not subvert something that he did not know anything about.

In what follows, we will briefly summarize the kind of city Tarsus had become by Paul's time with regard to its educational opportunities, as well as the kinds of educators Paul would have encountered during his visit there. This visit would have guaranteed an interaction with rhetoric, especially Aristotelian, which he later used when preaching to the Greeks and especially when composing his letters—all of which were written after this important visit to Tarsus.[4]

Tarsus as an Educational Center for Philosophy and Rhetoric

Paul declares himself a citizen of Tarsus in Acts 21:39, a city that he deems quite important (also Acts 9:11, 30; 11:25; 22:3; Gal. 1:21). This mention of Tarsus has given rise to a debate concerning Paul's education, particularly the kind of education he received and how that education might reveal something about the things he wrote. Because Tarsus had a reputation for its educational system, it is likely that Paul had

---

[4] According to Watson, most ancient letters were mixed types performing a variety of rhetorical functions. An epistle and a speech are certainly different modes of expression and are typically analyzed as such, and Watson suggests that "epistles utilize Ethos and Pathos almost exclusively" whereas speeches more frequently rely on Logos. However, as we will see, Paul makes use of the category of Logos in addition to Ethos and Pathos. See Duane F. Watson, "The Three Species of Rhetoric and the Study of the Pauline Epistles," in Paul Sampley and Peter Lampe (eds.), *Paul and Rhetoric* (London: Continuum International, 2010), 25–47, here 41–2.

some level of education or, at very least, interaction with Greek ideas during his childhood years. The argument then becomes about just how much education Paul received before he went to Jerusalem to study with Gamaliel. However, as mentioned, this chapter aims to establish a "middle ground" that states that Paul had his most meaningful interactions with Greek ideas after his conversion when he returned to Tarsus (Acts 9:28-30).

By the time of Paul's return, Tarsus had established itself as not only a center within the empire—the capital of Cilicia, according to Dio Chrysostom (*Or.* 33.17)—but also a hub of Greek philosophical teachers and ideas. Tarsus owes its establishment to the Argives and attaches itself to Perseus and Herakles, giving it a significant, and noteworthy, Greek pedigree (Dio Chrysostom, *Or.* 33.1). During Paul's life, Tarsus was considered to be one of the leading cities in the ancient eastern empire, a city with a strong economy and educational system whose success was well regarded until the time of the Byzantine Empire.[5] The educational system at Tarsus was well known, as is noted by Strabo (64/63 BCE–21 CE) in his *Geographica*:

> The people at Tarsus have devoted themselves so eagerly not only to philosophy, but also to the whole round of education in general, that they have surpassed Athens, Alexandria, or any other place that can be named where there have been schools and lectures of philosophers … Further, *the city of Tarsus has all kinds of schools of rhetoric*; and in general it not only has a flourishing population but also is most powerful, thus keeping up the reputation of the mother-city. (Strabo, *Geogr.* 14.5.13; LCL, our emphasis)[6]

It appears that Tarsus had a reputation for its schools of rhetoric, and Paul would have encountered their proponents during his return to Tarsus.[7] It is also, therefore, quite likely that Paul encountered Aristotelian categories of rhetoric during this time. Though Tarsus was not a representative of the Peripatetic school necessarily, Blumenfeld notes that many Stoics, who were versed in Aristotelian categories of rhetoric, stationed themselves at Tarsus, which created a philosophical milieu.[8] One of the more prominent names was Athenodorus Cananites (74 BCE–7 CE), who was a friend

---

[5] Mary E. Andrews, "Paul, Philo, and the Intellectuals," *JBL* 53 (1934): 150–66, here 151.
[6] Strabo also tells us that Tarsus was the home of many renowned teachers, including a certain rhetorician who taught Julius Caesar (14.5.14), as well as the Stoic philosophers Antipater, Nestor, and Archidemus. See also D. Litfin, *St Paul nd Rhetoric in Corinth,"Julius Caesar (14.5.14), as well as the Stoic p*, SNTMS 79 (Cambridge: Cambridge University Press, 1994), 119; Stanley E. Porter and Andrew W. Pitts, "Paul's Bible, His Education, and His Access to the Scriptures of Israel," *JGRChJ* 5 (2008): 11.
[7] Strabo also notes a number of grammarians and poets in Tarsus. These include Plutiades and Diogenes, who were traveling teachers. He also notes that Diogenes was known for his composition of tragic poetry, as were the grammarians Artemidorus, Diodorus, and Dionysides—the greatest of the tragic poets (Strabo, *Geogr.* 14.5.15). Certain noteworthy poets are also mentioned by Dio Chrysostom (*Or.* 33.5), and Philostratus tells us that the famous Neopythagorean philosopher Apollonius of Tyana was educated in Tarsus under the orator Euthydemus of Phoenicia at the age of fourteen (*Vit. Apoll.* 1.7).
[8] Bruno Blumenfeld, *The Political Paul: Democracy and Kingship in Paul's Thought* (London: T&T Clark, 2003), 31.

to the great rhetorician Cicero and who eventually became the governor of Tarsus (Strabo, *Geogr.* 14.5.14). Athenodorus was also known for tutoring Augustus (45–44 BCE), and the direction to reform the city to be governed by the university was given directly by Augustus. Athenodorus thus placed Tarsus under the rule of the university (Strabo, *Geogr.* 14.14), a reform that aimed to make the city famous for εὐταξία καὶ σωφροσύνη (order and good sense) (Dio Chrysostom, *Or.* 33.48). This gave way to many public lectures in the markets and at the city gates, a context that would have provided an opportunity for Paul to listen and to debate with these teachers.[9] Though much of what Athenodorus wrote about is now lost, he seems to have specialized in moral philosophy[10]—something that influenced his political successor, Nestor, and potentially Paul's own thoughts and writing.

Educational Models in Ancient Greece

Since it has been established that Tarsus was a center of teaching, especially for the purposes of rhetoric, it makes sense that Paul would have returned to Tarsus in order to hone his rhetorical skills. Rhetoric is important since the very definition of it includes persuasion, and the purpose of Paul's entire mission is to persuade his listeners to believe in the resurrected Jesus. It therefore follows that Paul would have wanted to improve this act of persuasion, especially since he had unsuccessfully interacted with the Hellenistic Jews in Jerusalem.

Aristotle (384–322 BCE) becomes important in this discussion precisely because of his influential work *Rhetoric*. As mentioned, Tarsus was home to a number of Stoic philosophers, many of whom knew and taught Aristotelian rhetoric. Among these teachers are, most notably, Antipater, Nestor, and Archidemus. In addition to philosophy, these teachers would have offered classes in rhetoric most likely because it was considered to be a part of the Greek educational system.

As Pitts and Porter suggest, the traditional view is that the Greek educational system was a three-tiered one.[11] The first was primary school, or *Ludus Litteratius*, in which the student was exposed to a number of Greek literary works. The second was grammar school, or *Schola Grammatici*, in which the student would learn to imitate the greatest Greek writers by writing their lines and studying their style. The third was the rhetorical school, or *Schola Rhetoris*, in which a student would learn to perfect their writing and speaking style so as to become like one of the literary greats. As the student

---

[9] Ibid., 32. As much is attested by Bird who says, "If Paul received even only the basic elements of a Greek education, that alone would have left him exposed to Greek philosophy, literature, and rhetoric to some degree." See M. Bird, "Reassessing a Rhetorical Approach to Paul's Letters," *ExpTim* 119 (2008): 374–79, here 378.

[10] David Ulansey, *The Origins of the Mithraic Mysteries: Cosmology and Salvation in the Ancient World* (Oxford: Oxford University Press, 1989), 69.

[11] For the entire argument, see Porter and Pitts, "Paul's Bible," 9–41. See also Andrew W. Pitts, "Paul in Tarsus: Historical Factors in Assessing Paul's Early Education," in Stanley E. Porter and Bryan Dyer (eds.), *Paul and Ancient Rhetoric: Theory and Practice in the Hellenistic Context* (Cambridge: Cambridge University Press, 2016), 43–67.

progressed sequentially through this system, a greater number of opportunities arose with regard to employment and further study.

Such opportunities may have been restricted based on social status, however. For example, Booth demonstrates that the educational model could have been a two-track model: the first track for students of low socioeconomic status, and the second for those of high status. Such is also noted by Kaster, who adds that high-status students may have completely forgone primary school and begun with grammar school. This meant that a Roman citizen, as was the case with Paul, would have begun grammar school between the ages of six–eight and finished by twelve or thirteen years of age. This mirrors the Jewish model, according to Davies, which begins at the age of five and concludes at thirteen—the age at which a young boy was welcomed into the Jewish community as a man. From there, a man would have studied the commandments at age thirteen and then the Talmud at fifteen.[12]

These models of education combined with the age ranges, argues Pitts and Porter, are evidence of "Paul being raised in a Jewish home in Tarsus and learning the Scriptures while being educated in the grammar school, and then, after his bar-mitzvah (or equivalent at the time), going to Jerusalem to complete his education in Jewish law and related matters."[13] It then follows that, if Paul were to receive any kind of education in Tarsus as a boy, he would have concluded grammar school at thirteen—the age he moved to Jerusalem to begin studying the commandments and eventually the Talmud. This is a fair assessment to make, and it fits the models of education provided to us by Kaster and Booth.

However, what seems to be left out of the assessment is that Paul, if he left for Jerusalem at thirteen, would have missed the rhetorical aspect of his early Greek education. This is not to say that he did not learn something about rhetoric during the early stages of his education in Tarsus or even in Jerusalem, for that matter. But, because he forwent the rhetorical aspect of Greek education, Paul may have thought it important to return there at a later age to continue in such training. Such a proposal fits with the thesis suggested earlier, which states that Paul returned to Tarsus to hone his rhetorical training before being summoned to Antioch to preach to the Greeks.

Aristotle's Rhetoric

But what would have such rhetorical training included, and is there sufficient evidence to conclude that Paul had a working knowledge of Greek rhetoric? In this section, it will be argued that Paul did indeed have a working knowledge of rhetoric, specifically that of Aristotle. It follows that the foundation of Paul's ability to persuade his Greek listeners would have to be something that they would have understood, and Aristotle's

---

[12] A. D. Booth, "The Schooling of Slaves in First-Century Rome," *TAPA* 109 (1979): 11–19; R. A. Kastor, "Notes on 'Primary' and 'Secondary' Schools in Late Antiquity," *TAPA* 113 (1983): 323–46.

[13] Pitts and Porter, "Paul's Bible," 16; see also W. D. Davies, *Paul and Rabbinic Judaism: Some Rabbinic Elements in Pauline Theology* (Philadelphia, PA: Fortress, 1980), 24–5.

categories of Logos, Pathos, and Ethos are well attested in Paul's speeches and in his letters.[14]

Rhetoric is the art of persuasion (πίστις), and Aristotle gives a full explanation of this art form in his *Rhetoric*. Rhetoric stands as a counterpart to dialectic, which—based on the Socratic method—is a model that aims to discover the truth of a matter through the investigative questioning of assumption. Rhetoric, on the other hand, is more specific: once a truth has been stated, a rhetorician either persuades or dissuades from that truth.[15]

In the opening chapter of Book 1, argumentative persuasion (πίστις) is defined as a sort of demonstration (ἀπόδειξις), and the rhetorical form of demonstration is the enthymeme (ἐνθύμημα). With regard to the act of persuasion itself, a good rhetorician has the ability to showcase three things. The first is evincing his personal character (ἦθος) which will make his speech credible; the second is the power to stir the emotions (πάθη) of the listeners; and the third is the ability to prove (λόγος) the truth by means of persuasive arguments (*Rhetoric* 1.2). These three ingredients, so to speak, are found in Paul's letters as he often makes specific mention of things related to each. This kind of specific detail in Paul's letters leads us to conclude that he must have had some working knowledge of Aristotelian categories of rhetoric so as to showcase them in his speeches and letters.

Ethos

The personal character, or Ethos, of a speaker is important in the art of persuasion. According to Aristotle, Ethos depends on the character of the speaker, and of this he says, "We believe good men more fully and more readily than others: this is true generally whatever the question is, and absolutely true where exact certainty is impossible and opinions are divided" (*Rhetoric* 1356a). At first read, one might interpret Ethos as an estimation of the speaker's character, which could be understood as an estimation of the speaker's moral character.[16] But, for Aristotle, Ethos has more

---

[14] Fairweather notes as much and suggests that Paul's use of rhetoric, especially in 1 Corinthians, is innovative and distinct. Watson agrees and calls Paul's use of rhetoric in 1 Corinthians a "Christ-based logic that diverges from pagan sophistic." See Janet Fairweather, "The Epistle to the Galatians and Classical Rhetoric: Part 3," *TynBul* 45 (1994): 213–43; Watson, "Three Species," 44.

[15] Betz also notes that most uses of ancient rhetoric have little to do with discovering the truth and are instead used to persuade the audience of a particular line of thought. This is probably why, in Athens, Paul begins with an inspection of certain altars devoted to certain gods: Paul need not persuade his audience of the existence of God but rather that their efforts are improperly directed. As much is also noted by Eriksson, who suggests that the speaker's awareness of the opposite argument, or the "polarity" of an argument, was necessary. See H. D. Betz, "In Defense of the Spirit: Paul's Letter to the Galatians as a Document of Early Christian Apologetics," in E. Schlüssler Fiorenza (ed.), *Aspects of Religious Propaganda in Judaism and Early Christianity* (Notre Dame: University of Notre Dame Press, 1976), 98–114, here 100; Anders Eriksson, "Contrary Arguments in Paul's Letters," in Stanley E. Porter and Dennis Stamps (eds.), *Rhetorical Criticism and the Bible: Essays from the 1998 Florence Conference*, JSNTSup 195 (London: Sheffield Academic, 2002), 336.

[16] Smith seems to focus more on the development of moral character as it relates to Ethos. Of it, he says, "Thus is not enough for a speaker to *be* good, a speaker must understand virtue; the virtue of the culture is one of the fonts (dwelling places) of *ethos*." However, this interpretation of the word "good" is incongruent with what Aristotle then says about being persuaded by what the speaker says,

to do with a speaker's presentation than his or her moral character. He goes on to say, "This kind of persuasion (Ethos), like the others, should be achieved by what the speaker says, not by what people think of his character before he begins to speak" (*Rhetoric* 1356a).[17] Thus, Aristotle issues a warning for those who might dismiss a speaker based on that speaker's perceived reputation without ever listening to what he or she has to say.[18] This is pertinent in the instance of a speaker who aims to persuade a crowd of something that they may already disagree with; there can be no doubt that the speaker's moral goodness would be called into question if they defend a reprehensible position.[19]

Paul's awareness of Ethos is shown in his admitted lack of it. For example, Paul says to the Corinthians:

> And coming to you, brothers, I did not announce the mystery (μυστήριον) of God to you with lofty arguments or wisdom. For I did not claim to know anything amongst you except Jesus Christ and his crucifixion. In weakness and with trembling I came to you, and my message and my announcement were not made with persuasive words but with a demonstration of the spirit and power, so that your faith (πίστις) might not rest in human wisdom but in God's power. (1 Cor. 2:1-5, translation ours)

Typically, the essence of the word πίστις regards the audience's belief in a God they had perhaps not otherwise known. But, as mentioned, this particular term has a certain currency with regard to rhetoric: argumentative persuasion (πίστις) regards a speaker's ability to persuade the audience of the argument that he or she is presenting. But Paul appears to subvert the typical displays of Ethos by claiming that his weakness in speech was actually powerful. He then draws attention to the audience's familiarity with ethos by his use of the subjunctive voice in his last point, which creates a level of prominence that any audience at this time, certainly familiar with the art of rhetoric, would have been drawn to and understood.

---

and not by what they think of his character before he begins to speak. It follows that what Aristotle means by "good" is not moral goodness. Instead, it makes more sense to interpret "good" in the sense of delivery: "We believe people with good delivery more fully and more readily than others." This places the emphasis of Ethos on the speaker's presentation and not on something arbitrary like his moral character—especially if the audience knows nothing of such things. See Craig R. Smith, "Ethos Dwells Pervasively," in Michael J. Hyde (ed.), *The Ethos of Rhetoric* (Columbia: University of South Carolina Press, 2004), 5.

[17] This is also why Ethos is listed first among the three (Ethos, Pathos, and Logos). Ethos therefore refers to the speaker's delivery itself, which adds to the potency of the logical component.

[18] This is precisely why Paul, in his letters to the Romans, especially in chapter 7, is able to present himself as lacking in a moral sense and yet continue to be persuasive in his presentation.

[19] This is certainly true with regard to Aristotle's three divisions of oratory: political, forensic, and ceremonial oratory of display. Of these, Aristotle says, "political speaking urges us either to do or not to do something … Forensic speaking either attacks or defends somebody … ceremonial oratory of display either praise of censures somebody" (*Rhetoric* 1358b). It is clear that moral character has little to do with Ethos and that a speaker's delivery is important for persuading an audience to a disagreeable position.

Paul continues to subvert the audience's expectations of what comes next by adding a mystical element to explain his lack of Ethos: the mystery of God stands apart from that ascertained through conventional means of wisdom. Such a statement debunks the kind of sophistry that the Corinthian people may have been accustomed to. For example, he says, "This is what we are speaking, not with wise logic from sophistic (σοφίας) men, but spiritual things through spiritual means" (1 Cor. 2:13, translation ours). Paul's use of Ethos is thus one of subversion, a process that is not possible without an awareness of how Ethos typically functions in speech.[20] Such a process indicates that Paul had become well versed in rhetoric, something that he would have learned at Tarsus.

The Ethos of Paul's presentations can also be found in his speech at Athens. In Acts 17:16-34, Paul begins to speak in Athens to a number of people, both Jewish and Greek. It should come as no surprise that Paul then begins to interact with Stoic and Epicurean philosophers—the likes of whom were also in Tarsus—who bring him to the Areopagus for the reason that they were hearing novel ideas and wanted to learn more about them (Acts 17:19). This means that the audience was persuaded, at least in part, by the Ethos of Paul's arguments and they wanted to hear more of his presentation. It is evidence that Paul had become aware not only of Stoic philosophy and their writings but also of a particular means of rhetorical Ethos that his audience knew and understood.

Pathos

The Pathos of argument is an appeal to emotion in order to persuade the audience or, as Aristotle puts it, the ability to put an audience into a certain frame of mind (*Rhetoric* 1356a). In a sense, it is the aspect of the argument that creates a level of personalization: the audience that is emotionally invested in a speech is one who is willing to be persuaded. However, this raises the question of which kinds of emotion are better for persuasion because "our judgments, when we are pleased and friendly, are not the same as when we are pained and hostile" (*Rhetoric* 1356a).

Therefore, to incite emotions is essential to a speaker's ability to persuade their audience. A speaker must know the different kinds of emotion, be able to describe them, to know their causes, and the ways in which they are excited (*Rhetoric* 1356a). More specifically, the speaker must know how to avoid rousing anger or, at least, be able to direct the anger to an appropriate place. About this, Aristotle says that a speaker must know three things: the state of mind an angry audience is in; the people toward whom the anger is usually directed; and why they get angry. He goes on to say, "It is not

---

[20] Watson argues that "linking a Pauline epistle to a particular rhetorical species is unwise and looking toward a Christian rhetoric may be a better solution." However, we suggest that, in order to break certain rules of rhetoric, one needs to be aware of those rules first, and Paul does exactly this by subverting certain expectations that he knows his audience has. While a "Christian Rhetoric" may possibly be a better solution, such a solution has its basis in tradition. See Watson, "Three Species," 47.

enough to know one or even two of these points; unless we know all three, we shall be unable to arouse anger in any one" (*Rhetoric* 1377ba).

In this case, Paul does not subvert the meaning of Pathos, but there is sufficient evidence that he became better at arousing the *right* kinds of emotion after his time at Tarsus. We find such evidence in Paul's lack of ability to direct a crowd's anger during the early parts of his ministry, something that, as mentioned, is a result of his lack of skill with regard to the categories of rhetoric (Acts 9:29). This lack of skill would have, no doubt, created a desire to know more fully how to persuade an audience. It can hardly be debated that Paul did not possess the ability to generate emotion, however, but he became acutely aware of which kinds of emotion were harmful to his message and learned how to direct it properly. Paul had been an effective persecutor of the church, and his actions in this regard created a sense of fear among other believers (Acts 9:13-14, 21, 26). Yet, Paul expressed a certain excellence of speech (Acts 9:22) though not enough to ease the fears and anger of those who knew him before.[21] What is more, his speech had not convinced any of the Hellenistic Jews living in Jerusalem (Acts 9:29), immediately after which he was sent to Tarsus to become more aware of the elements of rhetoric.[22]

Paul's use of Pathos can be found throughout his letters, especially within his letter to the Galatians. In it, he refers to a certain group of unnamed perpetrators who had introduced a gospel quite different from the one he had preached (Gal. 1:6). The issue here seems to be about the origin of the gospel: the "new" gospel has its origins in human thought, whereas the Gospel of Christ is of divine origin (Gal. 1:11-12).[23] Paul's strategy here is to rouse a certain level of Pathos in the form of anger by revealing the inauthenticity of this "new" gospel, which is a statement about its lack of truthfulness.

---

[21] In 1:13–2:14, Paul argues the case of his own story, making several key points. He begins by recounting his "earlier life in Judaism" (Gal. 1:13), when he "advanced in Judaism beyond many among my people of the same age, for I was far more zealous for the traditions of my ancestor" (Gal. 1:14) and became one who "was violently persecuting the church of God and was trying to destroy it" (Gal. 1:13).

[22] It is worth noting that Paul later establishes that he had suffered alongside those whom he previously persecuted, and he does so through a number of comments. In Galatians, he creates common ground between himself and his reader: "become as I am, for I also have become as you are" (Gal. 4:12). He then points out that he has suffered for the Gospel: "May I never boast of anything except the cross of our Lord Jesus Christ, by which the world has been crucified to me, and I to the world" (Gal. 6:14) and then remarks that "I carry the marks of Jesus branded on my body" (Gal. 6:17). These statements were attempts to ease the minds of those who knew Paul as a persecutor of the church, serving as an emotional appeal to remind his audience of the character they should ascribe to him. A modern example may also serve to elucidate this point: the Rev. Martin Luther King, Jr, in his 1963 speech entitled "I Have a Dream," echoes that sentiments of Paul:

> I am not unmindful that some of you have come here out of great trials and tribulations. Some of you have come fresh from narrow jail cells. And some of you have come from areas where your quest ... left you battered by the storms of persecution and staggered by the winds of police brutality. You have been the veterans of creative suffering. Continue to work with the faith that unearned suffering is redemptive.

[23] Paul contends that his message came directly from God, especially in such statements as "(God) was pleased to reveal his Son to me" and had "set [me] apart before I was born and called me through his grace" (Gal. 1:15).

Such appeal to emotion continues into the second chapter of Galatians, in which Paul continues to rouse Pathos, but this time toward Peter. The problem this time seems to be a level of hypocrisy that Paul detects in Peter's behavior, and his words are meant to stir a degree of anger against Peter and others.[24] This raises a number of questions about how Christianity began to distinguish itself from Judaism, particularly with regard to how a Christian ought to observe the Torah. Paul's rhetorical approach is to direct the crowds' anger toward the apparent hypocrisy by reinforcing the truthfulness of his original gospel, which is to say that Christ had given the gift of salvation for free and not through adherence to particular customs (Gal. 2:16).

Paul's attempts to rouse anger are also seen in his treatment of those who had been persuaded by the new gospel. After his customary greeting, Paul chastises the church in Galatia: "I am astonished that you are so quickly deserting the one who called you in the grace of Christ and are turning to a different gospel" (Gal. 1:6). He continues with his charge: "You foolish Galatians! Who has bewitched you? It was before your eyes that Jesus Christ was publicly exhibited as crucified!" (Gal. 3:1) and "I wish those who unsettle you would castrate themselves!" (Gal. 5:12). Each of these statements is meant to create a level of emotional distress and anger in his audience, which should then be directed toward the perpetrators of the new gospel. This pattern is in keeping with Aristotle's description of Ethos.

Logos

Logos is the aspect of persuasion that regards what is reasonable, and its purpose is to prove something as necessarily true or not. Of Logos, Aristotle says, "Persuasion is effected through the speech itself when we have proved a truth or an apparent truth by means of the persuasive arguments suitable to the case in question" (*Rhetoric* 1356a). Therefore an argument, if it is to make logical sense and be persuasive, must contain Logos.

The Logos of an argument is subdivided into two things: an induction and an enthymeme. An induction is the first part of the argument and is presented as an observation. For example, the induction "all dogs are animals" is presented as an observation, which is the apparent truth that the speaker looks to persuade of. However, in order to move the observation into the category of a logical argument, the speaker needs to add an enthymeme. Using the example provided, the speaker creates the argument by adding the enthymeme: "all dogs are animals, *therefore my dog is an animal.*" The addition of the enthymeme is what Aristotle calls a rhetorical

---

[24] Paul may have furthered his ad hominem against Peter by outlining Peter's qualifications. He states the authority of Peter, saying that "Peter had been entrusted with the gospel for the circumcised" (Gal, 1:7), which may serve to reinforce Paul's authority on the matter. Paul does not deny the validity of Peter's work but notes "he who worked through Peter making him an apostle to the circumcised also worked through me in sending me to the Gentiles" (Gal. 2:8). It also allows Paul, as the authority in the eyes of the reader, then to condemn Peter in the next paragraph when Paul says he opposed Peter face-to-face in Antioch, "because [Peter] stood self-condemned" (Gal. 2:11). Paul closes his recitation by again reaffirming his Jewish birth and upbringing.

syllogism, a process that he deems essential and rudimentary to all argumentation (*Rhetoric* 1356b).[25]

Such examples of rhetorical syllogisms can be found all throughout Paul's letters and certainly in Romans 3. Here Paul is arguing for righteousness in the form of a covenant between humanity and God, and it appears that he creates a number of rhetorical syllogisms on both sides of the argument in order to prove his point.[26] It is worth noting that Paul makes use of the term λόγια in this section (Rom. 3:2), which could have certain currency in this discussion.[27] It is possible that the use of λόγια here refers to the Law of Moses (Deut. 4:7-8), but it is also reasonable to conclude that λόγια is referring to the argumentative proof of God's existence and therefore his righteousness as it relates to Israel. This fits Paul's logic in that he argues that God's existence as a righteous God is necessarily true regardless of humanity's behavior. It may also therefore be true that Paul continues with this logic as he creates the rhetorical syllogism regarding humanity's righteousness as it relates to God's. For example, Paul's opponent could argue (and perhaps does): I am not righteous in my behavior (yet God's righteousness still exists), therefore God's righteousness is even more obvious given my lack of it. This line of thought buttresses the idea that a person ought not to be condemned for their behavior since God is being glorified by it (Rom. 3:7). However, Paul subverts this line of reasoning with his own argument: I am not righteous in my behavior (yet God's righteousness still exists), therefore my unrighteousness is even more obvious. And this is a necessary argument for Paul since he *must* argue that humanity is devoid of righteousness—even with the Law—so that he can justify preaching to those Gentiles who do not have the Law (Rom. 3:28).

Paul's use of Logos is also evident within his personal testimony. He was circumcised on the eighth day, an Israelite, from the tribe of Benjamin, a Hebrew of the Hebrews, a Pharisee, quite zealous, law-abiding and faultless (Phil. 3:5-6). Each of these designations are meant to alert his audience to the fact that, according to Jewish tradition, Paul was authoritative. Thus, the argument could be rendered: these traditions are authoritative and demand certain respect (and I have fulfilled these traditions), therefore I deserve respect and authority. Yet, Paul continues in a pattern of subverting common conceptions of what is considered logical: righteousness is a gift from Christ (and my supposed righteousness came from what I achieved), therefore my righteousness counts for nothing. So much is said in Phil. 3:7-8, in which the expectations of the audience are subverted by stating that any authority or respect they once esteemed should be done away with on the basis that it counts for nothing.

---

[25] This is an example of deductive reasoning, which is a general example followed by a specific enthymeme. A logical argument can also be inductive, which is a more specific example followed by a more general enthymeme: "my pit bull is vicious, therefore all pit bulls are vicious."
[26] It is possible that Paul is using a "straw-man" argument, especially in Rom. 3:5. However, it is also possible that he is reminiscing about the kinds of arguments that were presented to him during the Jerusalem Council in Acts 15. See Stanley E. Porter, *The Letters to the Romans* (Sheffield: Sheffield Academic Press, 2015), 80–6.
[27] Porter notes the rarity of this particular lexeme, though Paul makes use of its cognates at several other points (1 Thess. 2:4; 2 Thess. 1:10; 1 Tim. 1:11, 3:16; Tit. 1:3). See Porter, *Romans*, 84.

These sentiments are further extrapolated in the introductions to his letters. For example, Paul begins his letter to the Galatians by introducing himself as an Apostle, one sent from Christ and from God on a mission that did not originate in human effort (Gal. 1:1). One can understand these introductions as a subversion much in the same way that Paul's testimony subverts common logic, which could be rendered as: my message is based on a divine calling (because I am an Apostle), therefore my message ought to be highly regarded as an Apostle. Yet Paul renders his argument as such: my message is based on a divine calling (because I am an Apostle), therefore my message ought to be highly regarded as a servant. These conclusions are related to Ethos as much as they are to Logos, and appearance of these examples is to be regarded as evidence that Paul is aware of typical rhetorical categories, though he subverts what is typical.

Conclusions

In this chapter, we have sought to establish a number of things. The first is that Paul returned to Tarsus after a negative interaction with certain Hellenistic Jews. We argue that Paul used this time to hone his rhetorical skill and thereby establish himself as a rhetorician. This is plausible since, after his time in Tarsus, Paul began to preach to the Greek population of Antioch and establish the church there, after which he began his missionary journeys through Greece.

The second point that we have established is that Tarsus had become a center for rhetorical training by the time of Paul's arrival. Athenodorus had established the city as one that was operated by the university, and a number of well-known teachers of rhetoric had come there. What is more, these teachers, who were mostly Stoic philosophers, were versed in Aristotelian categories of rhetoric as described in the *Rhetoric*. It is therefore plausible that Paul spent time learning from these teachers and became well aware of Aristotelian rhetoric.

The third is that elements of Ethos, Pathos, and Logos—each described by Aristotle in his *Rhetoric*—are used by Paul in his letters. We used examples from Acts, Romans, Galatians, and 1 Corinthians to show that Paul made use of each of the categories; however, he subverted the typical usage of these categories. Though many scholars have noted the existence of these categories in Paul's letters, our position is that Paul showcased his knowledge of Aristotle through his subversion: a process that could only happen if Paul had become educated in Aristotelian rhetoric.

8

Early Christian "Binding Spells"? The Formulas in 1 Cor. 12:3 Read against the Background of Ancient Curse Tablets

Susanne Luther

The Use of Spells and Curses in Antiquity

Curses or binding spells were frequently used in antiquity[1] to assert a person's wishes and claims by trying to control opponents and competitors by inflicting physical, emotional, intellectual, or spiritual harm or even death.[2] Curse texts were written on a variety of materials, for example, papyrus, ostraca, shells, or metal sheets.[3] Curses and binding spells were also used in the form of inscriptions on buildings, boundary stones, grave epitaphs, or votive offerings. Of special interest in this chapter is a corpus of texts so far widely neglected in New Testament Studies: the *defixionum tabellae*, short *defixiones*, ancient curse tablets—thin lead tablets inscribed with curses, which were rolled up or folded, sometimes pierced by nails or needles, and often buried near shrines or temples or deposited in graves or wells.[4] The lead itself, originally simply a cheap writing material, became a carrier of meaning over time, for the cold of the lead, its weight, and its property of being easily meltable, for example, are associated with the desired magical effect on the victim.[5]

---

[1] For a more extensive overview of ancient curse tablets, cf. the introductory chapter entitled "*defixiones* und das Neue Testament: Definitionen—Realien—Problemfelder," in Michael Hölscher, Markus Lau, and Susanne Luther (eds.), *Antike Fluchtafeln und das Neue Testament. Materialität—Ritualpraxis—Texte*, WUNT (Tübingen: Mohr Siebeck, forthcoming).

[2] John Fotopoulos, "Paul's Curse of Corinthians: Restraining Rivals with Fear and *Voces Mysticae* (1 Cor 16:22)," *NovT* 56 (2014): 275–309, here 276.

[3] Cf. Kirsten Dzwiza, *Schriftverwendung in antiker Ritualpraxis anhand der griechischen, demotischen und koptischen Praxisanleitungen des 1.–7. Jahrhunderts*, Band I: Textteil (PhD dissertation, Erfurt, 2014), 53–66; Karl Preisendanz, "Fluchtafel (Defixion)," *RAC* 8 (1972): 1–29, here 3–4.

[4] Cf. Preisendanz, *Fluchtafel*, 5.

[5] Cf. Amina Kropp, *Defixiones: dfx. Ein aktuelles Corpus lateinischer Fluchtafeln* (Speyer: Kartoffeldruck-Verlag, 2008), no. 8.3/1: "Quom]od<o> i[l]<l>e plu<m>bus po<n>dus h<a>bet, sic et [E]ud<e>mus h<a>beat v[o]s iratus. Inter la<r>vas [---]ate ia<m> hostiat quam celeris<s>im<e>m[---]" ("As this lead has heaviness, so shall Eudemus experience your [heavy] anger and be with the spirits of the dead as soon as possible").

Curse tablets, a sort of miniature inscriptions,[6] were used in the context of black magic. As the terminology of the curse texts suggests, they were meant to bind (Greek: καταδέω), ban, or pierce (Latin: *defigere*) people through the words written on the tablet.[7] The recurrent threefold structure of the curses indicates a main agent, who performs an action in order to manipulate a target.[8] The Latin term *defixio* appears only in the sources from the sixth century CE onward, but today usually serves as a technical term for the Latin as well as the Greek practice of black magic by means of magical texts written on lead tablets.[9] Roughly two-thirds of the texts were written in Greek and one-third in Latin,[10] but they also used foreign languages or magical words and phrases (*barbara onomata* or *voces mysticae*)—either of them unintelligible to the reader but supposedly intelligible to the gods or spirits addressed.[11]

The aim of the ritual connected with these texts was to ban people with the help of divine and underworld powers and thus gain power, for example, over their lives, health, and wealth. Curse tablets are thus not expressions of spontaneous cursing but rather the material remains of a multistep process of a cursing ritual.[12] The rituals could be performed in a variety of ways: Curses could be uttered privately or publicly, individually or collectively, they could be formulated in an unspecific, general way or name specific misfortunes that were to happen to the target. Moreover, curse tablets were used in a broad variety of contexts, in legal and political disputes,[13] in matters

---

[6] Amina Kropp, *Magische Sprachverwendung in vulgärlateinischen Fluchtafeln (defixiones)*, ScriptOralia 135 (Tübingen: Gunter Narr Verlag, 2008), 19.

[7] Cf. Preisendanz, *Fluchtafel*, 1–2; Kropp, *Magische Sprachverwendung in vulgärlateinischen Fluchtafeln (defixiones)*, 39–41.

[8] Cf. John G. Gager, *Curse Tablets and Binding Spells from the Ancient World* (New York: Oxford University Press, 1992), 13–14, for typical structures of curse formulas.

[9] For the use of the terminology, cf. Preisendanz, *Fluchtafel*, 1–2; Kropp, *Magische Sprachverwendung in vulgärlateinischen Fluchtafeln (defixiones)*, 37–43.

[10] Cf. Jürgen Blänsdorf, "Die Verfluchungstäfelchen des Mainzer Isis- und Mater-Magna-Heiligtums," *Der altsprachliche Unterricht* 51 (2008): 68–70, 68; cf. also Kropp, *Magische Sprachverwendung in vulgärlateinischen Fluchtafeln (defixiones)*, 45.

[11] Fotopoulos, "Paul's Curse of Corinthians," esp. 282–9 and 304–6.

[12] Cf. Kropp, *Magische Sprachverwendung in vulgärlateinischen Fluchtafeln (defixiones)*, 104–5; cf., for example, the tablet that names the piercing and killing of a puppy just as the intended target is pierced and so on in Auguste Audollent, *Defixionum tabellae quotquot innotuerunt tam in Graecis Orientis quam in totius Occidentis partibus praeter Atticas in Corpore inscriptionum Atticarum editas* (Frankfurt a. M.: Minerva, 1967), nos. 111–12; translation in Gager, *Curse Tablets and Binding Spells*, 143–4, no. 53. First tablet:

> I denounce the persons written below, Lentinus and Tasgillus, in order that they may depart from here for Pluto and Persephone. Just as this puppy harmed no one, so (may they harm no one) and may they not be able to win this suit; just as the mother of this puppy cannot defend it, so may their lawyers be unable to defend them, (and) so (may) those (legal) opponents

Second tablet:

> be turned back from this suit; just as this puppy is (turned) on its back and is unable to rise, so neither (may) they; they are pierced through, just as this is; just as in this tomb animals/ souls have been transformed/silenced and cannot rise up, and they (can)not … [the rest is unreadable].

[13] Cf., for example, Gager, *Curse Tablets and Binding Spells*, 141–2, no. 51. Side A: "I inscribe Selinontios and the tongue of Selinontios, twisted to the point of uselessness for them. And I inscribe, twisted to the point of uselessness, the tongues of the foreign witnesses"; Side B: "I inscribe Timasoi and the

of love and marriage,[14] in business matters,[15] in case of loss or theft[16] as well as in sports competitions.[17] They were used by pagans, Jews, and Christians over almost a millennium (sixth century BCE–fifth century CE) throughout a vast geographical area of the ancient Near East, Egypt, and the Greco-Roman world.[18] Roughly seventeen hundred κατάδεσμοι or *defixiones* have been discovered from the ancient world,[19] most of them date to the period from the fifth century BCE to the second century CE.[20] Ancient literature testifies to the fact that the fear of harmful spells was widespread in ancient society,[21] especially as curses could not be taken back; they could only be countered, for example, by antidotes such as counterspells, amulets, or prayers.[22]

Ancient curse tablets—although so far widely neglected in New Testament study—are of special interest to New Testament scholars as a number of New Testament texts betray a close connection to formulas used on ancient *defixiones*. However, those curse formulations are used in the New Testament in a distinctively different context and with a clearly different purpose. This chapter will focus on curse formulas using ἀνάθεμα κτλ., which are found on ancient curse tablets and in the New Testament, by first exploring speech-ethical aspects of the use of curse language in the New

tongue of Timasoi, twisted to the point of uselessness. I inscribe Turrana and the tongue of Turrana, twisted to the point of uselessness for all of them." Cf. also, for example, ibid., 144–5, no. 54.

> Make Akeilios Phausteinos and Stephanos, my opponents in the matter concerning the slaves and concerning the personal property and concerning the papers and concerning the things of which they might accuse me; and concerning these matters may they neither think (about them) nor remember (them); and cool off their mind, their soul, and their passion, from today and from this very hour and for the entire time of (their) life.

[14] Cf., for example, ibid., 92, no. 25:

> I turn away Euboles from Aineas, from his face, from his eyes, from his mouth, from his breasts, from his soul, from his belly, from his penis, from his anus, from his entire body. I turn away Euboles from Aineas.

[15] Cf., for example, ibid., 159–60, no. 66:

> I have seized Mikiôn and bound his hands and feet and tongue and soul; and if he is in any way about to utter a harsh word about Philôn … may his tongue become lead. And stab his tongue, and if he is in any way about to do business, may it be unprofitable for him, and may everything be lost, stripped away, and destroyed.

[16] Cf., for example, Roger S. O. Tomlin, "The Curse Tablets," in Barry Cunliffe (ed.), *The Temple of Sulis Minerva at Bath*, vol. 2: The Finds from the Sacred Spring; Oxford University Committee for Archaeology Monograph Series 7 (Oxford: Oxford University School of Archaeology, 1988), 59–277, no. 10:

> Docilianus (son) of Brucerus (Brucetus?) to the most holy goddess Sulis. I curse him who has stolen my hooded cloak, whether man or woman, whether free or slave, that … the goddess Sulis inflict death upon … and not allow him sleep or children now and in the future, until he has brought my hooded cloak to the temple of her divinity.

[17] Cf. Gager, *Curse Tablets and Binding Spells*, 42–199.
[18] Cf. Kropp, *Magische Sprachverwendung in vulgärlateinischen Fluchtafeln (defixiones)*, 43–6.
[19] Cf., for example, the online database http://www.thedema.ovgu.de/.
[20] Fotopoulos, "Paul's Curse of Corinthians," 276–83.
[21] Cf., for example, Pliny, *Nat. hist.* 28.4.19; cf. further Christopher A. Faraone, "Aeschylus' ὕμνος δέσμιος (Eum. 306) and Attic Judicial Curse Tablets," *JHS* 105 (1985): 150–4; "The Agonistic Context of Early Greek Binding Spells," in Christopher A. Faraone and Dirk Obbink (eds.), *Magika Hiera: Ancient Greek Magic and Religion* (New York: Oxford University Press, 1997), 3–32.
[22] Cf. Gager, *Curse Tablets and Binding Spells*, 218–42.

Testament in general. Then the argumentation focuses on the specific use of ἀνάθεμα κτλ. on ancient curse tablets and in the Pauline letters, where forms of *reception* as well as of *transformation* can be detected. The results allow for inferences regarding the use of early Christian curse formulations in ecclesiological and sacramental contexts, and their role as defining markers of early Christian identity over against pagan magical practices.

Speech-Ethics and the Reference to Cursing in the New Testament

In the New Testament, cursing is usually mentioned in vice catalogues enumerating those forms of human speech that are prevalent in the early Christian communities, but are not desired, just like slanderous, lying, angry, or deceitful speech.[23] The author of the Letter of James, for example, instructs his readers with a view to cursing: "but no human being can tame the tongue, a restless evil, full of deadly poison. With it we bless the Lord and Father, and with it we curse (καταρώμεθα) the human beings who are made in the likeness of God. From the same mouth go forth blessing and cursing (κατάρα). My brothers, this ought not to be so" (Jas 3:8-10).[24] The New Testament writings repeatedly remind the addressees that their speech should be truthful (e.g., λαλεῖτε ἀλήθειαν ἕκαστος μετὰ τοῦ πλησίον αὐτοῦ; Eph. 4:25) and credible (πιστὰς ἐν πᾶσιν; 1 Tim. 3:11), that they are to be role models in the use of speech (τύπος γίνου τῶν πιστῶν ἐν λόγῳ; 1 Tim. 4:12), and their mere word—without the reinforcement by means of oaths—should suffice (ἐγὼ δὲ λέγω ὑμῖν μὴ ὀμόσαι ὅλως· ... ἔστω δὲ ὁ λόγος ὑμῶν ναί ναί, οὒ οὔ· τὸ δὲ περισσὸν τούτων ἐκ τοῦ πονηροῦ ἐστιν; Mt. 5:33-37; cf. Jas 5:12). The New Testament texts, in particular the Gospel of Matthew and the Letter of James, show a clear tendency to condemn inadequate language in general and cursing in particular and warn of the eschatological judgment for the violation of speech-ethical norms.[25]

Focusing on the Pauline letter it becomes evident that—as in other New Testament writings—speech-ethical admonitions are aimed at preventing the use of cursing and curse language. In Rom. 12:14 the author formulates a clear admonition: "Bless those who persecute you; bless and do not curse (them)" (εὐλογεῖτε τοὺς διώκοντας [ὑμᾶς], εὐλογεῖτε καὶ μὴ καταρᾶσθε). However, Paul's letters likewise indicate that the Pauline congregations were not only familiar with the practice of cursing and the use of curse language but that both were actually elements of and means toward the early Christian groups' identity construction. Paul is, for example, familiar with the idea that people are handed over into the hands of a god or demon: in 1 Cor. 5:5 the apostle proposes that the sinner be expelled from the community by the people who are gathered "in the

---

[23] Cf. Susanne Luther, *Sprachethik im Neuen Testament: Eine Analyse des Frühchristlichen Diskurses im Matthäusevangelium, im Jakobusbrief und im 1. Petrusbrief*, WUNT II/394 (Tübingen: Mohr Siebeck, 2015), 12–13 and 187–246.
[24] Translations here and in the following are my own.
[25] Cf. ibid., *passim*.

name of the Lord" (ἐν τῷ ὀνόματι τοῦ κυρίου [ἡμῶν] Ἰησοῦ) by way of being handed over to Satan (παραδοῦναι … τῷ σατανᾷ) for the destruction of the flesh (εἰς ὄλεθρον τῆς σαρκός), however, with the aim of saving the culprit on the day of the Lord (ἵνα τὸ πνεῦμα σωθῇ ἐν τῇ ἡμέρᾳ τοῦ κυρίου).[26] Adolf Deissmann has already pointed out the allusion to the ancient practice of cursing, which can be found in this passage, where Satan is named instead of an underworld deity of the pagan context.[27] What is striking here is that Paul does not criticize or at least problematize this way of dealing with the situation. Rather, he positively propagates this course of action in the case of ethical misconduct in the congregation and recommends it to demarcate the boundaries of ethical conduct in the Corinthian community.

These examples show a remarkable discrepancy between the "rejection" and forms of "reception" of curse traditions, which is particularly striking in the Pauline writings. On the one hand Paul criticizes and prohibits cursing and regards it as behavior that does not befit those who possess the Spirit of God (Rom. 12:14; cf. also 1 Cor. 12:3), but on the other hand the texts indicate that he as well as his communities have taken up elements of the ancient practice of cursing in their everyday life and speech (1 Cor. 5:5; cf. also Gal. 1:8-9; 1 Cor. 12:2-3, 16:21-22). This seems to indicate that Paul does not generally condemn cursing. The thesis to be proposed in the following derives from this discrepancy: While the "reception" of the curse tradition from the pagan context is evident from the Pauline letters, there are also indications of a "transformation" of the tradition into positive forms of "binding-spells" for use within the Pauline communities. While Paul, for example, receives the tradition of binding a person *down* to an underworld deity (1 Cor. 5:5), his writings also show that he transforms this tradition into a "binding-spell" that binds a person *into* Christ (1 Cor. 12:2-3). This thesis will be argued by focusing on the curse formula ἀνάθεμα.

---

[26] Cf. Jan Dochhorn, "Die Bestrafung des Unzuchtsünders in 1. Kor 5,5. Satanologische, anthropologische und theologische Implikationen," in Jan Dochhorn, Susanne Rudnig-Zelt, and Benjamin Wold (eds.), *Das Böse, der Teufel und Dämonen—Evil, the Devil, and Demons*, WUNT II/412 (Tübingen: Mohr Siebeck, 2016), 127–51. Dochhorn interprets this act in relation "zur kirchlichen und göttlichen Gerichtsbarkeit" (129), with the purpose of removing the sinner from the community through "einen gemeindlichen Rechtsakt":

> In 5,12–13a ist deutlich von einem, "Richten" (κρίνειν) der Gemeinde die Rede. Dieses Richten läuft auf den Ausschluß des Inzestsünders aus der Gemeinde hinaus (5,2.13b). Von diesem aber hieß es auch, daß er dem Satan übergeben werden sollte (5,5). Ein Unterschied zwischen beiden Aktionen wird nicht erkennbar, und so legt sich die Annahme nahe, daß der Ausschluß aus der Gemeinde und die Übergabe an den Satan ein- und dasselbe sind. (130)

Satan is read in analogy with the ὀλεθρεύων (Exod. 12:23) of the Passah tradition, but regards the Satan in this context as an agent of God, for "er agiert hier erkennbar im Rahmen eines von Gott gesetzten Geschehens. Durch ihn wird das Gemeindegericht, das in 1. Kor 5,12-3 mit dem Gottesgericht parallelisiert wird, faktisch wirksam" (149).

[27] Adolf Deissmann, *Light from the Ancient East: The New Testament Illustrated by Recently Discovered Texts from the Graeco-Roman World* (London: Hodder and Stoughton, 1910), 303–4; cf., for an interpretation of the text in this perspective, Peter Busch, "Christlich korrekt verfluchen in Korinth: 1 Kor 5 und die 'Gebete um Gerechtigkeit,'" in Michael Hölscher, Markus Lau, and Susanne Luther (eds.), *Antike Fluchtafeln und das Neue Testament. Materialität—Ritualpraxis—Texte*, WUNT (Tübingen: Mohr Siebeck, forthcoming).

The Use of ἀνάθεμα κτλ. in Ancient Curse Tablets

ἀνάθεμα, the Hellenistic form of ἀνάθημα, is repeatedly used in the Pauline letters. The term ἀνάθημα/ἀνάθεμα refers originally to "something dedicated or consecrated to the deity,"[28] but in classical Greek it denotes primarily the votive offering dedicated to a deity (given in a temple)—in this meaning it occurs, for example, in Lk. 23:5, but also repeatedly on ancient curse tablets.[29] In the LXX and in early Jewish literature the term stands mostly for חרם (*herem*) and designates "something delivered up to divine wrath, dedicated to destruction and brought under a curse";[30] ἀναθεματίζω designates the speech act by which something is anathematized or cursed.[31] The use of the terminology in the New Testament is based on its use in the LXX and early Jewish literature,[32] where ἀνάθεμα κτλ. bears a negative connotation in the sense of a curse or a self-cursing or self-binding action that often serves to reinforce one's words (e.g., Mk 14:71; Acts 23:12, 14, 21; Rom. 9:3). In this meaning it can also be found in the context of ancient *defixiones*, where the formula ἀνάθεμα is, for example, documented on a curse tablet from the first or second century CE found in Megara; ἀναθεματίζω is used twice in this text and ἀνάθεμα can be found at the end, in each case with the meaning "cursing" or "curse":[33]

ζωαφερ τὸν θαλασσσημον σεκντηαπαφονοχαι παιδικὸν Πανα[ίτι]ον ἐγγαμμένον κεχαιαμ [. κα]ταγράφομεν τοὺς εκαιπην ... ει τους αὐτὰ καὶ **ἀναθεματίζ[ομ]εν** αὐτούς. Ἀλθαία Κόρη ὀρεο[βαζ]αγρα Ἑκάτη ἀκρουροβορη Σελή[νη]. ιθιβι ... μη. τούτους **ἀναθεμα[τι]ζομεν**· σῶμα πνεῦμα ψ[υ]χὴν [δι]άνοιαν φρόνησιν αἴσθησιν ζοὴν [καρδ]ίαν λόγοις Ἑκατικίοις ὁρκίσμ[ασί]τε αβραικοις. ... κον δίκαι τ ... ους Γῆ Ἑκάτη ... ους [κ]ελευόμενοι ὑπ[ὸ] τῶν ἱερῶν ὀνομ[ά]των αβραικωντε ὁρκισμάτων· τρίχας κεφαλὴν ἐνκέφαλον [πρόσω]πον ἀκοὰς ὀφρ[ῦς] μυκτῆρας

---

[28] Cf. Johannes Behm, "ἀνάθεμα κτλ," *TDNT* 1 (1964), 354–5, 354.

[29] Cf. here Katell Berthelot, "The Notion of Anathema in Ancient Jewish Literature Written in Greek," in Eberhard Bons, Ralph Brucker, and Jan Joosten (eds.), *The Reception of Septuagint Words in Jewish-Hellenistic and Christian Literature*, WUNT II/367 (Tübingen: Mohr Siebeck, 2014), 35–52, esp. 36–40; texts, for example, in Audollent, *Defixionum tabellae*, nos. 35, 37. Nancy Pardee, "'The Curse That Saves' (Didache 16.5)," in Clayton N. Jefford (ed.), *The Didache in Context: Essays on Its Text, History and Transmission*, NovTSup 77 (Leiden: Brill, 1995), 156–76, 161, reckons with a Jewish curse formula or one influenced by Judaism, since the words ἀδωνεία and Ιαω appear in the text.

[30] Cf. Johannes Behm, "ἀναθεματίζω κτλ," *TDNT* 1 (1964), 355–6, 354; cf. also Stefan Koch, *Rechtliche Regelung von Konflikten im frühen Christentum*, WUNT II/174 (Tübingen: Mohr Siebeck, 2004), 161–2.

[31] Cf. Behm, "ἀναθεματίζω κτλ," 355–6; cf. Berthelot, "The Notion of Anathema in Ancient Jewish Literature Written in Greek," 40–6, for the use of the term in the LXX, esp. 46: "In the Septuagint, ἀνάθεμα has to a great extent freed itself from its Greek meaning and has become a semantic neologism or a semantic Hebraism, that is, a Greek term with a meaning that so far existed only in its Hebrew counterpart." In early Jewish literature, the Greek-Hellenistic meaning seems to have prevailed. Cf. Berthelot, "The Notion of Anathema in Ancient Jewish Literature Written in Greek," 46–50.

[32] Cf. Berthelot, "The Notion of Anathema in Ancient Jewish Literature Written in Greek," 50–1.

[33] Concerning the dating, cf. Pardee, "The Curse That Saves," 159. Fotopoulos, "Paul's Curse of Corinthians," 300; and Gager, *Curse Tablets and Binding Spells*, 183–4, however, date the curse tablet to the second century. Cf. also Adolf Deissmann, "Anathema," *ZNW* 2 (1901): 342.

οι … πρὸ σιαγόνας ὀδόντα[ς] … ψυχὴν στοναχεῖν ὑγεία[ν] … τὸν αἷμα σάρκας
κατακάει[νστον]αχεῖ ὃ πάσχοι καί … ἐπιορκίζω … καὶ τὴν [τ-]ριώνυ[μο]ν
Σε[λήνην …] καὶ α … σαι νύκτιον μέσον ὅταν τὸν [… σ]τρέφῃς καὶ τὰ θειάων
περιπ … ν οὐρανοδρόμε καρτερόχ[ειρ] θεωρητὲ κυανόπεπλε κα … οπετ…κατὰ
γῆν καὶ κατὰ [θά]λασ(σ)αν ἡ Εἰνοδ[ία ?] ἐνωνπα[ρατίτ]ομεν τούτο[υς] τοὺς κατὰ
… του α … κηκου … φανι. [κατα]γρά[φ]ομεν [εἰς] κολάσε[ις …] καὶ [ποι]νὴν καὶ
[τι]μ[ωρ]ί[αν] ες παρὰ … περὶ τῶν π … εχα τὸ σῶμα. **Ἀνέθεμα.**

(ZÔAPHER TON THALLASSOSÊMON SEKNTÊAPAPHONOCHAI the beloved child Panaitios inscribed (here?) ECHAIPEN … **We curse** those EPAIPÊN … them and we anathematize them. Althaia, Kore, OREOBAZAGRA Hekate Moon who devours its tail … ITHIBI … **we anathematize** them—body, spirit, soul, mind, thought, feeling, life, heart—with Hekatean words and Hebrew oaths … Earth Hekate … commanded by the holy names and oaths of the Hebrews—hair, head, brain, face, ears, eyebrows, nostrils … jaws, teeth … so that their soul may sigh, their health may …, their blood (and) flesh may burn and (let) him/her sigh with what he/she suffers" I invoke … also Moon, the triple-named, who (circulates?) in the middle of the night whenever the … walk about, who courses the heavens with a strong hand, the visible one with the dark-blue mantle … on land and sea, Einodia (?) …, we anathematize (?) them … and enroll them for punishments, pain and retribution … the body. **Anathema.**)[34]

A group of *defixiones* from Knidos in Asia Minor dating to the second to first century BCE uses the verb ἀνατίθημι.[35] These are tablets that were probably publicly displayed in the shrine of the Demeter and Kore, as indicated by the holes on the upper side of the tablet and the instructions in the text to return stolen or lost goods.[36] The verso of one of the tablets reads:

[ἀνατίθη]μι Ἁ[γ]εμόν[η] τὴν σπατάλην, ἣν ἀπώλεσα [ἐν]
[τοῖς κή]ποις τοῖς Ῥοδοκλεῦς, Δάματρι καὶ Κούραι καὶ θεοῖς [π]ᾶσ[ι]
[καὶ πάσ]αις· ἀποδόντι μὲν [ὅ]σια καὶ ἐλεύθερα, <καὶ> κομισαμένοις τ[ὸ]
[κόμισ]τρον, καὶ ἐμοὶ τῆι κομιζομένηι καὶ τῶι ἀποδιδόντι· [μὴ]
[ἀπ]οδιδόντι δὲ Δάματρος καὶ Κούρας καὶ θεῶν τῶν π[α]-
[ρὰ Δ]άματρι καὶ Κούρᾳ πάντων καὶ πασᾶν, καὶ εἴ που πρ[α]-
θῆι, ἐνθύμιον ἔστω Δάματρος καὶ Κούρας· **ἀνατίθημι** δὲ κ[αὶ]
[ὅτ]ωι πλέον ἐξέτεισα παρὰ τὸν σταθμὸν τὸν ὑπ' ἐμοῦ ἐξητ[η]-
μένον Δάματρι καὶ Κούραι· δέσποινα, ἐμοὶ δὲ
ὅσια

---

[34] For the Greek text, cf. Audollent, *Defixionum tabellae*, no. 41; for the translation, cf. Gager, *Curse Tablets and Binding Spells*, 183–4, no. 85. I have added bold font to the Greek and to the English translation.

[35] Texts in Audollent, *Defixionum tabellae*, no. 1–13; further cf. Wolfgang Blümel, *Die Inschriften von Knidos* (Bonn: R. Habelt, 1992), 85; texts in Blümel, *Die Inschriften von Knidos*, nos 147–59; cf. Pardee, "The Curse That Saves," 161.

[36] It is disputed whether these holes indicate that they were hung on a wall or whether they are proof of a piercing of the writing material in connection with the curse ritual, cf. Blümel, *Die Inschriften von Knidos*, 85.

ἀνατίθημι Δάματρι καὶ Κόραι τὸν τὴ-
ν οἰκία μου ἀκατά<σ>τατον ποιοῦτα καὶ αὐτὸ[ν]
κα<ὶ> νῦν καὶ τὰ ἐ<κ>είν[ο]υ πάντα· ἐμοὶ δὲ
[ὅ]σια καὶ ἐλε[ύ]θε[ρ]α ᾗ πάντως³⁷

In Blümel's edition of the text ἀνατίθημι on these tablets is translated as "Ich deponiere … den Fluch gegen," that is, "I deposit the curse against …."³⁸

Literature on the Pauline writings has repeatedly referenced the correspondence between Paul's use of the terminology and the use in the LXX and in early Jewish literature. This tradition-historical link is certainly not to be debated. Nevertheless, the following argumentation will focus solely on the references between the Pauline texts and ancient curse tablets, in order to consider whether this specific background in Greco-Roman religious practices can provide a deeper insight or a new focus for the interpretation of the Pauline text.

Elements of Reception: Ancient Curse Traditions in the Pauline Correspondence

Beyond the use of ἀνάθεμα κτλ. as referring to votive offerings or cursing in general, the New Testament also knows the use of the terminology in the form of curse formulas. Especially the Pauline writings are indicative of this particular use of the terminology. In Gal. 1:8-9 the apostle advises the addressees that "even if we, or an angel from heaven, should preach to you a gospel contrary to that which we preached to you, let him be cursed (ἀνάθεμα ἔστω). As we have said before, so now I say again: if anyone is preaching to you a gospel contrary to that which you received, let him be cursed (ἀνάθεμα ἔστω)." The first sentence is mostly considered as an *eventualis* or *irrealis*, the second as an effective *realis*.³⁹ The particular formulaic ending of each sentence can be read as a threat of banishment or of a verdict, which puts anyone who opposes the right teaching conveyed by the apostle under a curse; the specific form of this threat

---

³⁷ Blümel, *Die Inschriften von Knidos*, 92–4, no. 150, text on p. 93 (verso).
³⁸ Cf. ibid., 94; cf. further Pardee, "The Curse That Saves," 158–67, who states:

> From the combined evidence it is clear that at some point the word ἀνάθεμα developed beyond its original meaning of "offering" eventually to include the semantic field of cursing as well, that is, a "negative" side. From the evidence it also seems reasonable to conjecture that this development took place within the Jewish milieu. … The verb ἀνατίθημι which is used in the context of eliciting the aid of an underworld deity(-ies) against one's enemies, that is, with a negative meaning, is found only in several of the curse tablets from Cnidus …. The Septuagint, however, knows the verb ἀνατίθημι only in the original, positive sense. And never is a negative meaning for the noun ἀνάθεμα, nor is the verb ἀναθεματίζω itself, found earlier than the occurrences in the Septuagint. Thus the occurrence of the term ἀνάθεμα in a negative sense outside of Judeo-Christian literature is rare and late (Megara, first-second centuries C.E.; Amathous, third century C.E.?), while the negative meaning for the verb ἀνατίθημι in both literatures is peculiar to a single site. (167)

³⁹ Cf. Hans Dieter Betz, *Der Galaterbrief: Ein Kommentar zum Brief des Apostels Paulus an die Gemeinden in Galatien*, Hermeneia (München: Kaiser, 1988), 111.

is a conditional curse formula, which serves as a dramatic warning and intends to prevent conflict.⁴⁰

A similar conditional use of curse language can be found in Paul's autograph in 1 Cor. 16:21-22: "I, Paul, write this greeting with my own hand. If anyone does not love the Lord, let him be cursed [ἤτω ἀνάθεμα]." And he adds: μαράνα θά. Usually the Aramaic μαράνα θά is read here as a liturgical formula commonly used in the early church,⁴¹ but also—when read as an element of a curse or ban—as a request or prayer for justice in the eschatological judgment.⁴² The fact that in the Pauline text the curse formula is combined with these untranslated⁴³ and for the Corinthian addressees possibly unintelligible Aramaic words betrays a close parallel to ancient curse tablets. As John Fotopoulos has pointed out with reference to the *defixiones*, foreign, non-Greek words, βάρβαρα ὀνόματα, which were often taken from Hebrew, Aramaic, Coptic, or other ancient languages, were thought to be very powerful as they were—at least in the eyes of the majority of the Greek-speaking population—only understandable to the spirits addressed.⁴⁴ In the first century CE these *voces mysticae* were frequently used on curse tablets, amulets, or magical papyri particularly in pagan use. Moreover, not only the linguistic form, but also the content of these Aramaic words used by Paul—μαράνα θά—aligns with the ancient practice of calling on the gods to come and grant or fulfill a curse.⁴⁵

Hence, Paul's use of curse formulas in these examples remains within the common usage in Antiquity; the conditional curses are directed against those who defy the truth of the gospel he preaches and against those who attempt to corrupt the early Christian

---

⁴⁰ Koch, *Rechtliche Regelung*, 162, defines these sentences as "kasuistische Rechtssätze"; basically it can be stated that

> Der Fluch ist quasi eine ultima ratio der Rechtsprechung, die von Gott die Wahrung der Rechtsordnung erwartet. Funktion solcher ultima ratio samt der mit ihr verbundenen Drohung dürfte zudem der Versuch sein, Konflikte erst gar nicht zum Austrag kommen zu lassen, sondern sie möglichst zu vermeiden, indem mit einem Fluch über jeden potentiellen Täter gedroht wird. (163)

Cf. also ibid. (168-71); cf. further Kjell A. Morland, *The Rhetoric of Curse in Galatians: Paul Confronts another Gospel*, Emory Studies in Early Christianity 5 (Atlanta, GA: Scholars, 1995), 239. Cf. also in this respect Paul's conditional self-cursing in Rom. 9:3.

⁴¹ Cf. G. Bornkamm, "Zum Verständnis des Gottesdienstes bei Paulus," in *Das Ende des Gesetzes: Paulusstudien*, BEvT 16 (Munich: Kaiser, 1952), 113-32, here 124; cf. also Karl Georg Kuhn, "μαραναθά κτλ.," *TDNT* 4 (1967), 466-72, 469-70: "Linguistic research thus offers three equally possible meanings of μαραναθά: 1. The prayer 'Lord, come' as a petition for the parousia; 2. the confession 'our Lord has come' (into the world in lowliness), 3. The statement 'our Lord is now present' (i.e., in worship, and especially the Lord's Supper)."

⁴² For a discussion of form, composition, and traditions, cf. Wolfgang Schrage, *Der erste Brief an die Korinther*, EKKNT VII/4 (Zürich: Benziger, 2001), 464-5, 472-3.

⁴³ In other verses Paul adds a translation; cf. Rom. 8:15; Gal. 4:6; Hans-Josef Klauck, *Herrenmahl Und Hellenistischer Kult: Eine Religionsgeschichtliche Untersuchung Zum Ersten Korintherbrief*, NTAbh 15 (Münster: Aschendorff, 1986), 358-9, who also interprets these untranslated words in the syncretistic context of early Christianity.

⁴⁴ Cf. Fotopoulos, "Paul's Curse of Corinthians," 282-9, 303-8.

⁴⁵ Cf. Koch, *Rechtliche Regelung*, 166, who states that the combination of the letter ending and the curse indicates that "der mit dem Gebetsruf herbeigerufene kommende Herr ... den Fluch am Verfluchten Wirklichkeit werden lassen [wird]." Cf. also David E. Aune, "The Apocalypse of John and Graeco-Roman Revelatory Magic," *NTS* 33 (1987): 481-501, 491-3.

communities. They serve to corroborate his epistolary argumentation or are intended as a strategy of preventing conflicts by deterring misconduct and apprehending wrongdoing. Curses are also used as a warning from or even defense against any danger from outsiders, from false teachers and opponents. Hence, the Pauline use of the curse formula ἀνάθεμα and its formulaic context displays a number of similarities with written and spoken curses in the Greco-Roman world and presupposes that the apostle's addressees were familiar with the ancient curse practice; they may even have engaged in it themselves. The popularity of the curse practice in the world of Paul's addressees is supported by thirty-eight curse tablets—many dating from the first century CE—that have been found in ancient Corinth.[46]

Elements of Transformation: A Pauline "Binding Formula" in 1 Corinthians?

The key text, which shows the *transformative* reception of the ancient curse practice in Paul, is 1 Cor. 12:2-3: "You know that when you were still pagans, you were drawn with force to mute idols. Therefore I will let you know: No one who speaks in the Spirit of God says, 'Jesus be cursed,' and no one can say, 'Jesus is Lord,' except in the Holy Spirit."[47] The verses offer a juxtaposition of two formulaic statements, the formula ἀνάθεμα Ἰησοῦς = "cursed be Jesus!" and the formula κύριος Ἰησοῦς = "Jesus is Lord," whereby only those who do not have the Spirit of God can curse Jesus, but only those who have the Spirit can pronounce the κύριος formula. The use of the curse formula with respect to Jesus has therefore often been considered as a criterion by which one can recognize a person's affiliation or nonaffiliation with the Christian community, a criterion by which one can distinguish between those who possess the Spirit and those who do not.[48] It is worth noting that Paul does not prohibit or criticize the curse formula itself, but merely classifies it as an identification marker. That the first formula represents a curse seems obvious against the background of the ancient *defixiones*; usually the formula is translated in exegetical literature as "cursed be Jesus" or "Jesus is a curse."[49] Bruce Winter has presented another translation of the phrase with reference to the ancient practice of cursing:[50] his translation of ἀνάθεμα

---

[46] Cf. Fotopoulos, "Paul's Curse of Corinthians," 291–4.
[47] Ἐν is to be understood in the instrumental sense, not in the local; cf. Schrage, *Der erste Brief an die Korinther*, 123; Luise Schottroff, *Der erste Brief an die Gemeinde in Korinth*, THKNT 7 (Stuttgart: Kohlhammer, 2013), 241–2, who refers to a context where Christians cursed Jesus—the emperor cult, as mentioned in Pliny, *Ep.* 10.96; cf. also *Mart. Polyc.* 9. For Greek curse terminology, cf. Wolfgang Speyer, "Fluch," *RAC* VII (1969): 1160–288, esp. 1174–5.
[48] Cf. a critical reflection on this position in Schrage, *Der erste Brief an die Gemeinde in Korinth*, 124–5.
[49] This can be argued with a reference to Gal. 3:13: "Christ has redeemed us from the curse of the law by becoming a curse for us—for it is written: Cursed is everyone who hangs on wood" (Χριστὸς ἡμᾶς ἐξηγόρασεν ἐκ τῆς κατάρας τοῦ νόμου γενόμενος ὑπὲρ ἡμῶν κατάρα, ὅτι γέγραπται· ἐπικατάρατος πᾶς ὁ κρεμάμενος ἐπὶ ξύλου). However, this formula is difficult to explain but has been read, for example, as an ecstatic utterance. For an overview of different positions, see D. A. Carson, *Showing the Spirit: A Theological Exposition of 1 Corinthians 12–14* (Grand Rapids, MI: Baker, 1987), 27–30.
[50] Cf. Bruce W. Winter, *After Paul Left Corinth: The Influence of Secular Ethics and Social Change* (Grand Rapids, MI: Eerdmans, 2001).

Ἰησοῦς reads "Jesus [grants or gives] an anathema," based on an analogy with ancient curse tablets from Corinth, which also do not contain a verb.[51] In this rendering of the formula, Jesus would not be cursed like a human being but called upon as the God who causes the curse. Although Winter's translation is controversial, since ἀνάθεμα cannot be found on the Corinthian *defixiones* he used as comparative texts,[52] this does not fundamentally negate the possibility of his translation of the formula. But whether we now assume that the ancient hearers or readers of 1 Cor. 12:2-3, who were probably familiar with the ancient practice of cursing, understood the formula as Jesus causing a curse—for example, against the opponents of the community—or whether we adhere to the traditional translation, which reads ἀνάθεμα Ἰησοῦς as a curse directed toward Jesus, it is undisputed that we are dealing with a curse formula. From this perspective the question arises how the second formula, κύριος Ἰησοῦς, should to be read.

Based on its form and pragmatics the κύριος Ἰησοῦς formula is mostly interpreted as a creed or as a liturgical formula in exegetical literature.[53] In the following I do not want to suggest that these interpretations are incorrect; rather I want to open the text to a new interpretation and illustrate what an interpretation of 1 Cor. 12:3 against the background of ancient *defixiones* could accomplish for the understanding of the formula, that is, which connotations might have resonated in the κύριος Ἰησοῦς formula for those first listeners who were familiar with the ancient practice of cursing.

The structural juxtaposition of the two formulas in the Pauline argumentation suggests that the κύριος Ἰησοῦς formula has to be read in analogy with the ἀνάθεμα Ἰησοῦς formula.[54] If the latter is understood as a curse formula—either in line with Winter's interpretation or according to the conventional interpretation in scholarly exegesis—then the former has also got to be read in this context. This suggests that the κύριος Ἰησοῦς formula may be read as a "binding formula," in a pragmatical-functional analogy to the ἀνάθεμα Ἰησοῦς formula. The point of comparison then lies on a pragmatic or speech-act-theoretical level, not on the semantic or structural comparability of the two formulas. Paul's argumentation criticizes the use of the ἀνάθεμα Ἰησοῦς formula with reference to his addressees, but he commends the use of the κύριος Ἰησοῦς formula.

However, from the text in 1 Corinthians it remains unclear what this formula effects and in which contexts it might be used. But the literary context can provide clues to a possible interpretation of the formula as having an apotropaic or protective

---

[51] Ibid., 174–6. Winter bases his argument also on text-critical considerations; cf. ibid., 177.
[52] So the argumentation in David E. Garland, *1 Corinthians*, BECNT (Grand Rapids, MI: Baker Academic, 2003), 569. Following Garland, see also Joseph A. Fitzmyer, *First Corinthians: A New Translation with Introduction and Commentary*, AB 32 (New Haven, CT: Yale University Press, 2008), 456.
[53] Cf., for example, Koch, *Rechtliche Regelung*, 163–5, who speaks of the "Verfluchung als Gegenbekenntnis zum Christusbekenntnis" (173), thus indicating a self-exclusion from the congregation, for "Verfluchung und Kyriosbekenntnis schließen sich aus, das Kyriosbekenntnis ist aber konstitutiv für die Zugehörigkeit zur Gemeinde" (174); cf. also Fitzmyer, *First Corinthians*, 459.
[54] This has been called an "antithetische ... Analogiebildung des Paulus zum Bekenntnis κύριος Ἰησοῦς," cf. Schrage, *Der erste Brief an die Gemeinde in Korinth*, 116; or "an ad hoc construction on Paul's part to form an antithesis," Hans Conzelmann, *1 Corinthians*, Hermeneia (Philadelphia, PA: Fortress, 1975), 204.

function through the act of pronouncing the name of the Lord—κύριος Ἰησοῦς: first of all κύριος Ἰησοῦς is a name that was already used in early Christianity as a powerful formula. In the Synoptic Gospels there are narratives in which the name of Jesus plays a central role in the miraculous acts of the disciples (cf. Mt. 7:22; Lk. 10:17; Mk 16:17) or Jewish exorcists (cf. Mk 9:38-39; Lk. 9:49). In Acts, healings and exorcisms are accomplished through the pronouncement of the name of Jesus (cf., e.g., Acts 3:6, 16; 4:7, 10, 30; 16:18); Jas. 5:14 describes the practice or early Christian rite of performing healings through the "name of the Lord."[55] While in Acts the mere expressions "Jesus Christ" or "Jesus Christ of Nazareth" seem to have sufficed, the magic formulas of early Christianity grew in length in later manuscripts; for example, in the Old Latin variants of Acts 9:40 the formula is expanded to "*in nomine domini nostri Jesu Christi*," and in the time of Justin Martyr the phrase "crucified under Pontius Pilate" was added and introduced into the baptismal liturgy.[56] In later centuries the name of Jesus was regarded as so powerful that its use is documented on apotropaic amulets.[57] Even in the context of the pagan curse practice the name was received on curse tablets, for example, ὁρκίζω σε κατὰ τοῦ θεοῦ τῶν Ἑβραίων Ἰησοῦ Ἰαβα Ιαη Ἀβραωθ.[58] But as the increase in name components indicates, in the early days of Paul's writing to the Corinthians, the mere mention of the name κύριος Ἰησοῦς would have been enough to be understood as a magical formula.

[55] Cf. David E. Aune, "Magic in Early Christianity," *ANRW* II.23.2 (1980), 1507-7, here 1545; cf. also John A. Ziesler, "The Name of Jesus in the Acts of the Apostles," *JSNT* 4 (1974): 28-41; R. Zimmermann, "Wundererzählungen in den Akten der Apostel—eine Hinführung," in R. Zimmermann (ed.), *Kompendium der frühchristlichen Wundererzählungen*, vol. 2: *Die Wunder der Apostel* (Gütersloh: Gütersloher Verlagshaus, 2017), 8-14; Wilhelm Heitmüller, *Im Namen Jesu: Eine sprach- und religionsgeschichtliche Untersuchung zum Neuen Testament, speziell zur altchristlichen Taufe*, FRLANT 1/2 (Göttingen: Vandenhoeck & Ruprecht, 1903), esp. 236, 253.
[56] Cf. Aune, "Magic in Early Christianity," 1547-9.
[57] Cf. Felicity Harley, "Invocation and Immolation: The Supplicatory Use of Christ's Name on Crucifixion Amulets of the Early Christian Period," in P. Allen (ed.), *Prayer and Spirituality in the Early Church 2, Everton Park 1999* (Queensland: Australian Catholic University, 2003), 245-57. In Fotopoulos, "Paul's Curse of Corinthians," 307-8, we see that *defixiones*

> commonly invoke a wide variety of Greek, Roman, and foreign deities or other supernatural beings, and these deities or supernatural beings could be classified as heavenly or chthonic. It was also stated that spells and curses commonly invoke the spirits of those who have died prematurely or by violence. It is interesting to note that the Lord Jesus who executes the curse in 1 Cor 16:22 has many of these same characteristics. Lord Jesus has characteristics of a chthonic deity since he died, was placed in a tomb, and experienced the realm of Hades in his death (descending εἰς τὴν ἄβυσσον, Rom 10:7, then being the ἀπαρχή of those who have died after his resurrection from the dead, 1 Cor 15:20). However, the Lord Jesus is also a heavenly deity, having origins from heaven ὁ πρῶτος ἄνθρωπος ἐκ γῆς χοϊκός, ὁ δεύτερος ἄνθρωπος ἐξ οὐρανοῦ (1 Cor 15:47; cf. Phil 2:6) while also returning to heaven from where he will later arrive at his *parousia* ... Moreover, Jesus died by violence through his crucifixion, while also dying prematurely by human standards. These are all characteristics of deities and other supernatural beings that are especially valued in curse tablets where they are invoked to come and execute curses.

Cf. Aune, "Magic in Early Christianity," 1545.
[58] Cf. *PGM* IV.3019; cf. Richard Wünsch, *Antike Fluchtafeln* (Bonn: A. Marcus und E. Weber, 1912), 6 no. 1. The name of Jesus was used in four ways: as magical formula in (biblical) exorcisms, as formula in the context of baptism in the church fathers, as apotropaic formula on amulets and magical papyri, and as incantation on curse tablets.

Paul repeatedly associates "the name of the Lord" with faith and baptism: for example, in Rom. 10:13 we read, "For everyone who calls on the name of the Lord (τὸ ὄνομα κυρίου) will be saved"; 1 Cor. 1:15 deals with the problem in whose name the Corinthians were baptized; and in 1 Cor. 6:11 Paul writes, "You were washed, you were sanctified, you were justified through the name of the Lord Jesus Christ [ἐν τῷ ὀνόματι τοῦ κυρίου Ἰησοῦ Χριστοῦ] and in the Spirit of our God." The name of Jesus hence serves to "bind" a person into the community with God. Parallel to a binding of persons "down" to some god of the earth or the underworld or "up" to a celestial god, as it can regularly be found on ancient *defixiones*, Paul seems to indicate in this formula a similar way of effecting a kind of "positive binding spell"[59] when he introduces this positive binding formula that effects the binding of a person to the κύριος Ἰησοῦς.

If "curse" is defined as "a directly expressed or indicated utterance, which in virtue of a supernatural nexus of operation brings harm by its very expression to the one against whom it is directed"[60]—this means that the mere act of utterance of the formula already effects the curse. This can also be assumed for the Pauline use of the κύριος Ἰησοῦς formula, which positively effects the binding of a person in the name of Jesus. By pronouncing the name of Jesus, for example, but not only, in baptism—a positive "binding" is effected.

For the life after this first "binding" Paul uses the metaphor of "being in Christ" (εἶναι ἐν Χριστῷ). The formula occurs sixty-four times in the genuine Pauline letters and thirty-seven times in the form of ἐν κυρίῳ. This spatial metaphor ἐν Χριστῷ allows for an interpretation that the person over whom the name of Jesus is pronounced and who is thus "in Christ" is bound "to" him or bound "into" him. Paul's notion of "being in Christ" implies that believers are determined by Christ in all their being and doing. This aspect of determination by a god reveals close parallels with the practice connected with the use of ancient curse tablets. If the κύριος Ἰησοῦς formula in 1 Cor. 12:3 is therefore read as a kind of "binding formula," it becomes clear that Paul changes the direction in comparison with the conventional use of ancient *defixiones*: While in the Greco-Roman practice of cursing the object was "bound down" to a deity of the underworld, Paul binds the person "into" Christ and thus replaces the underworld with the divine sphere that in the Christian conception is associated with God.

If this observation is plausible, then further formulaic phrases containing the name of the Lord can also be read in this light, for example, the greetings at the beginning and at the end of the Pauline Epistles can be interpreted *beyond* their function as wishes, prayers, and blessings as a powerful, positive "placing under the protection of God" in close parallel with the pagan protective spells that bind people to—or even "up" to—the Lord and his protection through the mere but explicit utterance of the formula. Regularly repeated formulas such as Ἡ χάρις τοῦ κυρίου ἡμῶν Ἰησοῦ Χριστοῦ μετὰ τοῦ πνεύματος ὑμῶν (Gal. 6:18; Phil. 4:23; Phlm 25; slightly varied in Rom. 16:20;

---

[59] There is a close relationship between curses and prayers; curses even display semantic parallels to prayer texts. Cf. Gager, *Curse Tablets and Binding Spells*, 175–99; cf. also Lindsay Watson, *Arae: The Curse Poetry of Antiquity*, ARCA: Classical and Medieval Texts, Papers, and Monographs 26 (Leeds: Cairns, 1991).

[60] Friedrich Büchsel, "κατάρα," *TDNT* 1 (1964): 449.

1 Cor. 16:23; 2 Cor. 13:13; 1 Thess. 5:28) could from this perspective be read as having a protective, possibly also an apotropaic, function in analogy to the binding spells of ancient magic and the ancient curse tradition.

Results

Reading the Pauline literature from the perspective of ancient curse tablets, it becomes apparent that they display an ambivalent position concerning the ancient practice of cursing: on the one hand Paul distances himself from the ancient practice of cursing by criticizing the cursing of opponents as it was used by members of his communities (Rom. 12:14; 1 Cor. 12:3); on the other hand the embedding of Paul and his addressees in the ancient religious context manifests itself in other places where the reception of curse traditions or curse language can be detected (1 Cor. 5:5, 12:2-3, 16:21-22; Gal. 1:8-9). But besides these elements of reception a tendency toward a specific transformation of ancient curse traditions on a religious and literary level comes to the fore: in 1 Cor. 5:5, for example, Paul draws on a negative speech act as used in the ancient practice of cursing and probably familiar to the Corinthian community, by which a person is cursed and bound down to a deity. Also in this verse, this "cursing" of a member of the community is regarded as an act of judgment, ultimately with the purpose of saving the sinner from the eschatological judgment. A similar kind of positive transformation of the act of cursing can also be found in 1 Cor. 12:2-3, where the negative curse formula ἀνάθεμα Ἰησοῦς is countered by a positive formula to be used by the Christian audience, which may, drawing on the Pauline argumentation and theology, be interpreted as an act by which a person is bound "into" Christ through pronouncing the new formula that Paul advocates: κύριος Ἰησοῦς.

9

Paul as the Originator of Women Teachers within Religious Circles

Chris S. Stevens

Contemporary debates concerning the roles of males and females within the local church have diverted from the positive elements concerning corporate roles for all members within the Christian community. Taking a step back and addressing this important issue is important for contemporary theological debates, especially concerning the position of women within the local church. The focus of this chapter is to help situate female involvement within the Christian community with principal attention given to the largely ignored text of Tit. 2:3-5.

Over thirty years ago, while working on women's roles in the early church, Alan Padgett said there was very little scholarship devoted to Tit. 2:1-10.[1] Since that time some interest has explored later parts of Titus 2 concerning Christological features, but still little attention has been given to the exhortations at the beginning. Even current debates relating the roles and participation of women in the church have not given much attention to the text of Titus 2.[2] There are likely two contributors to the lack of attention given to the importance of the text. First, some neglect is an unfortunate consequence of debates concerning Pauline authorship of the Pastoral Epistles.[3] However, even if Paul did not write Titus, it still was created by and used

---

[1] Alan Padgett, "The Pauline Rationale for Submission: Biblical Feminism and the *hina* Clauses of Titus 2:1-10," *EvQ* 59 (1987): 41. For a survey of movements in the scholarly interest of women in the biblical world, see Carolyn Osiek, "Women in the Ancient Mediterranean World: State of the Question—New Testament," *BR* 39 (1994): 57-61. For an extensive, albeit dated, bibliography, see Phyllis Bird, "Women in the Ancient Mediterranean World: Ancient Israel," *BR* 39 (1994): 31-45.

[2] While devoted to women in Paul, some authors ignore Titus 2 altogether: Pamela Eisenbaum, "Is Paul the Father of Misogyny and Antisemitism?" *CrossCurrents* 50 (2000/2001): 506-24; George Bernard Shaw, "The Monstrous Imposition upon Jesus," in Wayne A. Meeks (eds.), *The Writings of St. Paul* (New York: Norton, 1972), 296-302; Elaine Pagels, "Paul and Women: A Response to Recent Discussion," *JAAR* 42 (1974): 538-49. Even an entire book devoted to the topic of women in the church gives surprisingly little attention to what is presented here to be a radically important passage. I refer to Andreas J. Köstenberger and Thomas R. Schreiner, eds., *Women in the Church: An Interpretation and Application of 1 Timothy 2:9-15* (Wheaton, IL: Crossway, 2016).

[3] While not the first, ever since Baur separated the Pauline corpus into Homologoumena and Antilegomena, 1-2 Timothy and Titus have been debated as to their Pauline authorship. See F. C. Baur, *Paul the Apostle of Jesus Christ: His Life and Works, His Epistles and Teachings*, 2 vols. (Grand Rapids, MI: Baker Academic, 2011), 1.256-57. The names and movements concerning Pauline authorship have been summarized by George W. Knight III, *The Pastoral Epistles*, NIGTC (Grand Rapids, MI: Eerdmans, 1992), 21-2.

in the early church, thereby reflecting early thought and influencing early practices. A second unfortunate contributor is that many contemporary commentaries do not give focused attention to Titus but merge their commentary with the other Pastorals.[4] While the debates concerning authorship and pseudonymity are outside the immediate purview of this chapter, it is posited that Titus deserves attention as an early document concerning the role of women within the ancient church.[5]

This chapter offers a fresh sociohistorical background to Tit. 2:3-5. Within its *Sitz im Leben*, Tit. 2:3-5 is a radical departure from the religious sociohistorical norms of the day. The absence of female involvement in positions of cultic perpetuation in other religious groups indicates Paul, or one from within the Pauline group, was both novel and innovative in exhorting women to teach within the Christian community.

Historical Background

The attempt to analyze the rites and practices of ancient religious groups is a difficult endeavor. The matter is further complicated when we consider sectarian cults, which is of prime interest in this chapter since such groups tended to keep their cultic practices to themselves or are misrepresented by their opponents.[6] There is even less evidence concerning the religious practices and participation of women since the socioreligious life of ancient women is typically overlooked. As Bird has remarked, the one thing we are confident about women in the ancient world is how little we know.[7] Kroeger summarizes the problem thus: "History is written by, for, and about men."[8] Even if one does not use a feminist hermeneutic of history, it is the experience in the research for this chapter that discussion of women within cultic settings was certainly not a priority of ancient writers.[9] Kroeger also notes that in some cases women had separate religions

---

[4] Many commentaries lump the Pastorals together. Here are just a few major series that do so: Hans Conzelmann and Martin Dibelius, *The Pastoral Epistles: A Commentary on the Pastoral Epistles*, trans. Philip Buttolph and Adela Yarbro, Hermeneia (Philadelphia, PA: Fortress, 1972); J. N. D. Kelly, *The Pastoral Epistles*, BNTC (London: Continuum, 1963); William D. Mounce, *Pastoral Epistles*, WBC 42 (Nashville, IL: Thomas Nelson, 2000); Knight III, *Pastoral Epistles*.

[5] Titus is part of the Pauline corpus. For a discussion regarding pseudonymity of the letters, see Stanley E. Porter, "Pauline Authorship and the Pastoral Epistles: Implications for Canon," *BBR* 5 (1995): 105–23; and for an understanding of a canonical grouping of the Pauline corpus, see Brevard Childs, *The Church's Guide for Reading Paul: The Canonical Shaping of the Pauline Corpus* (Grand Rapids, MI: Eerdmans, 2008), 7–10; Günther Zuntz, *The Text of the Epistles: A Disquisition upon the Corpus Paulinum* (London: British Academy, 1946), 14–17; and Harry Gamble, "Redaction of the Pauline Letters and the Formation of the Pauline Corpus," *JBL* 93 (1975): 403–18.

[6] Concerning the mystery religions such as the Eleusinian, Isis, and Mithraic, Ulansey notes that the "cult maintained strict secrecy about its teachings and practices, revealing them only to initiates. As a result of this secrecy, almost no literary evidence about the beliefs of Mithraism has survived." David Ulansey, "Solving the Mithraic Mysteries," *BAR* 20.5 (1994): 40. Furthermore, the term "cult" is not used in a pejorative sense in this chapter. It is used to refer to cultic and religious practices of groups that often broke with main lines practices of the period.

[7] Bird, "Women in the Ancient Mediterranean," 31.

[8] Catherine Kroeger, "The Apostle Paul and the Greco-Roman Cults of Women," *JETS* 30 (1987): 25–38, here 25.

[9] Many of the articles, entries, and monographs that discuss socioreligious features of the ancient world did not broach the topic of the role or participation of women.

and frequently worshipped in "different temples and on different days," with "feminine religiosity" occasionally "quite different from its masculine counterpart."[10]

Despite these obstacles to the historical investigation, enough evidence provides general insights into the religious life of women in the ancient world.[11] In this chapter, primary attention is given to female participation in religious circles and especially their potential role as teachers of other members in the group.[12]

Ancient Cults

There were many ancient cults in and around the ancient Mediterranean and Near East. There were also a number of popular goddesses who attracted widespread attention. From Mount Olympus came Artemis, Athena, and Aphrodite for the Greeks. Later these were called Diana, Minerva, and Venus, respectively, by the Romans. However, some of the oldest religions have their roots in Babylon and Persia and slowly evolved through syncretism across the Aegean. These cults either spread or had influence all across Egypt, Greece, and ultimately the Roman Empire. The following exploration of some of the more significant religious groups is not an attempt to be exhaustive, but representative, of important groups. Moreover, greater attention is on groups where greater female involvement is anticipated.

In an exploration concerning ancient female religious practices, it seems appropriate to begin with a cult centered around a goddess. Isis was a widespread cult and "arguably the most important of the mystery religions of the Roman Empire."[13] The Cult of Isis developed from the heart of the Egyptian cosmogonies.[14] The cosmogony tells of Geb (earth-god) and Nut (sky-goddess), who gave "birth to Osiris, Horus Fore-Eyed, Seth, Isis, and Nephthys."[15] Isis became exceptionally popular, and her fame spread throughout the Mediterranean. Within the Hellenistic period, as Magness notes, the goddess rose to supreme status: "Isis quickly became associated with Sarapis, who was worshiped with her as supreme lord."[16]

There are a number of connections between the Cult of Isis and early Christianity. First, Isis is said to be resurrected from the dead, and Diodorus Siculus records how

---

[10] Kroeger, "Cults of Women," 27.
[11] For a general overview of Hellenistic and Roman religions, see Everett Ferguson, *Backgrounds of Early Christianity* (Grand Rapids, MI: Eerdmans, 2003), 148–318.
[12] For the purposes of being as broad as possible, a teaching role includes any role of instruction, informing, training, or discipling other members in the same religious community to follow particular practices or learn particular information.
[13] Stanley E. Porter, "Resurrection, the Greeks, and the New Testament," in Stanley E. Porter and Michael Hayes (eds.), *Resurrection*, JSNTSup 192 (Sheffield: Sheffield Academic Press, 1999), 76; cf. Ferguson, *Backgrounds*, 266–8.
[14] Isis was part of "the spread of Egyptian thinking in the Graeco-Roman Mediterranean world." See Hans-Josef Klauck, *The Religious Context of Early Christianity: A Guide to Graeco-Roman Religions* (Minneapolis, MN: Fortress, 2003), 129.
[15] Papyrus Bremner-Rhind (1.9) cited in William W. Hallo and K. Lawson Younger, *The Context of Scripture* (Leiden: Brill, 1997), 1:15.
[16] Jodi Magness, "The Cults of Isis and Kore at Samaria-Sebaste in the Hellenistic and Roman Periods," *HTR* 94 (2001): 157–77, here 162.

she possessed a drug raising her son Horus too.[17] For this reason, she was beloved as the caring mother goddess who provided resurrection to her children.[18] A second connection exists between the Cult of Isis and the early cults of Mary, the mother of Jesus.[19] Third, there were many women involved in the cult, similar to early converts of Christianity observed in Acts, but Ferguson points out that inscriptions indicate "devotees were not primarily women."[20]

Women did play a significant role in the membership of the cult, including the role of priestess. In *The Lamentations of Isis and Nephthys*, found in Pap. Berlin 3008, is told the laments of Isis's priestesses over the death of Osiris.[21] Furthermore, the wall painting from *casa delle Nozee d'Ercole* at Pompeii depicts a priestess as a representative serving at a religious festival.[22] Heyob concludes from the painting that "in some instances, at Pompeii both a woman and a man seem to have been representatives of the cult on an equal basis."[23]

Undoubtedly, the Cult of Isis is the foremost example of female engagement within a religious community. Women were members, participants, and even priestesses. However, evidence indicates that men in positions of authority dominated the Cult of Isis.[24] It may seem surprising within a group gathered around a mother as the divine authority that there is no description of women taking positions of teaching. The women sang laments, but they were not teachers. Even the painting at Pompeii depicts a woman in a religious festival alongside men, indicating that while women were active participants, they were assistants to the primary rulership of men. In the end, it is unclear exactly what the Cult of Isis believed and taught, and to what degree women could participate, but what is clear is they were not in any teaching roles.

Contemporaneous with late Second Temple Judaism, the Greek world had a thriving religious center north of Athens. Delphi was the omphalos of Greek religion and politics. In the Greek mountains was a multistructured temple complex dedicated to Apollo. The temples also served as a treasury for Greece and a focal point for seeking divine guidance. From as early as the eighth century until the fourth century BCE, the Delphic Oracle was the most celebrated and authoritative oracle for the Greek world. Delphi is largely unique in the ancient world with the typical religious structures being inverted. While male prophets and priests dominated elsewhere, the central figure at

---

[17] Diod. Sic. 1.25.6: τὸ τῆς ἀθανασίας φάρμακον, δι' οὗ τὸν υἱὸν Ὧρον.

[18] Tobin clarifies that Isis was not viewed as a mother-goddess in the way the Greek Demeter was, but "the motherhood of Isis was more of a political symbol." Vincent Arieh Tobin, "Isis and Demeter: Symbols of Divine Motherhood," *JARCE* 28 (1991): 187–200, here 194.

[19] Some have recently challenged the connection between Mary and Isis as a misinterpretation of iconography. See Sabrina Higgins's reading of Tran Tam Tinh. Sabrina Higgins, "Divine Mothers: The Influence of Isis on the Viring Mary in Egyptian *Lactans*-Iconography," *JCSCS* 3–4 (2012): 71–90.

[20] Ferguson, *Backgrounds*, 273.

[21] Miriam Lichtheim, *Ancient Egyptian Literature: Volume III: The Late Period* (Berkeley: University of California Press, 1973), 116–22.

[22] Sharon Kelly Heyob, *The Cult of Isis among Women in Graeco-Roman World*, EPRO 51 (Leiden: Brill, 1975), 99.

[23] Ibid.

[24] Hardy Grant, "Who's Hypatia? Whose Hypatia Do You Mean?" *Math Horizons* 16 (2009): 11–15.

Delphi was the Pythia, a prophetess.[25] Within its historical context, Kurt Latte explains that the "functioning of a woman in Delphi, remains unexplained."[26]

Given the unique social inversion for a religious setting, it would seem prima facie an example of a woman in a position of religious authority. Greece turned to her as the means of hearing from the gods. Her access to the divine gave her authority to direct those who came to inquire of the gods. There are even instances of manipulation.[27] The Pythia undoubtedly occupied a powerful political and religious character during the time Delphi was influential.

However, closer examination makes it apparent that the Pythia is not regarded as possessing personal authority or viewed in any way a religious teacher; the Pythia was not a person but a position. The high priestess was called Pythia, and it was not the name of any person. Perhaps this is why Herodotus at times refers to her through nonhuman means, but more as a puppet of the divine, such as people "sent once more to the god to ask" their questions.[28] As Latte explains, it was believed that Apollo took possession of Pythia in much the same way he did the "Delphian rocks," and in essence, Pythia functioned as "the instrument of the god, no more."[29]

People came to Delphi with the intention of hearing from Apollo, not to inquire of the wisdom and teaching of the Pythia. Ultimately, the understanding was that "when questions were answered it was by Apollo's wisdom, not the woman's. She was simply Apollo's mouthpiece."[30] Even when the Pythia spoke, it was the male priest who gave the prophecy and interpretation. Indeed, socially Pythia was able to capture a position of power, but she was not respected, revered, or regarded as a teacher even within her socioreligious community.

Turning to the Greek pantheon, "Dionysus, the son of Zeus and Semele, is the most polymorphous of the Greek gods."[31] The followers of the god of wine garnered widespread attention among the ancient Greek poets such as Euripides. Dionysus, or Bacchus, was depicted as a phallic god famous for the processions of pallophoria and the wild revelry of his followers. The cult was predominately female, and Kraemer concludes that evidence for male participation in "the classical period is scant."[32]

---

[25] For a thorough discussion of the Pythian prophetess, see Herbert W. Parke and D. E. W. Wormell, *The Delphic Oracle* (Oxford: Blackwell, 1965), 10–35.

[26] Kurt Latte, "The Coming of the Pythia," *HTR* 33 (1940): 9–18, here 11.

[27] For instance, the Pythia commands Alyattes to rebuild the temple of Athena at Assesos prior to her inquiring of the gods on his behalf. Hdt., *Hist.* 1.19.3.

[28] Hdt. 1.67.2–3. Likewise, in Plato's *Phaed.* 244B., Socrates extols Pythia and other women as prophetesses, believing they "accomplish many wonderful things, both for individuals and the public when they are inspired, but when they are in their right mind, they do little or nothing."

[29] Latte, "Pythia," 17. See also Ferguson, *Backgrounds*, 214. In a first-century poem by Marcus Lucanus, Appius is furious when Pythia is "speaking with her own voice" and demands the god take ecstatic possession of her. Lucan, *Civil War* 161. For a full discussion of the poem, see Klauck, *Graeco-Roman Religions*, 186–8.

[30] James G. Sigountos and Myron Shank, "Public Roles for Women in the Pauline Church: A Reappraisal of the Evidence," *JETS* 26 (1983): 283–95, here 288.

[31] Klauck, *Graeco-Roman Religions*, 107.

[32] Ross S. Kraemer, "Ecstasy and Possession: The Attraction of Women to the Cult of Dionysus," *HTR* 72 (1979): 55–80, here 69. Nilsson notes that it is not until a latter transitional stage "between the old orgia, which were celebrated by women exclusively, and the new Dionysiac mysteries that were open to men as well as women." M. P. Nilsson, *The Dionysiac Mysteries of the Hellenistic and Roman*

The worshippers of Dionysus were known as "maenads," meaning "mad-ones," or simply Bacchae.[33] While difficult to determine if the activities portrayed by Euripides reflect actual cultic practices, according to Kraemer, there is evidence suggesting that "Euripides knew of the Dionysiac rites."[34] The precise understanding of the activities is elusive, but it points to societal and sexual role inversions.[35] The participants were regarded as being under Dionysiac possession. Kraemer explains that the cult

> enabled Greek women at least temporarily to defy their normal roles and participate in activities which were normally not permitted to them, within a framework which prohibited the exercise of any serious sanctions against them, since the possession was, in most instances, understood to be amoral and irresistible.[36]

Therefore, similar to Pythia the cult participants were empowered by possession. Their conduct was accredited to Dionysus and not to the women. The miraculous performances of the Bacchae were indicators of divine possession. As Kurt explains, the Bacchae "draw milk and honey from the fountains (e.g., Aeschin. Sphett. in Aristid. II 23 Dind.), they suckle fawns and panthers (Eur. Bach. 699ff.)," but these miracles are credited to Dionysus, not to the women.[37] So while there is some sense in which membership in the cult permitted particular freedom for the females, it is similar to the situation with the Pythia at Delphi.[38]

Although their artful depictions cannot ultimately determine the cultic activities and theology of the Dionysian cult, what is clear is that no teaching took place from a priestess. Instead, the activities were of women at the whims of Bacchus leading them along in an orgiastic frenzy. Like the Pythia their position of authority was not on account of their knowledge or ability; they were not viewed as having knowledge and experience to pass on. They were not responsible for perpetuating the cultic practices.

The Roman god of agriculture, woods, and fields had a cult dedicated to him. Silvanus was the protector of the forests and beasts. The majority opinion is that women were barred from any participation.[39] In counter-distinction, Dorcey contends that "the divinity certainly appealed to women, even though they were not as visible

---

Age (Lund: Gleerup, 1957), 8. Although there are three male characters in Euripides' play: Cadmus, the former king of Thebes; Tiresias, the blind seer; and Pentheus.

[33] A. Henrichs, "Greek Maenadism from Olympias to Messalina," *HSCP* 82 (1978): 121–60.

[34] Kraemer, "Ecstasy and Possession," 59–60.

[35] Dodds contends there is no evidence from the fifth- to fourth-century Athens concerning such rituals. E. R. Dodds, *Bacchae* (Oxford: Oxford University Press, 1959), xxii. Kraemer, on the other hand, says there is evidence for such misconduct; cf. Kraemer, "Ecstasy and Possession," 60.

[36] Kraemer, "Ecstasy and Possession," 80.

[37] Latte, "Pythia," 11.

[38] For instance, in Euripides, *Bacch.* 1114, Agave is called a priestess, but her conduct of tearing apart her own son is depicted as not under her own volition. Furthermore, Euripides, *Bacch.* 1124, records Agave foaming at the mouth, "not thinking as she ought, was possessed by Bacchus."

[39] R. E. Palmer, "Silvanus, Sylvester and the Chair of St. Peter," *PAPhs* 122 (1978): 222–47, here 222; G. Wissowa, *Religion und Kultus der Römer*, Handbuch der Klassischen Altertums-Wissenschaft (Munich: Beck, 1912), 214.

Paul as the Originator of Women Teachers 155

and active in this cult as men."⁴⁰ Despite this claim, there is evidence suggesting women were not involved and were indeed not in positions of authority to teach.

The most explicit statement about female participation is in *De AgriCultura* 83 from the early second century BCE. The text records Elder Cato referring to the exclusion of women from the religious group.⁴¹ Much later, Augustine in his *City of God* comments that "three gods are assigned as guardians to a woman after she has been delivered, lest the god Silvanus come in and molest her."⁴² It is highly unlikely women should find special affinity with a god who is known for attacking and molesting them. Rather women would have been fonder of the three unnamed protectors than Silvanus himself. While Dorcey may be correct that in certain places women were allowed some level of engagement, there is clear indication they did not serve a teaching role.

One of the most widespread mystery religions during the Roman Empire was the Mithraic cult. Practices and theology concentrated around the god Mithra, meaning "contract" or "mediator of a contract."⁴³ Greco-Roman Mithraism possibly developed out of older forms of Zoroastrianism from ancient Persia or perhaps the myth of Perseus slaying Medusa.⁴⁴ Whatever the precise origins, worship included a focus on the sun. Mithraism rose to prominence in the Mediterranean contemporaneous with Christianity and was popular in the Roman world in the first to the fourth century CE. The cult displays a few affinities with Christianity, including the essential belief in the immortality of the soul. Mithraism perhaps even had an influence upon Christianity in the selection of the date for Christmas. Before the time of Jesus, December 25 was celebrated as the birthday of Mithras.⁴⁵

Mithras was the channel for the god of light to wage cosmic war against darkness, so unsurprisingly Mithras became a "patron deity of the soldiers, who spread his worship everywhere from the Euphrates to Hadrian's Wall in distant Britain."⁴⁶ Though widespread across cultures and lands, there is very little evidence concerning female participation. The long-standing opinion among scholars has been that "Mithra forbade their (female) participation in his mysteries."⁴⁷ Burkert contends that Mithras by definition "stood for men's clubs in opposition to family life."⁴⁸ Moreover, Ulansey

---

⁴⁰ Peter Dorcey, "The Cult of Silvanus in the Roman World" (PhD dissertation, Columbia University, 1987); "The Role of Women in the Cult of Silvanus," *Numen* 36 (1989): 143–55, here 143.
⁴¹ *De AgriCultura* cited by Dorcey, "Role of Women," 144.
⁴² *City of God*, 6.9.
⁴³ Klauck, *Graeco-Roman Religions*, 40.
⁴⁴ The theory that Mithraism traces its roots to Persia was put forward by Franz Cumont, *The Mysteries of Mithra*, trans. T. McCormack (London: Kegan Paul, 1903). More recently the position is challenged by the suggestion that Mithraism is more a product of syncretism in the Hellenistic and Roman periods. See especially David Ulansey, *The Origins of the Mithraic Mysteries: Cosmology and Salvation in the Ancient World* (Oxford: Oxford University Press, 1991). Cf. Ferguson, *Backgrounds*, 289.
⁴⁵ H. F. Vos, "Religions of the Biblical World: Greco-Roman," in Geoffrey William Bromiley (ed.), *ISBE* (Grand Rapids, MI: Eerdmans, 1979), 4:116. During post-apostolic times, perhaps as late as the fourth century, Mithraism merged with the Roman worship of *Sol Invictus*, which was celebrated on December 25. Blomberg contends that "Christians took advantage of this 'day off' to protest against Mithraism by worshiping the birth of Jesus instead." Craig L. Blomberg, *Jesus and the Gospels: An Introduction and Survey*, 2nd ed. (Nashville, IL: B&H Academic, 2009), 36.
⁴⁶ Vos, "Religions of the Biblical World," 4:116.
⁴⁷ Cumont, *Mysteries of Mithra*, 173. See also the strong words of Klauck, *Graeco-Roman Religions*, 141.
⁴⁸ Harvard Walter Burkert, *Ancient Cults* (Cambridge: Cambridge University Press, 1987), 52.

concludes that "the cult's membership was made up especially of Roman soldiers, bureaucrats, and merchants. Women were excluded."[49]

More recently there has been an attempt to reanalyze the evidence. Jonathan David attempts to demonstrate that women were at least allowed in the club. David concludes that "women had significant dealings with the cult, and *perhaps* were even initiated into the rites."[50] Despite his diligent efforts, at best David is only able to contend that nothing explicitly excluded women from the cult, "but rather did not have occasion to engage in them."[51] The practical exclusion of women was perhaps due in part to the physical feats during initiation rituals.[52]

Whether or not women were allowed to join the Mithraic cults is ultimately difficult to conclude. It is perhaps possible that in particular locations at certain periods women were members and perhaps even engaged in the rites, but even if permitted to join, there is no evidence to support the idea that women were ever in a position of teaching or perpetuating these mysteries. Franz Cumont concluded in his extensive study, "among the hundreds of inscriptions that have come down to us, not one mentions either a priestess, a woman initiate, or even a donatress."[53] While more recent burial findings suggest that a wife of one of the members perhaps was also allowed to join, the overall picture is quite clear. Women did not serve a role in the teaching and perpetuation of the Mithraic cults.[54]

Hypatia was an astronomer and mathematician in Alexandria from 370–415 CE.[55] Her father Theon was an important figure in Alexandria and a powerful intellect that educated his gifted daughter in the hard sciences. Her reported beauty and intellect garnered tales of her to spread far and wide, and books continued to be written,[56] and there was even a modern Hollywood movie about her.[57] In events that continue to be debated, Hypatia was killed "by a mob consisting (at least mainly) of Christians."[58]

Despite her unfortunate end, we find in Hypatia a woman who rose to the level of teacher and instructor. In Alexandria, "Hypatia lectured in her own home, to a select group of students, and to a wide audience in public halls."[59] Socrates notes she even taught in public presence of magistrates and "neither did she feel abashed in coming to an assembly of men."[60] The peculiar nature of her privileges is noted in the words

---

[49] Ulansey, "Solving the Mithraic Mysteries," 41.
[50] See Jonathan David, "The Exclusion of Women in the Mithraic Mysteries: Ancient or Modern?" *Numen* 47 (2000): 121–41, here 129; my emphasis.
[51] Ibid., 139.
[52] Porter, "Resurrection," 76–7.
[53] Cumont, *Mysteries of Mithra*, 173.
[54] David believes he has found archeological evidence for at least one female initiate in the grade of Lea; David, "Exclusion of Women," 125.
[55] Her story is recounted by Socrates in *Hist. eccl.* 7.15.
[56] Charles Kingsley, *Hypatia: Or, New Foes with an Old Face* (London: J. W. Parker and Son, 1853).
[57] Alejandro Amenábar, "Agora" (Spain, 2009).
[58] Grant, "Who's Hypatia?" 14. The account by Socrates notes the ringleader of the mob was a reader named Peter, and Hypatia was killed in a church called Caesareum. The murder had consequences for Cyril of Alexandria and the Alexandrian church as a whole.
[59] Ibid., 12.
[60] Socrates Scholasticus, "The Ecclesiastical History, by Socrates Scholasticus," in Philip Schaff and Henry Wace (eds.), *Socrates, Sozomenus: Church Histories*, trans. A. C. Zenos, NPNF² (New York: Christian Literature Company, 1890), 2:160.

of Damascius, a sixth-century philosopher and admirer, "though a woman" she taught in public.[61]

Therefore, roughly three centuries after the birth of Christianity there is found a robust female teacher and instructor, albeit not within a religious setting. Even though she would have been imminently qualified, and had support from her father, Hypatia still was viewed as an outlier to the norms of society. She could be praised for her beauty, praised for her intellect and talents, but only reluctantly accepted as an instructor. Interestingly, it was Christians who killed her amid political rivalry.

Second Temple Judaism

There is no mention of women teaching in the Hebrew Scriptures or other Second Temple literature. A few places mention a minimal prophetical role for women. There are only five women referred to with the title of prophetess נְבִיאָה in the OT: Miriam (Exod. 15:20), Deborah (Judg. 4:4), the unnamed wife of Isaiah (Isa. 8:3), Huldah (2 Kgs 22:14), and the false prophet Noadiah (Neh. 6:14). In the NT there are only two further references: Anna (Lk. 2:36-38) and Jezebel (Rev. 2:20).[62] Unlike some other prophets, most notably Elijah and Elisha, none of these women gathered a following to train and teach the next generation. They did not have disciples who continued to carry out their role and function within the religious community, that is, no cultic perpetuation. So, whereas Moses discipled and passed his staff—literally and figuratively—to Joshua, and Elijah called, ordained, and discipled Elisha, Miriam did not train or pass along to anyone. Although Deborah was a pivotal character in Judges, after her song in Judges 5, she is not mentioned again in the Hebrew Scriptures.[63]

The absence of teaching and cultic perpetuation continues in later Second Temple Judaism where none of the Minor Prophets mention female instruction within the sphere of cultic activities in a positive manner. Closer to the period of early Christianity, Cohen notes that "women's Judaism remains elusive."[64] The little available evidence offers no examples of Jewish women involved in the knowledge aspects of the cultic community.[65] Even some of the outlier groups about whom a bit more is known did not have any female involvement, as Cohen also notes that "according to both Philo and Josephus, the Essenes excluded women altogether."[66]

Some of the Second Temple literature gives insights into the view of women. In 1 Esdras 4:13-32, Zerubbabel presents women as powerful rulers of the world, but not because of good qualities. Instead, their power is primarily because of their sexual

---

[61] Cited in Grant, "Who's Hypatia?" 12.
[62] Jezebel is not called a prophetess in the OT making the reference in Revelation unlikely to be an official office or role.
[63] The Babylonian Talmud minimally and rather offhandedly references Deborah in *b. Pesah.* 6a.
[64] Shaye J. D. Cohen, *From the Maccabees to the Mishnah* (Louisville, KY: Westminster John Knox, 2006), 75.
[65] As Ross Kramer points out, "Almost no examples of communities of Jewish women in late antiquity." Ross S. Kraemer, "Monastic Jewish Women in Greco-Roman Egypt: Philo Judaeus on the Therapeutrides," *Signs* 14 (1989): 342–70, here 342.
[66] Cohen, *Maccabees to the Mishnah*, 74.

nature.⁶⁷ Women are laughingly called stronger than wine because of their essential sexual nature and their importance to make babies for men. Likewise, Judith and Susanna are presented as wise and honorable.⁶⁸ However, unlike male Jewish prophets, their beauty is an important factor frequently highlighted.⁶⁹

There are some examples within Judaism of women in political positions of power such as Salome Alexandra who reigned in Israel from 76 to 67 BCE.⁷⁰ The situation was rare in Israel despite being commonplace in Asia. Arrian notes that Alexander appointed Hecatomnus' daughter Ada to the governorship over Caria and that government by women was common in Asia from the time of Semiramis onward.⁷¹ White notes that within Greek culture generally, female status greatly improved from the time of Alexander onward.⁷² Despite all the social progress, White concludes, "Greek women never achieved a position in society equal to that of men nor even equal to the position of women in Roman society."⁷³

Conversely, Philo contended women were unfit for public roles and said that any man who allies with a woman has "the reputation of effeminacy and a complete want of manly courage and vigor" as if castrated.⁷⁴ Cohen concludes, "What the rabbis and Philo mean is that women ought not to take a role in Jewish public life or to assert their authority in public."⁷⁵

It is, however, important to note that the female experience of Judaism was desirable compared to other experiences in other societies. Cohen notes, "Gentile women found Judaism attractive ... Gentile women converted to Judaism, and native Jewish women died for it."⁷⁶ However, while Judaism was attractive to women, they were certainly not taking roles as rabbis or other teaching positions within Second Temple Judaism.

Moving closer to the centuries around Paul, one interesting group is the Therapeutrides, supposedly on the shores of Lake Mareotis just outside Alexandria. Philo, our only evidence about the group, portrays them as pietistic and Essene-like so much so that "some scholars have suggested that the Therapeutae were the Egyptian

---

[67] Likewise, T.Reu. 5:1 "For evil are women, my children; and since they have no power or strength over man, they use wiles by outward attractions, that they may draw him to themselves." Cited from James H. Charlesworth, *The Old Testament Pseudepigrapha*, ABRL (Garden City, NY: Doubleday, 1983), 1.784.

[68] See Judith and Susanna. Nickelsburg even sees in Judith many parallel features in the wisdom tradition. George W. E. Nickelsburg, *Jewish Literature between the Bible and the Mishnah: A Historical and Literary Introduction* (Minneapolis, MN: Fortress, 2005), 102.

[69] Jdt. 8:7; Sus. 1:2, 7. Prophets and respectable males typically have no comment about their appearance. However, females often have a comment about their degree of beauty.

[70] Josephus, *J.W.* 1.110–12.

[71] Arrian, *Anabasis* 1.24.

[72] John L. White, "The Improved Status of Greek Women in the Hellenistic Period," *BR* 39 (1994): 62–79, here 63. See also Michael Grant, *From Alexander to Cleopatra: The Hellenistic World* (New York: Collier Books, 1982), 194–213.

[73] White, "Improved Status," 78.

[74] Philo, *On Special Laws*, 3.31. Cited from Charles Duke Yonge with Philo of Alexandria, *The Works of Philo: Complete and Unabridged* (Peabody: Hendrickson, 1995), 597.

[75] Cohen, *Maccabees to the Mishnah*, 72.

[76] Ibid., 73. See Josephus, *J.W.* 2.20.

branch of the Essenes, but the question cannot be decided."[77] Conversely, some have argued the Therapeutrides represent Philo's idealization of a contemplative community free some the restraints of society in order to purse wisdom.[78] Despite some obvious idealized remarks by Philo, the majority position sees *De Vita Contemplativa* recording details of a real community that was "very small and composed of certain people from an affluent, educated circle in Alexandria, a circle in which Philo himself participated."[79]

Real or not, the portrayal of the practices suggests how an ideal cultic group functioned. Philo explains the primary end was to purse wisdom through meditation upon the sacred writings and philosophies, τοῖς ἱεροῖς γράμμασι φιλοσοφοῦσι, and upon the works of ancient men who founded other sects, συγγράμματα παλαιῶν ἀνδρῶν.[80] Whereas the "Essenes excluded women altogether," the Therapeutrides had female members.[81] While women were viewed as possessing the same zeal and commitment to pursue wisdom, they were not regarded as equals.[82]

The people would meditate and live in their separate huts for six days, but on the seventh day, they gathered in the common worship center. There was a large partition wall separating the group into male and female sections. Philo explains this partition was because women were not permitted to teach. Only the eldest and most advanced in learning was permitted to come forward to teach, and the wall existed to separate the women for the sake of modesty while still being able to hear the voice of the speaker.[83]

Like other streams of Judaism, women do not play a positive role within the perpetuation of knowledge or cultic practices. In sum, Philo believes a woman is "a selfish creature and one addicted to jealousy," making it *natural* to exclude women from being in positions of teaching and leading.[84] Cohen concludes that "Ancient Judaism, like all other cultures and societies in antiquity, was *androcentric*."[85]

Socioreligious Background Summary

It is beyond the goals of this chapter to attempt a metanarrative of women's religion in the ancient world, but it summarizes their practical experience and functional roles within religious circles.[86] The survey indicates women did serve in some capacity

---

[77] Cohen, *Maccabees to the Mishnah*, 164, 240. Taylor sees the group as "likely unrelated to the sect of Essences in Judea." Joan E. Taylor and Philip R. Davies, "The So-Called Therapeutae of 'De Vita Contemplativa': Identity and Character," *HTR* 91 (1998): 3–24, here 24.
[78] E. R. Goodenough, *An Introduction to Philo Judaeus* (Oxford: Blackwell, 1962), 32. See also Taylor and Davies, "Therapeutae," 24; Kraemer, "Monastic Jewish Women," 347.
[79] Taylor and Davies, "Therapeutae," 24.
[80] Philo, *Contemplative Life*, 28–9.
[81] Cohen, *Maccabees to the Mishnah*, 74. See also Jodi Magness, *The Archaeology of Qumran and the Dead Sea Scrolls* (Grand Rapids, MI: Eerdmans, 2002), 163–87.
[82] τὸν αὐτὸν ζῆλον καὶ τὴν αὐτὴν προαίρεσιν ἔχουσαι (*Contemplative Life*, 32).
[83] *Contemplative Life*, 32–3.
[84] *Hypothetica* 11.14. Also, in *Hypothetica* 11.14–15, Philo says that women are very calculated in manipulating men and misleading them by sexual advances.
[85] Cohen, *Maccabees to the Mishnah*, 70.
[86] Bird notes that location, economic and social complexities, and stratification make generalization hazardous, but focusing on ancient sources as much as possible is the best historiographical practice. Bird, "Women in the Ancient Mediterranean," 34.

within ancient Greco-Roman and Jewish cultic practices. Sigountos concludes that "there was general agreement in the Greek world that women could function effectively as prophetesses and priestesses."[87] In answering the question of this chapter, however, the survey indicates women's roles were narrowly regulated. For centuries prior to, contemporaneous with, and subsequent to Paul women were restricted from roles of teaching generally and especially within religious settings.

The Greco-Roman religious world believed women could prophesy, but only as a product of being possessed by a god. Women were deemed deficient on account of their intelligence, sexual nature, and their purpose within society being to stay home to make babies.[88] Sigountos concludes that there is a "tension in the thought of Plato, Musonius, and Plutarch" and the like, as they are egalitarian in some respects, but "limited in the application of those ideas by the traditional notions of his respective society."[89] Within Jewish circles, Josephus and Philo are even more critical of women than in the wider Greco-Roman world.

Paul and the Role of Women

Some modern authors believe Paul and the writings bearing his name present a deplorable view of women like other ancient androcentric writings. Many would agree with Eisenbaum giving a positive affirmation to the question, "Is Paul the Father of Misogyny and Antisemitism?"[90] Similarly, Shaw says that Paul is the "eternal enemy of woman," and his "teachings were abominable where Jews and women are concerned."[91] Unfortunately, these authors do not interact with Tit. 2:3 in their critiques of Paul.[92]

The aforementioned Greco-Roman socioreligious background of women in religious circles must inform the interpretation of Paul. From the historical background, it is clear that Paul makes a radical break from societal norms and not only includes women but exhorts them to play a significant teaching role in the perpetuation of religious faith and practice. While largely ignored, the canonical Pauline Corpus contains a radically innovative socioreligious exhortation to women in Tit. 2:3-4.

There are no significant textual variants in the pericope of Tit. 2:1-10.[93] The section includes direct addresses and behavioral instructions to Titus (v. 1), older men (πρεσβύτας; v. 2), older women (πρεσβύτιδας; vv. 3-5), young men (νεωτέρους),

---

[87] Sigountos and Shank, "Public Roles," 288.
[88] Plato, *Phaed.* 244B.
[89] Sigountos and Shank, "Public Roles," 292.
[90] Eisenbaum, "Paul the Father," 506. Eisenbaum further explains that "from a feminist perspective Paul is an ally of Christian conservatives who wish to keep women in a subordinate position to men" (506).
[91] Shaw, "Monstrous Imposition," 299. See also Pagels, "Paul and Women," 538–9.
[92] The absence of interaction with Titus cannot be dismissed simply by calling it pseudonymous. For even if it were pseudonymous, it arises from within the Pauline camp and circulates as part of the Pauline corpus and, therefore, reflects positions regarding women within his camp.
[93] In Tit. 2:5 there is a variant of οἰκουργούς or οἰκουρούς. The former is the predominate reading adopted in NA[28] (א A C D), while the latter is in the majority of ancient texts. For οἰκουργούς BDAG offers "busy at home, carrying out household duties," and for οἰκουρούς "staying at home."

including Titus (vv. 6–8), and slaves (δούλους; vv. 9–10). For πρεσβύτιδας, BDAG has as "old(er) woman, elderly lady." Reference concerns the simple factor of age rather than social status or office.[94] Paul is addressing the generic group of older female members of the church community, just like he is addressing older and younger males.

Pertinent to the aims of this chapter, attention is given to the exhortation concerning the NT *hapax legomena* καλοδιδασκάλους. The word is a combination of the preformative καλο- and the stem διδασκαλ-. Louw-Nida gloss καλοδιδασκάλος as "teacher of what is good, teacher of what is right."[95] That Paul is coining a new word is evidenced by TLG reporting only four uses outside of the NT, but all are citations of Tit. 2:4.[96]

Paul exhorts women of age to teach, which is unprecedented in contemporary Greco-Roman religious practices. A few aspects of the exhortation indicate awareness that the content and nature of the exhortation are peculiar in the ancient world. First, Paul acts as a *logogenitor* to coin a new term. The use of a new term draws the attention of the letter's recipients to pay additional attention.

Second, the grammar designates the role of mature women within the church as equally important to the role and behavior of the male groups addressed. The use of the adverb ὡσαύτως signals addressee shifting while coordinating without subordination of vv. 2–3 and vv. 5–6.[97]

Third, the use of the root σώφρων is an attribute and behavior that is exhorted for both men and women. Paul references this characteristic a number of times in Titus: (1) the presbyters are to be σώφρονα, self-controlled and prudent (1:8); (2) older men are likewise to be σώφρονας (2:2); (3) young women are to become σώφρονας, precisely like the older men (2:5); (4) young men too are to be self-controlled σωφρονεῖν (2:6). While most of the uses are functional Complements (i.e., direct object) in their clauses—only Tit. 2:12 is an Adjunct—the use in 2:4 is the functional Predicator (i.e., main verb). Therefore, Paul exhorts all Christians to become wise and self-controlled, but only the mature women are exhorted to teach, train, and perpetuate this attribute and behavior within the community.

A fourth way Paul highlights the peculiar nature of the exhortation concerns the bulk of the presentation. The more common and expected the exhortation, the less the instruction that is necessary. For instance, the exhortation for Titus to teach sound doctrine is only eight words.[98] The exhortation for older men to be godly consists of twelve words. The instruction concerning young men in vv. 6–8 is directed to the young men and to Titus, who is himself a young man, about what qualities and behavior they

---

[94] Usage in Philo within contexts of taxes indicates age is the only factor involved. See Philo, *Spec.* 2.33 and Josephus, *Ant.* 7.142. Furthermore, for comment on how reference is made to a "non-official" function, see Conzelmann and Dibelius, *Pastoral Epistles*, 140.

[95] J. P. Louw and Eugene Albert Nida, *Greek-English Lexicon of the New Testament Based on Semantic Domains*, 2 vols. (New York: United Bible Societies, 1988), 33.239. BDAG likewise has "teaching what is good," and LSJ has "teacher of virtue."

[96] Basil of Caesarea's *Regulae Morales*, Origen's Commentary on John, and John Chrysostom's homilies on Titus.

[97] While v. 9 lacks the coordinating adverb, the new social group is still addressed by an acc. pl. noun.

[98] Word counts based on NA^{28}.

must obtain. The exhortation to the collective two-party group is a combined thirty-one words. Similarly, the exhortation to slaves, not often directly addressed in religious texts, contains twenty-eight words.

However, the exhortation solely to the older women is the largest for any of the demographic groups within the early church at thirty-four words. The extra degree of detail is necessary on account of the peculiar nature of the exhortation. The unique and unprecedented exhorting of women to teach in the Greco-Roman world requires Paul to give fuller instructions. Prior to Christianity, such instruction simply did not occur.

Neglecting Tit. 2:3

The pro-feminist interpretations mentioned earlier are not the only ones neglecting to interact with Tit. 2:3. In an article with the primary thesis being that women cannot teach, it is remarkable that Grudem does not even reference Tit. 2:3. The matter is especially exceptional considering Grudem emphasizes the root διδασκ- for teaching in the NT, διδασκαλία, διδάσκαλος, and διδάσκω.[99] If one wanted a complete view of the NT perspective on teaching, then καλοδιδάσκαλος must be included since it has the same root with a preformative.[100] The simple locutionary reading of Tit. 2:3 must be incorporated into discussions about women in the church specifically, and Paul's views on sex generally. This single verse represents Christianity as departing from other Greco-Roman religious practices and Judaism too.[101]

In Tit. 2:3 Paul is exhorting the mature women to serve the local church by teaching and mentoring the next generation of Christian women to perpetuate particular cultic and membership practices. Within its social and religious setting, the exhortation is a radical development departing from contemporary religious attitudes. What is truly amazing is that Paul does not exhort a select few gifted women who are set apart for a particular task. Instead, the exhortation is that just as all women are not to be to slanderers or drunkards, so also all older women are to serve in perpetuating discipleship and teaching what is good within the Christian community.

Paul exhorts Titus to equip all disciples in sound doctrine. Part of that discipleship is exhorting the older women in the church to be engaged in the discipling and further teaching in the church. The task is not for a select few, the exhortation is for all women to gain the proper wisdom and fulfill particular duties and roles within the religious community.

---

[99] Wayne A. Grudem, "Prophecy—Yes, but Teaching—No: Paul's Consistent Advocacy of Women's Participation without Governing Authority," *JETS* 30 (1987): 11–23, here 17–18.

[100] Interestingly, *TDNT* includes καλοδιδάσκαλος with the entry for διδάσκαλος. Likewise, Louw-Nida, *Greek-English Lexicon of the New Testament*, lists the former at 33.249 under διδασκαλία and διδάσκω at 33.224.

[101] The distinctiveness of Christianity in the ancient world is highlighted in a recent book by Larry W. Hurtado, *Destroyer of the Gods: Early Christian Distinctiveness in the Roman World* (Waco, TX: Baylor University Press, 2016).

Conclusion

In the past three decades scholarship has begun to address what Bird said are "'black holes' in our view of ancient Israel and its neighbors and discern the warp in the visible spectrum of images."[102] Previous explorations of female religious experience center around the binary categories of inclusion or exclusion rather than focusing on the form and role of participation within the community. This chapter brings cross-cultural and cross-cultic experiences to bear on the biblical data. Having a better understanding of the religious experiences and roles of women in the ancient Mediterranean undoubtedly sheds light on passages about women in the Bible. This chapter has highlighted one essential factor behind Tit. 2:2-3, namely, Paul was the radical originator of women teaching within the religious community. Further work on Paul must necessarily coordinate this information with other pertinent passages, most notably 1 Tim. 2:12. Alas, that exploration must await a subsequent paper.

By the time Titus is written, Paul has worked alongside the likes of Euodia, Syntyche, and Phoebe. He has seen over the years how beneficial and trustworthy these women are for the strengthening and expansion of the ministry. Paul learned the theological truths he articulated in Gal. 3:28, Rom. 12:4-5, and Col. 3:15 about the church members being equal in one body. He learned that mature and godly women like Priscilla had the wisdom and skills to teach others, even correcting the rhetorically powerful Apollos in Acts 18:26. Given what Paul learned theologically and what he experienced personally in ministry, Paul exhorted women to draw upon their unique gifting and image bearing for the benefit of the local church. For Paul, serving the local body is not for a select few or a select sex. All women should be taught sound doctrine and then exhorted and nourished to grow and mature in order to teach and disciple the following generations.

---

[102] Bird, "Women in the Ancient Mediterranean," 31.

10

The Secret of the Hidden Cross: The Form, Meaning, and Background of the Hellenistic Hymn Quoted in 1 Tim. 3:16

Roy D. Kotansky

More than fifty years ago in a landmark study, Robert H. Gundry explicated the meaning of the famous Christological hymn of 1 Tim. 3:16 in a thoroughgoing fashion by first analyzing the various strophic configurations proffered for the composition, then offering a trenchant exegesis of the individual lines, and finally grounding the confession within its larger theological and historical milieu.[1] His lasting contribution was to explain the meaning of the hymn's sequential layout as a depiction of Jesus's working through various spatial environments: Earth (lines 1, 4–5)—Underworld (2–3)—and Heaven (6), in order to show a largely Judean-based theology absent the cross but conspicuous for its "theology of cosmic triumph over the 'angels.'"[2] Though written a half century ago, the enduring nature of Gundry's work is testament to the full-dress character of his exegetical and theological rigor. In the analysis presented here, we pay homage to Gundry's work by adopting his three-pronged approach as a springboard for updating some recent work and introduce an entirely new set of rhetorical and theological proposals that aim to bring the whole hymn into fresh light within its own cultural milieu.[3]

The hymn is introduced by the phrase "By common confession, great is the secret (τὸ μυστήριον) of piety," followed by the introductory relative pronoun ὅς, which does not form part of the hymn proper:[4]

---

[1] R. H. Gundry, "The Form, Meaning and Background of the Hymn Quoted in 1 Timothy 3:16," in W. Ward Gasque and Ralph P. Martin (eds.), *Apostolic History and the Gospel: Biblical and Historical Studies Presented to F. F. Bruce on His 60th Birthday* (Grand Rapids, MI: Eerdmans, 1970), 203–30.
[2] Ibid., 218–19: "A Palestinian theology of the cross is entirely missing," with comparison to 1 Pet. 3:18–19 (see also 213–14); cf. next note and discussion at the conclusion of this chapter.
[3] As a former pupil of Dr. Gundry's, a present colleague, and abiding friend, I devote this heartfelt contribution to him and his more than sixty years of dedicated biblical scholarship. I also wish to acknowledge the help of Arthur Droge, Clare Rothschild, and Craig Evans in shepherding this chapter to its completion.
[4] 1 Tim. 3:16: καὶ ὁμολογουμένως μέγα ἐστὶν τὸ τῆς εὐσεβείας μυστήριον· ὅς, κτλ. The relative pronoun is problematic, for "the mystery" is neuter (τό), leaving no antecedent for ὅς, prompting some to suggest a fragment; cf. Gundry, "Form and Meaning," 211, n. 3; 219, with n. 4. The variant ὅ in the Western tradition (D* lat) cannot be easily dismissed, and the widely found θεός requires no comment. Regardless, I. Howard Marshall, *A Critical and Exegetical Commentary on the Pastoral*

Line 1: ἐφανερώθη ἐν σαρκί
Line 2: ἐδικαιώθη ἐν πνεύματι
Line 3: ὤφθη ἀγγέλοις
Line 4: ἐκηρύχθη ἐν ἔθνεσιν
Line 5: ἐπιστεύθη ἐν κόσμῳ
Line 6: ἀνελήμφθη ἐν δόξῃ

Form

We begin with Gundry's analysis, who writes of the notoriety of various commentators' "schematizations" over the years, from those who see six individual lines laying out a "more or less chronological progression," to others who advocate two strophes of three lines each (lines 1–3 + 4–6), or three strophes of two lines each (1–2 + 3–4 + 5–6)—the view most championed by those at the time of Gundry's writing.[5] His summary also proves useful in getting us up-to-date before exploring our more recent analyses.

Typical of the six-lined chronological approach are the views of Henry Alford and C. K. Barrett, the former of whom explains the individual strophic lines as follows:[6]

Line 1: Birth of Jesus
Line 2: Baptism (with receipt of the Holy Spirit) + Temptation
Line 3: Ministry of Jesus by angels, after the Temptation
Line 4: Apostolic preaching during Jesus's life
Line 5: Initial faith of the Disciples
Line 6: The Ascension

Gundry rightly faults Alford for the forced, unnatural readings that he must bring to his interpretation in order to sustain a strictly chronological sequence that ends with the Ascension in line 6; the reference to Jesus's being preached ἐν ἔθνεσιν (line 4) can hardly refer to the narrow preaching of the Apostles within Judaism (cf. Mt. 10:5-6), any more than their believing ἐν κόσμῳ (line 5) can be accredited to the faith of the pioneering disciples—both require a more global realization.[7] Alford is having to "squeeze the universe into a ball," to quote T. S. Eliot, in order to fit more tightly all the schemata of lines 1–5 before the wrap-up of the Ascension in line 6.[8] Thus, Gundry

---

Epistles, ICC (Edinburgh: T&T Clark, 1999), 523, equates the mystery with Christ, as one must (see later, sec. "Background"), even though properly the Greek must read μυστήριον, ὅ; cf. Philip H. Towner, *The Letters of Timothy and Titus* (Grand Rapids, MI: Eerdmans, 2006), 278.

[5] Gundry, "Form and Meaning," 203.
[6] Henry Alford, *The Greek Testament*, 4 vols. (London: Rivingtons and Deighton, Bell, 1865; repr. Chicago: Moody, 1968), 3:334; see Gundry, "Form and Meaning," 203–4; C. K. Barrett, *The Pastoral Epistles* (Oxford: Clarendon, 1963), 65–6; cf. Marshall, *Pastoral Epistles*, 500; Brice L. Martin, "1 Timothy 3:16—a New Perspective," *EvQ* 85 (2013): 105–20, esp. 108.
[7] Gundry, "Form and Meaning," 203–4.
[8] "Would it have been worth while, / To have bitten off the matter with a smile, / To have squeezed the universe into a ball / To roll it toward some overwhelming question, / To say: 'I am Lazarus, come from the dead, / Come back to tell you all, I shall tell you all'" (*The Love Song of J. Alfred Prufrock* [1917], by T. S. Eliot [lines 90–5]).

keenly observes that Jesus's baptism, temptation, and ministry by angels "appear to be unlikely points of emphasis for a hymnic précis of Jesus's ministry."[9] The difficult ἐδικαιώθη ἐν πνεύματι (line 2) would seem, rather, to refer to the resurrection, as C. K. Barrett and others have it. But for the final line, Barrett tries to accommodate a carpet too chronologically large for Alford's exegetical room, not by sheering the rug but by enlarging the room. For him the reference to being taken up in glory (ἀνελήμφθη ἐν δόξῃ) in line 6 must refer to the final consummation in the End-Times, that is, to Jesus's victory in his Parousia (cf. 1 Cor. 15:25; Phil. 2:10-11).[10] Thus we have in lines 1–6, Incarnation—Resurrection—Ascension—Mission of the Church—Success of the Mission—Final Exaltation. Again, Gundry counters:

> The chief flaw here is that "taken up in glory" most naturally refers to the ascension rather than the consummation. Indeed, ἀναλαμβάνω describes the ascension in Acts 1:2, 11, 22 [and Mk 16:19], and in view of these parallels the noun ἀνάλημψις almost certainly refers to the ascension in Luke 9:51. (Cf. 24:51)[11]

Thus the chronological problem of line 6's Ascension remains—so long as we adhere to any intra-textual "proof-texting" to explain line 6's ἀνελήμφθη. But we need not have to—indeed should not have to—as we shall have occasion to discuss later.

Two-Strophe Theories

A division of the hymn into only two strophes (I–II) of three lines each, in some respects, seems the most natural of all—certain internal problems notwithstanding. It takes, in the example of W. Lock, the following form:[12]

Strophe I (lines 1–3): Incarnation in Flesh—Vindication in Spirit—Watched by Angels
Strophe II (lines 4–6): Proclaimed among the Nations—Believed in the World—Taken up in Glory

The first strophe, then, would represent the life of Jesus as seen on earth; the second, the life of the ascended Lord as lived in heaven.[13] Here, again, problems of interpretation remain, even though we shall champion a more complex version of just such a two-strophe analysis in this chapter. But for the moment, Lock's view that ὤφθη ἀγγέλοις refers to the "angelic observation of our Lord's earthly ministry"[14] seems improbable,

---

[9] Gundry, "Form and Meaning," 204, concluding, "Besides, angels appeared to Jesus throughout his earthly ministry, not he to them."
[10] Ibid., in reference to Barrett, *Pastoral Epistles*, 65–6.
[11] Gundry, "Form and Meaning," 204, with n. 2, remarking further on the chronological inconsistencies of the views of W. B. Wallis and R. A. Knox, for example.
[12] W. Lock, *The Pastoral Epistles* (Edinburgh: T&T Clark, 1924), 45; see Gundry, "Form and Meaning," 204–5; Marshall, *Pastoral Epistles*, 500–1, with n. 9 (citing, further, Seeberg and Fee); followed with minor variations by Mounce and again Fee, as cited in Martin, "New Perspective," 108.
[13] Gundry, "Form and Meaning," 204–5.
[14] Ibid., 205.

and his insistence on making the third line of each strophe fit too tightly into his scheme of "seen on earth" / "seen from heaven" creates inconcinnities in respect of the chronology of the third segment of each strophe—a problem that continues to plague all interpretations of the hymn. Put somewhat differently, Gundry notes that the antithesis "angels" / "nations" forms a poor bridge among the three groups "flesh" / "spirit," "angels" / "nations," and "world" / "glory."[15]

The problem of the third line in each of the two-strophe analytical schemata—particularly that of the second strophe, the Ascension in line 6—continues to hobble a correct understanding of the hymn's structure, a necessary prerequisite toward a proper exegesis of the individual lines of the whole composition. Its position at the end throws akilter the otherwise complete chronological "sequelae" of the hymn, which shows a rather regular, temporally governed arrangement. For this reason, H. von Soden's view, which otherwise aligns rightly with Lock's in presenting strophe I (lines 1–3) as representing Jesus's career on earth, and strophe II (lines 4–6) as the "results on earth through the church,"[16] has to come up with an aberrant interpretation for ἀνελήμφθη ἐν δόξῃ (line 6) in order to make the chronology of the two-strophe theory work: the "taking up" of Jesus, he maintains, must refer to the "taking up" on behalf of men of Jesus in faith—a virtually impossible interpretation.[17] It is just not natural and cannot be sustained by the Greek. Similarly, to get around the chronological problem of line 6, E. F. Scott, who also takes up a two-strophe identity but sees a "refrain" added to each strophe (lines 1–2 + 3 and lines 4–5 + 6), has to interpret the "taken up in glory" as a kind of final glory following the Parousia and Last Judgment.[18] But this suffers from the same problems as the others, in reattributing to the sense of ascending (ἀνάλημψις) something that it does not carry, namely, the doctrine of the παρουσία. The final Advent of Jesus cannot, in any context, be associated with his Ascension; besides, the verb ἀνελήμφθη is in the past tense—it is a literary fait accompli—something that makes no sense if applied to a future Parousia and Judgment.[19] The view of W. J. Dalton

---

[15] Ibid.: "The second of the three antitheses ... breaks down any strict division into two strophes by bridging the supposed boundary between them." As we shall see, later, however, there are no real antitheses to imagine, just vertical parallels among elements within each strophe, with only a horizontal "bridging" of the final element in each of the two strophe, so that "seen by angels"/"taken up in glory" form a parallel.

[16] Ibid. (with n. 4), herewith cited, in reference to H. von Soden, *Kolosser, Epheser, Philemon, Pastoralbriefe*, 2nd ed. (Tübingen, 1893), 237, and further, M. Albertz, *Die Botschaft des Neuen Testaments* (Zollikon-Zürich: Evangelischer Verlag, 1952), 1/2:132, who holds similar views.

[17] See Gundry, "Form and Meaning," 205, who is correct in noting that (1) this view is already contained in line 5's "believed on in the world"; (2) δόξῃ (line 6) contrasts with κόσμῳ in line 5; and (3) ἀναλαμβάνω in the sense of appropriating one's faith in Jesus can never be used in the personal sense that von Soden's wayward interpretation requires.

[18] E. F. Scott, *The Pastoral Epistles*, The Moffatt New Testament Commentary (New York: Harper and Brothers, n.d.), 41–2; B. S. Easton, *The Pastoral Epistles* (New York: Scribner's, 1947) 136; see Gundry, "Form and Meaning," 205; Marshall, *Pastoral Epistles*, 500–1. Scott's concept of a "refrain" comes closest to what we suggest in this chapter.

[19] A point slightly missed by Gundry, "Form and Meaning," 205–6, who, though noting the incorrect attribution of line 6 to final glory, focuses rather on the supposed antithesis "world" / "glory" in lines 5–6, as if this disallows a separation of line 6 from line 5. But there is no antithesis between "world" and "glory," for the whole phrases include "*believed on* in the world" and "*taken up* in glory"—not as close a match as "*proclaimed* among the Gentiles" (4) with "*believed on* in the world" (5). Gundry (presumably, with others) creates false antitheses between lines 3–4 and 5–6 (1–2 is correct) (206

is essentially the same as that of Scott, who, in opting for a two-strophe scheme, is probably also correct in not linking lines 3-4 and 5-6 with the "three-strophers" but rather—in seeing lines 3 (Appearance to Angels) and 6 (Taken up in Glory) as parallel—suggests that the refrain in line 6 repeats that of line 3.[20] Before we return to our own version of the two-strophe theory, a summary of the three-strophe theory will demonstrate that, though the most popular of all, it proves the least likely to explain the structure of the 1 Tim. 3:16 hymn.

Three-Strophe Theories

The basic division of the hymnic verse comes in its simplest form as three couplets of two lines each, with the following pairs: (1) lines 1-2, with "flesh" / "spirit" paralleling one another; (2) lines 3-4 ("appeared to angels" + "preached among the nations") paralleling; and (3) lines 5-6 ("believed on in the world" / "taken up in glory") matching up.[21] But a close examination of this schema quickly reveals its insurmountable faults: clearly the couplet "flesh" / "spirit" starts out with a great match, but why force such unnatural couplets on the rest? Appearance to Angels (3) + Preaching to the Nations (4) not only shows no correspondence whatsoever, other than sequential— something denied by the "three-strophers," anyway—it also breaks up the rather natural pairing of the adjacent lines in "he was proclaimed to the nations" (ἐκηρύχθη ἐν ἔθνεσιν, line 4) and "he was believed on in the world" (ἐπιστεύθη ἐν κόσμῳ, line 5). The resultant pairings after lines 1-2, sc. "angels" / "Gentiles" (3-4) and "world" / "glory" (5-6), not only prove awkward, ungainly, and unlikely but they do disservice to the full range of each of the phrases, which speak of an "appearance" (ὤφθη) (3) vis-à-vis a "proclamation" (ἐκηρύχθη) (4)—in addition to the mention of angels (ἀγγέλοις) versus "nations" (ἐν ἔθνεσι)—and, moreover, of a "believing" (ἐπιστεύθη) (5) vis-à-vis a being "taken up" (ἀνελήμφθη) (6). Such unnatural pairings, following lines 1-2, cannot be salvaged by simple pronouncements about what the lines actually say, without demonstrable indications that the twosomes validate a thesis for such pairings, sc. "The third couplet indicates the acceptance of Christ both in the world and in heaven."[22]

---

n. 1). The more likely grouping for the whole, as we shall see later, is 1-2 + 4-5 + 3-6, with the last two "dovetailing" to bridge an otherwise neat bifurcation. This intentional overlapping is meant to highlight events culminating in the heavenly realms (as per Dalton in next note).

[20] Ibid., 205 n. 1, on W. J. Dalton, *Christ's Proclamation to the Spirits*, AnBib 23 (Rome: Pontifical Biblical Institute, 1965), 90 n. 19, with additional reference to J. N. D. Kelly, *The Pastoral Epistles* (New York: Harper & Row, 1963), 92, who, though keenly observing that line 3 describes the "ascension through the sphere of angelic powers" (Gundry, "Form and Meaning," 205 n. 1), rejects the two-strophe view. A final view of Sir Robert Falconer, *The Pastoral Epistles* (Oxford: Clarendon, 1937), 137, is rightly rejected by Gundry in oddly bridging, horizontally, the competing elements of the two strophes (206).

[21] As espoused, for example, by Kelly, *Pastoral Epistles*, 92; cf. Gundry, "Form and Meaning," 206; Marshall, *Pastoral Epistles*, 501-3; Martin, "New Perspective," 108-9, citing also Andrew Y. Lau, *Manifest in Flesh: The Epiphany Christology of the Pastoral Epistles*, WUNT II/86 (Tübingen: Mohr Siebeck, 1996), 91, among other commentators.

[22] Or "the second couplet indicates the appearance of Christ to angels and the proclamation of him to mankind," in Gundry's ("Form and Meaning," 206) summarizing of Kelly, in both instances. But neither statement offers any kind of proof toward establishing a nexus with a supposed theory of couplets.

It does no such thing, for being "taken up in glory" (ἀνελήμφθη ἐν δόξῃ, 6) not only says nothing of the *acceptance* of Christ, it has no bearing at all on Jesus being "believed on in the world," as if there were some systematic theological reason that preaching and belief has allowed Jesus to gain entrance into heaven. For this reason, Gundry is no doubt correct in seeing neglected, if not more powerful, parallelism between lines 1 and 6 and 4 and 5—that is, between an initial manifestation in the flesh and a final exaltation in glory; and between proclamation and reception.[23] But, once again, lines 3 and 6, which themselves parallel, whether "spatial" or "chronological," harry the scheme.[24]

A Two-Stanza Scheme, with a Twist

This brings us to our own interpretation, which we introduce with an observation on the ancient phenomenon of syllable-count. Isocolon—the equality of syllables—is a well-known rhetorical actuality of classical Greek composition. Gundry already cites Eduard Norden (followed by Spicq) in noting the apparent absence of it in this hymn as an indication of "an early Palestinian Jewish matrix rather than a 'Hellenistic' one."[25] But there is little reason to see this hymn, if even stemming from a Jewish milieu, as having to be a *translation* of a Semitic original; it could well have derived from a Hellenistic Jewish milieu that composed in Greek, albeit with a strong Semitic mindset and grammatical-structural *Hintergrund*—that is, one showing verbs coming first, aorist passives, no contrastive μέν/δέ constructions, and so on—yet still remaining highly Hellenized in outlook.[26] In fact, the pervasiveness of the passives—used with every single verb in the creed—is odd even for a Semitic composition and may have more to do with the peculiar anonymity of the hymn's subject-matter than with anything else, a topic we take up in greater detail later. Aorist passives such as these are often used as circumlocutions for the handiwork of God, the avoidance of whose Name may be seen as a conventional gesture of respect within orthodoxy in sidestepping the utterance of the ineffable *Shem*. But such a reticence might not apply here at all, since the unspoken subject of the passive verbs is hardly God—or at least not exclusively Him, as the divine agent behind the actions of the verbs—but rather *human* justifiers (depending upon

---

[23] Ibid., 208–9, though, again, not so much between lines 2 and 3, as mentioned earlier. Gundry then goes on to describe elaborations on the three-strophe theme à la Dibelius, Conzelmann, Jeremias, Spicq, and Schweizer, which need not concern us here, since the discussion to follow somewhat vitiates the details of their individual arguments (206–9). Gundry also summarizes and critiques the views of Jeremias, Spicq, and Deichgräber (207 n. 2, with bibliographical references in n. 1), pertaining to somewhat balky parallels to Egyptian enthronement ceremonies.

[24] Ibid., 207: "The movement of thought is spatial rather than chronological because one important point is that the Saviour has reunited heaven and earth." But such a reunion can also be chronologically expressed. Further, the attempt to link lines 3–4 and especially lines 5–6 seem particularly forced with the three couplets interpretation (cf., e.g., ibid., 207: "And in lines 5 and 6 the singing church praises the victory of Christ").

[25] Ibid., 220, with n. 4, on E. Norden, *Agnostos Theos: Untersuchungen zur Formengeschichte religiöser Rede* (Leipzig: Teubner, 1913), 254–7; and C. Spicq, *Les épîtres pastorales* (Ébib; Paris: J. Gabalda, 1947), 108.

[26] Gundry, "Form and Meaning," 220–1.

how we interpret ἐδικαιώθη in 2), *human* proclaimers (4), and *human* believers (5). Only line 6's ἀνελήμφθη (was taken up) has an indubitable agent in God.[27]

Semitic composition aside, the decidedly Hellenistic use of isocolon in our hymn, as noted by Norden, Spicq, and even Gundry, may be more pervasive than formerly thought. What has not been previously noticed is that this hymn's entire composition is made up a single large-scale isocolon, showing the entirety of 1 Tim. 3:16—minus its introductory ὅς (or ὅ)—dividing perfectly into two equal parts of 22 syllables each: Stanza I = 5 + 3 + 5 + 4 + 2 + 3 (= 22 syllables) and Stanza II = 4 + 4 + 4 + 3 + 4 + 3 (= 22 syllables). Consider the following schematic diagram:

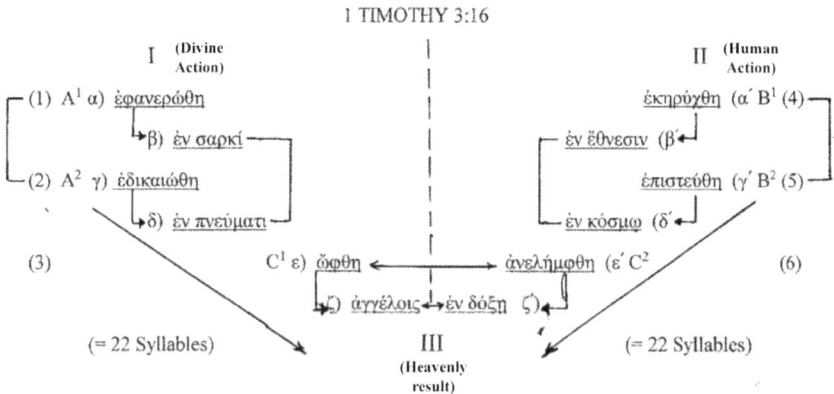

This chart adumbrates the partition of the Timothy hymn into its two respective components, based upon the identification of a kind of "double helix" composed of a 22 + 22 syllabic isocolonic configuration.[28] The left side (strophe I) in the figure shows the first three lines (of 22 syllables) of the hymn, cascading downward, with the individual phrases labeled sequentially and capping in the Appearance to Angels (line 3). The right side (strophe II), equally of 22 syllables, provides the final three verses (4–6)—similarly running downward—with a climax in the Ascension of line 6. The identification of this 22 + 22 syllable isocolon will ensure that the hymn is to be divided exactly into a *two*-strophe schema of equal syllabic parts, making the 3-line + 3-line configuration the only truly viable strophic layout—but with a twist. The basic pattern will be A-A-C::B-B-C and not the expected A-B-C::A'-B'-C' (or A-B-C-D-E-F), so that the twin C-couplets (labeled above C¹ and C²), coming at the end of each stanza, will "dovetail" to form a type of bridge joining the two ends. Lying in separate strophes

---

[27] Both ἐφανερώθη (1) and ὤφθη (3) are more nondescript and work better in a "middle" rather than "passive" sense: "He manifested himself" (1) and "He made himself seen" (or "was made seen/visible") (2)—this last, in English, having no aorist passive equivalent is usually rendered "appeared." But see discussion on p. 194.

[28] A¹⁻² + C¹ represents strophe **I** and B¹⁻² + C² represents strophe **II**. The Greek letters α, β, γ/α', β', γ', and so on are added further to identify individual words or phrases. Arabic numerals, (1), (2), and so on identify original line numbers. We superimpose at the bottom (to be inverted, later) a third category (**III** = C¹ + C²) around which the other two appear to "wrap," as if around a pole or column, as they "descend." This third category, however, is not a separate strophe, as discussed later.

(I and II), this dovetailing will create a discrete apex—here momentarily shown at the bottom—that, with its matching elements, crowns the whole hymn with a climactic glorification of Christ in the heavenlies. Thus, as an overlapping pair, the two will form what we label as a third, independent category (III), even though the double strophic pattern remains intact, with each part, C^1 and C^2, falling to the side of its own strophe, I and II, respectively.

In terms of classification, this twofold stanzic arrangement of three lines each, in the first instance, gives what we refer to as the *divine action* (strophe I), or *divine sphere*, of the hymn—what occurs in respect of Jesus's life ($A^{1-2} + C^1$), from the point of view of the nonhuman agency of God. Next, in the second instance, we have what amounts to the *human action* (strophe II) of the hymn, that following Jesus's life, death, and resurrection—when he is kerygmatically preached *about* and believed *upon*—but it is something that although holding true for the preaching apostles and accepting believers does not apply so much to his ascension ($B^{1-2} + C^2$):

I (Divine Action/Sphere)

Line 1: Incarnation (A^1 α-β)
Line 2: Death/Resurrection (A^2 γ-δ)
Line 3: Appearance to Angels/Glorification (C^1 ε-ζ)

II (Human Action/Sphere)

Line 4: Proclamation among the Nations (B^1 α-β)
Line 5: Reception (Belief on) in the World (B^2 γ-δ)
Line 6: Ascension (C^2 ε-ζ)

Put slightly differently, the first strophe (I, lines 1–3) deals with the *divine*, or heavenly, action upon Jesus, when he lived as a human being on the earth-plane; the second strophe (II, lines 4–6) captures the *human* action upon Jesus, as he lives as a divine figure in the heavenly plane. The first addresses the *divine* Manifestation, Vindication, and Appearance of Jesus in the human sphere; the second, the human Preaching *about*, Reception *of*, and the *taking up* of Jesus from among humans, into the divine sphere.[29] The third element in strophes I and II can thus be seen to cap each stanza with a matching *glorification* of Jesus ($C^1 = C^2$):

$A^1/A^2 + C^1$ = Divine Action → Leading to Human (= Jesus) Result → Glorification
$B^1/B^2 + C^2$ = Human Action → Leading to Divine (= Jesus) Result → Glorification

But herein lies the twist. The concluding lines of each strophe (3 and 6 = $C^1 + C^2$) do not, respectively, fall within their own purview as concrete examples of our just-mentioned taxonomy of *God acting* versus *human acting* upon the person of Jesus.

---

[29] That is, when Jesus is taken up, after having lived and taught as a *resurrected human being* among his human disciples, for a period of time—perhaps even years, as this hymn suggests—as we discuss later. It must be remembered that the figure of Jesus as a resurrected being differs from that of Jesus as an *ascended* being.

For in the first strophe with the appearance of Jesus to angels (line 3) and in the second strophe with the ascension of Jesus (line 6), our divine/human roles seem to have been reversed. In strophe I—our "God-acting" stanza—it is the *human* being, Jesus, who now makes *himself* to appear (ὤφθη) to the angels (line 3 = C^1); whereas in strophe II—the "Human-acting" stanza—it is Jesus himself who is acted upon by God (ἀνελήφθη) (line 6 = C^2). Thus, the two C-sections uniquely cap the individual parts of their own strophes by forming a bridge that crowns the whole of the hymn's cosmic drama. Each in turn transposes the divine/human compartmentalization within their own columns to emphasize and elevate the hymn's tall lyrics by bringing the story of Jesus into its final resting place in the heavenlies. But the recapitulating third element of each of the two strophes (namely, $C^{1,2}$ = lines 3, 6), though of heavenly import, individually, still belongs in their respective columns (or strophes), since the appearance to angels aligns Jesus somewhat with the earth-plane (see later), whereas his being taken up in glory aligns him with the heavenly plane. Thus, this "Heavenly Result," or Glorification, of $C^1 + C^2$, though not a separate strophe, will be seen to top off each of the two stanzas (I–II), like coping stones, with its own built-in category as a self-contained unit, III. Both $C^1 + C^2$ will simultaneously remain in their own proper stanzas, I and II, respectively. One can look at the whole as if a large "angel-food cake" of two halves (I–II) with a thick, heavenly icing covering the top and joining the two halves of the inner caking, sliced evenly down the middle.

This newly shaped schema, demonstrating an extraordinary division of the Christological hymn into two equal parts, presents a uniquely interweaving juxtaposition of a Jesus who, in the first instance, is being divinely acted upon (I), followed by a post-resurrection Christ, who, in the second instance, is being humanly acted upon by a believing group of energetic disciples and converts (II). All of this is somehow being secretly recorded in a hymn that not only lacks any designated figures, divine or human, but also mentions no name of Jesus himself. At the quickening crescendo of this mysterious figure's elevation to the "heavenly" spheres, the third, hidden, category (III) of our diagram summarizes in an almost visual manner the whole of the hymn by crisscrossing the roles of man and god in its presentation of a human being who appears to angels and then turns into a divine figure exalted to the supernal realms. The "secret" of the hymn remains not only in the absence of an unnamed cross but in the lack of a named Jesus.

The Ancient Art of "Visual Poetry" or *Technopaignion*

Technopaignion, or "Visual Poetry," as it is sometimes called, represents a special class of figured drawing whereby lesser-known writers—mostly bucolic poets, as well as later prose authors—produced poems, entitling them after certain commonplace shapes.[30] The "play" in such writing was the technique whereby the poems themselves would be graphically written out in the shapes of the works that carried their titles—hence, the

---

[30] Christine Luz, *Technopaignia. Formspiele in der griechische Dichtung*, Mnemosyne Supplements 324 (Leiden: Brill, 2010); Luis Arturo Guichard, "Simias' Pattern Poems," in M. A. Harder, R. F. Regtuit,

name τεχνοπαίγνιον. It was also a widely popular form of writing in the early Roman Imperial period (and later), along with acrostics, palindromes, isopsephia, and similar wordplays.[31] Examples of such Hellenistic poets and their works include Simias of Rhodes's (third century BCE) *Wings*, *Axe*, and *Egg*; Dosiadas' *Altar* (of Hellenistic date or later); Ps.-Theocritus' *Syrinx* (of Imperial date); and Besantinus's *Altar*.[32]

A particularly good representation of such a *technopaignion* is that preserved in Simias's *Axe*, a poem shaped in the form of a double axe, as best presented in the diagrammatic text and translation of Guichard's, given here. The writing begins broadly at the top and narrows down with each subsequent line diminishing, only to expand again after the apex:[33]

1	Phocian Epeius in gratitude for her strong device, to the virile goddess Athena
3	Then when he burnt to ashes with fire-breathing doom the holy city
5	a man who was not reckoned among the Achaean chieftains,
7	But now he was entered on the path of Homer,
9	thrice blessed he whom with a gracious
11	This blessedness
12	ever breathes.
10	mind you watchest over.
8	thanks to you, holy Pallas of many counsels,
6	but an unknown one who carried water from the pure fountains.
4	of the Dardinae and dashed down from their seats the gilded kings,
2	gave the axe with which of old he laid in ruin the high, god-built towers.

But as the reader will soon note from the line numbers to the left, the poem is not to be read sequentially, from top to bottom, but rather with the lines alternating between the upper and lower parts, as they form the rough shape of a double-ax, with the upper half *descending* in its diminution of lines, and the lower half *ascending* toward the center. The role of the axe (πέλεκυν, 2) in the poem, moreover, is actually of only modest import, as an altogether different religious narrative dominates the story line;

---

and G. C. Wakker (eds.), *Beyond the Canon*, Hellenistica Groningana 11 (Leuven: Peeters, 2006), 82–104; S. Strodel, *Zur Überlieferung und zum Verständnis der hellenistischen Technopagnien* (Frankfurt, 2002); Dick Higgins, *Pattern Poetry: Guide to an Unknown Literature* (Albany: State University of New York Press, 1987), 19–24, who also mentions the later Greek Magical Papyri (175; discussed later); G. Wojaczek, *Daphnis. Untersuchungen zur griechischen Bukolik* (Meisenheim: Hain, 1969); "Bucolica analecta," *WJA* 5 (1979): 81–90; "Bukolische Weihegaben. Die Figurengedichte von Simias, Theokrit und Dosiadas," in P. Neukam (ed.), *Motiv und Motivation* (München: Bayerische Schulbuch-Verlag, 1993), 125–76.

[31] Luz, *Technopaignia*.

[32] Cf. Guichard, "Simias' Pattern Poems," 84, with n. 7, who also writes of an extensive tradition of visual poetry, that is to say, texts that in a broad sense try to represent the shape of objects. Although this sort of poetry has been commonly considered in terms of literary oddity, erudite experiment, and avant-garde, recent studies have demonstrated its continuity from Antiquity to modern times, the Greek poems being the first examples preserved.

[33] Ibid., 87, which slight modifications to the punctuation. The *Egg*, for example, is shaped oppositely, with the short lines coming first at top and bottom and expanding in the middle to form an ovoid shape; see the text and translation in ibid., 94–5.

indeed in the case of the *Egg*,³⁴ the word "egg" itself is not even mentioned in the poem. Such shapes focus more on the novelty of the "wing-shaped"—or other—patterns. Remarkably, what has not been noted, as far as can be determined in the case of this particular poem, is that the *Axe*, just like the Timothy hymn, also presents a perfect isocolon of 78 syllables for each of its upper and lower halves.³⁵

Such shapes of the bucolic poems are regularly represented visually in later manuscripts of authors such as Simias, and despite different manuscripts showing variations on the shapes of these poems—with at least four different layouts for the *Axe* itself—it becomes clear from Hephaestion, the second-century metrician, that figured writing was intended to be written to enhance its visual effect, even if the actual manuscripts do not always depict the intended shapes.³⁶ This will have important implications for the preservation of our hymn in its own form of writing.

For now, even if the configuration of the Christological hymn does not form an actual shape of an *Axe* or an *Egg*—or even a cake mold, for that matter—in our preserved manuscripts, its arrangement of parallel *stichoi*, precise phrasing, and balanced isocola seems to presuppose a text that was formerly built upon just such a tradition of "figured writing." We know from the earlier discussion that such compositions as these (called λέξις γραφική or graphic speech) focused on the manner in which the actual writing was to be presented—not in terms of calligraphic writing, per se, but in terms of the way that such patterns or shapes could be graphically presented, whether the pattern was acrostic, palindromic, chiastic, or truly "visual." In the same manner that Simias's *Axe* can be seen to form a kind of double "pyramidal" shape, one inverted to another, despite its being called an "axe," so too can the Timothy hymn be viewed as a single pyramid, but with its twin bases now representing the starting point of each of our two identified strophes, as the lines individually ascend upward (1a → 3b + 4a → 6b):

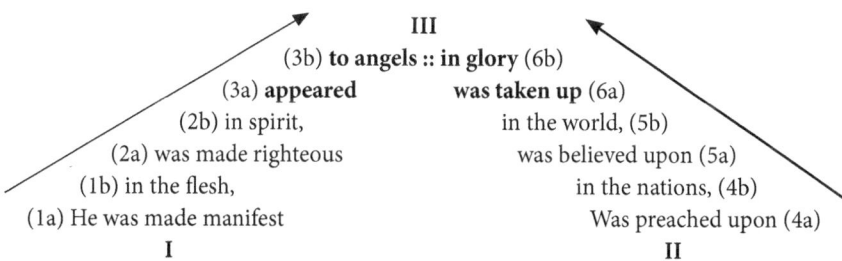

---

³⁴ See n. 33.

³⁵ That is, if ἱεράν (3) were read as 3 syllables, or conversely if ἵλαος (10) were read as 2 (yielding 77 syllables each). This attention to isocolon in the Hellenistic examples adds weighty credence to the thesis that the isocolonic configuration of the 1 Timothy hymn will contribute to its interpretation as an example of *technopaignia*.

³⁶ Ibid., 87–8, with n. 21, on Hephaestion, *Ench. metr.* (p. 62.5–6 Consbruch): "Of this shape are also Simias' *Egg* and other poems" and the scholion on Theocritus (p. 343.7–10 Wendel): "The reader should place the last kolon after the first, then the second from the beginning, and after this the second from the end, and continue on this way until coming to the middle." Guichard also gives the Greek of all such passages. For the manuscript illustrations, see Guichard, "Simias' Pattern Poems," 88–9, 100 (Plate 1): *Parisinus suppl. gr. 384*, f. 28v (s. X²/²), Bibliothèque nationale de France; 102 (Plate 3): *Vaticanus gr. 434*, f. 3r (s. XIII–XIV), Biblioteca Apostolica Vaticana.

In this case, we have inverted our original diagram given earlier to present it as a now upright "pyramid"—or to retain our earlier imagery, a raised, layered "cake"—but we realize, based upon the liberties afforded such visual writing, that our "cake" had been baked upside down all along. Now our hymn, if we can imagine it being diagrammed on its presumably original sheet of papyrus, is to be sung from its beginning in the lower left of the hymnal page (I), then rising to the first of two climaxes in the heavenly appearance of Jesus to the angels. Next, with the second strophe (II), beginning anew at the lower-right corner, the song will climb in its subsequent verse to come to full apogee, as graphically presented in the model's upper-left corner in a line (6a–b), which ends with the Lord's ascension (III).

Some Examples from Ritual Invocations

Such pyramidal visual shapes, as is well known, were also a common feature—using ancient Greek vowels and other syllabic configurations—of the widely studied Greek Magical Papyri and kindred texts.[37] Although our hymn is not a "magical" text, per se, its configuration does share a connection with such broadly disseminated ritual texts; their examples further demonstrate how visual and figured writing extended well beyond the bucolic examples of their Hellenistic forebears. For example, *PGM* I.12–19 presents just such a pair of pyramidal shapes, the one ascending, the other descending, that is, as an inverted pair composed of an incrementally expanding set of the diminishing seven vowels:[38]

[37] On *technopaignion* in ancient magic, see Luz, *Technopaignia*, 213–22; C. A. Faraone, *Vanishing Acts on Ancient Greek Amulets: From Oral Performance to Visual Design* (London: Institute of Classical Studies, 2012), 4–5.

[38] H. D. Betz, ed., *The Greek Magical Papyri in Translation, including the Demotic Spells*, 2nd ed. (Chicago: University of Chicago Press, 1992), 3, with Greek text in K. Preisendanz, *Papyri Graecae Magicae. Die griechische Zauberpapyri*, 2 vols. (Stuttgart: Teubner, 1973–4), abbreviated *PGM*, followed by papyrus number and line. Faraone, *Vanishing Acts*, 4–5, 78, discusses the possibility that magic borrowed the technique from the poets.

The key here is to see that though the papyrus instructions at first identify the writing of the vowels in a simple linear fashion, as follows: α εε ηηη ιιιι οοοοο υυυυυυ ωωωωωωω (*PGM* I.11), it next specifies that the vowels should actually be *written* in specific shapes, that is, by making two pyramidal κλίματα, "inclinations," or "ladders," as shown on the illustrated papyrus (*PGM* I.11–19).[39] The actual writing will thus take on an especially figural shape. The magic spell, in which this configuration is used, involves a ritual to acquire the assistance of a heavenly deity, named inter alia as "the holy Orion" (ὁ ἅγιος Ὠρίων, *PGM* I.29). That the shape of the descending and ascending pyramids is meant to assist, as a kind of heavenly ladder, the very arrival of the summoned god is proved by the fact that within the invocation, the "ladder" sequence of vowels is to be uttered again, this time naming the god in the vocative, along with the command that he "come to me," and so on (α εε ηηη ιιιι οοοοο υυ[υυυ]υ ωωωωωωω ἧκέ μοι, κτλ.; *PGM* I.26). This shows that such technical, figured writing was meant to provide a type of manuscript "map"—or in the case of the Timothy hymn, a song-sheet, so to speak—to help in the proper interpretation and understanding that the shape of the composition was intended to play.[40] In the two cases here—the configuration of the Christ-hymn and the pattern of vocalic "magical" invocation—are both meant to narrate how a heavenly figure comes down and ultimately ascends after playing out an assigned role, although the differences between the two types—the one Christian, the other pagan—prove somewhat different in the individual import and the religious context in which they are grounded. But the two not only appear to share a common literary device, they no doubt reflect a shared concept of divine descension and ascension.

Another invocational prayer, *PGM* IV.1167–1226, infused with strong Jewish elements such as that with which the prayer ends ("I call upon you, the one on the gold leaf … the great God, the one who shone on the whole world, who is radiant at Jerusalem, lord," etc.) also seems to build upon this tradition of a "ladder" of vowels that reaches to heaven. The text, after the invocation, immediately continues with a series of vowel-permutations beginning and ending with Ἰάω (= יהו). The vowels, parenthetically labeled in the manuscript as consisting of "100 letters," are identified just before the Jerusalem invocation as a kind of heavenly stairway:

> Creator of the world, creator of the universe, lord, god of gods, MARMARIŌ IAŌ. I have spoken your unsurpassable glory, you who created gods, archangels, and decans … I invoke your hundred-lettered name *which extends from the sky* (ἀπὸ τοῦ στερεώματος) *to the depth of the earth*; save me, for you are always rejoicing in saving those who are yours, etc.[41]

The prayer, which is said to deliver one even from death, also opens with a hymn of praise to the largely Jewish creator God—blended, to be sure, with other, diverse

---

[39] See LSJ, s.v. κλίμα. The sense is uncertain, but assuredly has to do with the figure's shape; cf. Betz, *Greek Magical Papyri*, 3 n. 5. For the various names of these figural shapes, see Faraone, *Vanishing Acts*, 1–2, who also discusses examples of them presented in linear fashion (13–14).
[40] See n. 44.
[41] Betz, *Greek Magical Papyri*, 61 = *PGM* IV.1200–1213; my italics.

syncretistic elements. The fact that the prayer next turns to ask that the "Father of the world" (πατέρα κόσμου; IV.1170) come to the petitioner (δεῦρό μοι; 1171), and later that "Heaven be opened" (ἀνοίγηθι, οὐρανέ; 1180), suggests that the 100-lettered name was meant to serve as a visualizing device representing the ladder whereby God is able to descend to earth in order to help the praying candidate. It also hints that other, palindromic names of God, such as AŌ EY ĒOI AIOĒ YEŌA (1183), within the prayer contain just the right amount of vowels to allow them to be shaped into "heavenly" pyramids, by having one letter added (or removed) with each successive line:

α
ω ε
υ η ο
ι α ι ο
η υ ε ω α

Or,

α ω ε η υ
ο ι α ι
ο η υ
ε ω
α

A late antique Greco-Aramaic amulet on a silver *lamella* (leaf), preserving a long bilingual exorcism for John (Ἰωάννης) son of Benenata, also contains in its upper-middle (Greek) section various groupings of vowel-pyramids, mostly in descending order, among which occurs the divine name Ιαω, also in pyramid formation.[42] Below this can be read the Aramaic equivalent for "Father," Αββα, Αββα, Αββα, Αββα, but in a rectangular shape. What proves noteworthy about this particular grouping of vowels is the presence of long columns of η's, ε's, and α's to the left of the wing-figured formations. These would seem to allude to the opening exorcistic formula on the silver leaf which begins in Aramaic, "I bind this amulet from Jerusalem, in the name of Yah" (lines 7–8) and continues with the naming of the angels Penan'el and Joel, "who is with the chariot of Yah, and *who causes the pillars of heaven and earth to shake*" (line 10, italics added). Here we have a clear indication that the "pillared" columns of vowels on the silver exorcism, which were no doubt chanted or sung (as well as written), were meant to represent the heavenly pillars that do indeed shake.[43] A set of unexplained slash-marks, ////////////, right after this reference to shaking,

---

[42] R. Kotansky, J. Naveh, and S. Shaked, "A Greek-Aramaic Silver Amulet from Egypt in the Ashmolean Museum," *Le Muséon* 105 (1992): 5–24, esp. 8, lines at 6a. The text is composed of thirty-seven long lines written across the width of the tablet.

[43] The cosmic shaking itself is no doubt intended as a like-by-like (*similia similibus*) action made to reinforce the efficacy of the exorcism itself, whose opening lines refer to the *shaking* of the "filthy spirit from the 248 limbs" of the possessed bearer of the charm. On the phenomenon of written and spoken amulets, see R. D. Kotansky, "Textual Amulets and Writing Traditions in the Ancient World," in David Frankfurter (ed.), *Guide to the Study of Ancient Magic*, RGRW 189 (Leiden: Brill, 2019), 507–54.

would also seem to depict either the pillars themselves or more likely the shaking of the cosmos itself. We introduce these examples to show that in certain hymnic contexts, configurations of vowels, or other formulas, were regularly shaped into a sort of figured writing in order to portray graphically narrative features of the hymn or invocation. Again, our Timothy hymn shows a plausible nexus with these papyrus invocations, as well as some connection with the tradition of the bucolic poetry; it also appears to preserve a hymn that, in its displaying a marked isocolon of syllables with a distinctive A-A-C + B-B-C pattern, could easily lend itself to being graphically depicted as a dually strophed hymn, dovetailing upward to its dramatically heavenly climax in the manner of the more mystic configurations of the Magical Papyri. As a hymn that was presumably sung early on within the pre-Pauline Christian communities, it is only natural that the matching "ascensions" of Jesus in 1 Tim. 3:16, preserved in the climatic C-portions isolated in our earlier analysis, should come at the "heights" of the song's apogee, pictorially represented at the apex of the pyramidal stairway to heaven, showing an ascended Jesus on top in his appearance to angels.[44] Thus, the singing itself can be seen to reach the very heights of heaven, from which supernal realms Jesus himself also rules. Perhaps, too, we can imagine the hymnal tones starting low on the musical scale (whether seen or heard), then rising steadily to the higher registers of the human voice as it sings the song's refrain and tells of the glory of Jesus's appearance to heavenly angels and his ascension to the heights of the celestial worlds above. Ours is no longer just a strictly chronological ordering of prosaic verses; it reaches a distinctive crescendo in the rising climax in the glorification and exaltation of Jesus, presented in a "figured" formation of markedly mystico-magical proportions.

Meaning

The Individual Elements

Having examined the form of our Timothy hymn, we turn to some particulars of the individual lines, which Gundry especially, and subsequent commentators, have carefully analyzed. We do not intend to hash out anew the long history of exegesis that these lines have endured, but rather to focus on how our new identity of the hymn's isocolon and its subsequent division into a two-strophe composition affect our understanding of the hymn's individual components. With the view that our hymn can be divided neatly into two stanzas of 22 syllables each (I–II), topped by a bridging pair of heavenly "choruses" (III), it becomes clear that the composition will follow a rather strict sequential pattern. Based upon much of modern exegesis, it becomes clear that the meaning of lines 2 and 3, and to a lesser degree line 1, remains difficult, not to speak

---

[44] It is also possible that the graphic depiction could be "visually" imagined, as it was sung. Faraone, *Vanishing Acts*, 10, gives examples (*PGM* II.1–2, 5–6) of *speaking*, not writing, a name in its proper "pyramidal" shape or "winged-formation" (πτερυγοειδῶς), even though it is written out only linearly. Forming a mental picture of the step-pyramidal shape of the Timothy hymn earlier, I have determined, aids in its easy memorization, so that "figured" writing can also take on shape simply as "figured" singing.

of the chronology of line 6. We also maintain that, because of the sharp isocolonic division, the arrangement of the hymn lends itself most readily to a chronological sequence, as argued by the original six-verse schemers. That means that the Ascension in line 6 will represent the culmination of the entirety of the hymn, a matter we take up in greater detail here.

Line 1: *Manifestation in Flesh.* The standard explanation of this line takes it as a reference to the incarnation, but upon closer examination matters are not so straightforward. For Gundry, ἐφανερώθη "probably refers to the entire earthly career of Jesus right up to his ascension, not to his birth alone,"[45] thus taking the aorist as a constative aorist. But constative aorists are not used of Jesus in lines 2–3, and such a use would rob the sequence of its true chronological sense. We cannot have the chronology of these lines blending one into another, with ἐφανερώθη ἐν σαρκί overlapping ἐδικαιώθη ἐν πνεύματι (2)—not to speak of ἀνελήμφθη ἐν δόξῃ in line 6. A more discrete and punctiliar force of the verbs makes better sense, as we shall see later. Even if Gundry's broad incarnational chronology may take the interpretation further than others, he is absolutely correct in challenging Stanley's view that line 1 refers to the crucifixion (alone) and not to the incarnation.[46] The discussion illuminates the troubles with the phrase, for here chronological problems are seemingly encountered from the very outset. The use of φανερόω "for the incarnate ministry of Jesus"[47] (cited by Gundry in Jn 1:31; Heb. 9:26; 1 Pet. 1:20; and 1 Jn 1:2, 3:5, 8) does not provide the closest parallels in that references to the "flesh" are absent, plus there remain strong doubts that they refer to Jesus's incarnation.[48] The mentions of σάρξ applied to a human lifetime lose their force when attached to the aorist passive ἐφανερώθη, but there can be no doubt that the noun refers to the human experience. The verb φανερόω, on the other hand,

---

[45] Gundry, "Form and Meaning," 209–10. Further, Marshall, *Pastoral Epistles*, 523–5, with reference to, but not emphasis on, the preexistence of Christ, plus the remark, "The most that can be said is that the historical event of the incarnation is in mind" (524).

[46] Gundry, "Form and Meaning," 209, with n. 1, on D. M. Stanley, *Christ's Resurrection in Pauline Soteriology*, AnBib 13 (Rome: Pontifical Biblical Institute, 1961), 237, with additional references and discussion. Gundry (210) further challenges the views of Descamps, Dupont, and Schneider, in seeing line 1 as a reference to Jesus's *corporeal* post-resurrection appearances (on which, see further later).

[47] Gundry, "Form and Meaning," 209.

[48] Jn 1:31 refers to Jesus's being "revealed to Israel" through the agency of (ἵνα = διὰ τοῦτο) John's actions, namely, a revelatory baptism; it has nothing to do with Jesus's incarnation, much less his birth. 1 Jn 1:2 uses the verb of the manifestation of ἡ ζωή (ἡ αἰώνιον), "(eternal) life," as a circumlocution for Jesus, with no reference to "flesh" or incarnation per se; and even if the passages in 1 Jn 3:5, 8, do refer to the "manifestation" of Jesus, it is again surprisingly vague on incarnational language. If Jn 1:31 serves as our guide, then these latter references in 1 John will also refer to Jesus's "manifestation"—that is, his "unveiling" at the commencement of his ministry in baptism—and not to his incarnation. These passages all seem to depend upon a Markan, or pre-Markan, concept of an arrival of Jesus as the "coming one" (ἔρχεται, Mk 1:7). Heb. 9:26 and 1 Pet. 1:20, building upon a common eschatological tradition, may also be mirroring this tradition as well. Thus ἐφανερώθη ἐν σαρκί remains a unique expression. The reference in Martin, "New Perspective," 111, to *Epist. Barn.* 12:9 (read 12:10), "manifested in the flesh," looks like a paraphrase of 1 Tim. 3:16. A closer look at the passage that reads, "Again, see Jesus, not as son of man, but son of God, but *in form*, having been manifested in flesh" (τύπῳ δὲ ἐν σαρκὶ φανερωθείς) suggests that the addition of the phrase "but in form" aims to explain a less-than-straightforward phrase. In *Epist. Barn.* 15:9, as noted by Martin (n. 45), φανερωθείς is used of the resurrection appearances (see later and n. 79).

as we shall see further later, will flow more readily when used of the resurrection of Jesus, not of his incarnation.

Line 2: *Vindication in Spirit*. The phrase ἐδικαιώθη ἐν πνεύματι is even more problematic than that of line 1, as Gundry observes, who correctly challenges interpretations that understand ἐδικαιώθη to mean "divinized."[49] For such a sense, we would have expected, for example, ἐδοξάσθη ἐν πνεύματι, "he was *glorified* in spirit," not "*vindicated* in spirit," but that is not what we have—or ever did.[50] The difficulty is that we are working with two expressions—ἐν πνεύματι and ἐδικαιώθη—that prove discomforting. They do not seem to go well together. The parallelism between ἐν σαρκί and ἐν πνεύματι, under normal circumstances, should help to elucidate each contrastive passage, but such overly abstract interpretations as "in the fleshly, corporeal, or earthly sphere," for the former, and "in the spiritual or heavenly sphere," for the latter, fail to take into account the contextual and individualistic nature of the phrases.[51]

For ἐδικαιώθη in line 2 one has to ask what "vindication in the spirit" really means. Adhering more to a locative sense for the datives, Gundry questions the views that see reference to Jesus's "anointing with the Spirit at baptism ... his miracles, exorcisms, preaching, and spotless life through the Holy Spirit"[52] and the even more widely held view that line 2 refers to the resurrection *by the agency of the Holy Spirit*, since the datives cannot be instrumental.[53] Owing to the inherent difficulties in the phrase, Gundry turns to a novel preference suggested by 1 Pet. 3:18-19, namely, that Jesus's

---

[49] Gundry, "Form and Meaning," 210: "The meaning of 'vindicated in spirit' (line 2) lies in doubt." Cf. Marshall, *Pastoral Epistles*, 524, with n. 76; Martin, "New Perspective," 112, writes, "Scholars disagree on the meaning of each word," and reports the variety of translations and interpretations.

[50] As argued by E. Schweizer, *Lordship and Discipleship* (London: SCM, 1960); and A. Descamps, *Les Justes et la Justice dans les évangiles et le christianisme primitif hormis la doctrine proprement paulinienne* (Louvain: Publications Universitaires, 1950), 87-9, with Gundry's criticism, "Form and Meaning," 210, with n. 3 (cf. 207 n. 1).

[51] The two, much like the parallels in 1 Pet. 3:18 (later), thus argue more for datives of reference. So, rightly, Gundry, "Form and Meaning," 211, who, however, allows for the locative as well. But a translation such as "he was vindicated in the spiritual sphere" seems too obtuse to warrant any real plausible sense. In the end, Gundry seems to favor the view that line 2 "refers to that vindication in spirit prior to the resurrection" (214; cf. 211 n. 2); that is, in going to the "abyss in spirit-form to proclaim his triumph [he] thus enjoyed vindication before the hostile spirits there" (213); see discussion in the chapter with n. 54.

[52] Ibid., 212. When Marshall, *Pastoral Epistles*, 526, writes, "The occasion of the vindication is amply indicated in the testimony of the early church" (citing in n. 84, Rom. 1:4; 1 Cor. 2:1-9; Phil. 2:5-11; Col. 2:8-15; Eph. 1:20-21; Acts 2:22-36, 3:11-15, 4:10-12, 10:34-43; 1 Pet. 3:21-22) and speaks of "Jesus' vindication before hostile powers," not a word is said of vindication, nor a hint of vindication in the spirit among the references. Martin, "New Perspective," 113, presents interpretive possibilities from the earthly ministry to the resurrection, and everything in between, but his view that the line refers to Jesus being declared righteous "by the Spirit" is condemned by the strict spatial/locative sense required by the twin flesh/spirit phrases.

[53] Gundry, "Form and Meaning," 212, although he opts for a reference to the resurrection "in the realm of the spirit with reference to the spiritual nature of Christ's glorified body." Marshall, *Pastoral Epistles*, 525, writes: "The phrase may refer to the means or agent of vindication, i.e. the Holy Spirit ... if vindication and resurrection are identical"—they are not—and choose rather the human mode/sphere versus the supernatural. In any event, "vindication in spirit," as a reference to the resurrection, cannot stand, as we will show later.

vindication refers to his descent into the infernal world in the time between his death and resurrection.[54]

But the problem, it seems, lies in the verbs themselves, not in the datives. We have seen some of the issues attending ἐφανερώθη, in the first phrase of line 1. Worse is the sense of ἐδικαιώθη in line 2. With the second line referring to the resurrection, how is that sense to be construed with the verb δικαιόω? This verb would seem to suggest that Jesus somehow needed *justification* or *vindication* for a life well lived, and if so, how did that occur in the realm of the spirit? Did the resurrection, in a sense, *validate* the life he had experienced in the flesh?[55] That might represent a theology hard to come by in the New Testament. Jesus's life, often referred to as being spotless and sinless in the Scriptures, is hardly one requiring justification, although the centurion's declaration at the cross that Jesus was δίκαιος in Lk. 23:47 (cf. Mt. 27:19) stands out as an exception. But here Jesus is judged righteous "in the flesh," not "in the spirit."

We might find help by beginning with a different definition for δικαιόω than that usually touted for this passage. What comes to mind as a workable option is the sense found for the verb in Aeschylus, *Agamem*. 393, where δικαιωθείς means "proved" or "tested"—something more specialized than that related to mere chastisement alone.[56] The verb also occurs in a similar sense in the LXX of Ezek. 21:18 (13), where it translates the Hebrew בחן (to test).[57] But this may not be the exact definition we are looking for. The root of δίκη, from which our verb derives, can carry the sense of "judgment; punishment," as well as "justice," "atonement," "satisfaction"; it is captured in the cognate meaning of δικαιόω—*do a man right*, or *do justice*, that is, *chastise, punish; pass sentence on* (LSJ, s.v., def. III. 1). Although it is akin to the definition *pronounce and treat as righteous, justify, vindicate* (LSJ's def. III. 3), it is just different enough to warrant closer inspection. But any new sense of the verb would not be intended to go with its phrase ἐν πνεύματι, as shown in our hymn. For reasons to be explained later, we believe that the verbs of the two phrases in lines 1 and 2 got switched at an earlier stage of the hymn's transmission, and this may well solve the incongruities of both phrases. The expressions would have formerly read ἐδικαιώθη ἐν σαρκί (1) and ἐφανερώθη ἐν πνεύματι (2), respectively, so that we have instead, "he was *tested* in flesh and *made manifest* in spirit."

That is, Jesus was *put to the test* in his fleshly life, as a human, then made manifest in spirit form in his resurrection. That testing would have included the temptation, the

---

[54] Gundry, "Form and Meaning," 213–14, 218–20. For critique, see Marshall, *Pastoral Epistles*, 525 (with references in n. 79). What is not addressed, however, is the opaqueness, even obscurity, of the sense of what "vindicated" (ἐδικαίωθη) means. In what manner is Jesus needing vindication, and why in the netherworld? Marshall (following Hofius) suggests vindication by God, but an appeal to "vindication on the OT model" (citing Rom. 3:4 = Ps. 50 [51], etc.) is remote and provides few hopeful parallels in respect of Jesus (525). See later and the discussion in n. 65.

[55] Gundry, "Form and Meaning," 219: "In any case, the emphasis on vindication implies the humiliation of his suffering and death."

[56] LSJ, s.v., δικαιόω, def. I, citing A. *Ag*. 393 (lyr.): κακοῦ δὲ χαλκοῦ τρόπον / τρίβῳ τε καὶ προσβολαῖς / μελαμπαγὴς πέλει δικαιωθείς, κτλ. ("Like base metal beneath the touchstone's rub, *when tested* he showeth the blackness of his grain") (trans. H. W. Smyth, LCL), in a simile on greed.

[57] LXX ὅτι δεδικαίωται, κτλ. "Because *it is* a testing, and what if *the sword* despises even the scepter?" (trans. NKJ Version).

"agony" in the garden, the trial, and the crucifixion—in a sense, all that made Jesus human, indeed the totality of his life.[58] But ἐδικαιώθη can also refer more narrowly to Jesus's being *punished*, or even *condemned* to die, in the specific sense of his trial and crucifixion.[59] Here, we may well begin to uncover the "secret" of the missing Cross: it may lie in the trial of Jesus being intentionally disguised in the switched language of this would-be Passion element.

If such an alignment of ἐδικαιώθη with ἐν σαρκί makes better sense for our hymn, even more so will be the (re)placement of ἐφανερώθη with ἐν πνεύματι, the clearer representation for the resurrection to be expected in this line. The verb is used with just this sense in the resurrection appearance stories of Mark and John. In the longer ending of Mk 16:9, we read: Ἀναστὰς δὲ πρωῒ πρώτῃ σαββάτου ἐφάνη πρῶτον Μαρίᾳ τῇ Μαγδαληνῇ, κτλ. ("Having arisen on the first day of the week, he *appeared* first to Mary Magdalene," etc.) (W reads ἐφάνη, but without πρῶτον). But this cognate, φαίνω, is matched even more perfectly in the variant reading of D (Codex Bezae), which now reproduces the same verb as that found in 1 Tim. 3:16: sc., ἐφανέρωσεν πρώτοις Μαρίᾳ τῇ Μαγδαληνῇ, κτλ. ("he *manifested* (himself) in the first instance to Mary Magdalene," etc.); see also Acts 10:40: καὶ ἔδωκεν αὐτὸν ἐμφανῆ γενέσθαι ("But God raised him on the third day and made him *to become manifest*"). An even better match is found in Mk 16:12, followed by that of v. 14, in the Longer Ending, where in the first instance we read of the two anonymous disciples to whom Jesus appeared while the disciples were walking in a field: ἐφανερώθη ἐν ἑτέρᾳ μορφῇ ("he *appeared* to them in another form"). The same form of the aorist passive is used in 16:14, when Jesus appears to the eleven disciples as they reclined at dinner: τοῖς ἕνδεκα ἐφανερώθη. The identical verb transpires in the "longer ending" of John, where the resurrection of Jesus is introduced as follows: "After these things Jesus *manifested himself* [ἐφανέρωσεν ἑαυτόν] again to his disciples at the Sea of Tiberias, and he *manifested* (himself) in the following manner [ἐφανέρωσεν δὲ οὕτως]" (21:1). The exact aorist passive form of the verb as that of our hymn comes about in the summary of the pericope at Jn 21:14: τοῦτο ἤδη τρίτον ἐφανερώθη Ἰησοῦς τοῖς μαθηταῖς ἐγερθεὶς ἐκ νεκρῶν ("This was already the third time that Jesus *was manifested* to his disciples, having been raised from the dead"). These forms of "manifestation" emerge as technical terms in the communities that produced the resurrection appearance stories in Mark and John; they record manifestations of Jesus as the supernatural display of a risen figure in a spirit-body (ἐν πνεύματι here: ἐν ἑτέρᾳ μορφῇ in Mk 16:12; cf. ἐγείρεται σῶμα πνευματικόν in 1 Cor. 15:44).[60] The strength of this use of φανερόω has not been lost on early commentators

---

[58] Cf. *Epist. Barn.* 5:1: "The Lord endured to deliver up his flesh to corruption" (ὑπέμεινεν ὁ κύριος παραδοῦναι τὴν σάρκα εἰς καταφθοράν), in reference to his atoning death.

[59] See T. Muraoka, *A Greek-English Lexicon of the Septuagint* (Louvain: Peeters, 2009), s.v. δικαιόω, 170, def. 3. *to consider in court and pronounce judgment*, where our passage from Ezek. 21:13 is cited, but with the rather idiosyncratic translation, "a verdict is out"; cf. LSJ, s.v., def. III.1, "pass sentence on."

[60] This is not to deny the resurrection of Jesus in bodily form, although Lk. 24:39 goes out of its way to have Jesus state that a hypothetically raised πνεῦμα would not have "flesh and bones" (σάρκα καὶ ὀστέα), as Jesus now does. Although Paul calls the raised body πνευματικόν and not of σάρξ καὶ αἷμα, in 1 Cor. 15:44, 50, he cannot be held responsible for not knowing such passages as Lk. 24:39 or Jn 20:19-31, which aim at countering arguments that Jesus was a *phantasma* and not *somatically*

who aver that line 1 "refers to Christ's *post-resurrection appearances* to people" and not to his incarnation, even though this would overlap incongruently with line 2.[61] It is only a step closer to switch the verbs. In this manner, the two verses, thus properly rectified, would appear more grounded in historically concrete data: the trial and crucifixion of Jesus and his subsequent resurrection, a verbal concretization whose deficiency all commentators seem to wrestle with (see the further the discussion in the section "Background").

Line 3: *The Appearance to Angels.* The hymn's *manifestation in spirit* is followed most naturally by an *appearance to angels*. This expression of Jesus's materialization, albeit to angels, for which ὤφθη is a technical term in early Christianity, only makes sense following the resurrection of Jesus after his condemnation to death on the cross (cf. Lk. 24:34; Acts 9:17, 13:31, 26:16; 1 Cor. 15:5-8). But why an appearance to angels and not to humans, that is, specifically women and disciples?[62] Gundry writes of ὤφθη ἀγγέλοις that it is "surely not to angels in the sense of human, apostolic messengers who had witnessed the risen Christ" and proceeds to expose the weaknesses of several positions, such as the appearance of Jesus during his incarnation—or even before it— where in a number of passages angels are said to be observing Jesus.[63] Thus the sense of ὤφθη is misconstrued in these contexts, faltering on the simple observations that the aorist passive must refer to Christ appearing to angels and not to angels *watching* Jesus. This also disturbs the otherwise clean chronology of the hymn which our twofold stanza now requires. An appearance to angels at his ascension and investiture at the right hand of God seems the most common interpretation, with particular reference to the work of Rudolf Bultmann.[64] But this competes with, and therefore confounds, the neat chronological parallelism of our two-stanza schema, culminating with the C^1-C^2 heavenly crowning.[65] But Gundry's insight that the ἀγγέλοις of line 3 could refer to Jesus's appearance to the fallen angels of the netherworld to whom he preached,

---

raised. This may represent a later emphasis; our hymn is closer in time to the Pauline and deutero-Markan concepts.

[61] Towner, *Letters*, 279, n. 38; my italics. See Gundry, "Form and Meaning," 210 (with references in n. 22).

[62] See, for example, R. D. Kotansky, "The Resurrection of Jesus in Biblical Theology: From Early Appearances (1 Corinthians 15) to the 'Sindonology' of the Empty Tomb," in B. E. Reynolds, B. Lugioyo, and K. J. Vanhoozer (eds.), *Reconsidering the Relationship between Biblical and Systematic Theology in the New Testament*, WUNT II/369 (Tübingen: Mohr Siebeck, 2014), 83–107, where ὤφθη is paramount.

[63] Gundry, "Form and Meaning," 214, citing 1 Pet. 1:12; Eph. 3:10; Lk. 2:2-25; Mk 1:13, 16:5-8; Mt. 4:11, 28:2-7(?); Jn 20:12-13; Acts 1:10-11(?), with bibliographic references in nn. 3–5.

[64] Gundry, "Form and Meaning," 214, in reference to R. Bultmann, *Theology of the New Testament* (New York: Scribner, 1955), 2:153; further Marshall, *Pastoral Epistles*, 526–57; Towner, *Letters*, 282.

[65] Hinted at in Gundry, "Form and Meaning," 215, who wisely counters the potential redundancy of pairing line 3 + line 6 with the observation that "line 6 refers to the ascension as such; line 3 would refer to angelic observation of it." But Gundry settles on his own pairing of line 2 with line 3, so that the former "refers to vindication through descent in hades," in order to support his view that ἀγγέλοις must have in mind the imprisoned spirits of Jude 6, a proposition that remains plausible but which the arguments of this chapter offer an alternative for (see ibid., 215, 208–9, 212–13; further, n. 66).

according to Jude, has not been widely discussed and might teeter—but not fall—on other grounds.⁶⁶

One cannot rule out entirely that ἀγγέλοις might hide a double entendre invoking both angelic and human messengers, that is, the men and women recorded in the gospels to whom Jesus appeared after his resurrection.⁶⁷ But our new interpretation of line 2 as a reference to the appearance of Jesus (ἐφανερώθη ἐν πνεύματι) might include post-resurrection appearances to various groups of believers, even if specifics are not mentioned.

The same verbal form ὤφθη, of line 2, is used in a seriatim list of post-resurrection onlookers in 1 Cor. 15:5-8 who experience appearances of Jesus, none of them specifically women.⁶⁸ Even though the use here in our hymn of the same formula with ἀγγέλοις is unparalleled (as much in this hymn is), the expression may share a tradition with the gospel versions of the resurrection of Jesus that *do* include women. In Mk 16:1 we are told that Mary Magdalene, Mary the mother of James, and Salome rose early to anoint the body of Jesus at the tomb. When they enter the empty tomb they see the figure of a "young man" (νεανίσκος) seated on the right and dressed in a white robe (Mk 16:6). They famously do not see Jesus, nor experience a post-resurrection appearance of him at all but are told that he is risen (ἠγέρθη), that "he is not here" (οὐκ ἔστιν ὧδε), and that Peter and the disciples will see him later in Galilee (ἐκεῖ αὐτὸν ὄψεσθε; Mk 16:6-7).

The point of all this is that in at least two of the canonical versions—that of Luke and John—two angelic figures greet the women (or woman, in John) who come to the tomb. A third account, told indirectly in Luke 24 when Jesus appears anonymously to an anonymous two, recounts the story of the women's (γυναῖκές τινες; v. 22) visit to the tomb with a description of their own "vision of angels" (ὀπτασίαν ἀγγέλων ἑωρακέναι; v. 24). I believe that it is these tomb-side angels, whether two or more, that become the recipients of the vision of the post-resurrected Jesus. With the exception of the Gospel of John, none of these tomb-side events is accompanied by an appearance of Jesus to the women—not a one. But there may well have been an initial appearance by Jesus to the angels *at the tomb*—the very angels of the hymn's ὤφθη ἀγγέλοις. There are good reasons to believe this, even though it is not recorded that Jesus explicitly appeared to the angels *at the tomb*.⁶⁹ One is that the details of the tomb-side angelic figures

---

⁶⁶ Cf. Marshall, *The Pastoral Epistles*, 525, 527. It is true that ἀγγέλους does occur in Jude 6 of "fallen angels" imprisoned in the underworld, just as they appear in 2 Pet. 2:4 in a parallel passage. But in these contexts their identity is unmistakable in the way they are described; in the sins and errors that they commit; and in the judgment that they await. The additional parallel in 1 Pet. 3:19 refers to these same as πνεύματα—the deceased souls of those who perished in the Flood.

⁶⁷ On human messengers, see R. W. Micou, "On ὤφθη ἀγγέλοις, 1 Tim iii.16," *JBL* 11 (1892): 201–5, and the references to Holtzmann, Seeberg, and Metzger, in Marshall, *Pastoral Epistles*, 526–57 n. 87; Towner, *Letters*, 281.

⁶⁸ See Kotansky, "Resurrection of Jesus."

⁶⁹ The technical nature of the verb makes such a tomb-side appearance inevitable. The remarks by Marshall, *Pastoral Epistles*, 526-7, that the verb is not limited to heavenly appearances and therefore not technical fails in respect to those cases were it does refer to visions and appearances—and *are* technical. Although Marshall is correct to point out "the better known tradition of Christ's exaltation and appearance to the heavenly hosts in the spiritual realm" (527) to best contextualize the line—further referencing their subjection and worship of Christ—the phrase ὤφθη ἀγγέλοις is never found, nor even alluded to, in any of the passages he cites (527 n. 91). The appearance to angels

indicate an intimate and close proximity of the angels to the whole event of the post-resurrected Jesus. Besides the fact that the stone is rolled away (Mk 16:3—in Mt. 28:2, by angelic agency), Mark attests that the angelic figure (νεανίσκον) was "seated at the right" (καθήμενον ἐν τοῖς δεξιοῖς; 16:5), a feature echoed in John's reference to the two angels, again seated (καθεζομένους), "one *at his head*, one *at his feet*, where the body of Jesus had lain" (20:12). This contrasts with the two disciples who had just entered the empty tomb to find the linen cloths and the head-napkin (σουδάριον), but neither Jesus, nor angels (20:5-7).[70]

The reason that Jesus's appearance to the angels is not laid out is that Mark, and especially John, are interested in having the women become *messengers* themselves of the news that Jesus is risen. The angels can only tell the women what must be true for them—that the angels themselves become the first attesters of the risen Jesus and had seen him: they sit on the very spot of his risen body, exclaim his resurrection, point to his absence, and tell them to report the report; the women are now to become messengers to the messengers. This is what John aims to emphasize by having Mary Magdalene herself become the discipular "*angel-*"*messenger* (ἀγγέλλουσα τοῖς μαθηταῖς; 20:18) of the two *angelic messengers* (δύο ἀγγέλους; 20:11), although in this case she herself has already seen Jesus (20:11-17). In the older Markan version, though, there was no appearance of Jesus to Mary or to the others. This is why ὤφθη ἀγγέλοις is made to stand as it does, in the Timothy hymn, and, at least for proto-Mark, why it represents the *only* true post-resurrection vision: the angels saw the risen Jesus and were his first messengers (ἄγγελοι). For this reason, too, Luke can only describe, in lieu of a resurrection appearance, the women's "vision of angels" (ὀπτασία ἀγγέλων; 24:23) that actually precedes the very vision to the anonymous men—again being two (δύο). Regardless, the format of the Timothy hymn's lines 1–3 will still be seen to echo remarkably the Markan sequence: Jesus *crucified* (τὸν ἐσταυρωμένον; 16:6), that is, condemned; *raised* (ἠγέρθη; 16:6), that is, made manifest; and *seen* (ἐκεῖ αὐτὸν ὄψεσθε; 16:7), that is, appeared, although this last now becomes a proleptic vision: the vision to the angels is to be transferred to a vision by the *male* recipients. Nevertheless, ἐσταυρωμένον = ἐδικαιώθη (1) + ἠγέρθη = ἐφανερώθη (2) + ὄψεσθε = ὤφθη (3). This, then, will pave the way for the hymnic lines that follow in 4–5.[71]

Line 4: *Proclamation to the Nations*. The kerygmatic preaching and reception of the gospel follows next and comes naturally upon an appearance to angels, since it is they who inaugurate the message, as seen earlier. This is less clear in Mark, but the

at the tomb may still be viewed as "in the spiritual realm"—in respect of the majority of angels (see earlier)—but more sepulchrally oriented in respect of the one (or two) who announce him.

[70] See Kotansky, "Resurrection of Jesus," 93–107.
[71] Further, the statement "He is not here" (Mk 16:6; Mt. 28:6; Lk. 24:6) is meant to add further emphasis that the women are *unable* to experience a seeing of the raised Jesus; they become messengers *to be believed*, just as their reporting of the good news (and its belief) become models of the hymn's next lines. It is also possible, we may add, that the one, or two, angels in the gospel accounts are just the remnants of a larger group of angels who witnessed the raising of Jesus within the heavenly sphere (cf. Towner, *Letters*, 282) and that the ones that were left behind alone remained to tell of the miraculous events. Gould, "Pastor's Wolves," 253–4 (see n. 90 in this chapter), rightly observes on ὤφθη ἀγγέλοις that "in the Gospel story there were angels around the tomb ... their high calling was to have been witnesses of the Lord's coming forth from the tomb."

command of the angelic youth, "But go, tell his disciples and Peter" (ἀλλὰ ὑπάγετε εἴπατε τοῖς μαθηταῖς αὐτοῦ καὶ τῷ Πέτρῳ; 16:7) can be understood to include the kerygmatic kernel, "(you seek) Jesus of Nazareth, *crucified, raised*" (Ἰησοῦν ... τὸν Ναζαρηνὸν τὸν ἐσταυρωμένον, ἠγέρθη; 16:6). The Shorter Ending of Mark, in contrast to the famous line of Mk 16:8, has the unidentified women use the Johannine-like language of "angelic" message to report to the Petrine group what occurred, even though the heavenly "messenger" in Mark was a νεανίσκος: "And they reported ... all that they had been told" (πάντα δὲ τὰ παρηγγελμένα ... ἐξήγγειλαν; 16:8+). In the accumulated longer versions in Mark, reportage is repeated (ἀπήγγειλεν [16:9] ... ἀπήγγειλαν [16:12]) but met with unbelief. In the Shorter Ending, Jesus commissions the Petrine group with the κήρυγμα of salvation (16:8+). Marshall writes that the aorist "sums up an ongoing process which in principle has already decisively taken place" (cf. 1 Tim. 2:1-7; Gal. 2:2).[72]

Line 5: *Belief in the World*. As with the previous line, the sense of accomplishment is finished, at least in the post-Pauline world (see discussion to follow). That does not mean that all evangelizing and all response are completed, only that ἐν κόσμῳ signifies the gospel reaching the circum-Mediterranean world and beyond and suggests a gospel that may have reached Spain, if indeed (as tradition has it) Paul preached there before his ultimate demise (Rom. 15:24, 28).[73]

Line 6: *The Ascension to Glory*. "The hymn closes with a rather enigmatic phrase ... if the ascension of Christ is in view (cf. Gundry, 204; Spicq, 474), a straight chronological understanding of the piece comes to grief," writes Marshall.[74] But this can only hold true if we insist upon specific "proof-texting" that necessitates the production of unnatural harmonizations. Exegesis of this kind should be avoided, for it deprecates the intent, purpose, and scope of individual writers and disallows readings and interpretations that aim to arrive at the truth of what the original language of its composers and compilers originally contemplated. Thus, we must eschew the forced interpretations that ἀνελήμφθη must refer to the final enthronement, final glory of Christ, or the Parousia.[75]

The strict chronological order, and language, of the hymn requires the reader to take ἀνελήμφθη in line 6 as an indubitable reference to exactly what it claims to be: the Ascension, even if the chronology does not match up with that given in the account of Acts 1:1-11. But we need not use this scriptural reference as our guide

---

[72] Marshall, *Pastoral Epistles*, 528; cf. Townes, *Letters*, 282–3.
[73] Understandably, Marshall, *Pastoral Epistles*, 528 (like others), sees "the world" in a more universal sense, sc. "the world of humanity into which Christ came." Here, however, because of the parallelism with line 4, κόσμος must have a more geographical sense, as becomes clear in our discussion on line 6 later.
[74] Ibid., 528; Townes, *Letters*, 284: "the reference frustrates a neat chronological sequence."
[75] Gundry, "Form and Meaning," 216. Marshall's reference to "the installation and exaltation of Christ to the realm of glory, *for which the event of the ascension stood as a symbol*" (*Pastoral Epistles*, 528–9) cannot be sustained by the Greek. The theory of an Egyptian, or other, enthronement story does not hold up; cf. Gundry, "Form and Meaning, 207–8; Martin, "New Perspective," 109, with n. 31.

to interpreting 1 Tim. 3:16. Some chronological ambiguity is already present within Luke-Acts itself, and elsewhere in the New Testament, so that this may well open the door for a broader understanding of the timing of this important post-resurrection event. In Acts, the same form of the verb as here occurs (ἀνελήμφθη), first in 1:2, in respect of the ascension as narrated earlier in the author's "first book" (sc., Lk. 24:50-51), and then, with a different verb ἐπήρθη ("he was lifted up"), when told of Jesus's ascension into a cloud at the disciples' gathering in Acts 1:6. Major textual problems occur at Lk. 24:51 where, following the verb διέστη (ἀπέστη D), the phrase καὶ ἀνεφέρετο εἰς τὸν οὐρανόν is omitted in ℵ* D it sy^s, no doubt "in order to relieve the apparent contradiction."[76] A second problem arises with the reading at Acts 1:2, whose variants are wrought with complicated and profound difficulties of their own.[77] For our purposes, it is sufficient to observe that according to Lk. 24:50 Jesus was "carried up into heaven" on the very same (late) evening of his resurrection, if one does a careful reading of Lk. 24:1 ("*first day* of the week, early dawn") and 24:13 ("*that very day*"), followed by 24:29 ("*evening*"—with a disappearance at 24:31) and 24:33 ("*that same hour*"; cf. v. 36), with 24:50 (a walk to Bethany, following a second eating, 24:41-43). This differs from Acts 1:3, 9, where Jesus ascends, following a forty-day period of post-resurrection appearances, including teaching.

In Mark, whose endings are variable anyway, there is additional ambiguity in respect of the timing of the Ascension. In the Shorter Ending of Mark (post 16:8), after the women "reported to those with Peter" (τοῖς περὶ τὸν Πέτρον), Jesus—rather cryptically with no mention of his arrival or appearance—is simply stated as sending out the Petrine party with the message of the gospel. Nothing is said of a subsequent ascension. Did it occur much later? In the Longer Ending, after the Commission with additional instructions (16:14-18), it is said that Jesus was "taken up (ἀνελήμφθη) into heaven, and that he sat down at the right hand of God" (16:19), following indeterminant temporal references (μετὰ δὲ ταῦτα [16:12]; ὕστερον [16:14]). In Mt. 28:16-20, there is no direct reference to the Ascension, for after the Great Commission (28:16-20), Jesus is said to remain with the disciples until the end of time: "And behold, I am with you all the days until the consummation of the Age." Nor does John's Gospel narrate an ascension; and although implying a return (21:22-23), nothing is said of his leaving or his absence.

Thus within the gospel records, tradition portrays the ascension of Jesus as occurring soon after, on the very night of, the resurrection (Luke); to a short time later (short Mark); to as long as forty days afterward (Acts); and, last, to not at all (long Mark, John), or never (Matthew). This same temporal ambiguity is expressed even more so in our noncanonical, Patristic, and gnostic sources. Thus, the *Gospel of Peter* 5:10-11 has Jesus ascend (ἀνελήμφθη) immediately upon his death on the cross;[78] whereas the *Epistle of Barnabas* 15:8 records a tradition of celebrating the ascension on

---

[76] Metzger, *Textual Commentary*, 190.
[77] Ibid., 273–7, devoting five pages to this well-known difficulty.
[78] καὶ ὁ κύριος ἀνεβόησε λέγων Ἡ δύναμίς μου, ἡ δύναμις, κατέλειψάς με· καὶ εἰπὼν ἀνελήμφθη—text in H. B. Swete, Εὐαγγέλιον κατὰ Πέτρον: *The Akhmîm Fragment of the Apocryphal Gospel of St. Peter* (London: Macmillan, 1893; repr. Eugene, OR: Wipf and Stock, 2005), 11–12.

the eighth day after the resurrection.[79] The *Apocryphon of James* tells of an ascension five hundred and fifty days after Jesus rises.[80] And in the *Pistis Sophia*, Jesus spends a full eleven years instructing his disciples, of which the whole gnostic treatise proves its result.[81] At the end of that tractate, we read the following:

> They preached the *Gospel* (εὐαγγέλιον) of the Kingdom in the whole *world* (κόσμος) while Christ *worked* (ἐνεργεῖ) with them through the word of confirmation and the signs which followed them and the marvels. And in this way the Kingdom of God was known upon the whole earth and in the whole *world* (κόσμος) of Israel, as a witness to all *peoples* (ἔθνος) which exist from the places of the East to the places of the West.[82]

Even though the *Pistis Sophia* does not spell out the actual ascension at the end of the tract, the strength of its very opening line containing an incipit of an eleven-year teaching cycle implies that Jesus would have returned to heaven following the *completion* of the long teaching period and the *summation* of the disciples' preaching mission and worldwide reception. Just like the account in 1 Tim. 3:16, then, the activity of spreading the gospel and its reception is spoken of as having been accomplished: the *Pistis Sophia*'s Gospel of the Kingdom has been preached in the "whole world" and made known; the Christ-hymn's gospel has been *proclaimed* among the nations and *believed on* in the world. The sequence and chronology of the two are thus the same, even though reasons to assume any direct gnostic influence upon 1 Tim. 3:16 might be limited. But even more significantly, in both the *Pistis Sophia* and the hymn, Jesus does not ascend until the full dissemination of the gospel, and that is exactly what we unmistakably have in the chronology of line 6 of the latter. The hymn thus reflects a tradition of the disciples having fulfilled, more or less, the kerygmatic commission. Then, and only then, do we have Jesus ascend to heaven, and not vice versa. This will best explain how we are to interpret the chronological sequence of ἀνελήμφθη in our celebrated hymn's culminating line: it is a reference to the Ascension following many

---

[79] *Epist. Barn.* 15:9: ἐν ᾗ (sc. ἡμέρα, the 8th) καὶ ὁ Ἰησοῦς ἀνέστη ἐκ νεκρῶν καὶ φανερωθεὶς ἀνέβη εἰς οὐρανούς.

[80] That is, one-and-a-half years afterward; see NHC I, 2.19-20 (cf. I, 15.5-6, 14-15, 35), in James M. Robinson, ed., *The Nag Hammadi Library in English*, 3rd ed. (San Francisco: Harper & Row, 1988), 29–37, esp. 30, 36–7. In these cases, Jesus appears after the resurrection specifically to instruct the disciples in esoteric teachings; cf. *The Book of Thomas the Contender* (NHC II, 7), 138.24 (Robinson, *Nag Hammadi Library*, 201); *The Sophia of Jesus Christ* (NHC III, 4), 91.10-13; 119.8-11 (Robinson, *Nag Hammadi Library*, 222, 243); *The Dialogue of the Savior* (NHC III, 5), 120.1 (Robinson, *Nag Hammadi Library*, 246); *The Letter of Peter to Philip* (NHC VIII, 2), 140.15-23 (Robinson, *Nag Hammadi Library*, 436f.); see also Craig A. Evans, "Jesus in Gnostic Literature," *Biblica* 62 (1981): 406–12, esp. 407, who has kindly brought my attention to Iain Gardner and Jay Johnston, "The *Liber Bartholomaei* on the Ascension: Edition of Bibliothèque Nationale Copte 132 f. 37," *VC* 64 (2010): 74–86, among other works.

[81] 1.1: "*But* (δὲ) it happened that after Jesus had risen from the dead he spent eleven years speaking with his *disciples* (μαθήτης)," in Carl Schmidt and Violet MacDermot, eds., *Pistis Sophia*, NHS 9 (Leiden: Brill, 1978), 3.

[82] Carl Schmidt and Violet MacDermot, eds., *Pistis Sophia*, NHS 9 (Leiden: Brill, 1978), 771. Here, we have recorded the Greek loanwords into Coptic, which no doubt reflect the original Greek translation as well.

years of preaching and believing in the world, both "East and West," just as we find mirrored in "shorter" Mark's ἀπὸ ἀνατολῆς καὶ ἄχρι δύσεως (following 16:8 in L Ψ 099 and others) and in the *Pistis Sophia*.

Background

We have seen earlier how the expression "he was manifested in the flesh" (ἐφανερώθη ἐν σαρκί), in combining two somewhat oxymoronic elements, "manifestation" and "flesh," creates better sense if read as a description of the resurrection, ἐφανερώθη <u>ἐν πνεύματι</u>, "he was made manifest *in spirit*," having suggested a switch of the verbs in lines 1 and 2, respectively.[83] Conversely, line 2's ἐδικαιώθη, which is even more unsuitable and difficult to interpret with ἐν πνεύματι, finds a better match if read with line 1's ἐν σαρκί. Here, though, ἐδικαιώθη would have to be understood as "condemned" or "tried," rather than "vindicated," since "vindicated in spirit" (or, "vindicated in flesh") yields rather labored exegesis. Additionally, as the earlier examples show, ἐφανερώθη is more commonly used of the resurrection, thus providing in ἐν πνεύματι a further eligible counterpart, just as ἐδικαιώθη ἐν σαρκί would seem to unravel a rather knotty expression in the canonical version's ἐδικαιώθη ἐν πνεύματι:

"He was <u>condemned</u> in the flesh,	= Crucifixion
was made <u>manifest</u> in the spirit,	= Resurrection
appeared to angels.	= Heavenly Appearances
Was proclaimed among the nations,	= Preaching to the Gentiles
was believed on in the world,	= Belief in him in the world
was taken up in glory.	= Ascension to Heaven

Once the proposed switch is made, producing the improved <u>ἐδικαιώθη</u> ἐν σαρκί + <u>ἐφανερώθη</u> ἐν πνεύματι, and showing Jesus's being *tried*—indeed *condemned*—in the flesh and then being made manifest in his resurrection, the rest seems to fall more naturally into shape. Each line now carries its own, distinct, kerygmatic element, with line 1, and especially 2, no longer producing their formerly lumpish phrases capturing impossibly long periods of time. There is something about the logical flow and cadence of this new reading that alleviates the strained meaning of the older, canonical word order and appears to bring more orderliness to the whole. Christ's manifestation in the spirit as a resurrected figure, following his condemnation in the flesh (trial, crucifixion, and death), sets the stage for the whole of the hymn to stand on surer footing. Thus the chronology suggested by the earlier diagram allows the sequence of kerygmatic events

---

[83] One expects to be "begotten" in the flesh, not "manifested" (or "made to appear"), as Jn 1:14; Rom. 1:3, 8:3, and so on make clear; see Gundry, "Form and Meaning," 209. 1 Jn 1:2: Ἰησοῦν Χριστὸν <u>ἐν σαρκὶ</u> ἐληλυθότα; and Rom. 8:3: <u>ἐν ὁμοιώματι σαρκὸς</u> ἁμαρτίας are particularly relevant.

to unfold naturally, from death to ascension.[84] The realignment also offers an improved parallel with the well-known text of 1 Pet. 3:18-19, where θανατωθεὶς μὲν σαρκί, ζῳοποιηθεὶς δὲ πνεύματι ("*having been put to death* in the flesh, but *made alive* in the spirit") perfectly matches our new ἐδικαιώθη ἐν σαρκί, ἐφανερώθη ἐν πνεύματι ("he was *condemned* in the flesh [but] made *manifest* in the spirit").[85] It is also supported by Rom. 4:25, ὃς παρεδόθη διὰ τὰ παραπτώματα ἡμῶν καὶ ἠγέρθη διὰ τὴν δικαίωσιν ἡμῶν ("who was *handed over* [= *put to death*, RSV] for our trespasses and *raised* for our justification"). These parallels are difficult to ignore.

Such exchanges of lines (or words) are not new to the exegesis of this hymn. Within the early history of interpretation of 1 Tim. 3:16, Weiss, with little success, once attempted, for example, to switch lines 5 and 4, in order to create a better chronological consistency for line 6—a switch that our new reading and interpretations now obviate, since anything other than straightforward chronology is no longer an issue.[86] But why, we must ask, do we find these changes at the beginning of the Timothy hymn? If the hymn originally read, "He was *condemned* in the flesh," but "was *made manifest* in the spirit," who felt the need to change this to a more obfuscating, "He was *made manifest* in the flesh," but "was *vindicated* (?) in the spirit"? A possible answer—but not necessarily the only one, as we shall see—may lie in the background of the Pastoral Epistles in general, and in that of our Christological hymn in particular, in which there was an effort to combat some form of incipient Jewish Gnosticism or proto-Gnosticism, a heresy identified among the opponents and thought to be reflected in the Epistles' often eristic language.[87]

---

[84] Each of the aorist passives is no longer to be interpreted variably (constative in some cases, punctiliar in others), but each aims to accentuate the singularity of their individual kerygmatic happenings: Death—Resurrection—Appearances—Preaching—Believing—Ascension.   Even ἐκηρύχθη and ἐπιστεύθην, although constative, are viewed as completed actions in the past. The kerygmatic age, at least initially, is closed.

[85] See, for example, Gundry, "Form and Meaning," 213–14, who interprets the hymn differently, introducing additional elements of the Petrine hymn—like the *descensus ad inferos*—into the Timothy hymn. On the parallel, too, in *Diognetus* 11.3, see Marshall, *Pastoral Epistles*, 500 n. 6, who feels the passage is based upon 1 Tim. 3:16. But the differences seem too great to suggest direct borrowing.

[86] That is, reading "He was believed on in the world (5) / He was preached among the nations (6) / He has taken up in glory." B. Weiss, *Die Briefe Pauli an Timotheus und Titus*, KEK, 5th ed. (Göttingen: Vandenhoeck & Ruprecht, 1902), 237, as cited in Gundry, "Form and Meaning," 205 n. 3.

[87] Cf. 1 Tim. 1:3-4, 6-7, 19-20; 4:1-3, 7; 6:3-5, 20 (ἡ ψευδώνυμος γνῶσις!); 2 Tim. 2:14, 16-18; 3:6-9; 4:3-4; Tit. 1:9-16; 2:12; 3:9. That the opponents are gnostics is a long-held view; see Marshall, *Pastoral Epistles*, 47–50. One of its greatest proponents, G. Haufe, "Gnostische Irrlehre und ihre Abwehr in den Pastoralbriefen," in K.-W. Tröger (ed.), *Gnosis und Neues Testament* (Gütersloh: Mohn, 1973), 325–39, claimed "an enthusiastic soteriology which saw baptism as burial and resurrection with Christ and argues that it must be *assumed* that the motif of redemptive *gnosis* was linked to this understanding of baptism" (Marshall, *Pastoral Epistles*, 48, who, however, counters rather too succinctly and ineffectually in writing, "but this assumption is unfounded and with it the scheme collapses"). See, further, W. Schmithals, "The Corpus Paulinum and Gnosis," in A. H. B. Logan and A. J. M. Wedderburn (eds.), *The New Testament and Gnosis: Essays in Honour of Robert McL. Wilson* (Edinburgh: T&T Clark, 1983), 107–24; J. Roloff, "Pfeiler und Fundament der Wahrheit," in E. Grässer and O. Merk (eds.), *Glaube und Eschatologie* (Tübingen: Mohr Siebeck, 1985), 229–47; M. Goulder, "The Pastor's Wolves: Jewish Christian Visionaries behind the Pastoral Epistles," *NovT* 38 (1996): 242–56.

To explain this more carefully, we turn first to the second of the two phrases of our putative originals, sc. *ἐφανερώθη ἐν πνεύματι (*he was _made manifest_ in spirit"). I. Howard Marshall, in summarizing the views of one of the most famous of gnostic proponents nowadays, Walter Schmithals, writes in respect of the "Pastoral"-opponents:

> The resurrection has been spiritualised and the opponents believe that they belong to the limited group who experience the redemption of their bodies and (in the mind of the author) are self-conceited. From this enthusiasm flow their ascetic tendencies and depreciation of creation, and their desire for emancipation from the earthly, and their disinterest in the life of the world. They may have denied the humanity of Jesus, (etc.).[88]

Such a phrase as our original "he was _made manifest_ in spirit" may have been thought to provide too much fuel to the hypothesized gnostic fire in appearing to "spiritualize" the resurrection, even though this can hardly have been a concern of the original writer of the hymn.[89] A change to "vindication" (ἐδικαιώθη) in the spirit, difficult as the phrase may be, may well have alleviated the potential problem.

On the other hand, the resultant conversion from _manifestation_ in spirit to _vindication_ in spirit would then have forced line 1's alteration from _condemnation_ in the flesh to the canonical _manifestation_ in flesh, since what we have is a matching pair of switched verbs. The interchanging of the aorist passives would have armed orthodoxy with a two-pronged attack against any incipient heterodoxy, since an original _condemnation in flesh_ might have contributed too easily to gnostic sloganeering about the evils of the material world and could have helped their cause by identifying Jesus, or someone like Jesus, as a person worthy of judgment or condemnation _in the flesh_, since the σάρξ, for the Gnostics, represented an inimical human state—something to be loathed, denied, and transcended. Safer to work such a corporeal phrase into something more like a _manifestation_ in the flesh, although this, too, might have been seen to contribute somewhat to a docetic view of Christ, as well. But here orthodoxy at least retains an emphasis on σάρξ, and since Jesus's human status is not to be denied, we plainly have the lesser of two editorial evils, albeit the possibilities for various gnostic misrepresentation remain.[90]

---

[88] Marshall, _Pastoral Epistles_, 48; Schmithals, "_Corpus Paulinum_"; see notes to follow.

[89] On such a "spiritual resurrection," see _The Treatise on the Resurrection_ (NHC I, 4), 45.39–46.2 (Robinson, _Nag Hammadi Library_, 55); _The Sophia of Jesus Christ_ (NHC III, 4 and BG 8502, 3), 91.10–12: "the Saviour appeared, not in his previous form, but in the invisible spirit. And his likeness resembles a great angel of light" (Robinson, _Nag Hammadi Library_, 222; cf. [9]4.24–9[5].1–3, p. 224), even though the tractate goes on to describe the body as "pure (and) perfect flesh." Cf. Mk 16:12, ἐφανερώθη ἐν ἑτέρᾳ μορφῇ, discussed earlier.

[90] Cf. Goulder, "Pastor's Wolves," 250-5 (see n. 71), who sees in 1 Tim. 3:16 an attempt to combat incipient Jewish gnostic visionaries and writes of the author of 3:16, "to his opponents Christ was a divine aeon who took possession of the human Jesus for a period" (252). He further writes on the gnostic Cerinthus' antithetical view that "Christ was a _heavenly spirit_ and not a man, distinct from and superior to the human Jesus" (252; my italics), thus supporting how our hymn's putative original "he was manifested _in spirit_" might have proved worrisome (cf. 254–5, with ref. to 2 Tim. 2:18; my italics); cf. also, for example, Epiphanius, _Pan._ 26.20.5.

We envision that the original hymn got slightly altered because its first two lines aligned too readily with gnostic views that may have deprecated the flesh and spiritualized the resurrection. In the hymn's original wording, Jesus's being condemned in the flesh and manifested in the spirit would have been perceived as contributing to gnostic tendencies and predilections so that orthodox editors felt safe to rework the verbs to read, "He was manifested *in the flesh*" and was "condemned (that is, 'vindicated') *in the spirit*," although these rearranged terms produced the awkward expressions that we now encounter in all our current manuscript witnesses.[91]

A broader picture addresses the issue of the hymn's cultural background and, by extension, its perceived place of origin. R. H. Gundry, again, addresses this in some detail, opting for a more Palestinian Christian milieu and less of a "Hellenistic" one.[92] We have seen earlier, however, that certain features of the hymn's grammar need not point to a strictly Semitic backdrop, but rather one that favors a more spacious Hellenistic (if indeed Jewish) linguistic milieu; that is, the hymn was composed in Greek, even if we find cases, for example, of the aorist passive.[93] Besides, the identification of the precise 22-syllable isocolon schema of this hymn shows a wary cognizance of Greco-Roman rhetorical (if not magico-religious) features, and Gundry is keen to observe that the hymn's lines 4 and 5 "point to a community concerned with widespread evangelism and to a time when that had already started and gained some success."[94] In the end, he posits as a possible place of origin Syrian Antioch.[95]

We have seen earlier how the form of the Christological hymn in 1 Tim. 3:16 shows some structural and linguistic similarities to the kerygmatic elements in Mark and John, especially in respect of the tomb-side events and appearance of angels. In particular we noticed an absence in the original version of canonical Mark of any post-resurrection appearance stories. Instead, we find a presumed manifestation of angels to the women

---

[91] It is likely, however, that the suggested "original" form of the hymn was never recorded in written form and that both versions were orally interchangeable, as suggested later. But the argument that there can be no textual basis for a change such as that proposed here is countered by the prospect of uncertainty in respect of the early text of the NT; see R. D. Kotansky, "The Early Papyri, 'Gospel-Parallel' Variants, and the Text of the New Testament in the Second Century," in Craig A. Evans and Jeremiah J. Johnston (eds.), *Scribes and Their Remains*, SSEJC 21; LSTS 94 (London: T&T Clark, 2020), 224–80.

[92] Gundry, "Form and Meaning," 216–22, rightly arguing, for example, against Hellenistic θεῖος ἀνήρ concepts (220) and, earlier, against Egyptian enthronement motifs (207–8); cf. Marshall, *Pastoral Epistles*, 504.

[93] But this is common enough in Greek, and even the author of 1 Timothy employs it readily (1 Tim. 1:11, 13, 16; 2:7, 13, 14 [*bis*]; 3:10; 4:14; cf. 2 Tim. 1:9, 10, 11, 16; 4:17 [*bis*]; Tit. 1:3; 3:7), and no one claims that the Pastoral Epistles are Semitic in origin.

[94] Gundry, "Form and Meaning," 221.

[95] Ibid., 221–2, arguing that a hymn arising out of persecution was "reapplied" to "the rising threat of incipient gnosticism, described in 4:1ff. (cf. the Colossian heresy)," where—he further adds—the "stress on incarnation ... now counters docetism and asceticism," just as the emphasis on universalism "now contradicts gnostic esotericism" (222). Gundry's notion of persecution (221 n. 7)—correct in our view—is echoed in the notion of "the motif of triumphant vindication," as argued by O. R. B. Wilson, "A Study of the Early Christian Credal Hymn of 1 Timothy 3:16" (unpublished doctoral thesis, Southern Baptist Theological Seminary, Louisville, KY, 1954), 38–43 (*non vidi*). Wilson, on the other hand, focuses on the confessional nature of the hymn, which suggests persecution. We find the persecutional element rather in the "secrecy" (μέγα μυστήριον) of the hymn's intentionally opaque language (see further later).

who come to the tomb, angels who somehow stand in lieu of a bodily appearance of the risen Jesus to the tomb-goers. Even though a promise of an appearance to the disciples in Galilee acts as a proxy for the lack of appearances at the tomb, the absence is starkly evident and well known. The appearance of two angels in John's gospel, moreover, seems to stand as a substitute for, and a confirmation of, the individual materialization of Jesus to Mary Magdalene, in the form of the gardener;[96] the angels, nonetheless, act as true ἄγγελοι—etymological "messengers"—of the resurrection's kerygmatic report. This, we have argued, is what seems to be reflected in the hymn's ὤφθη ἀγγέλοις of line 3. Can this observation contribute to the thesis that the Timothy hymn stemmed from an early Christian milieu that shared a background and communal commonality with Mark's Gospel, both in its canonical form and in its subsequent addenda?

We noticed earlier how ἐφανερώθη ἐν πνεύματι as a resurrection formula parallels remarkably the Markan ἐφανερώθη ἐν ἑτέρᾳ μορφῇ in 16:14 and elsewhere (Mk 16:9). We have also observed that the Timothy hymn does not present a powerful incarnational statement in line 1, even if we were to retain its "canonical" word order. "He was manifested *in the flesh*," we noted, would seem a rather unusual way to describe a birth, or a begetting, which is one more reason to adopt a reading that places ἐφανερώθη *with spirit*, and not *with flesh* (and, conversely, ἐδικαιώθη with flesh). All of this seems to accord well with a Markan, or "pre-Markan," supposition that the gospel does not know, let alone record, anything akin to a birth narrative. The Timothy hymn, too, in speaking albeit rather vaguely of a trial, or condemnation, of Jesus in his earthly life—followed by an appearance in spirit-body after his crucifixion—is pursuing the same sort of Markan narratival tradition that knows neither of a birth (or early life) of Jesus nor an appearance of him in resurrected form at the tomb-side, apart from angels. Nor does it acknowledge, we may add, anything like a Johannine preexistence of Jesus—all of that has been taken away by our rereading of the hymn to create a rather straightforward kerymatic outline, albeit one still rather opaquely explicated. If it preserves nothing of the complexities and theological richness that we find, for example, in the celebrated Philippians hymn, our *chanson* still keeps intact its condemning to death, manifestation in spirit form, appearance to angels, and subsequent attention to the whole program of the gospel's dissemination.[97] All of these similarities between the hymn and Markan—or para-Markan—textual traditions suggest an origin of this early Christological masterpiece in the Eternal City of Rome itself, the most likely place for Mark's own provenance and composition.[98]

The lack of concrete kerygmatic elements attached to the life of Jesus in the hymn still requires attention for they remain conspicuously absent in the Timothy passage. Why is this so? Why does the hymn speak of being "*manifested* in the flesh" (if we follow the canonical version), and not merely being "*begotten* from the seed of David, according to the flesh" (τοῦ γενομένου ἐκ σπέρματος Δαυὶδ κατὰ σάρκα), as we find,

---

[96] Kotansky, "Resurrection of Jesus," 93–107.
[97] The only thing missing in the Mark parallels is the ascension, unless we accept the longer ending where Jesus is "taken up into heaven" (ἀνελήμφθη εἰς τὸν οὐρανόν; 16:19).
[98] As cogently argued recently by Brian J. Incignieri, *The Gospel to the Romans: The Setting and Rhetoric of Mark's Gospel*, BibInt 65 (Leiden: Brill, 2003).

for example, in Rom. 1:3? And why does it speak of Jesus being "vindicated in spirit" rather than simply being "raised from the dead" (ἠγέρθη ἐκ νεκρῶν)? Although the restored version's *"condemned in the flesh"* and *"made manifest in the spirit"* clearly alleviate these unclarities, concrete historical anchoring of the kind that we expect in confessional material is flagrantly absent in the hymn. Not only is there no reference to the crucifixion of Jesus, proper—although ἐδικαιώθη ἐν σαρκί makes it somewhat clearer—the post-resurrection appearances in ὤφθη ἀγγέλοις remain vague. The second part of the hymn, with references to preaching and believing, and ultimately ascending, are also formed with the same broad strokes as the first part. Our hymn is no Baroque landscape but an Impressionist (or Cubist) mural. Where is mention made of the preaching *disciples* or the believing *masses* whose naming would provide both the *subjects* of the promulgators and the *objects* of the converted? Where is the very name of Jesus, or that of Christ, or even of the Son of God? Indeed, all the subjects remain mysteriously absent and hidden in the obtuse aorist passives, where in each part they seem to bear a different subject.[99] The historical kerygmatic details so often found in Acts, Paul, and the other hymns, such as the naming of Jesus of Nazareth, his crucifixion (with mention of Pontius Pilate), his being raised up by God, his ascension and/or return, are paradoxically noticeable in their nearly complete nonappearance in the hymn.[100]

A plausible response to the application of such indirect language in our hymn, especially the lack of even the mention of Jesus Christ, or his crucifixion, may be found in a simple answer: persecution. A theory that the hymn arose from a context of worshipping Christians who faced harsh persecution may well explain the hymn's uniquely formulated language, although this could be just so much hugger-muggery. But a threat of trials could be related to, and offer an explanation as to why, the hymn is introduced to readers at the beginning as a μυστήριον: "*And by common confession, great is the secret of our piety.*"[101] The hymn, in being introduced as if it were a great *mystery*, intends to keep something under rather tight wraps. But what the "secret" of the hymn is, or of the religious piety that it seeks to embody, we are not told, and that is why it must remain a secret, perhaps one that is revealed only to a select few.

The quagmire surrounding the two verbs, "he was condemned" (ἐδικαιώθη) versus "he was manifested" (ἐφανερώθη), which we suggest got switched, may provide a partial solution. We propose that the verbal swap may *not* have been due to any scribal (or pre-scribal) manuscript change—whether willful or erroneous, after all. Rather, we proffer that the two were intentionally variable to begin with. Due to the nature of early Christian communal singing as an oral phenomenon, the hymn may not have been subject to textual fixity. Either phrase could have been used in singing, and both indeed probably were. Only when the early hymn was written down as "1 Tim. 3:16" did its text become immovable. Each phrase could have been sung antiphonally, with

---

[99] Possibly, *God* in section I (A^1–A^2); *Man* in II (B^1–B^2); and *Christ* in III (C^1–C^2)?
[100] Cf., for example, Acts 2:22-36; 3:11-26; 4:8-12, 27-28; 5:29-32; 10:34-43; 13:26-41; 17:31; 26:23; Rom. 1:3-6; 1 Cor. 15:3-7; Phil. 2:6-11; 1 Tim. 2:5-7; 1 Pet. 3:18-22; Heb. 1:3, and so on.
[101] See n. 4, and Marshall, *Pastoral Epistles*, 521–3; emphasis added. On the thorny issues of the authorship of the Pastorals, which we cannot address here, also see Marshall, *Pastoral Epistles*, 57–92.

"he was condemned" coming first, at one given time, and "he was manifested" coming second, at another. Or, it is possible that the phrase "he was condemned in the flesh," if the original, proved to be the more "secretive," whereas the other became the more common, or widespread, as if each were sung by variable groups within a spiritual Christian *gnōsis*. Conversely, the phrase "manifested in the flesh" could have been the version sung openly out of fear of persecution (or because of secrecy for secrecy's sake) with the whole hymn itself, in its singing, intentionally mitigating any direct historical reference to the Passion of Jesus—especially to the Cross.

Coincidentally, when the two variant readings of the hymn that we have suggested are presented in single lines, the strophes show a distinct chiastic pattern, creating a large "X" resting between them:

1 He was <u>condemned</u> in the flesh,   He was <u>made manifest</u> is spirit
                                X
2 He was <u>manifested</u> in the flesh,   He was <u>"justified"</u> in the spirit

Here we are reminded that the ancient derivation of the name *chiasmus* comes directly from the Greek letter "X"—a Cross. Chiasm, whether written out fully in Greek texts or merely "visualized" in linear configuration, was recognized by knowledgeable auditors and readers of ancient texts as a valid, if not "secret," technique of writing. This is much the same as we find with the "figured" writing of our own hymn, whether it was physically laid out in "patterned" writing or preserved linearly. In the mind's eye, the variant readings would thus form a distinctive—and no longer secret—figure: a Cross, once it has been recognized and pointed out as such by insiders.

If we look again at the shape of the "figured writing" (*technopaignion*) of the hymn, we see that this too might support, within its own configuration, this self-same reference to a secret Cross:

| ΑΓΓΕΛΛΟΙ<u>C</u>ΕΝΔΟΞΗ |
ΩΦΘ<u>Η</u>	ΑΝΕΛΗΜΦΘ<u>Η</u>
ΕΝΠΝΕΥΜΑΤ<u>Ι</u>	ΕΝΚΟCΜΩ
ΕΦΑΝΕΡΩΘ<u>Η</u>	<u>Ε</u>ΠΙΣΤΕΥΘ<u>Η</u>
<u>Ε</u>ΝCΑΡΚ<u>Ι</u>	ΕΝΕΘΝΕΣ<u>Ι</u>
<u>Ε</u>ΔΙΚΑΙΩΘ<u>Η</u>	ΕΚΗΡΥΧΘ<u>Η</u>

We saw earlier how this hymn, based upon its isocolonic division, allows a bifurcation into two equal parts (I–II), parts that overlap in such a way that an apex, enclosing the heavenly elements of angelic appearance and ascension, stands as a kind of "hidden," third category (III) bridging the other two equal parts. The shape of the hymn, if drawn out syllabically and according to the arrangement of its individual components, lends itself to being viewed as a "step"-pyramid, once inverted. It produces an image to be read from bottom to top—a configuration that can be shown to symbolize the upward ascent of Jesus from the earthly sphere to the heavenly. Such figured writing, as noted, also finds support in certain ritual texts, especially those comprised of sung vowels that emblemize the ascent (and descent) of divine beings from earth to heaven (and vice versa). Such an arrangement, in the case of our hymn, might also suggest that the composition, as originally chanted, could be felt to rise in pitch with an increasingly higher cadence, as the "narrative" of its stanza tells of the elevation and glorification of Jesus.

As Gundry himself observed, the initial elements of each of the phrases of the hymn's six stanzic lines is comprised of a series of assonating vowels, as underlined above: ε-ε-ε-ε-ω-α + ε-ε-ε-ε-α-ε.[102] With the suggestion that these might somehow relate, ritualistically, to the aforementioned papyrus texts, the sounding out of these vowels probably formed a part of early Christian hymns in some heterodox and gnostic circles, and their strategic placement here can be seen to contribute to the mystical appreciation of vowel assonance in the ancient world. But in addition to the initial string of vowels, we can also identify the same in the *final* elements of each phrase: sc., η-ι-η-ι-η + ϲ + η-ι-η-ω-η-η. Each of these phrases ends, as well, in a vowel, with the remarkable exception of the final *sigma* at the end of ΑΓΓΕΛΟΙϹ (= Σ), a consonant that occurs in a phrase found in the very middle of the "heavenly" stanza of line 3, along with the following ΕΝΔΟΞΗ. We suggest that the presence of this solitary -C- (sigma) is no accident; indeed, we tender the proposition that this apical sigma, crowning the very top of the hymnic "pyramid" itself and standing in direct contrast to the series of assonating vowels ascending to it, may have been meant to represent nothing other than an abbreviation for the word for "CROSS." That is, C(TAYPOC) = σταυρός serves as the missing and all-important kerygmatic element of our Christological hymn. What is more, if one were to draw a line from this sigma, top to bottom, it would divide in half each of the two "sides" (I and II) of the depicted hymn (left and right), based upon our identified 22-syllable arrangement. This vertical line, as shown in the earlier figure, would produce the very upright of the Cross we are looking for. Similarly, if one were also to draw, as seems natural, a horizontal line separating the distinctively heavenly element III ($C^1 + C^2$), from its lower components (I and II), this would provide the crossbar (*patibulum*) of the Cross, as indicated just above. The whole would depict, through the design of the hymn's layout, a completed σταυρός, hidden to all but the "initiated" few.[103] This σταυρός, as well as the "X" described above, is what we hold to be the very "secret" (τὸ μυστήριον) of the Christian's piety indicated in the hymn's opening formula—and as symbolized by the very shape—or the absence of shape—of the hymn itself, as we have hypothetically constructed in our chapter here.[104] Less secret

---

[102] Gundry, "Form and Meaning," 212: "The string of ἐν's may come from a desire for similar sound without the requirement of identical sense."

[103] Similarly hidden but unnamed references to the Cross have been detected elsewhere in the text of the NT, notably in the alliterative assonance of repeating *T*'s at Heb. 2:14, which cryptically refers to the Cross, known to be *T*-shaped; see Thomas E. Schmidt, "The Letter *Tau* as the Cross: Ornament and Content in Hebrews 2,14," *Bib* 76 (1995): 75–84, for comparable features; see also E. Dinkler, *Signum Crucis. Aufsäze zum Neuen Testament und zur Christlichen Archäologie* (Tübingen: Mohr Siebeck, 1967).

[104] Marshall, *Pastoral Epistles*, 503, writes:

> Rather, the text is an exposition of the "mystery," i.e. of what was secret but has been revealed; this secret is now seen to be the Saviour himself, and the church is the body to whom the secret has been revealed that he has been revealed in flesh in the world and then vindicated

but showing a remarkable confluence with the structure of our strophic verses is the potential layout of the celebrated Philippians hymn, mentioned in passing elsewhere in this chapter. The lines of Phil. 2:6-11, if laid out in a pattern similar to that of 1 Tim. 3:16, also yield a perfect isocolon—this time of 90 syllables each,[105] with the cosmic "descent" of Jesus occupying a downward ladder ending in v. 8's "becoming obedient to the point of death." This then turns upward to "ascend" toward a summating "Jesus Christ is Lord to the glory of God the Father" (v. 11), which matches the opening of the hymn in v. 6. This same step-pyramid configuration, which like the 1 Timothy hymn could serve as an aid for memorization, is composed of nine lines of "descending" text followed by nine lines of "ascending" text, with the phrase "but death on a *cross*" (θανάτου δὲ σταυροῦ) resting at its apical bottom.[106] A similar such structure, albeit it being a collection of thirteen hymns and not a lone song, has been identified in the Dead Sea Scroll's *Angelic Liturgy: Songs of the Sabbath Sacrifice* (4Q400–4Q407, 11Q17, Mas1k). Here the "structure of the composition as a whole" divides into three sections of *Songs 1–5*, *Songs 6–8*, and *Songs 9–13* in such a way that "the whole can be visualized as a pyramidal structure, in which the seventh *Song* serves as a climatic focus."[107]

---

and exalted as proof of his position. Admittedly, even the vindication is hidden: these statements are statements of faith about what has happened in heaven.

Based upon our new analysis, however, we would say that it is not the vindication that is hidden but rather the Cross itself—that is, the crucifixion.

[105] Provided we omit the τό before ὄνομα in v. 9 with D F G K L P Ψ 075 0278 81 104 365 630 1175ᶜ 1241 1505 1881 2464* Cˡᵉˣ ᵀʰᵈ

[106]

	I (Descent)	II (Ascent)	
6	"Who in the form of God being	To the glory of God the F."	
	Not a thing to be grasped to be thought	Jesus Christ is Lord	
	Equal to God	And every tongue confess	11
7	But he emptied himself	In heaven, on earth, etc.	
	The form of a slave taking	Every knee should bow	
	In the likeness of man becoming	That in the name of Jesus	10
	In aspect being found as a person	That is above every name	
8	He humbled himself	And bestowed on him a name	
	Becoming obedient unto death	Wherefore God exalted him	9
	(90 syll. →) **But a death on a cross** (90 syll. ↑)		
	III (Cross)		

The fact that this hymn divides equally into two parts of 90 syllables each, with an apical reference to the historical Cross, provides added weight to the prospect that the hymn in 1 Timothy also preserves a reference to the Cross, albeit in a more covert manner.

[107] See James H. Charlesworth and Carol A. Newsom, eds., *The Dead Sea Scrolls: Hebrew, Aramaic, and Greek Texts with English Translations*, vol. 4B: *Angelic Liturgy: Songs of the Sabbath Sacrifice* (Tübingen: Mohr Siebeck, 1999), 3 (here we have added the Roman numeral labels to their three sections):

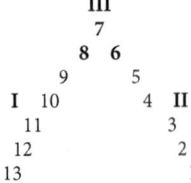

The need for "secrecy" conveyed by 1 Tim. 3:16's "cross" may have arisen out of a challenging situation that saw the church facing formidable persecution among its house and tenement churches, although this is something that we can by no means be certain of. The historical developments in Rome following the Great Fire of 64 CE, when the emperor Nero (r. 54–68 CE) blamed the urban Christians for the citywide conflagration for which he himself was responsible, forms one possible backdrop to the resultant religious persecution and could have occasioned the initial need for first-century believers to maintain a heightened level of awareness in monitoring their ecclesial gatherings and in conducting their day-to-day lives, although the context of our hymn may point to a later period.[108] One is reminded of the well-established use of the "fish"–acronym ΙΧΘΥΣ (= "Jesus Christ, Son of God, Saviour") as a code word for self-identifying Christians who needed to supervise their lives with secrecy in the face of a program of growing anti-Jewish/Christian sentiment throughout the Empire. A well-known second-century gem in the British Museum contains an early Crucifixion scene preserving syllables pointing to a Christian hymnic invocation that, inter alia, disguises in similar code form a reference to the figure on the Cross as "the blameless lamb" (ἀμνὸς ἄμωμος; cf. 1 Pet. 1:19).[109] Could the purportedly visual structure of our hymn in 1 Timothy and its variant verses also disguise, as its hidden secret, a message of the Cross that it now intends to disclose in the hymn's singing and citation? We believe so. At least the concealed σ(ταυρός), and other features that we have discussed, might point in the direction of such a contingency.

The group of songs shows a configuration remarkably similar to that which we suggest for the single 1 Timothy hymn. The editors further write that the songs were recited "as the praxis of a communal mysticism" during which "the community ... is led through a progressive experience" that "produces an anticipatory climax at the center of the work" (4), that is, with the apical song number 7.

[108] On the fire of 64 CE and subsequent persecution, see Incignieri, *Gospel to the Romans*, 156–207, who rightly points out that even after 70 CE Christians in Rome were still fearful of persecution. Indeed, it was not until the time of Trajan (98–117 CE) that empire-wide persecutions of Christians officially let up (cf. Eusebius, *Hist. eccl.* 3.33). Thus, if our hymn has a Roman "persecutorial" origin, it might well have arisen in the time of the reign of Domitian (81–96 CE), or even later. But we must remember that comparable Christological hymns such as that of the pre-Pauline Phil. 2:6-11 were thought to be composed as early as the forties CE, as the relative date of the epistle itself suggests (fifties CE).

[109] In the form σοαμ νωαμ = ἀμνὸς ἄμω(μος); see R. D. Kotansky, "The Magic 'Crucifixion Gem' in the British Museum," *GRBS* 57 (2017): 631–59, esp. 638–9. The inscription on the obverse, surrounding the Crucifixion scene, reads in full: Υἱὲ, / πατήρ, Ἰη/σοῦ Χριστέ, σοαμ νωα/μ, ωαωι, α/ϝηιουω, / ἀρτάννα / λυσίου / [υ]ἱ[οῦ] ("O Son, Father, O Jesus Christ, SOAM NŌAM, ŌAŌI, AEĒIOYŌ, O cross-(beam) of the redeeming Son!") The lines are composed of varying iambic meters.

11

"Out with the Christians ... Out with the Epicureans!" Atheism and Constructing the Other in Antiquity

Richard A. Wright

Around the year 180 CE, the satirist Lucian responded to a request from a friend that he provide an account of the life of a certain Alexander, a man who established himself as a priest/prophet for the god Asclepius. Lucian believed Alexander to be a charlatan. He tells the friend that he is embarrassed that his friend would make a request to document the life of such a scoundrel; and he was also embarrassed for himself that he had fulfilled the request (*Alex.* 1–2).

According to Lucian, Alexander concocted an extravagant plan to scam foolish simpletons out of their money. There came a time when people began to see through the charade—primarily Epicureans (*Alex.* 25).[1] Alexander went on the attack by warning the citizens of Pontus that the area had become overrun by atheists and Christians spreading scandalous reports about him; he also spoke out against Epicurus (*Alex.* 25). He later moved to Rome. As part of an expanding menu of cultic options, Alexander introduced a set of mysteries modeled after those of Eleusis. On the first day of the mysteries, a proclamation was read: any atheist, Epicurean, or Christian must immediately leave; then an antiphonal cry was raised: "Out with the Christians"; to which the response came: "Out with the Epicureans" (*Alex.* 38).

My interest for this chapter is not in Lucian's characterization of Epicureans and Christians.[2] Rather, I use Lucian's text as an invitation to think about the circumstances in which educated people living in antiquity might apply the label "atheist." I let Lucian's

---

[1] Lucian indicates that Epicurus and Metrodorus were men with skeptical minds who had keen insight and were able to see through deceit (*Alex.* 17). Epicureans appear to thwart Alexander in chapters 45–7. The work ends with a tribute to Epicurus (*Alex.* 61).
[2] It is fascinating to see the different roles Christians play in Lucian's writing. In *The Passing of Peregrinus*, they are the foolish and gullible. In *Alexander*, they are among those who can see through Alexander and are placed on the same level as the Epicureans who are the ostensible heroes of the story. For a brief, recent, description of the challenges presented by Lucian and his usefulness for understanding non-Christians' perceptions of Christians in the second century, see John A. North, "Pagan Attitudes," in James Carleton Paget and Judith Lieu (eds.), *Christianity in the Second Century: Themes and Developments* (Cambridge: Cambridge University Press, 2017), 265–80. For a full discussion of *Alexander the False Prophet*, see U. Victor, *Lukian von Samosata: Alexandros oder der Lügenprophet, Eingeleitet, herausgegeben übersetzt und erklärt* (Leiden: Brill, 1997).

treatise set the end point for my investigation. I do not look at authors who write after the second century. Lucian also suggests the parties to be compared. By bringing Christians, Epicureans, and atheists into comparison, Lucian must have expected his readers to understand the logic of the comparison.[3] I use this scene, therefore, to explore the degree to which the application of the label "atheist" to Epicureans and Christians might help us understand the use of that term in antiquity.

I begin by looking at the application of the label "atheist" to Epicureans. I turn next to literature dealing with Christians. I conclude with a few general observations about how this exploration shapes our understanding of the label "atheist."

Epicurean Atheists

By the time that Lucian wrote, Epicurus and his followers had long been labeled as atheists.[4] It is important to remember that the term "atheist" could be used by intellectuals to describe a philosophical position that asserts that gods do not exist. Used in this way, the label is, or can be, neutral. Neither Epicureans nor Christians fit into this category. But the term became a descriptor of a social category into which intellectuals placed other intellectuals whose ideas about the gods they disagreed with. Tim Whitmarsh observes, "Atheism is not just a philosophical position willingly assumed by consenting adults; it is also a social category constructed by self-styled protectors of religious orthodoxy as a receptacle for those whose beliefs they do not share."[5] And, one might add, they do not like.

It is in this sense that "atheist" is used in the literature we are examining. Given the application of this label, one might expect to find charges of atheism against Epicurus arising out of opposition to his theology or concern about deviant religious practices; something like what we see in Plato's *Apology* against Socrates.[6] This, however, was not the case. Anti-Epicurean sources say nothing about charges of atheism.[7] Epicurus seems to have enjoyed popular support—or at least there is no evidence that he

---

[3] Tim Whitmarsh has argued that Lucian did not think Christians were atheists ("'Away with the Atheists!' Christianity and Militant Atheism in the Early Empire," in Paget and Lieu, *Christianity in the Second Century*, 288–90). This is not the space for me to debate that issue, though I am not persuaded by all of the arguments he puts forward. For my purpose in this chapter, it does not matter whether Lucian believed them to be atheists. One does not need Lucian to wonder whether Christians might have been perceived as atheists in antiquity. One finds this label used of Christians in the second century. Lucian provides a convenient launching point for the comparison of Christians, Epicureans, and atheism. Whitmarsh also points out that his is the only place in ancient literature where Christians and Epicureans are brought into comparison (290 n. 30).

[4] Marek Winiarczyk provides a detailed list in "Wer galt im Altertum als Atheist?" *Philologus* 128 (1984): 157–83, see esp. 168–70. Whitmarsh attributes the origins of the use of the term with a negative sense to fifth century BCE Athens. Tim Whitmarsh, *Battling the Gods: Atheism in the Ancient World* (New York: Alfred A. Knopf, 2015), 124.

[5] Whitmarsh, *Battling the Gods*, 116. Whitmarsh suggests that the negative sense of the term had its origins in the political desire to stigmatize individuals (124).

[6] For the charge that Socrates does not acknowledge the gods (*Apol.* 18C, 23D); that he does not acknowledge the gods of the city but rather new daimonian (*Apol.* 24C).

[7] An observation made by Dirk Obbink, "The Atheism of Epicurus," *GRBS* 30 (1989): 187–223, here 202–3.

aroused the anger of the general populace.⁸ Diogenes Laertius records that Epicurus was well respected by his fellow citizens. He writes: "Our philosopher has abundance of witnesses to attest his unsurpassed goodwill to all people—his native land, which honoured him with statues in bronze; his friends, so many in number that they could hardly be counted by whole cities, and indeed all who knew him" (10.9).⁹ Philodemus, using a bit of hyperbole, makes the same point:

> He was inoffensive to them, so that not only did he not engage in any lawsuit against anyone, he did not even have a quarrel. In fact, while some philosophers were prosecuted for their way of life and for their teachings, and some were exiled from city, some even from league, and put to death, and all became the butt of writers of comedy, only Epicurus magnificently secured protection for himself together with those who dwelt with him according to the genuine precepts of the school, without falling prey to the virtue-hating and all-harassing mouth of comedy.¹⁰

Epicurus participated in traditional cults and encouraged his followers to do likewise. Various sources indicate that Epicurus and individual Epicureans offered sacrifices and dedications, were initiated into mysteries, and celebrated the calendrical festivals and rites of personal and ancestral cults.¹¹

---

⁸ Plutarch asserts that the reputation of Epicureans as irreligious people was known to all humanity (*Non Posse*, 1100D). Some Epicureans were expelled from cities outside Athens, but the reasons derived from Epicurean hedonism, not theology (see the list of incidents in Obbink, "Atheism," 204 n. 59).

⁹ Translations of classical authors, unless otherwise indicated, are taken from the Loeb Classical Library—with occasional modifications.

¹⁰ Philodemus, *On Piety* 1505-32; cf. Dirk Obbink, ed. *Philodemus: On Piety I: Critical Text with Commentary* (Oxford: Clarendon, 1996). All translations and references to *On Piety* are to the Obbink edition unless otherwise noted.

¹¹ Diogenes Laertius records that words could not describe Epicurus's piety toward the gods (10.10). Philodemus reports that he participated in city festivals and sacrifices and was initiated into both the city's mysteries (see *On Piety* 28, 30, and 31; Obbink, *Philodemus*). In *On Frank Criticism*, frag. 6, Philodemus indicates that Epicurus rebuked Pythocles for causing Leonteus to stumble with respect to the gods. *Philodemus: On Frank Criticism*, introduction, translation, and notes David Konstan et al. (Atlanta: SBL, 1998). Also see P. Oxy. 215:

> But you, O man, consider it a thing of the greatest blessedness to discern properly that which we can conceive as preeminent among existing things; marvel at this notion and reverence it in freedom from fear, and then [sacrifice piously while participating in such rites] just as [they do] when they intend to worship, but instead not belittling in religious observance an entity of such sanctity in relation to your happiness. (Quoted from Obbink, "POxy. 215 and Epicurean Religious Theoria," *Atti del XVII Congresso Internaz. di Papirologia* ? [1984]: 611-12)

Catherine J. Castner has argued that we may possess inscriptional evidence of cultic participation by some Epicurean women. Seven women appear in various sources as members of Epicurus's school during his lifetime. Four names of these hetairai are found in contemporary inscriptions. The four made dedications to healing gods at about the time the school was founded or soon after. Catherine J. Castner, "Epicurean Hetairai as Dedicants to Healing Deities?" *GRBS* 23 (1982): 51-7, here 51. Pamela Gordon has commented on the difficulties associated with this evidence, "Remembering the Garden: The Trouble with Women in the School of Epicurus," in John T. Fitzgerald et al. (eds.), *Philodemus and the New Testament World*, NovTsup 111 (Leiden: Brill, 2004), 234-7; also, *The Invention and Gendering of Epicurus* (Ann Arbor: University of Michigan Press, 2012), 100-3.

Perhaps Epicurus only went through the motions of cultic activity but did not in fact believe in the existence of gods (which his opponents asserted to be the case). Epicurus, though, explicitly affirmed that gods exist. After a brief introductory statement in his *Letter to Menoeceus*, Epicurus writes: "First of all, believe that god is an incorruptible and happy being, as common opinion of the world dictates ... For there are gods; for our knowledge of them is distinct" (123).

Epicurus makes reference to "common opinion," but his theology was in its details constructed to combat "common opinion." Having stated that the gods do in fact exist, he qualifies that statement by saying "But they are not of the character which people in general attribute to them" (*Ep. Men.* 123).

Epicurean gods were exemplars of the Epicurean good life. The first of the *Kuriae Doxae* states that: "A blessed and imperishable being neither has trouble itself nor does it cause trouble for anyone else; therefore, it does not experience anger or indebtedness, for such feelings indicate weakness." One of the consequences of this definition of happiness for these beings is that they cannot be bothered by requests from human beings; they do not answer prayers; they do no harm to, but neither do they help, human beings.

In what appears to be an attempt to pre-empt the application of the label "atheist," Epicurus claims

> that person is not impious who discards the gods believed by the many, but the one who applies to the gods the opinions entertained by the many. For the assertions of the many about the gods are ... false opinions. (*Ep. Men.* 123–4)[12]

If, then, Epicurus was not an atheist—he certainly did not consider himself to be one and apparently none of his contemporaries did either—why did this label get attached to him? I introduce two of Epicurus's critics: Cotta, one of the spokesmen in Cicero's *De natura deorum* (written around 45 BCE); and Plutarch (who wrote in the first century CE).

Cotta argued that Epicurus's beliefs *about* the gods actually destroyed religion.[13] He said that Epicurus

> destroyed the very foundations of religion, and overthrew—not by main force like Xerxes, but by argument—the temples and the altars of the immortal gods. Why, what reason have you for maintaining that men owe honor to the gods, if the gods not only do not honor men, but care for nothing at all? "But deity possesses an

---

[12] Obbink, though, denies any indication in Epicurus' writings of a response to a charge of impiety ("Atheism," 203–4). There certainly is no evidence of a charge of impiety or atheism in this passage, but the language does suggest an attempt to avoid being labeled as such.

[13] Cicero's *Nat. d.* 1.85. See Obbink for the suggestion that the charge of atheism had its origin in the skeptical Academy ("Atheism," 208–20). Sextus Empiricus included Epicurus at the end of a long list of atheists that he presented to show that belief in the gods' existence was not universal; in this way the skeptics argued that the dogmatists' appeal to a universally accepted opinion about the gods was not legitimate (215–16). Since Carneades liked to use lists of atheists, and since he had a hand in the expansion of the catalogue (through Clitomachus), he may have included Epicurus in the list. If so, Carneades may be the ultimate source for the atheism of Epicurus (218).

excellence and pre-eminence which must of its own nature attract the honor of the wise." Now how can there be any excellence in a being so engrossed in the delights of his own pleasure that he always has been, is, and will continue to be entirely idle and inactive? Furthermore how can you owe piety to a person who has bestowed nothing upon you? or how can you owe anything at all to one who has done you no service? Piety is justice towards the gods; but how can any claims of justice exist between us and them, if god and man have nothing in common? Holiness is the science of divine honor; but I fail to see why the gods should be worshipped if we neither have received nor hope to receive benefit from them. (*Nat. d.* 1.115-116)

Epicurus had claimed that religious ritual ought to continue because the nature of the gods deserved it. Cotta denied that claim. The nature of the Epicurean gods did not warrant piety.

This was the case for two reasons. First, a god so intent on its own pleasure that it became inactive did not deserve honor. Second, religion must be understood as a cooperative exchange between gods and humans. Human beings owe nothing to gods who do nothing for them. There must be some hope of benefit from the gods or there is no reason to honor them. By eliminating divine beneficence, Epicurus cuts out the very essence of religion. Epicurus calls god "good" but denies the very essence of goodness: beneficence. Cotta argued:

Epicurus however, in abolishing divine beneficence and divine benevolence, uprooted and exterminated all religion from the human heart. For while asserting the supreme goodness and excellence of the divine nature, he yet denies to god the attribute of benevolence—that is to say, he does away with that which is the most essential element of supreme goodness and excellence. For what can be better or more excellent than kindness and beneficence? Make out god to be devoid of either, and you make him devoid of all love, affection or esteem for any other being, human or divine. It follows not merely that the gods do not care for mankind, but that they have no care for one another. (*Nat. d.* 1.121)

It should be noted that Cotta does not deny that Epicurus and Epicureans actually participated in cults. In fact, he acknowledges that they do.[14] This participation, though, is merely pretense. It reveals a lack of courage on the part of the Epicureans. They ought to deny the existence of the gods as the result to which their theology logically leads. (*Nat. d.* 1.85). Epicurean theology empties their actions of any content.

By the end of his speech Cotta accepts Posidonius's assertion that Epicurus did not, in fact, believe in the gods. He states:

"But Epicurus (you will tell me) actually wrote a treatise on holiness." Epicurus is making fun of us, though he is not so much a humorist as a loose and careless writer. For how can holiness exist if the gods pay no heed to man's affairs? … It is

---

[14] See *Nat. d.* 1.85; also 1.86.

doubtless therefore truer to say, as the good friend to us all, Posidonius, argued in the fifth book of his *On the Nature of the Gods*, that Epicurus does not really believe in the gods at all, and that he said what he did about the immortal gods only for the sake of deprecating popular odium. (*Nat. d.* 1.123)

Cotta asserts that Epicurus only pretends to believe the gods exist in order to avoid popular outrage.[15] In the final analysis, Epicurean religion was not religion at all. If the gods are not involved in human affairs there can be no point to continue to participate in cultic activity (*Nat. d.* 1.3).

Two aspects of Cotta's argument appear also in Plutarch. First, Plutarch argued that Epicurean theology emptied religion of any meaning. The gods must be understood as benefiting human beings or religion has no content. He writes:

For it is better that our belief about the gods should include an intermixture of a certain emotion that is part reverence and part fear, than that, by trying to escape this, we should leave ourselves no hope of divine favour, no confidence in prosperity, and in adversity no refuge in God. (*Sua. viv.* 1101B–C)

Plutarch accuses Epicurus of playing word games with religion:

It is this disjoining of one word from another that works harm and fills your lives with a godless negligence and recklessness, when you tear away from the gods the appellations attached to them and by that single act annihilate all sacrifices, mysteries, processions and festivals. To whom shall we offer the Sacrifice Before the Ploughing, the Sacrifice for Deliverance? How shall we hold the ceremonies of the Bearing of Light, of the Revels, and of the Prenuptial Rites, if we leave ourselves no Lady of Nuptials, no Reveller, no Bearer of Light, no Guardian of the Ploughing, and no Deliverer? These views affect matters of the highest and gravest import, and the error in them involves reality, not a set of vocables or the conjunction of meanings or the accepted usage of words. (*Adv. Col.* 1119E–F)

The very vocabulary used to call on the gods describes their functions in the lives of the people. The removal of these descriptors from the divine names, in effect, takes away the involvement of the gods and therefore the reasons for sacrificing to them.

Second, because Epicurus denies that gods respond to human cultic activity, Plutarch doubts the sincerity of Epicurean religious practices:

This indeed is why they imagine that the superstitious attend sacrifices and initiations not because they like to but because they are afraid. Here the Epicureans are themselves no better than they, since they do the same from fear and do not even get the measure of happy anticipation the others have, but are merely scared

---

[15] Cotta's statement is implicit evidence that Epicurus was accepted—or at least not attacked—by the populace. Cotta indicates that if the crowd knew what Epicurus believed, they would be outraged; they were not, apparently, outraged.

and worried that this deception and fooling of the public might be found out, with an eye to whom their books on the gods and on piety have been composed. (*Sua. viv.* 1102C)

The Epicureans only participate in cultic activities out of fear that they will be discovered as impious or atheists. Plutarch believes the Epicureans are duplicitous—they put on a show out of fear of public outrage.

Plutarch adds two additional elements to the critique beyond what we saw from Cotta in Cicero. First, he attacks Epicurus's assessment of what is wrong with popular religion. Contrary to Epicurus's claim, Plutarch asserts that most people are not frightened by religion. Religion is a joy to human beings. He writes:

No visit delights us more than a visit to a temple; no occasion than a holy day; no act or spectacle than what we see and what we do ourselves in matters that involve the gods, whether we celebrate a ritual or take part in a choral dance or attend a sacrifice or ceremony of initiation. (*Sua. viv.* 1101D-E)

Rather than terrorizing people, religion is a great source of joy—but only for those who believe in divine providence (*Sua. viv.* 1102A). Those few who are frightened benefit from this fear. It prevents them from doing wrong:

Now we should, I grant you, remove superstition from our belief in the gods …; but if this proves impossible, we should not cut away both together and kill the faith that most men have in the gods. This is no terrifying or grim faith, as these men pretend, when they traduce providence as if she were some foul witch to frighten children with or unrelenting Fury out of tragedy hanging over our heads. No; among mankind a few are afraid of God who would not be better off without that fear; for since they fear him as a ruler mild to the good and hating the wicked, by this one fear, which keeps them from doing wrong, they are freed from the many that attend on crime. (*Sua. viv.* 1101C-D)

Finally, Plutarch is concerned about a social dimension to cultic activity that was not raised by Cotta. For Plutarch, it is unimaginable that a city could exist without religious practices that pay honor to the gods who, in turn, supply good fortune to human beings. Apart from this reciprocal relationship no government can survive:

In your travels you may come upon cities without wall, writing, king, houses or property, doing without currency, having no notion of a theatre or gymnasium; but a city without holy places and gods, without any observance of prayers, oaths, oracles, sacrifices for blessings received or rites to avert evils, no traveller has ever seen or will ever see. No, I think a city might rather be formed without the ground it stands on than a government, once you remove all religion from under it, get itself established or once established survive. Now it is this belief, the underpinning and base that holds all society and legislation together, that the Epicureans … proceed directly to demolish. (*Adv. Col.* 1125E-F)

The Epicureans posed a threat to civilization as Plutarch understood it. Epicurus had attacked the very foundation of civilization.

From the Epicurean evidence, I want to make four observations about the label "atheist." First, the application of the label is part of an exercise carried out by intellectuals toward other intellectuals. Cicero and Plutarch are well-educated men directing their criticism toward another well-educated man. All of these men came from essentially the same location in the socioeconomic hierarchy.

Second, all of the participants in this exercise used the term "atheist" to construct another person or group as "other." Even Epicurus engaged in this exercise and used the label against others in an attempt to distinguish his ideas and practices from those of "others." He attacked, for example, the fifth-century atheists, including Prodicus, Diagoras, and Critias, for removing the divine from the things that exist, thereby contrasting his own position from that of true atheists.[16]

Third, theological ideas are of primary importance. Each author indicated that what one says about the gods matters; words make a difference. Finally, and directly related to point three, fourth: appropriate behavior (properly honoring the gods) does not override problematic theology. It did not matter to Cotta or Plutarch that Epicureans participated in cultic activities. Epicurean theology emptied those activities of their proper function.

The Problem with Christians

No Greek or Roman author before Lucian associates Christians explicitly with atheists. Of course, few Greek or Roman authors paid any attention to Christians at all. If we look at the non-Christian authors in the second century who construct Christians as "other" and Christian authors who defend themselves against that construction, we find three distinct strategies: (1) non-Christian authors who attach a label to Christians—but not the label "atheist"; (2) one non-Christian author (Celsus) who constructs Christians as "other" but does so apart from the use of any label; and (3) Christian authors who defend themselves against the use of a label: "atheist."[17] Even though only one of these sets of authors actually uses the label "atheist" in their writings, the writings concerning

---

[16] See Obbink, who cites book 12 of Epicurus's Περὶ φύσεως (P. Herc. 1077 18; "Atheism," 204). Whitmarsh comments that the precariousness of Epicurus's own theological position might have been the motivating factor for his attack on others (*Battling the Gods*, 209).

[17] Galen, also writing in the latter half of the second century, does not fit easily into this discussion. He had a mixed response to the Christians. In a commentary on Plato's *Republic*, preserved only in Arabic, Galen observes that although Christians sometimes derive their faith from parables and miracles, at other times they act like philosophers. Galen seems to have been impressed primarily by how Christians handled death and how they exercised sexual restraint. For the text and commentary, see R. Walzer, *Galen on Christians and Jews* (London: Oxford University Press, 1949). For a reassessment of the Arabic evidence that calls into question the authenticity of part of the quotation provided in Walzer, see Stephen Gero, "Galen on the Christians: A Reappraisal of the Arabic Evidence," *OCP* 56 (1990): 371–411. Even with Gero's corrections, Galen's qualified, favorable assessment of Christian actions still stands. See also the recent discussion by Rebecca Flemming, "Galen and the Christians: Texts and Authority in the Second Century," in Paget and Lieu, *Christianity in the Second Century*, 171–87.

Christians taken as a whole can inform our understanding of the use of that term in antiquity. I take each strategy in turn.

Non-Christian Descriptions

Those non-Christian authors who attached a label to Christians did not use the label "atheist." Instead, they chose to label Christians as *superstitio*.[18] Pliny the Younger in a letter to the Emperor Trajan (written between 111 and 113 CE), Tacitus, in the *Annales* (written somewhere between 115 and 120 CE), and Suetonius, in *Nero* (written around 121 CE) all label the group of people who followed Jesus a superstition. Both Tacitus and Suetonius used the label in connection with descriptions of events during the reign of the emperor Nero.

The Greek and Latin terms translated "superstition" could refer to a variety of different kinds of beliefs, behaviors, or circumstances. Richard Gordon has argued the term *superstitio* was used against deviant groups in contrast with sacrificial religion. Sacrificial religion was rational, appropriate, coherent, and effective. Non-sacrificial or new religious groups or foreign religions were labeled superstitious.[19] Plutarch offers support for such an understanding of the label. In his *De Superstitione*, for example, he describes superstition as an "emotional idea" (δόξαν ἐμπαθῆ; 165B–C, 167B), contrasting such behavior with rational religious practices. He also associates it with foreign religions (171B–E).[20] The second-century authors under consideration in this chapter also illustrate elements highlighted by Gordon.

Tacitus introduces his readers to Christians in his discussion of the fire that swept through Rome in 64 CE. In this description, he emphasizes the foreign roots of the group. He characterizes Christians as "a destructive superstition" (*exitiabilis superstitio*) that, having been suppressed at the death of their leader, "broke out again not only in Judaea, the first source of the evil but even in Rome, where all things hideous and shameful from every part of the world find their center and become popular" (*Ann.* 15.44). From the description it is clear that Tacitus has no stomach for the group, but his interest is not really in the Christians per se but rather in what Nero's treatment of the group revealed about Nero's own suspect character. He later notes that when Nero

---

[18] In what follows, I treat these terms as independent of one another. One must keep in mind, though, that some ancient authors understood there to be overlap between the terms. For example, both Plutarch and Seneca, while drawing distinctions between atheism and superstition, acknowledge the similarity between the two concepts. In *De Superstitione*, Plutarch writes, "It occurs to me to wonder at those who say that atheism is impiety, and do not say the same of superstition" (169F). He also argues that "the atheist has no part in causing superstition, but superstition provides the seed from which atheism springs, and when atheism has taken root, superstition supplies it with a defense, not a true or a fair one, but one not destitute of some speciousness" (171A). For Plutarch, superstition is a worse state than that of atheism. In a discussion of superstition, Seneca questions, "What difference is there between denying the gods and dishonouring them?" (*Ep.* 123.16).

[19] Richard Gordon, "Religion in the Roman Empire: The Civic Compromise and Its Limits," in Mary Beard and John North (eds.), *Pagan Priests: Religion and Power in the Ancient World* (Ithaca, NY: Cornell University Press, 1990), 237.

[20] For a detailed discussion of the use of the term, see Grodzynski, "Superstitio," *REA* 76 (1974): 36–60. See also Dale Martin, *Inventing Superstition: From the Hippocratics to the Christians* (Cambridge, MA: Harvard University Press, 2007).

put members of the group on trial as the arsonists responsible for the fire, Christians were convicted not of arson but of "hatred of humanity."[21] I suggest, but do not defend here, that the expression "hatred of humanity" might be connected to Christian deviant religious practices that tended to separate them from the rest of the city.[22]

Suetonius provides very little information in his description of the Christians. He writes, "[Nero] likewise inflicted punishments on the Christians a kind of people who held a new and *maleficae* superstition" (*Nero*, 16.2).[23] *Maleficus* could be used by an author to indicate a criminal, but the term could also refer to a magician or an enchanter—that is to say, a religious deviant. Suetonius's use of the term leaves open the possibility that he was disturbed by deviant religious practices of Christians. But one cannot say with any certainty; Suetonius says nothing more about the group.

The first author to show any detailed interest in this group was Pliny the Younger. Pliny finds himself in circumstances where he must decide how to adjudicate Christians who have been brought forward for trial. What was only hinted at in Suetonius becomes explicit in Pliny. He knows crimes have been associated with Christians but wonders whether actual crimes must be proven or whether he can punish them on the basis of the name alone (*Ep.* 10.96.2). He refers the matter to the Emperor Trajan. In summarizing his assessment of the group, he labels them a distorted and excessive superstition (*superstitionem pravam et immodicam*; *Ep.* 10.96.8).

That the group could be considered foreign also appears in Pliny's letter. He begins his discussion of his current procedure by describing an interrogation at the end of which, if the person persists, he or she is executed. The punishment presumes that the person under trial is not a Roman citizen. This is made clear by a second type of person who is on trial and is also a Roman citizen; such persons were sent to Rome (*Ep.* 10.96.3–4).

The focus of Pliny's attention is on their religious deviance. He comments that they sing hymns to Christ as a god (*Ep.* 10.96.7). But what is particularly troubling to Pliny

---

[21] Brent Shaw has recently challenged the historicity of Tacitus's description of Nero's actions against the Christians. He doubts that Nero could have identified a group of Christians in the early sixties much less believed them to be worthy of punishment as Christians. Brent Shaw, "Myth of the Neronian Persecution," *JRS* 105 (2015): 73-100. Christopher Jones issued a rebuttal in *New Testament Studies*: "The Historicity of the Neronian Persecution: A Response to Brent Shaw," *NTS* 63 (2017): 146–52. Shaw responded to the response: Brent Shaw, "Response to Christopher Jones: The Historicity of the Neronian Persecution," *NTS* 64 (2018): 231–42. For my purposes, whether Nero actually persecuted Christians does not matter. My interest is in the fact that Tacitus chooses to label the group a superstition.

[22] For a detailed discussion of this issue, see Richard A. Wright, "Christians, Epicureans, and the Critique of Greco-Roman Religion" (PhD dissertation, Brown University, 1994). Erich Gruen suggests that Tacitus chooses the label "superstition" because he viewed it "in terms of religious belief and observances, without any suggestion of ethnic characteristics." Erich Gruen, "Christians as a 'Third Race': Is Ethnicity an Issue?," in Paget and Lieu, *Christianity in the Second Century*, 238. I would agree that Tacitus chose the term because of Christian religious observances or practices but (1) question what in the passage suggests that Tacitus is concerned with Christian belief, and (2) it seems to me that the fact that Tacitus connects the movement to Judea does at least raise the possibility that he understands there to be a connection between this group and Jewish ethnicity.

[23] *genus hominum superstitionis novae ac maleficae*. Shaw, rightfully, points out that in Suetonius's description of Nero's actions, no connection is made between to the fire of 64 CE. And, conversely, when Suetonius describes the fire, he does not mention the Christians. Shaw, "Myth," 83–4.

is their refusal to honor the gods. Pliny also explicitly connects Christian behavior to the health of the sacrificial economy in his province. Activity in the temples and meat markets began to improve after Pliny took action against the Christians (*Ep.* 10.96.10). Pliny's requirement that Christians sacrifice to the image of the emperor and that they denounce Christ indicates his concern to correct religious deviance.

Our final non-Christian author under consideration, Celsus, does not use either the label of "superstition" or that of "atheist" in connection with Christians. He does, though, call attention to the kinds of behaviors identified by Pliny: He observes that they refuse to swear by the genius of the emperor (*Cels.* 8.65–68); they do not have any altars or temples, and they do not participate in the Roman feasts (*Cels.* 8.17–21). He indicates that these behaviors put the empire at risk in multiple ways. They risk bringing down divine anger by not paying proper respect to the gods (*Cels.* 8.55). He suggests that even if the world were to turn to the Christian god, that god would not fight for the empire, and even if he did—based on how ineffectively he has fought for the Jews—he would not be much help (*Cels.* 8.69). Christians themselves shirk their obligations and will not participate in the military. He claims Christians are united against the rest of the humankind (*Cels.* 1.1, 2.4, 3.14, and 8.2–5). From Celsus's perspective, Christians threaten the order and safety of the empire.

All of these non-Christian authors focus on Christian behavior. With the exception of Celsus, who does not provide a label for the group, none of these authors show any awareness of—or interest in—Christian ideas about their god. Tacitus and Pliny indicate that the group is foreign; Pliny explicitly and Suetonius implicitly indicate a connection between the group and crimes; Pliny and Celsus explicitly and Tacitus and Suetonius implicitly are worried about religious deviancy. All of these concerns fit neatly into ancient descriptions of superstition, and that is the label used by these authors.

Christian Descriptions

When we turn to Christian authors writing in the second century, it is not surprising that we see the apologists defending themselves against the kinds of behaviors called out by the non-Christian authors previously considered: possible criminal activities, immoral behavior (though no particular immoral act is listed in these non-Christian authors), and religious deviancy. These Christian authors, though, do not defend themselves against the label "superstition" but the label "atheism." I briefly illustrate with two apologists: Justin (whose first apology was written between 155 and 157 CE) and Athenagoras (whose *Legatio Pro Christianis* was written around 176–7 CE).[24]

---

[24] I focus on these two apologists. The label "atheist" also appears in the *Martyrdom of Polycarp*. In this text, the governor attempts to get Polycarp to say "away with the atheists" in reference to Christians. Polycarp refuses and instead uses the expression against the mob that has assembled against him. The scene does not provide much help with respect to understanding characteristics of an atheist. See Whitmarsh, "Away with the Atheists," for a discussion of the rhetorical work the label performs in the *Martyrdom of Polycarp*. Whitmarsh also discusses other Christian literature, including Justin and Athenagoras.

Justin makes three moves that are pertinent to our consideration of atheism. First, with respect to accusations of crimes, he insists that such charges be proven. Judges ought not return verdicts on the basis of the name "Christian" alone (*1 Apol.* 4).

Second, in his response to the label "atheist," Justin accepts that Christians are indeed atheists—but only with respect to the gods of popular piety. Christians do believe in the one true God (*1 Apol.* 6).[25] Justin asserts that Christians have been accused as atheists not because of their theological ideas (a point I will return to shortly) but only because they do not participate in civic cultic activities. He writes, "And this is the sole accusation you bring against us, that we do not reverence the same gods as you do, nor offer to the dead libations and the savor of fat, and crowns for their statues, and sacrifices" (*1 Apol.* 24).[26]

Third, Justin attempts to convince his reader to turn their attention to Christian theological ideas. Near the beginning of his *Apology*, he writes, "It is our task, therefore, to afford to all an opportunity of inspecting our life and teachings, lest, on account of those who are accustomed to be ignorant of our affairs, we should incur the penalty due to them for mental blindness; and it is your business, when you hear us, to be found, as reason demands, good judges" (*1 Apol.* 3).[27] The content of Christian teaching is moral and rational—comparable to the best in non-Christian authors. Justin writes, "If, therefore, on some points we teach the same things as the poets and philosophers whom you honour, and on other points are fuller and more divine in our teaching, and if we alone afford proof of what we assert, why are we unjustly hated more than all others?" (*1 Apol.* 20).[28]

In Justin, Christians practice a rational religion (*1 Apol.* 13). It is their accusers who are irrational. In fact, these people are controlled by their passions. Justin writes, "In our case, who pledge ourselves to do no wickedness, nor to hold ... atheistic opinions, you do not examine the charges made against us; but, yielding to unreasoning passion, and to the instigation of evil demons, you punish us without consideration or judgement" (*1 Apol.* 5).[29]

There is overlap in the way that Athenagoras interacts with the label "atheist" with how Justin did. Like Justin, Athenagoras insists that charges are brought against Christians because of the name alone (*Leg.* 1). He writes, "But for us who are called Christians you have not in like manner cared; but although we commit no wrong ... you allow us to be harassed, plundered, and persecuted, the multitude making war upon us for our name alone."[30] He pleads that Christians be granted the same benefit as any other person: that they be tried on the basis of specific accusations and either released, if proved unfounded, or punished for the specific crime (*Leg.* 2). He says,

---

[25] Whitmarsh observes that Justin is the only Christian author who accepts the label "atheist" before qualifying its meaning. Whitmarsh, "Away with the Atheists," 287.
[26] *ANF* 1:171. Additional citations of the charge of atheism can be found in Justin, *1 Apol.* 6, 9, 10, 13; *2 Apol.* 3.
[27] *ANF* 1:163.
[28] *ANF* 1:169. For more detailed points of comparison with non-Christian authors, see *1 Apol.* 20–3; 59–60. Because of my interest in the label "atheism," I focus narrowly on Christian ideas. The discussion could easily be expanded, though, to include discussions of virtuous and pious behavior.
[29] *ANF* 1:164.
[30] *ANF* 2:129.

"What, therefore, is conceded as the common right of all, we claim for ourselves, that we shall not be hated and punished because we are called Christians …, but be tried on any charges which may be brought against us, and either be released on our disproving them, or punished if convicted of crime."[31]

In contrast with Justin, Athenagoras denies that Christians are atheists. But like Justin, Athenagoras claims that the only reason people label Christians as atheists is because of their cultic deviance. He writes:

> But, as most of those who charge us with atheism, and that because they have not even the dreamiest conception of what God is, and are doltish and utterly unacquainted with natural and divine things, and such as measure piety by the rule of sacrifices, charges us with not acknowledging the same gods as the cities, be pleased to attend to the following considerations. (*Leg.* 13)

He admits that Christians do not acknowledge the same gods as the cities and that they do not make sacrifices. But that does not mean one should conclude Christians are atheists. People who make such charges are ignorant of the true nature of God.

Christians cannot be atheists, Athenagoras argues, because they do in fact believe in a god—a god who is similar in some ways to the gods of the philosophers.[32] He questions why poets and philosophers testify to a single god with some of the same attributes (such as being uncreated and eternal) but are not called atheists (*Leg.* 5–6). In a move similar to one we saw in Epicurus, Athenagoras contrasts Christian theology with true atheists such as Diagoras who openly declared that there is no god (*Leg.* 4).

The intelligent reader should not be carried away by popular and irrational opinion against Christians. He writes: "If I go minutely into the particulars of our doctrine, let it not surprise you. It is that you may not be carried away by the popular irrational opinion, but may have the truth clearly before you … Allow me here to lift up my voice boldly in loud and audible outcry, pleading as I do before philosophic princes" (*Leg.* 11).[33] Again, like Justin, Athenagoras distinguishes Christian ideas from the irrationality of the people. He appeals to the rationality of the emperor to recognize the rationality of Christianity. Like Justin, Athenagoras insists that Christian theology is rational. Like Justin, he attempts to redirect non-Christian attention from behavior to theology; in which context Christian behavior makes sense.

These Christian writers acknowledge that what troubles non-Christians is Christian behavior. Justin and Athenagoras claim this concern with behavior is the cause of them being labeled atheists. In their response to non-Christian accusations, these Christian authors address the behaviors that non-Christians labeled superstitious, but they do so without addressing the label "superstition." Justin and Athenagoras address crimes associated with the group. They also address the religious practices that bothered non-Christians. They emphasize the rationality of their religion; Christian religious

---

[31] *ANF* 2:130.
[32] Athenagoras takes up the points in chapter 5 and the philosophers in chapter 6 of *Legatio pro Christianis*.
[33] *ANF* 2:134.

practices are not irrational. These writings show awareness of what non-Christians find problematic. But the authors are unwilling to defend themselves against the label "superstition" attached to those behaviors.

Instead, Christian authors defend themselves against the label "atheist." But, as we saw in the Epicurean material, the label "atheist" operates where theological ideas are in question, not behavior. How are we to make sense of this?

Tim Whitmarsh has argued that non-Christians did not make accusations of atheism against Christians. Christians themselves introduced that label into their rhetoric for their own purposes in defining themselves against non-Christians. He writes, "Its primary purpose is to cement Christian self-definition against the non-Christian 'other,' not the other way around."[34] Christians claim the label but redefine it to strengthen their own self-understanding and, in turn, use it against those who do not accept their god.

Whitmarsh's argument is persuasive, but I think there is an additional element at work in the Christian rhetorical strategy. Justin and Athenagoras introduce the label as part of their attempt to shift attention from Christian religious deviance to their theological ideas. If opponents would listen to Christian theology, they would see that Christian cultic practices are consistent with that theology. The apologists write to draw attention to Christian ideas. As part of their attempt to get their ideas heard, they take on the label "atheist" because that is the pejorative term used in a discussion of ideas about the gods; not superstition.

Conclusion

Given what we have seen in a rather complicated set of texts that construct Epicureans and Christians as "other," what light do these texts shed on the circumstances in which the label "atheist" was put to use in antiquity? A few brief observations follow and serve as my conclusion.

First, both labels we have encountered in this literature—"atheist" and "superstition"—belong to a portfolio of terms used by intellectuals to construct some individual or group as "other." The terms can overlap but were not used to label the same category of people. Superstition was applied to people already identified as "other" either because of their foreignness or religious deviance or both.[35] Superstition appears to have carried a much more pejorative connotation about the intellectual abilities of the person or group so labeled.

Second, in contrast to superstition, "atheism" was a label used by intellectuals against intellectuals. Epicurus, Cicero, and Plutarch all come from roughly the same well-educated, social location. Athenagoras and Justin come from roughly that same location and were attempting to engage readers in that social location. It is perhaps because of the association of the label with intellectual debates concerning ideas about

---

[34] Whitmarsh, "Away with the Atheists," 285.
[35] Other factors might enter into the equation, but these two were the ones most present in our literature.

the gods that Justin and Athenagoras defend themselves against being atheists and not against being a superstition. Even though their arguments show awareness of the non-Christian concerns about behaviors these authors label superstitious, they do not specifically address that label.

Third, the label "atheist" primarily stigmatizes a person's or group's theological ideas. Cotta and Plutarch were unimpressed that Epicurus and his followers practiced traditional piety. They were bothered by Epicurus's theology, the content of which logically (to their way of thinking) required a denial that the gods exist. And even though Justin and Athenagoras connected the term to Christian behavior, in their writings, the label operates within a larger rhetorical context attempting to get the reader to focus on Christian theological ideas. So, in a sense, the label is still connected to arguments about what can properly be said about a god. Pliny, Tacitus, and Suetonius were not interested in Christian ideas or theology, and so they do not label Christians as atheists.[36]

In the final analysis, even though no non-Christian author appears to have labeled Christians "atheists," Christian attention to the rhetorical use of that label is consistent with how we see it being applied to Epicurus and his followers. Christian authors in the second century, by claiming that label, rather than the one applied to them, demonstrate their shared understanding with other intellectuals who used the label as a tool to mark "others."

---

[36] In contrast to the other non-Christian writers, Celsus did pay attention to Christian theological ideas. To take just one example, in *Cels.* 4.71, Origen indicates that Celsus knows Christian Scripture and ridicules Christians for attributing passions to God: "Celsus, not understanding that the language of Scripture regarding God is adapted to an anthropopathic point of view, ridicules those passages which speak of words of anger addressed to the ungodly, and of threatenings directed against sinners" (*ANF* 4:529). Celsus has read Christian Scripture and attacks ideas Christians have about their god. But because Celsus did not label Christians as atheists or superstitious people, this fact does not help us with our understanding of either term.

12

Jinn and the Myth of the Shepherd

Jonathan Poletti

Reviewing the discovery narrative of the Dead Sea Scrolls leaves us with many unanswered questions. The narrative centers on a shepherd or goatherd. What was his name? Visiting Qumran in 1952, the Jesuit scholar Robert North inquired and later reported: "Muhammad Dib was the name of the first scroll-finder, according to Dr. William Reed, who as director of the American School employed him in the 1952 cave-search at the time of my visit there." But another source provided different names. North adds in a footnote that "the experienced Ta'amira foreman Ibrahim Sawriyya assured me in a visit to the Ta'amira desert that the names of the first two discoverers were Ahmad and Jum'a."[1]

Around 1949 Najib S. Khoury, an Arab Christian in Bethlehem, writes an account of the discovery, which was later published. He does not know the shepherds, but he has them "from the el-Ibayyat family from the Nawawrah clan which in turn belong to the el-Ta'amireh tribe who live sometimes on the hills of Judea and sometimes near the Dead Sea."[2] Such specificity is unusual, as histories of the scrolls tend to exotic flights. John C. Trever's 1965 memoir, *The Untold Story of Qumran*, recalls the find being disclosed to him in March 1948: "All the more like a tale out of the *Arabian Nights*, their story threw me into a state of confusion."[3]

If the setting is a cave outside Bethlehem, the story could be the birth of Jesus as told in the *Protoevangelium of James* (18:1). Indeed, the Ta'amireh may have witnessed that event. Mary Grey suggests: "They are the best candidates we have for the Shepherds of the Nativity story, and they themselves support the idea that they were once Christian, pointing as evidence to the remains of the Byzantine church in Tekoa."[4] The Qur'ān

---

[1] Robert North, "Qumran and Its Archeology," *CBQ* 16 (1954): 426–37, here 428 n. 11.
[2] Sherman Johnson, "The Finding of the Scrolls," *AThR* 39 (1957): 208–17, here 213. For background on Khoury, see Vernon G. Elgin, *Holy Hitchhiking Foreign Highways* (Bloomington, IN: AuthorHouse, 2010), 146.
[3] John C. Trever, *The Untold Story of Qumran* (Westwood, NJ: Fleming H. Revell, 1965), 76.
[4] Mary Grey, *The Advent of Peace: A Gospel Journey to Christmas* (London: SPCK, 2010), 64. For further biblical suggestion: Delia Khano, a local memoirist, notes a Ta'amira belief that Tamar of Genesis 38 is their progenitor, and sees further evidence of the tribe's Christian past. See Delia Khano, *By Eastern Windows*, 3rd. rev. ed. (Ramallah: Guiding Star, 1995), 62. A Tamar region south of the Dead Sea is noted in Ezek. 47:19 (cf. 48:28). Harmut Stegemann sees the tribe as the Odomera of 1 Macc. 9:58–73. See Harmut Stegemann, "Qumran: Founded for Scripture. The Background and Significance of the Dead Sea Scrolls," *Proceedings of the British Academy* 97 (1998): 1–14, here 2.

identifies the birthplace of Jesus as "a remote place" (19.16, 22), but among Muslims it is regularly seen, following Christian tradition, as a desert near Bethlehem.[5] Through either tradition, the shepherds may understand their workplace to have been the birthplace of the Christian messiah.

But to return to the question of their names: G. Lankester Harding, director of the Department of Antiquities of Jordan, in his 1949 media disclosure of the discovery, did not name the shepherds, but in a 1955 revision he identifies them as "Mohammed edh Dhib and Ahmed Mohammed."[6] Bedouin male names come in three or four parts: personal name, father's name, grandfather's name (optional), or clan ascription.[7] If the discoverer was Ahmad or Ahmed, then "Ahmed Mohammed" may be his name. He would be Ahmed, Mohammed's son. If from the Ibayyat family, his name may have been Ahmed Mohammed el-Ibayyat. We refer to him as "Muhammed edh-Dhib," but his name may not be known.

William H. Brownlee, investigating the scrolls' early movements, found that edh-Dhib had attended a Lutheran school in Beit Sahur, near Bethlehem.[8] In light of this education and edh-Dhib's dexterity with Western references to time, Brownlee considered him "not illiterate."[9] Abu Salim, a sheikh of the Ta'amireh, noting he had attended the same school, tells Brownlee that edh-Dhib "had indeed attended school, but only for a short while." However, a Ta'amireh guide informed Brownlee that "edh-Dheeb is illiterate."[10]

Unfortunately there are few ethnographic studies of the Ta'amireh, but we might find help for resolving these apparent contradictions in nineteenth-century Christian travelogues. In 1841, Edward Robinson observed the tribe's avoidance of literacy: "the Ta'âmirah stand degraded by it in the eyes of their brethren." This is the usual Bedouin way. But, he notes, the sheikh here exists in a separate category: "The learning of the tribe is confined to the Khatîb, no other individual being able to read or write." Their sheikh is "more than an ordinary Sheikh; he could read and write; and was likewise the Khatîb or orator and Imâm of his tribe."[11] Evidently, Ta'amireh sheikhs following that period had been willing to allow broader education—by Christian teachers—but were overruled. Henry Baker Tristram, in 1873, notes that "on the complaint of the Moslem

---

[5] See Geoffrey Parrinder, *Jesus in the Qur'an* (Oxford: Oneworld, 1995), 76. See also Stephen Shoemaker, "Christmas in the Qur'ān: The Qur'ānic Account of Jesus' Nativity and Palestinian Local Tradition," *JStAI* 28 (2003): 11–39, here 16–17.
[6] G. Lankester Harding, "Introductory: The Discovery, the Excavation, Minor Finds," in D. Barthélemy and J. T. Milik (eds.), *Qumran Cave 1*, DJD 1 (Oxford: Clarendon, 1955), 4.
[7] See Alexander Borg and Gideon M. Kressel, "Bedouin Personal Names in the Negev and Sinai," *ZAL* 40 (2001): 32–70, here 42.
[8] Possibly the Evangelical Lutheran School, founded in 1901 by German missionaries.
[9] William Hugh Brownlee, "Edh-Dheeb's Story of His Scroll Discovery," *RevQ* 3 (1962): 483–94, here 489.
[10] William Hugh Brownlee, "Some New Facts Concerning the Discovery of the Scrolls of 1Q," *RevQ* 4 (1963): 417–20, here 418–19.
[11] E. Robinson and E. Smith, *Biblical Researches in Palestine, Mount Sinai and Arabia Petraea* (London: John Murray, 1841), 178. See also Ignaz Goldziher, *Muslim Studies*, vol. 1, ed. S. M. Stern, trans. C. R. Barber and S. M. Stern (London: George Allen & Unwin, 1967), 107.

religious authorities, the Christian school established among the Ta'amirah has been broken up."[12]

These observations predate edh-Dhib, but questions remain. Had he gone to school in training to be a sheikh? If so, would that indicate that his father was a sheikh? Perhaps. "The position of tribal sheikh is often passed down from father to son," notes Scott Weiner of Gulf Arabs.[13] A Ta'amirah with school experience, unless a sheikh, might be read as shameful in a culture that has made, as M. C. A. Macdonald puts it, "the positive choice to remain non-literate."[14]

Trever and Brownlee

Most information about the shepherd derives from accounts by two Old Testament scholars, John Trever and William Brownlee, who in 1947–8 were colleagues at the American Schools of Oriental Research in Jerusalem and worked to authenticate, photograph, and publicize the four scrolls purchased by the Syrian Archbishop-Metropolitan Athanasius Y. Samuel. Neither met edh-Dhib, but Brownlee, in 1957, published the 1956 interview, which had been conducted by Khoury.[15] In 1961 Trever issued a skeptical reply, finding such new disclosures by Bedouin informants unreliable, as they take "considerable pleasure from complicating the story or inventing some new angle."[16] In late 1961 Trever obtained new interviews with two men identified as the shepherd-discoverers. He featured them in his 1965 book. The effect was to call into question the 1956 interview. In 1962 and 1963 Brownlee published two more papers on the scrolls' early movements.[17]

Despite the skepticism expressed in the new interviews (Esther Eshel regarded them of "doubtful authenticity,"[18] and according to Jutta Jokiranta they were "probably already modified in the 'Bedouin tradition'"[19]), Trever's new information seems to have prevailed, and a photograph of the 1961 interviewees has been a standard image used to document the discoverers for history. A photograph of the shepherds taken in 1949 at the cave is mostly available in scholarly sources. What does this photograph reveal? The shepherd identified as edh-Dhib in 1949, though his shawl or keffiyeh is partly covering his face, would not appear to be the man identified as edh-Dhib

---

[12] Henry Baker Tristram, *The Land of Moab: Travels and Discoveries on the East Side of the Dead Sea and the Jordan* (New York: Harper & Brothers, 1873), 92.
[13] Scott Weiner, "Kinship Politics in the Gulf Arab States," *Arab Gulf States Institute*, Issue Paper no. 7 (2016): 8.
[14] M. C. A. Macdonald, "Literacy in an Oral Environment," in Piotr Bienkowski, Christopher Mee, and Elizabeth Slater (eds.), *Writing and Ancient Near Eastern Society: Papers in Honour of Alan R. Millard* (New York: T&T Clark, 2005), 47.
[15] William H. Brownlee, "Muhammad Ed-Deeb's Own Story of His Scroll Discovery," *JNES* 16 (1957): 236–9.
[16] John C. Trever, "When Was Qumrân Cave I Discovered?" *Rev Q* 3 (1961): 141.
[17] See earlier, nn. 9 and 10.
[18] Esther Eshel, "Review of *The Dead Sea Scrolls in Perspective*, by John C. Trever," *JAOS* 126 (2006): 273–6, here 274.
[19] Jutta Jokiranta, "Review of *The Dead Sea Scrolls in Perspective*, by John C. Trever," *DSD* 18 (2011): 98–9, here 98.

in 1961.[20] Another photo of the discoverer appears in Paul W. Lapp's archeological report.[21] The man in the 1949 photo may well have become, twelve years later, the Lapp photo subject, but neither bears much resemblance to the 1961 interviewee.

In 1993 Trever's researcher Anton Kiraz died, and in 2005 Kiraz's son George A. Kiraz published his father's correspondence as *Anton Kiraz's Archive on the Dead Sea Scrolls*. Here we learn that Kiraz had no prior knowledge of the shepherds but only interviewed two men who were sent to him by the mayor of Bethlehem, a city then within the borders of Jordan. Kiraz notes a motive for this assistance: "These people are cross with Kando and Canawati, because they have exploited them."[22] That these interviews were set up as a retaliation against the well-known dealer of the scrolls, and another merchant in Bethlehem, is a drama we may be unable to unpack. But one should take note now that no other identification of the shepherds by scholars seems to have been pursued.

The 1961 interviewee is identified as Muhammad Ahmad El-Hamed, called 'edh-Dhib' as a nickname. He is described as a shepherd who also does day labor. He does not mention working in any scroll-related excavation. Archeological reports mention edh-Dhib doing that work, naming him, according to Lapp and Frank Moore Cross,[23] as Muhammed edh-Dhib Hassan. Reports by Harding, Roland de Vaux, and John Allegro also describe interactions with Muhammed edh-Dhib (spelled variously) in the course of Qumran excavations.

The behavior of Kiraz's 1961 interviewees was different from any noted before. They required significant remuneration for themselves and an intermediary prior to speaking, provoking at one point a standoff of sorts. The shepherds in 1949 had been "liberally tipped" and in 1956 "remunerated" in an environment perceived as friendly.[24] Kiraz later realizes that the second shepherd, identified as Jum'a Muhammad, had for the occasion of the interview added "Ahmad" in his name "to coincide with what has been published." Kiraz notes the 1961 interviewee identified as edh-Dhib had a "wife and four daughters" in 1964.[25] Dominique Barthélemy noted the shepherd-discoverer in 1952 was unmarried.[26]

Finding no points of identification between the original shepherds and the 1961 interviewees, we set aside the Kiraz interviews with the two purported discoverers, and reprioritize Brownlee's papers as guides. Kiraz's work is valuable and his 1961

---

[20] See Joan E. Taylor, Dennis Mizzi, and Marcello Fidanzio, "Revisiting Qumran Cave 1Q and Its Archaeological Assemblage," *PEQ* 149 (2017): 295–325, here 301. For another photo from the same location, with an older man, see Millar Burrows, *The Dead Sea Scrolls* (New York: Viking, 1955), plate 1.

[21] Paul W. Lapp and Nancy L. Lapp, "Discoveries in the Wâdī Ed-Dâliyeh," *AASOR* 41 (1974): 1–106, here plate 102.

[22] George A. Kiraz (ed.), *Anton Kiraz's Archive on the Dead Sea Scrolls* (Piscataway, NJ: Gorgias, 2005), 69.

[23] Frank Moore Cross, "The Discovery of the Samaria Papyri," *BA* 26.4 (1963): 109–21, here 114 n. 4.

[24] Brownlee, "Edh-Dheeb's Story of His Scroll Discovery," 483 n. 1.

[25] Kiraz, *Anton Kiraz's Archive*, 115, 151.

[26] See Weston Fields, *The Dead Sea Scrolls: A Full History: Volume One, 1947–1960* (Leiden: Brill, 2009), 126–7. Trever keeps up with the 1961 interviewee. In a 1989 interview he calls him "Akmed el-Hamid" and notes he had retired to Amman on the reverse dowries of his five daughters. See Ron Grossman, "Dead Sea Squabbles," *Chicago Tribune*, December 20, 1989, Section 5, 5.

interviewees, if not the discoverers, might be expected to provide details of an identity being impersonated. The man identified as edh-Dhib, that is, "the Wolf," says this name originally referred to his father. This is helpful, as is Kiraz's 1966 interview with an older and well-established man, encountered in Bethlehem, who speaks without remuneration and is identified as Khalil Musa, a third Ta'amireh man involved in the discovery. If this account is accurate, then Jum'a is Musa's son, and edh-Dhib is Musa's nephew. Musa adds, in Kiraz's paraphrase: "El Deeb was an orphan and poor and he was very young too. He was a goatherd, he didn't have for himself any flock."[27]

The Ta'amireh did not track birth dates, but in 1952 edh-Dhib's age was guessed as "less than 25";[28] in 1963, he was thought to be 33.[29] The shepherd would seem to have been born around 1929, and in 1947, he would be around 18. Is "very young" descriptive of age 18? Barthélemy uses the phrase of edh-Dhib when he was around age 23.[30] However, the ethnographer Richard T. Antoun, in a 1967 study of male life cycle in a Jordanian village, says of young men at age 15: "At this time, unless he is a student, he always appears in public clad in full headdress consisting of the Bedawin shawl and headband, and never bareheaded. He endeavors to grow a full mustache as a sign of his incipient manly status." Antoun emphasizes the orphan is socially marginal. "The term 'orphan' (*qarut*) is, indeed, a synonym for misfortune in village circumstances."[31]

Shepherds and Geopolitics

Regular insinuations have been made of the cave having been discovered amid smuggling operations, but the shepherd narrative is durable across early retellings. Note these less-cited references:

- Khoury's *c.* 1949 letter says the shepherds "discovered a small opening which was a door to a small cave."[32]
- Rosine Nimeh-Mailloux, a longtime Canadian schoolteacher and memoirist, claimed to be Kando's niece and said she plied family members for information about the discovery. In her narration, Musa tells Kando: "My nephew, a shepherd in Wadi Qumran, found this in a cave. He was looking for his goat."[33]
- The novelist Meyer Levin, in the January 1957 issue of *Esquire*, purporting to recall what E. L. Sukenik of the Hebrew University told him in 1950, narrates Sukenik's first hearing the find-story: "The Bethlehemite had himself talked with the goatherd who had been in the cave. Some rocks had shifted, revealing the opening,

---

[27] Kiraz, *Anton Kiraz's Archive*, 204.
[28] Fields, *The Dead Sea Scrolls*, 127.
[29] Brownlee, "Some New Facts Concerning the Discovery of the Scrolls of 1Q," 419.
[30] Fields, *The Dead Sea Scrolls*, 126–7.
[31] Richard T. Antoun, "Social Organization and the Life Cycle in an Arab Village," *Ethnology* 6 (1967): 294–308, here 295–6.
[32] Johnson, "The Finding of the Scrolls," 213.
[33] Marty Gervais, "Lively Tale of Old Scrolls," *Windsor Star*, November 19, 1999, 3. Gervais is a Canadian poet and professor at the University of Windsor.

which had been sealed during all these centuries. Inside, there had been a number of jars, some of them broken. There was nothing left now in the cave, he was sure, only a few shards and fragments of scriptures."[34]
- In a memoir reprinted in *The Message of the Scrolls*, Sukenik recalls, of November 1947 in Bethlehem, a second hearing of the shepherd story from the dealer Faidi el-Alami: "I had already heard it but it was a good tale."[35]
- In his 1966 memoir, *Treasure of Qumran*, Samuel recalls hearing the tale from Kando: "A goat lost in a rocky desert, a shepherd tossing an errant stone, caves and caches—these seemed the fabrics of fiction, did they not?"[36]
- Roland de Vaux recalls in 1971: "Later in 1952, I had as one of my laborers Muhammad adh-Dhib, the Bedouin who had been the first to enter the cave, and I made him tell me his story in the presence of his comrades who verified it."[37] In 1959 de Vaux had footnoted his belief that edh-Dhib's 1949 disclosure was "spontaneous" and had been repeated for him in 1952.[38]

After comparing many accounts, it appears no one knows when the find occurred. The reports are largely conjecture. In his 1966 book Samuel placed the find "some weeks" prior to April 1947, but in a 1949 narration he had not mentioned learning a date.[39] Sukenik notes in a 1955 book that he received no information on this point: "Presumably the discovery took place some time in the late spring of 1947."[40] This is problematic, for an Associated Press report of Sukenik's news conference of April 26, 1948, had the discovery happening "several months ago."[41] The resulting dating of the find to the winter of 1946–7 became dominant.

Discovered antiquities could of course be claimed by the state, but amid rapidly changing regimes and borders, alterations to the find-story could lead to suggestions of a new owner. This seems to be in play in the following announcements:

- The scrolls were discovered, says the April 10, 1948, press release from Yale University, "preserved for many centuries in the library of the Syrian Orthodox Monastery of St. Mark in Jerusalem."[42] In this scenario, the scrolls belong to the Syrians.
- On April 25, 1948, the *New York Times* says the find was made "some time ago in a hillside cave near En-Geddi" by Bedouins who "realized the value of their

---

[34] Meyer Levin, "The Seven Scrolls of Professor Sukenik," *Esquire* 47 (January 1957): 144.
[35] Yigael Yadin, *The Message of the Scrolls*, ed. James H. Charlesworth (New York: Crossroad, repr., 1992), 22.
[36] Athanasius Yeshue Samuel, *Treasure of Qumran: My Story of the Dead Sea Scrolls* (Philadelphia: Westminster, 1966), 145.
[37] Roland de Vaux, *The Bible and the Ancient Near East* (New York: Darton, Longman & Todd, 1971), 183.
[38] R. de Vaux, "Les manuscrits de Qumrân et l'archéologie," *RB* 66 (1959): 87–110, here 88 n. 3.
[39] Athanasius Yeshue Samuel, "The Purchase of the Jerusalem Scrolls," *BA* 12.2 (1949): 26–31.
[40] E. L. Sukenik, ed., *The Dead Sea Scrolls of the Hebrew University* (Jerusalem: Magnes, 1955), 13.
[41] "Biblical Texts Found in Judea Believed of 2,000 Years Ago," AP wire story, *Baltimore Sun*, April 27, 1948, 4.
[42] "Earliest Known Manuscript of Isaiah Discovered," RNS news release, *Living Church*, June 6, 1948, 9.

discovery and brought the manuscripts to the American School of Oriental Research in Jerusalem."[43] In this version, the scrolls are part of the British Mandate Palestine, which dissolves weeks later.

- On April 26, 1948, Sukenik holds his news conference, apparently stimulated by the *Times* story. He might have read that story as the American scholars trying to clean up the problem of having appeared to aid the Syrians in an illegal operation, while evading the thorny Jordanian problem. His purpose in the announcement may have been to prevent Samuel from exporting and selling the scrolls internationally, thus making a sale to the Hebrew University more likely.
- G. Ernest Wright, in the September 1949 issue of the *Biblical Archaeologist*, recalls a conversation in London the prior July: "It was found, said Mr. Harding, in 1937 by a bedouin searching for a lost goat!"[44] As this news update begins with talk of "the former 'Transjordan,' now deceased," the scrolls' legal situation may have been in mind. With Transjordan, a British mandate territory, terminating in May 1946, would Britain assert ownership? Some readers might wonder what Harding was doing in London.
- On August 9, 1949, Harding formalizes Jordanian provenance in an article in the *London Times*, which discloses the shepherd narrative. He locates the find in "late summer or autumn of 1947," which is curious, as he had said the same in an update in the July *PEQ*, when the shepherds, he noted, had not yet been located. Harding there criticized Trever in particular: "He encouraged, and openly rejoices in, the smuggling of the documents out of the country; they are now in America."[45]
- In the 1955 revision to his report, Harding redates the discovery to "early in the summer of 1947,"[46] telling Brownlee this owed to new interviews with "the Bedouins" done at the Wady Murabba'at excavations in 1952.[47]
- The October 23, 1956, interview by edh-Dhib places the discovery in 1945, in Transjordan.
- Trever recalls that in 1958 he was taken to meet Bisharah Canavati, a Bethlehem merchant, who tells him the scrolls were found in 1942.[48]
- Brownlee records that Khoury told him, in 1960, another story in "that the first scroll discovery was in 1938," being kept "hidden for years, before being brought to light, because they were obtained through murder."[49]

---

[43] Julian Louis Meltzer, "10 Ancient Scrolls Found in Palestine," *New York Times*, April 25, 1948, 6L.
[44] G. Ernest Wright, "Archaeological News and Views," *BA* 12.3 (1949). 64. On possible British interest in the 1Q Scrolls, note Khoury's 1949 letter: "I am told by the man concerned (Khalil Quando) that some Britishers asked him secretly to bring back those scrolls in America and they will give him as much money as he wants?" (Johnson, "The Finding of the Scrolls," 217). Nimeh-Mailloux has a similar note: "Uncle Khalil had made a deal for them to be sold to the British from the Diocese of St. Mark in the old city of Jerusalem." See Gervais, "Tale," 3.
[45] G. Lankester Harding, "The Dead Sea Scrolls," *PEQ* 81 (1949): 112–16, here 116.
[46] Harding, "Introductory: The Discovery, the Excavation, Minor Finds," 4.
[47] Brownlee, "Some New Facts Concerning the Discovery of the Scrolls of 1Q," 420.
[48] Trever, "When Was Qumrân Cave I Discovered?" 137–9.
[49] Brownlee, "Edh-Dheeb's Story of His Scroll Discovery," 493 n. 28.

- Trever's 1965 book dates the discovery to November 1946, which brings it back to Jordan. That the 1961 interviews on which he relies were set up by a Jordanian official might seem to be a conflict of interest.

To finish situating evidence of the shepherd, we have to ask if the 1956 interview can be believed. Is it even an "interview"? There are no questions. Is it plausible that Khoury decided, nine years later, to invite a statement on the circumstances of the discovery? No reason for doing so was offered.

We might consider this scenario: Harding was fired weeks earlier, late September 1956, in a purge of British officials from Jordan's government.[50] Perhaps he arranged the interview in retaliation, having learned years earlier the find took place in Transjordan. But the mayor of Bethlehem, in setting up the 1961 Kiraz interviews, was focusing on Kando and Canavati. How would they be disadvantaged by new interviews about the discovery? If the primary focus of the 1961 interviews was to confirm that find was in Jordan, then perhaps the merchants had been behind edh-Dhib's 1956 interview that had located the find in Transjordan.

In view of Cross's descriptions, from early 1967, of cloak-and-dagger efforts by Kando to sell the Temple Scroll for a higher price than Jordanian controls allowed,[51] another scenario could be as follows: Kando had been trying to establish a new provenance for the Temple Scroll so as to sell it internationally. He had employed for this purpose, Cross says, a Washington, DC, law firm. A legal strategy might have involved enlisting edh-Dhib to establish the find in Transjordan. With a further claim the Temple Scroll had come from Cave 1, its ownership might seem sufficiently confused to enable a sale.[52] Harding's exit from the Department of Antiquities might have seemed like the occasion to make such a move.

Was edh-Dhib in 1956 just proffering, with the 1945 discovery date, a legal fiction? That would not be established, in that nothing he said has been disproved. The glaring problem with taking seriously his dating is that he would not sell the scrolls. They were sold two years later, he says, by his uncle. Trever dismissed the interview over this point: "For a Bedouin to retain an antiquity 'in a skin bag' hanging on a wall 'for more than two years,' when he knows he could get even a few plastres for it in the market place, seems quite unthinkable."[53]

Let us keep in mind the possibility of a two-year gap between when the shepherd found the scrolls and when they were sold as we delve into the discovery narrative, alert to some little-noticed details—such as the jinn.

---

[50] See Jason Kalman and Jaqueline S. du Toit, *Canada's Big Biblical Bargain: How McGill University Bought the Dead Sea Scrolls* (Montreal: McGill-Queen's University Press, 2010), 82.

[51] See Hershel Shanks, ed., *Frank Moore Cross: Conversations with a Bible Scholar* (Washington, DC: Biblical Archaeology Society, 1994), 136.

[52] The Kando family long maintained, as to Weston Fields, that the Temple Scroll was found in Cave 1. See Fields, *The Dead Sea Scrolls*, 535 n. 64. Khoury's 1949 letter spoke of "more scrolls" (Johnson, "The Finding of the Scrolls," 217). Allegro told a story of Kando burying scrolls from the first cave in his garden to discover they turned to "lumps of sticky glue." John Marco Allegro, *The Dead Sea Scrolls* (Harmondsworth: Penguin, 1956), 19. Could this be a cover story in case the Temple Scroll was remembered?

[53] Trever, "When Was Qumrân Cave I Discovered?" 141.

Jinn and Panic

Harding's 1955 report, revising his 1949 report, has a new disclosure: his narration, he says, is a "considerably condensed version"[54] of what he was told. He does not say what kind of details had been left off, but upon learning about Bedouin people in proximity to caves, we might start to develop ideas. Raphael Patai notes: "The underground realm of wells, cisterns and caves is the world of the jinn."[55]

Many descriptions of Bedouin suggest a general idea of nature being populated by entities either favorable or hostile to human life. Samuel M. Zwemer, in *The Influence of Animism on Islam* (1920), notes: "Constantly one is told of some tree or grove, 'a very strong spirit lives there,' but if you ask its name or origin none can be assigned. Its existence and power are undoubted, and many tales of the mischief it has caused will be quoted in proof."[56]

Historically in Palestine, caves have been a particular focus of spirit inhabitation. We might even mention Mk 5:2-3, where the man with an "unclean spirit" lived in tombs, openings cut into rock and discussed as caves (cf. Isa. 65:4 LXX). Ada Goodrich-Freer, in Jerusalem in 1907, notes caves "are inhabited by saint or jinn as the case may be."[57] In 1927 Taufik Canaan observes that caves are "considered by the Mohammedans to be the abiding places of *djinn*."[58] Such observations, if varying in details, are common.

From the Arabic root "to be hidden," jinni is the singular form; jinn the plural (though jinns is often seen); jin, djinn, or genie are also used. Learning what exactly the Ta'amireh believed about them now seems unlikely. We certainly feel their fear. In Harding's 1949 report, the shepherd is "nervously apprehensive"[59] in approaching the cave. In the 1955 version, that disappears, but here they "nervously investigated"[60] the jars. No reason for this anxiety is noted.

In 1956 two narrations of the Qumran cave discovery mention *jinn*. In his 1956 book, Allegro describes the rock hitting a jar, as the shepherd flees "in a frantic desire to put as much distance between himself and this jinn-ridden cave as possible."[61] The same year, Cross offers, "when the fear of jinn or hyenas finally gave way to the lure of buried gold, the shepherd crept into the cave."[62] Neither scholar is said to have interviewed the shepherd. They may have read Harding's report with context picked

---

[54] Harding, "Introductory, the Discovery, the Excavation, Minor Finds," 4.
[55] Raphael Patai, *Arab Folktales from Palestine and Israel* (Detroit, MI: Wayne State University Press, 1998), 49 n. 12.
[56] Samuel M. Zwemer, *The Influence of Animism on Islam: an Account of Popular Superstitions* (New York, NY: The Macmillan Company, 1920), 143.
[57] H. H. Spoer and A. Goodrich-Freer, "The Powers of Evil in Jerusalem," *Folklore* 18 (1907): 54–76, here 69.
[58] Taufik Canaan, *Mohammedan Saints and Sanctuaries in Palestine* (London: Luzac, 1927), 45–46.
[59] G. Lankester Harding, *London Times* (August 9, 1949): 5.
[60] Harding, "Introductory, the Discovery, the Excavation, Minor Finds," 4.
[61] Allegro, *The Dead Sea Scrolls*, 16.
[62] Frank M. Cross, "The Scrolls from the Judaean Desert," *Arch* 9 (1956): 41–53, here 42.

up along the way. They may see a suppressed panic in Ta'amireh people later excavating in caves. Lapp notes "their usual frantic manner."[63]

Consider a 1933 report by W. F. Albright of a dig in Moab. He investigates a spot that the company's Bedouin guide, a sheikh named Mohammed, thinks must have "treasure." They go in, to find a tomb, and a cave:

> The cave was partly empty, but none of the Bedouin dared go in, until Dr. Gordon, who was in charge, taunted them with their cowardice and questioned their claim to call themselves "lions" (*nahna isbâ'* is their favorite cry). Then all the workmen near the entrance made a rush, and entered the cave in such a tangle of arms and legs that the *jinn* were quite frightened away.[64]

Jinn are discussed in the Qur'ān, but as Clinton Bailey observes in a 1982 study of Bedouin religious practices, Islam is "but one of several belief systems practiced by them simultaneously,"[65] and local ideas about jinn can vary widely. As Ahmed K. Al-Rawi notes, a form of jinn, more of a ghoul, was thought to have "inhabited the desert, a highly desolate area where the imagination played a very important role in people's experience of the being."[66]

Talking with Bedouin brothers in the Negev for a 1979 book, Moshe Piamenta asks about jinn. One brother explains: "There is a man of (under) ground, I mean a demon—*basmala*—that comes out in the guise of a shadow, in secluded passages, such as secluded forests, or woods, or valleys, where people do not live." This man's brother relates an encounter with such a being: "I cannot describe him. He had no human form. I hit him with a stone and God saved me from him."[67]

Into the Cave

Wright, Khoury, and Canavati suggested the cave was found in 1937, 1938, and 1942, respectively. These might all be true. Bedouin may have known of the cave previously and understood it to be inhabited. The shepherd's "discovery" might be a story of his different values, of the new possibilities he created.

Let us follow him as he goes in search of his goat. "You always made me pay for every missing animal," Jacob says to Laban in Gen. 31:39 (NET). In *Bedouin Culture in the Bible*, Clinton Bailey notes that "shepherds are held accountable for any injuries

---

[63] Lapp and Lapp, "Discoveries in the Wâdī Ed-Dâliyeh," 10. See N. L. Bragazzi and G. Del Puente, "Panic Attacks and Possession by Djinns: Lessons from Ethnopsychiatry," *Psychology Research and Behavior Management* 5 (2012): 185–90.

[64] W. F. Albright, "Soundings at Ader, a Bronze Age City of Moab," *Bulletin of the American Schools of Oriental Research* 53 (1934): 13–18. See also Cyrus H. Gordon, *The Living Past* (New York: Norton, 1941), 47–9.

[65] Clinton Bailey, "Bedouin Religious Practices in Sinai and the Negev," *Anthropos* 77.1/2 (1982): 65–88, here 66.

[66] Ahmed K. Al-Rawi, "The Arabic Ghoul and Its Western Transformation," *Folklore* 120.3 (2009): 291–306, here 294.

[67] Moshe Piamenta, *Islam in Everyday Arabic Speech* (Leiden: Brill, 1979), 36.

caused to animals under their care."[68] If unable to find the missing goat, we might infer, he knows he will be punished. He might be apprehensive not just for the goat but for himself. "The good shepherd lays down his life for the sheep," Jesus says in Jn 10:11. This is not wisdom unique to Christians; this is the life of shepherds.

In the 1956 interview, edh-Dhib narrates: "As I was roaming, I came upon a cave with its entrance open at the top like a cistern." The cave would later be expanded, but in the 1949 photo there are two openings: a triangular slit at the bottom, and a round portal that would be above his head. Was it raining? In 1955, Millar Burrows records talk about the cave discovery: "One story has it that they took refuge from a thunderstorm in a cave. Another story is that a runaway goat jumped into the cave."[69] Goats are averse to rain, and a shepherd may suspect his goat sought shelter in the cave, if the search happened in a storm.

In the usual narration he throws a stone into the cave. This might be to roust out the goat, or test for wild animals, but stone-throwing often seems to come up in jinn lore. Note Zwemer: "The good angels throw stones at them, that is, shooting stars, and the common name given to these demonic transgressors is therefore 'the stoned ones.'"[70]

The shepherd may flee, but comes back, perhaps with Jum'a. They know the goat is not in the cave. The goat might remain a motivator even so. Perhaps going into the cave is an effort to find something to replace the goat, to alleviate the shepherd's punishment. Perhaps the loss of the goat, and its presumed death, suggests some logic of divine replacement is at work. These are people who sacrifice animals to invite divine blessing.[71]

There are defenses against jinn. They include charms, amulets, and reciting from the Qur'ān. What seemed helpful in the Albright narration was the lion. Does this suggest the Bedouin used an animal as spiritual protector? Jinn and animals have complex associations, and if the lion seems to be an emblem of "courage," the animal with real power against the jinn is the wolf. A manual of Islamic spiritual medicine notes the "virtual consensus that the jinn are afraid of wolves, and they cannot appear in wolf form."[72]

The shepherd, then, has a unique status. He is doing the human activity of shepherding, while adopting a "wolf" protector, who is also his father. The "Muhammed the Wolf" who enters the cave is both of them. If the shepherd's father had been a sheikh, this man's public status as a "wolf" might have indicated a gift in dealing with jinn. In a harrowing 2011 report on belief in jinn among Bedouin in the Negev desert, Longina Jakubowska explains: "Sheikhs vary in their reputation and specialization and command different degrees of authority over the spirits. Minor cases of affliction

---

[68] Clinton Bailey, *Bedouin Culture in the Bible* (New Haven: Yale University Press, 2018), 29.
[69] Burrows, *The Dead Sea Scrolls*, 4.
[70] Zwemer, *The Influence of Animism on Islam*, 126.
[71] See Bailey, "Bedouin Religious Practices in Sinai and the Negev," 74.
[72] Abu'l-Mundhir Khaleel ibn Ibraaheem Ameen, *The Jinn and Human Sickness: Remedies in the Light of the Qur'an and Sunah* (Riyadh, Saudi Arabia: Darussalam, 2005), 34. See Robert Lebling, *Legends of the Fire Spirits: Jinn and Genies from Arabia to Zanzibar* (New York: I.B. Tauris, 2010), 95.

can be treated by sheikhs with less experience while more serious ones demand the attention of a powerful healer."[73]

Goodrich-Freer noted that families of sheikhs "are considered to possess a hereditary gift of dealing with jinn and other spirits, and are resorted to by Christians and Moslems alike."[74] If a father had this ability, his son might also (or at least wonder if he does). Though edh-Dhib will never become a sheik, he may be a spiritual figure in his own right. He seems to attain a new idea of resilience to spirit possession, a noted ability of jinn. He goes into caves and is not harmed. Does edh-Dhib communicate this idea to his tribesmen? His narration of the cave entrance might have had, for them, the suggestion that a human can face the jinn and prevail. The scrolls' excavations seem to have required that belief.

Charms and Sandals

The shepherds are often said to be disappointed with finding manuscripts instead of "treasure." J. van der Ploeg, in one of the more detailed scholarly reconstructions of the discovery, thinks they were "well pleased with their find"[75]—but the shepherds' initial view of the scrolls and their value may not be known. We seem to know that they have seen such objects before. Trever recalls a clerk at Canavati's shop telling him that when he was a boy, he saw scraps of leather burned that he later understood to have been scrolls.[76] Then a Ta'amireh tribesmen later tells Eric Mitchell how scrolls had been used "as wipes to clean a baby's bottom."[77]

Such uses seem to imply a lack of interest or lack of respect for the scrolls, but do they? Bedouin remedies for diaper rash, as Aref Abu-Rabia discusses, involve spiritually valued objects applied to afflicted infants.[78] Bailey describes magical practices for maladies involving incense and burning. Such practices have been widespread. Yoram Bilu and Yehuda C. Goodman note, of dybbuk exorcism in traditional Jewish culture, that manuscripts with mystic symbols (whose meaning need not be understood) were "burnt down and put before the victim's nostrils to scorch and suffocate the possessing spirit."[79] If scrolls were understood to be magical objects, taken after all from a jinn dwelling, they would seem to have been highly valued.[80]

---

[73] Longina Jakubowska, "The Invasion of Jinn Spirits: Modernity and the Bedouin," in A. Malewska and E. Klekot (eds.), *Anthropology and Modernity* (Warsaw: DIG, 2010), 121–35, here 131.

[74] Spoer and Goodrich-Freer, "The Powers of Evil in Jerusalem," 58. See also Philip Hermans, "Struggling with the Jinn: Moroccan Healing Practices and the Placebo Effect," in Christiane Timmerman et al. (eds.), *Moroccan Migration in Belgium: More Than 50 Years of Settlement*, CeMIS Migration and Intercultural Studies 1 (Leuven: Leuven University Press, 2017), 307–28, here 317.

[75] J. van der Ploeg, *The Excavations at Qumran* (London: Longman, Green, 1958), 5.

[76] Trever, "When Was Qumrân Cave I Discovered?" 137.

[77] Eric Mitchell, "A Brief History of the Dead Sea Scrolls," *SwJT* 53.1 (2010): 3–14, here 4.

[78] Aref Abu-Rabia, *Indigenous Medicine among the Bedouin in the Middle East* (New York: Berghahn, 1991), 119.

[79] Yoram Bilu and Yehuda C. Goodman, "What Does the Soul Say?: Metaphysical Uses of Facilitated Communication in the Jewish Ultraorthodox Community," *Ethos* 25.4 (1997): 375–407, 398.

[80] In a May 9, 1883, letter, Wilhelm Shapira describes Bedouin chased into a cave by enemies to find scrolls some viewed as charms. See Shlomo Guil, "The Shapira Scroll Was an Authentic Dead Sea Scroll," *PEQ* 149 (2017): 6–27, here 9.

Edh-Dhib may himself view the scrolls as having magical ability. In the 1956 interview, he says: "I kept the leather with me until I returned to our house, where I put it in a skin bag and hung it up in a corner. The skin bag remained hanging for more than two years." Bailey notes the greatest defense against evil was a *hijāb*, "an amulet in the form of Qur'anic quotations written down and placed in a leather pouch."[81] If edh-Dhib had created a bag to function as this kind of amulet, he had given the scrolls the status of scripture. The shepherd's uncle may take the scrolls in payment for the goat. Musa may suspect the area is about to become a war zone, and a sale in early 1947 makes sense.

Edh-Dhib's ability to read would not seem to be important, unless, as Brownlee supposed, his early schooling had cultivated interest in books. That edh-Dhib could not read the scrolls is assumed. But as he is often said, with puzzling emphasis, to be illiterate, we ought to touch on evidence cited for that view. In the 1956 interview, edh-Dhib narrates his return from the cave: "When I reached my companions, I showed them what I had found and gave each of them a piece of the leather, so that they might use it for their sandal straps."

That he actually meant this was immediately doubted. The scrolls were "too brittle to make good sandal scraps,"[82] notes Brownlee. Trever adds that the shepherd saw "how brittle the leather was and abandoned such a thought, even if it occurred to him."[83] Then John Allegro's 1956 book has Kando suggesting the scrolls "might serve as raw material for his cobbler's business."[84] Brownlee sees this as "a facetious bit of bargaining."[85]

In a 1959 newspaper interview, Kando recalls: "They brought the first pieces to me in 1947. When they need money they bring me more pieces." He refers to "old things" and "old papers," when seeming to speak of scrolls.[86] To refer to valuables in terms of their basic materiality would seem to be a strategy to avoid publicly discussing the illegal activity of finding and selling antiquities.

The scrolls are often said in later treatments to have been brought to Bethlehem in view of a quick sale, but early on they were said have been brought to a sheikh. In Samuel's memoir this is noted in a scene when he observes the scrolls were in Hebrew: "Kando muttered disappointedly. It was not his mistake, he insisted. When the sheikh of the Ta'amireh had brought them to him, he had used an old Arabic expression which said, 'Ancient things are in Syriac.'"[87] If the effect will be to classify the documents as Christian, the sheik may be indicating they are even older.[88]

Not much more is known about edh-Dhib, after the few mentions in archeological reports. Allegro notices him in a 1958 article: "If this young man today shows no more

---

[81] Bailey, "Bedouin Religious Practices in Sinai and the Negev," 83.
[82] Brownlee, "Muhammad Ed-Deeb's Own Story," 238.
[83] Trever, "When Was Qumrân Cave I Discovered?" 141 n. 20.
[84] Allegro, *The Dead Sea Scrolls*, 18.
[85] Brownlee, "Edh-Dheeb's Story of His Scroll Discovery," 486 n. 7.
[86] Charlotte Ebener, "The Dead Sea Scrolls Come through Kando, the Shoemaker," *Herald-News*, April 21, 1959, Passiac, NJ, 12.
[87] Samuel, *Treasure of Qumran*, 144.
[88] See Brannon Wheeler, "Arab Prophets of the Qur'an and Bible," *JQS* 8.2 (2006): 25.

signs of wealth than a gold watch strapped to his wrist, the chiefs of his tribe have risen to eminence among Jordan's business tycoons."[89] In the c. 1962 photo on the last page of the Lapp report, he is not wearing a keffiyeh. For a Western person this would be of no consequence, but seeing a Bedouin man so disrobed in public is unusual. We are seeing his private self. He looks into the camera, holding a bit of scroll. His end, like that of his goat, is not known.

Conclusion

The early narratives of the scrolls feature dynamic interplay of races, cultures, scriptures, and religious traditions. As Jewish, Christian, and Muslim interests were present, there were also the Bedouin, moving between them. To reflect on the bits and pieces of evidence that is sometimes, like the scrolls themselves, compromised, we are invited to explore a magical world. We can examine and reexamine the details and testimony of every participant, even the boy who began it all, but it is unlikely we shall ever get to the truth. The ambiguities and uncertainties surrounding the first discoveries of the scrolls near Qumran are not unlike the convoluted and contradictory stories we have heard relating to the discoveries of the Coptic codices in Egypt.

---

[89] John Allegro, "The Dead Sea Scrolls—a Survey," *Rationalist Annual* (1958): 5.

Contributors

Peter G. Bolt, Sydney College of Divinity

Frederick E. Brenk, S.J., Arrupe House Jesuit Community

Craig A. Evans, School of Christian Thought, Houston Baptist University

Roy D. Kotansky, Scholar of New Testament and Classics

Elina Lapinoja-Pitkänen, doctoral student, University of Helsinki

Susanne Luther, Faculty of Theology and Religious Studies, University of Groningen

Jeff Pettis, New Brunswick Theological Seminary

Jonathan Poletti, independent scholar

Chris S. Stevens, Scholar of New Testament Theology and Linguistics

Alexa Wallace, graduate student, The College of Emmanuel and St. Chad

Adam Z. Wright, The College of Emmanuel and St. Chad

Richard A. Wright, Abilene Christian University

Index of Modern Names

Abrams, D. 34
Abu-Rabia, A. 228
Africa, T. W. 100
Albertz, M. 168
Albright, W. F. 226–7
Alford, H. 165–7
Al-Rawi, A. K. 226
Allegro, J. 220, 224–5, 229–30
Allen, P. 146
Allen, W. C. 110
Allison Jr., D. C. 105, 111
Amenábar, A. 156
Andrews, M. E. 125
Antoun, R. T. 221
Arnaoutoglou, I. 32
Ascough, R. S. 23, 24
Audollent, A. 136, 141
Aune, D. E. 120, 143, 146
Aus, R. D. 121
Austin, W. G. 33
Arav, R. 39
Avery-Peck, A. J. 111

Bailey, C. 226–7, 229
Baldassare, I. 8
Barag, D. 97
Barber, C. R. 218
Barrett, C. E. 1
Barrett, C. K. 166–7
Barthel, P. 101
Barthélemy, D. 218, 220
Baur, F. C. 149
Beard, M. 83, 209
Becker, E. 63
Beekmann, S. 59
Behm, J. 140
Berner, U. 83
Berthelot, K. 140
Betz, H. D. xii, 39, 42, 85, 128, 142, 176–7
Bienkowski, P. 219
Bilu, Y. 228

Bird, M. 126, 150
Bird, P. 149, 159, 163
Blänsdorf, J. 136
Bloch, R. 84
Blomberg, C. L. 155
Blümel, W. 141, 142
Blumenfeld, B. 125
Boardman, J. 49
Bolt, P. G. xi, 42, 54, 59
Bommas, M. 5
Bons, E. 140
Bonz, M. P. 114
Booth, A. D. 127
Borg, A. 218
Bornkamm, G. 143
Bouillet, M. N. 113
Brashear, W. 48
Bragazzi, N. L. 226
Bravo, B. 42, 52
Brenk, F. E. x, 4, 8, 17, 40, 41, 44–6, 55
Bricault, L. 2, 6, 15, 24
Brooke, G. J. 121
Brown, C. G. 83
Brown, P. 55
Brown, R. E. 99, 111
Brownlee, W. H. 218–21, 223, 229
Bruce, F. F. 165
Brucker, R. 140
Bryant, C. D. 63
Büchsel, F. 147
Bultmann, R. 184
Burket, H. W. 155
Burrows, M. 220, 227
Busch, P. 139
Busen, L. A. 63
Buttolph, P. 150

Campbell, J. 62, 66
Canaan, T. 225
Carlston, C. E. 119

Carson, D. A. 144
Cary, E. 84, 92, 107, 114
Castner, C. J. 203
Charlesworth, J. H. x, 54, 111–12, 158, 198, 222
Childs, B. 150
Chilver, G. E. F. 93
Clark, K. 108
Clausen, K. B. 1
Cline, R. 103
Cohen, J. D. 157–9
Cohn, N. 64
Cole, S. E. 6
Collins, J. J. 98
Colson, F. H. 108
Conzelmann, H. 145, 150, 170
Cotter, W. 120–1
Cox, R. J. 4
Crawley, R. 85
Cross, F. M. 220, 224–5
Cumont, F. 103, 155–6
Cunliffe, B. 137

Dabrowa, E. 106
Dalton, W. J. 168–9
Daly, R. J. 111
Daniel, R. W. 39, 50
Danker, F. 74, 104
David, J. 156
Davies, P. R. 159
Davies, W. D. 105, 127
de Caro, S. 11
de Vaux, R. 220, 222
Deichgräber, R. 170
Deissmann, A. 47, 139–40
Del Puente, G. 226
de Ruggiero, P. 89
Descamps, A. 180–1
Dibelius, M. 150, 170
Dinkler, E. 197
Dittenberger, W. 104
Dochhorn, J. 139
Dodds, E. R. 154
Doran, R. 99
Dorcey, P. 155
Douglas, M. 55, 71
Downing, F. G. 121
Droge, A. 165
Dunand, F. 15

Dupont, J. 180
du Toit, J. S. 224
Dyer, B. R. 123
Dzwiza, K. 135

Easton, B. S. 168
Ebener, C. 229
Eisenbaum, P. 149, 160
Eitrem, S. 56–7
Elgin, V. G. 217
Eliot, T. S. 166
Elliott, J. K. 111–12
Engelmann, H. 24–7, 35
Eriksson, A. 128
Erler, M. 4
Eschel, E. 219
Evans, C. A. xi, 62, 98, 100, 111, 165, 189, 193
Evans, C. F. 59
Evelyn-White, H. G. 41
Everett, A. 89
Ezquerra, J. A. 36

Fairclough, H. R. 114
Fairweather, J. 128
Falconer, R. 169
Faraone, C. A. 47–9, 137, 176
Farmer, W. R. 99
Farnell, L. R. 55
Feder, F. 17
Feder, S. 63
Fee, G. D. 167
Feldman, A. 121
Feldman, L. H. 41
Ferguson, E. 15153, 155
Ferrill, A. 97
Fields, W. 220, 221
Fiorenza, E. S. 128
Fitzenreiter, M. 17
Fitzgerald, J. T. 203
Fitzmyer, J. A. 6, 86, 145
Flemming, R. 208
Foerster, W. 39, 47
Foster, B. O. 115
Fotopoulous, J. 135–7, 140, 143–4, 146
Foucart, P.-F. 23
France, R. T. 105
Frank, G. 111

Frazer, J. G. 63, 113, 115
Frye, N. 67

Gager, J. G. 49, 51, 136–7, 140–1, 147
Gallarte, I. M. 121
Gamble, H. 150
Gardner, I. 189
Garland, D. E. 145
Garland, R. 49
Gasparini, V. 1, 4, 8, 16, 32
Gasque, W. W. 165
Gero, S. 208
Gervais, M. 221, 223
Geyser-Fouché, A. 98
Gnuse, R. K. 102
Goldsworthy, A. 87, 89
Goldziher, I. 218
Golvin, J.-C. 2
Goodenough, E. R. 159
Goodman, M. 99
Goodman, Y. C. 228
Goodrich-Freer, A. 225, 228
Gordon, C. H. 226
Gordon, P. 203
Gordon, R. L. 36, 209
Gordon, R. 63
Goulder, M. 186, 191–2
Grant, H. 152, 156–7
Grant, M. 158
Grässer, E. 191
Green, J. B. 39
Green, S. J. 84
Grey, M. 217
Grodzynski, D. 209
Grossman, R. 220
Grudem, W. A. 162
Gruen, E. S. 4, 210
Grüll, T. 109
Guichard, L. A. 173–5
Guil, S. 228
Gulick, C. B. 84, 86
Gundry, R. H. 165–71, 180–2, 184, 187, 190–1, 193, 197
Gurtner, D. M. 108

Haase, W. 40, 46, 48, 120
Hall, E. S. 25
Hallo, W. W. 151
Hagner, D. A. 105

Hansen, M. H.. 24
Harder, M. A. 173
Harding, G. L. 218, 220, 223–5
Harland, Philip A. 23–5, 27, 29, 31–2, 36
Harley, F. 146
Harris, R. 79–80
Hart, G. 25, 37
Haufe, G. 191
Haslam, A. S. 33–4
Hata, G. 41
Hays, M. 151
Heinze, R. 42–3
Hendricks, O. M. 77
Henrichs, A. 39, 58, 154
Hermans, P. 228
Heyob, S. K. 152
Hicks, R. D. 107
Higgins, D. 174
Higgins, S. 152
Hinton, J. 63
Hogg, M. A. 34
Hölscher, M. 135, 139
Holtzmann, H. J. 185
Hopfner, T. 57
Hopkins, K. 87
Hurtado, L. W. 162
Hyde, M. J. 129

ibn Ibraaheem Ameen, A.-M. K., 227
Incignieri, B. J. 194, 199
Isbell, C. D. 39

Jackson, H. M. 108
Jacobus, H. R. 101
Jakubowska, L. 227–8
James, M. R. 54, 111
Jameson, M. H. 55
Jefford, C. N. 140
Jeremias, J. 170
Johnson, S. 217, 221, 224
Johnston, J. 189
Johnston, J. J. 193
Jokiranta, J. 219
Jones, B. W. 97
Jones, C. 210
Joosten, J. 140
Jordan, D. R. 39, 48–52, 55, 57
Jung, C. 62

Kalman, J. 224
Kambitsis, S. 49
Kastor, R. A. 127
Kelly, J. N. D. 150, 169
Kent, R. G. 113
Kessler, D. 17
Keulen, W. H. 4–5
Khano, D. 217
Khoury, N. S. 217, 219, 221, 223–4, 226
King, J. E. 119
Kingsley, C. 156
Kiraz, A. 220–1
Kiraz, G. A. 220–1
Kirchner, S. 17
Kister, M. 101
Klauck, H. J. 143, 151, 153, 155
Klekot, W. 228
Kloppenborg, J. S. 23–4, 26
Klostermann, E. 110
Knibb, M. A. 54
Knight, G. W. 149–50
Knox, R. A. 167
Koch, S. 140, 143, 145
Kok, J. 34
Kondakov, N. P. 57
Kondoleon, C. 16
Konstan, D. 203
Köstenberger, A. J. 149
Kotansky, R. D. xii, 39, 55, 178, 184–6, 193–4, 199
Kraeling, C. H. 58
Kraemer, R. S. 153–4, 157
Kressel, G. M. 218
Kroeger, C. 150–1
Kropp, A. 135–7
Kuhn, K. G. 143
Kurtz, D. C. 49

Lampe, P. 111, 124
Lane, A. N. S. 39
Langton, E. 47
Lapinoja-Pitänen, E., x–xi
Lapp, N. L. 220, 226
Lapp, P. W. 220, 226
Latte, K. 153, 154
Lattimore, R. 96
Lau, A. Y. 169
Lau, M. 135, 139

Lebling, R. 227
Lembke, K. 1–3, 5–9, 15, 20
LePort, B. 100
Levick, B. 96
Levin, M. 221–2
Lewy, H. 58, 84
Lichtheim, M. 152
Liebeschuetz, J. H. W. G. 93
Lieu, J. 24, 201–2, 208, 210
Lifton, D. 125
Lindsay, W. M. 113
Lion, H. A. 113
Litwa, M. D. 120
Lock, W. 167
Logan, A. H. B. 191
Longenecker, R. N. 23, 59
Louw, J. P. 161–2
Lugioyo, B. 184
Luke, T. S. 97
Luomanen, P. 34
Luther, S. xi, 135, 138–9
Luz, C. 173, 176
Luz, U. 111

Magness, J. 151, 159
Malaise, M. 15
Malewska, A. 228
Malinowski, B. 64
Maltomini, F. 39
Mark, Joshua J. 37
Marshall, I. H. 165–6, 168–9, 180–2, 184–5, 187, 191–3, 195, 197
Martin, D. 209
Martin, M. W. 123
Martin, R. P. 165–6, 169, 180–1, 187
Matthews, S. 121
Matyszak, P. 66–8
MacBain, B. 84
MacDermot, V. 189
MacDonald, D. R. 73, 75, 78, 80
MacDonald, M. C. A. 219
MacPherson, J. 67, 68
McCormack, T. 155
McEleney, N. J. 99
McGuckin, J. A. 78
McKnight, S. 39
McLean, B. H. 26–7, 37
Mee, C. 219
Meeks, W. A. 149

Meltzer, J. L. 223
Merk, O. 191
Merkelbach, R. 26, 98
Metzger, B. M. 185, 188
Meyboom, P. G. P. 2, 9–10, 12, 18
Micou, R. W. 185
Miles, M. M. 1
Milik, J. T. 218
Millard, A. R. 219
Miller, F. J. 113, 115
Minas-Nerpel, M. 2
Minns, D. 117
Mitchell, E. 228
Mol, E. 6
Moore, C. C. 63
Moorman, E. 1, 3–4, 6, 8, 13
Morgan, M. G. 94, 96
Morland, K. A. 143
Moser, C. 16–17
Mounce, W. D. 150, 167
Moyer, Ian S. 26, 29, 31, 35
Muraoka, T. 183
Muscettola, S. A. 11
Müskens, S. W. G. 8
Myers, C. 77

Naerebout, F. G. 3
Naumann-Steckner, F. 19
Naveh, J. 178
Nestle, W. 100
Neukam, P. 174
Neusner, J. 111
Newman, H. I. 101
Newsom, C. A. 198
Nickelsburg, G. W. E. 53–4, 158
Nida, E. A. 161–2
Nilson, M. P. 153
Nock, A. D. 97
Norden, E. 170–1
Noreña, C. F. 97
North, J. 24, 83, 201, 209
North, R. 217

Obbink, D. 47–8, 202–4, 208
Ogilvie, R. M. 47
Olson, E. T. 33
Osgood, J. 87
Osiek, C. 149

Padget, A. 149
Päffgen, B. 19
Page, D. L. 55
Pagels, E. 149, 160
Paget, J. C. 201–2, 208, 210
Palmer, R. E. 154
Pardee, N. 140–2
Parke, H. W. 153
Parrinder, G. 218
Parsons, M. C. 123
Parvis, P. 117
Patai, R. 225
Paton, W. R. 87
Pearce, S. 4
Pérez, G. A. 99
Perrin, B. 85, 107, 116
Pettis, J. 78
Pfeiffer, S. 1, 4
Phillips, C. R. I. 47
Piamenta, M. 226
Pitts, A. W. 124–7
Podlecki, A. J. 83–4
Podvin, J.-L. 24
Poletti, J. xii
Pollini, J. 6
Porte, D. 120
Porter, S. E. 61, 123–7, 133, 150–1, 156
Potts, T. F. 6
Poyser, G. H. 113
Preisendanz, K. 39, 49, 135–6, 176
Pritchard, J. B. 39, 109
Prufrock, J. A. 166
Pyysiäinen, I. 34

Quack, J. F. 17
Quarles, C. L. 110

Rajak, T. 24
Reed, W. 217
Regtuit, R. F. 173
Reinink, G. J. 54
Reynolds, B. E. 184
Richards, K. H. 86
Riggs, C. 2, 5, 10
Ripat, P. 84, 88
Robinson, E. 218
Robinson, J. M. 189
Robinson, S. E. 54
Rolfe, J. C. 87–8, 91–2, 100

Roloff, J. 191
Ross, R. C. 86
Rothschild, C. 165
Rousseau, J. J. 39
Roussel, P. 23-7
Rusch, A. 23

Sampaolo, V. 8, 10-13, 16
Sampley, P. 124
Samuel, A. Y. 222, 229
Sanders, J. A. x
Sansone, D. 93
Schaff, P. 156
Schmidt, C. 189
Schmidt, T. E. 197
Schmithals, W. 191-2
Schneider, B. 180
Schottroff, L. 144
Schrage, W. 143-5
Schreiner, T. R. 149
Schrijvers, P. H. 10
Schwartz, D. R. 100
Schweizer, E. 170, 181
Scott, E. F. 168
Scott, K. 96
Scurlock, J. A. 40
Seeberg, A. 185
Shackleton Bailey, D. R. 5
Shaked, S. 178
Shank, M. 153, 160
Shanks, H. 224
Shaw, B. 210
Shaw, G. B. 149
Shneidman, E. S. 63
Shoemaker, S. 218
Shultz, R. 63
Sigountos, J. G. 153, 160
Slater, E. 219
Sloan, P. T. 100
Smith, C. R. 128-9
Smith, E. 218
Smith, J. Z. 46
Smith, M. 41, 47, 58, 85, 86
Smith, W. D. 55
Smyth, H. W. 182
Sokolowski, F. 39, 103
Solmsen, F. 86
Speyer, W. 144
Spicq, C. 170-1

Spier, J. 6
Spoer, H. H. 225, 228
Stadler, M. 4
Stanley, D. M. 180
Stegmann, H. 217
Stein, R. H. 119
Sterling, G. E. 4
Stern, S. M. 218
Stevens, C. xi-xii
Strodel, S. 174
Sukenik, E. L. 221-3
Sutherland, C. H. V. 97
Sweet, H. B. 188
Swetnam-Burland, M. 3-4, 6, 8-13, 18-19

Tajfel, H. 33-4
Takács, S. A. 1, 16
Talbert, C. H. 100
Tanaseanu-Döbler, I. 83
Taraporewalla, R. 97
Tardieu, M. 84
Taylor, J. E. 159, 220
Theissen, G. 56
Thomas, R. 19
Thompson, R. C. 40
Thompson, W. G. 120
Tiede, D. L. 97
Timmerman, C. 228
Tobin, V. A. 152
Tomlin, R. S. O. 137
Towner, P. H. 166, 184, 186-7
Tran tam Tinh, V. 8, 152
Trever, J. C. 217, 219-20, 223-4, 228-9
Tristram, H. B. 218-19
Tröger, K. W. 191
Trumbower, J. A. 111
Turner, J. C. 33-4
Twelftree, G. H. 39

Ulansey, D. 126, 150, 155-6
Uro, R. 34

van der Horst, P. W. 53
van der Ploeg, J. 228
van Eck, E. 38
van Haarlem, W. 19
van Henten, J. W. 101
Vanhoozer, K. J. 184
van Kooten, G. 101

Várhelyi, Z. 17
Vernant, J.-P. 42
Versluys, M. J. 1–2, 6–7, 15, 24
Versnel, H. S. 48, 51, 56
Veymiers, R. 1, 8, 15, 16, 32
Victor, U. 201
Vidman, L. 37
Vittozzi, G. C. 1, 3, 7, 20
Vlastos, G. 84–5
von Soden, H. 168
Vos, H. F. 155

Wace, H. 156
Wakker, G. C. 174
Wallace, A. xi
Wallis, W. B. 167
Walzer, R. 208
Wardle, D. 96
Warmington, E. H. 113
Watson, D. F. 123–4, 128, 130
Watson, L. 147
Wedderburn, A. J. M. 191
Weiner, S. 219
Weiss, B. 191
Wendel, C. 175
West, D. S. 59
Wellesley, K. 94
Wheeler, B. 229
White, J. L. 158
Whitmarsh, T. 202, 211–12, 214
Wight, K. 19
Wild, R. A. 26, 36
Williams, G. 1

Williams, R. 38
Williamson, J. B. 63
Wilson, O. R. B. 193
Wilson, R. McL. 191
Wilson, S. G. 23, 26
Winiarczyk, M. 202
Winter, B. W. 144–5
Wissowa, G. 154
Witherington III, B. 123
Witt, R. E. 37
Wojaczek, G. 174
Wolmarans, J. L. P. 106
Woolf, G. 24
Worchel, S. 33
Wormell, D. E. W. 153
Wright, A. Z. xi, 61, 70
Wright, G. E. 223, 226
Wright Knust, J. 16–17
Wright, R. A. xii, 210
Wünsch, R. 39, 146

Yadin, Y. 222
Yarbro, A. 150
Yoon, D. I. 61
Younger, K. L. 151

Zalta, E. N. 33
Zenos, A. C. 156
Ziebarth, E. 23
Ziesler, J. A. 146
Zimmermann, R. 146
Zuntz, G. 150
Zwemer, S. M. 225, 227

Index of References

HEBREW BIBLE/OLD TESTAMENT

Genesis
1	70
3	71
4	70
16:7	103
19:15	103
21:17	103
22:11-15	103
32:1	103
40–41	102

Exodus
10:21-23	107
10:22	107
12:23	139
15:20	157
19:18	108
24	118
27:16	108
34:29	118

Leviticus
9:22-24	76
9:24	76

Numbers
24:17	98, 101, 120

Deuteronomy
4:7-8	133
32:17	52, 54

Joshua
1:6	70

Judges
4:4	157

1 Samuel
2:26	105

2 Samuel
4:10	104

1 Kings
10:1-2	105
10:25	105
18:37-39	76
18:39	76
19:11-12	108

2 Kings
1:9	78
1:10	73, 75
1:12	73, 75–6
2:11-12	78
22:14	157

Nehemiah
6:14	157

Job
9:6	108

Psalms
2:7	70
18:7	109
51	182
72:10-11	105
74:13-17	65
77:18	109
91:6	52
96:5	52
97:4	109
106:37	52, 54

Isaiah
6:1-6	80–1

6:4	109	1:22-23	100, 102
7:14	100	1:23	108
8:3	157	2:1-2	101
13:21	52	2:2	101
24:20	109	2:5-6	102
34:14	52	2:10-11	101
40:9	105	2:11	105
52:7	105	2:12	101
60	105	2:13	102
60:5-6	105	2:15	102
61:1	105	2:17-18	102
65	52, 56	2:19-20	102
65:3	52	2:22-23	102
65:4	225	2:23	102
65:11	52	3:13-17	119
66:24	99	3:17	70
		4:1-11	71
Ezekiel		4:3	71
21:13	182–3	4:6	71
21:18	182	4:11	184
47:19	217	5–7	70
48:28	217	5:21-26	70
		5:27-30	70
Daniel		5:33-37	138
7:9-10	119	7:1-12	70
10:6	118–19	7:22	146
		8:29	57
Joel		8:31	40
3:16	109	9:20-22	72
		10:1-4	74
Micah		10:5-6	166
4:7	105	15:18	70
4:8	105	16:1-8	112
		17:1-8	76, 119
Haggai		17:2	118
2:6	109	17:5	70
		17:6	74, 76
Zechariah		25:41	57
13:2	40	27	112
14	111	27:19	102, 109, 182
14:4-5	111	27:45	107
		27:51-54	110
NEW TESTAMENT		27:51-53	110–11
		27:51	108, 111
Matthew		27:52-53	110–11
1:1	70	27:53	110–11
1:18	70, 100	27:54	111
1:20	100	27:56	73
1:21	100	27:62-66	112

28:1-8	112	5:7	56, 106
28:2-7	184	5:8	40
28:2-4	112	5:9	56, 106
28:2	108, 111, 186	5:10	56
28:3	78	5:12-13	106
28:4	112	5:12	40
28:6	186	5:13	40
28:9	112, 118	5:15	40
28:16-20	112, 118, 188	5:16	40
28:17	118	5:17	106
28:19	118	5:18	40
		5:25-43	72
Mark		5:35-43	77
1:1	70	6:7	40, 54
1:7	180	6:13	40
1:9-11	119	6:14-29	54
1:12-13	71	6:14-16	58
1:13	70, 184	6:49	58
1:20	73	7:24-30	57
1:21-28	55, 77	7:25	40
1:23	40	7:26	40
1:24-25	55	7:29	40
1:24	55	7:30	40
1:26	40	8:11	107
1:27	40, 55	8:31	77
1:29-30	77	9	40
1:32-34	54	9:2-8	73–4, 76, 119
1:32	40	9:2	78
1:34	40	9:3	118
1:39	40, 54	9:4	76
1:40	72	9:5-7	77
3:11	40, 54	9:7	70
3:13-19	73–5, 78	9:8	81
3:15	40, 54	9:14-29	57
3:16	74	9:17	40
3:17	74	9:20	40
3:22-30	54	9:22	57
3:22-23	54	9:25	40, 57
3:22	40, 58	9:26	58
3:30	40, 54	9:27	58
4:38	57	9:29	57
4:40	57	9:38-39	146
4:41	57	9:38	40, 54, 58
5	71	10:9	77
5:1-20	56, 58, 106	10:32-45	78
5:1	56	10:35-40	73
5:2-3	225	11:14	106
5:2	40	11:20-21	106
5:4	55, 106	13:1-37	78

13:1-9	77	4:3	71
14:32-42	77	4:9	71
14:32-41	74	5:1-11	73
14:38-40	77	5:12	72
14:71	140	6:12-16	74
15	110	8:29	40
15:27	78	8:31	57
15:33	107	8:43-48	72
15:38	108, 110	9:28-36	76, 119
15:39	109–10	9:28-29	78
15:40	73	9:29	74, 81, 118
16:1	185	9:35	70
16:3	186	9:49	146
16:5-8	184	9:51-56	73–5
16:5	112, 186	9:51	74, 167
16:6-7	185	9:52-56	75, 77–8
16:6	185–7	9:52	74
16:7	112, 187	9:53	74
16:8	187–8, 190	9:54	74–5
16:9	40, 183, 187, 194	10:17	146
16:12	183, 187–8, 192	19:12-24	38
16:14-18	188	19:13	56
16:14	183, 188, 194	19:27	38
16:17	40, 146	22:25-26	104
16:19	167, 188, 194	23:5	140
		23:44-45	107
Luke		23:44	107
1:8-20	102	23:45	108
1:16-17	103	23:47	182
1:21-23	102	24	185
1:24-25	102	24:1-10	112
1:26-33	103	24:1	188
1:35	70	24:4	112, 118
1:39-41	103	24:6	186
1:46-55	103	24:13-27	118
1:57-66	103	24:13	188
1:67-79	103	24:15-16	118
2	103	24:22	185
2:1	103	24:23	186
2:2-25	184	24:24	185
2:8-20	103	24:29	188
2:10-11	104	24:31	118, 188
2:36-38	157	24:33	188
2:40-52	105	24:34	184
2:52	105	24:36	188
3:1-20	103	24:39	59, 121, 183
3:21-22	119	24:41-43	188
3:22	70	24:44-49	112
4:1-13	71	24:50-53	112

24:50-51	117, 188	4:27-28	195
24:50	188	4:30	146
24:51	167, 188	5:29-32	195
		7:55-56	118
John		8:9-24	58
1:14	190	8:12	58
1:29-34	119	9:3-8	118
1:31	180	9:11	124
9:2	71	9:13-14	131
10:9	72	9:15	124
20:5-7	186	9:17	184
20:11-29	112	9:21	131
20:11-17	186	9:22	131
20:12-13	184	9:26	131
20:12	186	9:28-30	123, 125
20:14-16	118	9:29	131
20:17	117	9:30	124
20:18	186	9:40	146
20:19-31	183	10:34-43	181, 195
20:19-23	118	10:38	104
20:26-29	118	10:40	183
20:28-29	118	11:19-26	124
20:28	112	11:25	124
21:1	183	12:21-23	98
21:14	183	13:26-41	195
21:22-23	188	13:31	184
		15	133
Acts		15:22-29	6
1:1-11	187	16:18	146
1:2	167, 188	17:16-34	130
1:3-8	112	17:19	130
1:3	188	17:22-23	86
1:6-11	74	17:23	86
1:6	188	17:31	195
1:9-11	112, 118	18:26	163
1:9	118, 188	19:13-17	58
1:10-11	184	21:39	124
1:11	167	22:3	124
1:22	167	22:21	124
2:22-36	181, 195	23:12	140
3:6	146	23:14	140
3:11-26	195	23:21	140
3:11-15	181	26:16	184
3:16	146	26:23	195
4:7	146	28:11	78
4:8-12	195		
4:9	104	Romans	
4:10-12	181	1:3-6	195
4:10	146	1:3	190, 195

1:4	118, 181	2 Corinthians	
1:14-15	124	4:16	71
3	133	13:13	148
3:2	133		
3:4	182	Galatians	
3:5	133	1:1	134
3:7	133	1:6	131–2
3:28	133	1:7	132
4:25	191	1:8-9	139, 142, 148
7	129	1:11-12	131
8:3	190	1:13–2:14	131
8:15	143	1:13	131
9:3	140, 143	1:14	131
10:7	146	1:15-16	124
10:13	147	1:15	131
12:2	71	1:21	124
12:4-5	163	2:2	187
12:14	138–9, 148	2:8	132
15:18-21	124	2:9	124
15:24	187	2:11	132
15:28	187	2:16	132
16:20	147	3:13	144
		3:28	163
1 Corinthians		4:6	143
1:15	147	4:8	54
1:22	83	4:12	131
2:1-9	181	5:12	132
2:1-5	129	6:14	131
2:13	130	6:17	131
5:5	138–9, 148	6:18	147
6:11	147		
10:20–22	54	Ephesians	
10:20	54	1:20-21	181
12:2-3	139, 144–5, 148	3:7-9	124
12:3	139, 145, 147–8	3:10	184
15:3-7	195	4:8-10	110
15:3	71	4:25	138
15:5-8	184–5		
15:14	71	Philippians	
15:20	111, 146	2:5-11	181
15:25	167	2:6-11	195, 198–9
15:44	183	2:6	120, 146, 198
15:47	146	2:8	198
15:50	183	2:10-11	167
16:21-22	139, 143, 148	2:11	198
16:22	146	3:5-6	133
16:23	148	3:7-8	133
		4:23	147

Colossians		Titus	
1:18	111	1:3	133, 193
2:8-15	181	1:9-16	191
3:15	163	2	149
		2:1-10	149, 160
1 Thessalonians		2:1	160
2:4	133	2:2-3	161, 163
4:16-17	118	2:2	160–1
5:28	148	2:3-5	149–50, 160
		2:3-4	160
2 Thessalonians		2:3	160, 162
1:10	133	2:4	161
		2:5-6	161
1 Timothy		2:5	160–1
1:3-4	191	2:6-8	161
1:6-7	191	2:9-10	161
1:11	133, 193	2:9	161
1:13	193	2:12	161, 191
1:16	193	3:7	193
1:19-20	191	3:9	191
2:1-7	187		
2:5-7	195	Philemon	
2:7	193	25	147
2:12	163		
2:13	193	Hebrews	
2:14	193	1:3	195
3:10	193	2:14	197
3:11	138	9:26	180
3:16	133, 165–6, 169, 171, 179–80, 183, 188–9, 191–3, 198–9	James	
		3:8-10	138
4:1-3	191	5:12	138
4:7	191	5:14	146
4:12	138		
4:14	193	1 Peter	
6:3-5	191	1:12	184
6:20	191	1:19	199
		1:20	180
2 Timothy		3:18-22	195
1:9	193	3:18-19	110, 165, 181, 191
1:10	193	3:19	185
1:11	193	3:21-22	181
1:16	193	4:6	110
2:14	191		
2:16-18	191	2 Peter	
2:18	192	2:4	185
3:6-9	191		
4:3-4	191	1 John	
4:17	193	1:2	180, 190

3:5	180	Tobit	
3:8	180	3:8	52
4:18	63	3:17	52
		6:7	52
Jude		6:13	52
6	185	6:14	52
		6:15	52
Revelation		6:17	52
1:12-16	119	8:3	52
2:20	157		
3:12	77	PSEUDEPIGRAPHA	
9:20	54		
16:14	40	Apocalypse of Adam	
18:2	52	1:4	54
18:12	40		
22:4	77	1 Enoch	
		19:1	53
APOCRYPHA		99:7	53-4
Baruch		Jubilees	
4:7	52	10:1	40
4:35	52	22:16–23	54
1 Esdras		Odes of Solomon	
4:13-32	157	42:10	110
		42:11	110
Judith			
8:7	158	Sibylline Oracles	
		3.334–6	101
1 Maccabees		8.47	54
1:48	40	8.384	54
9:58-73	217	8.386	54
		8.393	54
2 Maccabees			
3:22-26	79	Testament of Benjamin	
3:25	79	5:2	40
3:26	79		
9:4	99	Testament of Job	
9:5-9	99	3:3-4	54
9:9	99		
9:10	99	Testament of Levi	
9:12	99	10:3	108
10:29-30	79		
10:30	79	Testament of Reuben	
		5:1	158
Susanna			
1:2	158	Vita Prophetarum	
1:7	158	12:12	108

Qumran

1QS
4.21-22	40

11Q5
19.13-15	40

Babylonian Talmud
Pesahim
6a	157

Yoma
39b	108

Jerusalem Talmud
Sota
6.3	108

Philo
De vita contemplativa
28-9	159
32-3	159

De fuga et inventione
De gigantibus
6-12	53
16	53, 55

Hypothetica
11.14-15	159
11.14	159

Legatio ad Gaium
65	53

De somniis
1.135-41	53

De specialibus legibus
2.33	161
3.31	158

De vita Mosis
1.123	108

Josephus
Antiquities
2.11-86	102
7.142	161
8.45-49	53, 57
13.314	53
13.317	53
13.415-16	53
17.1	53
18.195-202	99
18.195	119
19.343-4	99
19.345	99
19.346	99, 119
19.350	99

Jewish War
1.23	98
1.82	53
1.84	53
1.110-12	158
1.599	53
1.607	53
1.656	100
2.20	158
3.400-2	98
3.351-3	102
4.618	104
4.624-5	98
4.656	104
5.69	106
5.135	106
5.207-12	108
6.47	53
6.289-91	98
6.293-6	108
6.312-15	98
6.313	98
7.185	53, 57

Apostolic Fathers
Epistle of Barnabas
5:1	183
12:9	180
12:10	180
15:8	188
15:9	180, 189

Diognetus
11.3	191

Index of References

Ignatius
Smyrnaeans
3.2   59

Martyrdom of Polycarp
9   144

CLASSICAL WRITERS/CHRISTIAN WRITERS

Acts of Pilate
11:1-2   107

Acts of Thomas
10   110–11
32   110–11
156   111

Aelius Lampridius
Commodus Antoninus
16.1–2   88

Aeschylus
Agamemnon
393   182

Choephori
125   41

Persae
354   41
620   41
630   41, 49
642   41

Apocryphon of James (NHC I, 2)
2.19–20   189
15.5–6   189
15.14–15   189
15.35   189

Appian
Bella civilia
2.115–16   88

Apuleius
Metamorphoses
9.27–8   5
11.11   18
11.22   5
11.27   6
11.28–30   4

Aristotle
Poetica
1449b   65

Rhetorica
1.2   128
1356a   128–30, 132
1356b   133
1358b   129
1377ba   131

Arrian
Anabasis
1.24   158

Athenagoras
Legatio pro Christianis
1   212
2   212
4   213
5–6   213
5   213
6   213
11   213
13   213

Book of Thomas the Contender (NHC II, 7)
138.24   189

Callimachus
Hymnus in Apollinem
1   109

Cassius Dio
Historia romana
44.18.1–4   88
51.16.3–5   17
61.35.1   92
61.36.2   92
64.8.1   98
66.1   97
66.2   98

Cicero
De divinatione
2.40   96

De natura deorum
1.3	206
1.85	204–5
1.86	205
1.115–6	205
1.121	205
1.123	206
2.71	86

De republica
1.41.61	113
6.22	107

Claudius Ptolemy
Centiloquy
§100	101

Clement of Alexandria
Stromata
5.14.127	41

De AgriCultura
83	155

Descensus Christi ad Inferos
5:1	109
7:1	112

Dialogue of the Savior (NHC III, 5)
120.1	189

Dio Chrysostom
Orationes
33.1	125
33.5	125
33.48	126

Diodorus Siculus
Bibliotheca historica
1.25.6	152

Diogenes Laertius
Vitae philosophorum
4.64	107
7.151	43
8.31-32	40
10.9	203
10.10	203
10.123	204
10.123–4	204

Dionysius of Halicarnassus
Antiquitates romanae
2.56.6	107
2.63.2–4	114

Ennius
Annales
Frag. 64	113
Frags. 114–15	113
Frag. 116	113
Frag. 118	113
Frags. 119–20	113

Epicurus
Epistula ad Menoeceum
Apud Diog. Laert.	204
Apud Diog. Laert.	204

Peri Physeōs
12	208

Epiphanius
Panarion
26.20.5	192

Euripides
Alcestis
843–4	41
1003	41
1140	41

Bacchae
585–93	109
699–701	154
1114	154
1124	154

Eusebius
Historia ecclesiastica
2.7.1	109
3.33	199

Gospel of Peter
5:10-11	188
5:15	107
5:18	107

10:39-40	112	Justin Martyr	
10:41	110	*1 Apologia*	
		3	212
Hephaestion		4	212
Enchiridion de Metris		5	212
62.5-6	175	6	212
		9	212
Herodotus		10	212
Historiae		13	212
1.19.3	153	20-3	212
1.67.2-3	153	20	212
6.98.3	108	21.1-3	117
		24	212
Hesiod		59-60	212
Opera et dies			
121-6 41-2, 45		*2 Apologia*	
155	49	3	212
Theogonia		*Letter of Peter to Philip* (NHC VIII, 2)	
669	49	140.15-23	189
Homer		Livy	
Ilias		*Ab urbe condita*	
2.353	84	1.16.1	114
2.786-7	103	1.16.2-3	115
3.121	103	1.16.3	118
8.170-71	84	1.16.6-7	115
13.821-3	84	1.16.7	118
18.61	40		
18.182	103	Lucan	
23.103-4	43	*De bello civili*	
		161	153
Odyssea			
4.540	49	Lucian of Samosata	
10.190-91	50	*Alexander pseudomantis*	
11.475-76	43	1-2	201
24.15-204	44	7	101
		17	201
Homeric Hymns		25	201
33	78	38	201
		45-7	201
Hymn to Demeter		61	201
35	49		
		Philopseudes	
Jerome		9	58
Epistula		16	55
120	108		

Martial
Epigrams
2.14	5
8.81	5
10.48	5

Martyrdom and Ascension of Isaiah
9:17	110

Nonius Marcellus
De compendiosa doctrina
120.1	113

Origen
Commentarium in evangelium Matthaei
12:36	78

Contra Celsum
1.1	211
2.4	211
3.14	211
4.71	215
8.2–5	211
8.17–21	211
8.55	211
8.65–68	211
8.69	211

De principiis
i. prol. 8	59

Ovid
Fasti
2.478	115, 117
2.487	113
2.493–95	115
2.493	107
2.505–9	115
2.511	115

Metamorphoses
1.5–9	65
1.736–46	10
9.140	67
14.811–28	115
14.811	115
14.814	113
15.671–2	109

Paterculus, Marcus Velleius
Historiae
2.41.1	87, 100
2.57.1–2	88, 109
2.59.6	90
2.71.2	89

Philodemus
De libertate dicendi
Frag. 6	203

De pietate
28	203
30	203
31	203
32	203

Philostratus
Vita Apollonii
1.7	125
3.38	55, 57
4.20	55, 57

Pistis Sophia
1.1	189

Plato
Apologia
18C	202
23D	202
24C	202

Cratylus
398A	41
398B–C	42
407E	103

Leges
717B–718A	42

Phaedo
107D–108B	42
244B	153, 160

Respublica
364B	51
427B	42
469A	42
540C	42

Symposium		
202D–203A	42	
655A	44	
Timaeus		
42D	45	
61C	45	
69C–D	45	
90A–C	42	
90A	45	
Pliny the Elder		
Naturalis historia		
2.30.97	88	
15.83	96	
28.4.19	137	
Pliny the Younger		
Epistulae		
10.96	144	
10.96.2	210	
10.96.3–4	210	
10.96.7	210	
10.96.8	210	
10.96.10	211	
Plutarch		
Adversus Colotem		
1119E–F	206	
1125E–F	207	
Alexander		
73–4	85	
75.1–2	85	
Antonius		
11.3	89	
16.4	89	
22.2	90	
33.2	89	
34.1	89	
55.3	90	
60.2–3	89	
60.2	108	
63.6	109	
Brutus		
36–7	46	
37	46	

Caesar		
1.2	87	
49.11	45	
63.1–2	88	
63.3	88	
63.5–6	88, 102, 109	
63.6	88	
63.7	88	
68.2	88	
69.3–4	107	
69.4	88	
Camillus		
21.2	46	
Consolatio ad Apollonium		
109C–D	22	
Crassus		
22.4	46	
De defectu oraculorum		
415A	44	
415B	42	
417B	42	
418B	57	
418E	56	
419F	45	
431B	43	
431E	43	
De E apud Delphos		
393E–394C	4, 8	
De facie in orbe lunae		
941F	86	
943A	45	
944C	45	
De genio Socratis		
575A–598F	86	
577D	86	
580A–B	86	
582B	86	
586F	86	
591C	40, 45	
591D	45	
591E	45	
591F	45	

593C–D	86	*Publicola*	
593D–E	45	13.4	46
594E	86		
		Quaestiones romanae et graecae	
De Iside et Osiride		§51, 277A	44
357A–D	12		
360E–F	45	*Romulus*	
378A	4, 8	27.5–6	115
382A–C	17	27.6	107
382F–384A	13	27.8	116
		28.1–3	116
De superstitione			
164E–171F	85	Polybius	
164E	85	*Historiae*	
165B–C	209	3.112.8–9	87
165B	85	6.56.6	86
165E–F	86		
166A–B	86	*Protevangelium of James*	
167A	86	18:1	217
167B	209		
167D–E	86	Ps.-Apollodorus	
169F	209	*Bibliotheca*	
171A	209	2.4.8–2.7.7	67
171B–E	209	2.6.1–2.7.7	68
		3.16.1–Epitome 1.23	68
De tranquillitate animi		Epilogue 1.24	69
474B	41		
		Ps.-Clementines	
Dion		*Libri recognitionum*	
2 45–6		II.13	58
12	45	II.15	58
Galba		Ps.-Phocylides	
23.4	94	100–102	53
24.2–3	94	100–101	49, 53
		149	53, 58
Non posse suaviter vivi secundum Epicurum		150	53, 58
1100D	203		
1101B–C	206	Ps.-Plato	
1101C–D	207	*Axiochus*	
1101D–E	207	364A	120
1102A	207		
1102C	207	Seneca	
		Epistulae	
Parallelae graecae et romanae		123.16	209
308A	44		
		Servius	
Pelopidas		*Ad Virilii Aeneidem commentarii*	
31.2–3	107	6.763	113

Index of References

Sextus Empiricus
Adversus mathematicos
9.74   43

Socrates Scholasticus
Historia ecclesiastica
7.15   156

Sophia of Jesus Christ (NHC III, 4)
91.10-13   189
91.10-12   192
119.8-11   189

Statius
Silvae
3.2.107-16   5

Thebais
7.65   109

Strabo
Geographica
1.2.8   86
14.5.13   125
14.5.14   125-6
14.5.15   125
14.14   126

Suetonius
Augustus
6   90
29.3   90
31.1   90
91.1   90
91.2   90
93   90
94.1   100
94.2   90
94.3   89, 102
94.4   89, 102
94.5-6   90
94.7   90
94.8-9   90
94.11   90
95-6   90
96.2   90
97.1   90
97.3   91
99.1-2   91

Caligula
12.1   91
57.1-3   91
57.3   92
57.4   92
58.2-3   92
59   92, 109

Claudius
7   92
22   92
46   92, 98

Galba
1   93, 106
4.1   93
4.2   93
4.3   94
8.2   94
9.2   94
9.4   94
18.1-3   94
18.1   94
18.2   108
19.1   94

Julius
1.3   87
6.1   87
7.2   87, 100
81.1   88
81.2   88
81.3   88, 102, 109
81.4   88
88.1   88, 117

Nero
6.1-2   92
7.1   92
16.2   210
19.2-20.2   94
23   94
34.4   92
36.1-2   93, 102
36.1   92
36.2   93, 102
40.2   93
40.3   94
46.1   93

48.2	93	16.14	93
56	93		
		Historiae	
Otho		1.10	96
4.1	94	1.62.2–3	95
4.4–5	94	2.1	96
4.4	94	2.78.2	96
6.1–2	95	2.78.3	96
7.2	95	2.50.2	94
8.3	95	5.13	108
9.3	95		
		Tertullian	
Tiberius		*Ad nationes*	
14.1	91	3.2.9	117
14.2	91		
14.3–4	91	Theophilus	
19	91	*Ad Autolycum*	
67.1–4	91	3.27	117
69	91		
74	91, 108	Thucydides	
75.1	91	*Historiae*	
		3.89.1–2	108
Vespasianus		7.50.4	85
4.1–2	96		
4.5	96, 101	*Treatise on the Resurrection* (NHC I, 4)	
5.2	96	45.39–46.2	192
5.4	96		
5.6	96	Varro	
5.7	94, 96–7	*De lingua Latina*	
7.1	97	5–10	113
7.2–3	97	7.6	113
25	97		
		Vergil	
Vitellius		*Aeneid*	
3.2	95, 102	1.275–7	114
8.2	95	1.286–9	114
9.1	95	1.290	114
10	95	6.763	113
14.5	95	6.777–89	114
18	95	6.789–92	114
Tacitus		*Georgica*	
Annales		1.467–8	88, 107
2.69	51	1.498–9	114
11.11	92	1.503–4	114
14.9	92		
14.22	93, 98	Xenophon	
15.44	209	*Hellenica*	
15.47	93	4.7.4–7	84

Index of References

INSCRIPTIONS AND PAPYRI

L'Année Épigraphique
106	103

BGU
628	109

British Museum Papyri
10685C	40

Corpus Inscriptionum Iudaeae/Palaestinae
III, 2335	106

Corpus Inscriptionum Latinarum
III, 30	106
XI, 4639	51
XIV, 24	103

Defixionum Tabellae
22	52
25	52
26	52
29	52
30	52
31	52
32	52
33	52
34	52
35	52, 140
37	140
38	52
51	141
111–12	136
198	52
234	52
235	52
237	52
238	52
239	52
240	52
242	52, 56
249	52
271	52, 56

Defixionum Tabellae Atticae
99	49, 52
102	52

Greek Magical Amulets
52	57

Inscriptions de Delos
1403	29
1412	29
1416	29
1417	31
1434	29
1435	29
1440	29
1442	29
1452	29
2039	30–1, 33, 37
2075	30, 37
2076	30, 37
2077	30–3, 37
2078	29–31, 33, 37
2079	30–1, 33, 37
2080	30–1, 33, 37
2081	30–1, 33, 37
2085–86	30, 37
2085	37
2086	37
2087–88	29–30, 37
2087	36
2617	30
2618	30

Inscriptiones Graecae
XI, 4 510–1349	25
XI, 4 129	26
XI, 4 1215	30–1
XI, 4 1216	27
XI, 4 1217	27, 31
XI, 4 1220	27
XI, 4 1221	27
XI, 4 1223	28
XI, 4 1224	30
XI, 4 1225	30
XI, 4 1226	28, 31, 33, 37
XI, 4 1227	28
XI, 4 1228	28, 32, 37
XI, 4 1229	28, 37
XI, 4 1230	27
XI, 4 1243	30, 33
XI, 4 1247	27
XI, 4 1249	30, 37
XI, 4 1250	30, 37

XI, 4 1252	27	IV.369–70	50
XI, 4 1290	27, 31, 33	IV.396–7	50
XI, 4 1299	25–7, 35	IV.435	49
XI, 4 1305	33	IV.442–8	50
XI, 4 1307	31	IV.446	49
		IV.458–62	50

Inscriptiones Graeca ad Res Romanas Pertinentes

I, 901	104	IV.1167–1226	177
III, 719	104	IV.1170	178
IV, 309	104	IV.1171	178
		IV.1180	178
		IV.1183	178
		IV.1200–1213	177

Inscriptiones Latinae Selectae

107	104	IV.1247–48	57
113	104	IV.1254	57
8759a	106	IV.1390–98	50
		IV.1474–5	50
		IV.1786	57

Inscriptions de Pergamon

336	25	IV.1849–50	49
		IV.1968–70	50
		IV.2031	50

Orientis Graeci Inscriptiones Selectae

458	104	IV.2060	50
655, iii, 36	96	IV.2647	58
		IV.3015	57
		IV.3019	146

Papyri Berlin

3008	152	IV.3040	57
		V.1–53	57
		V.304	48

Papyri Bremner-Rhind

1.9	151	V.334	50
		V.370–446	57
		VII.348–58	57

Papyri Graecae Magicae

I.1	49	VII.394	48
I.11–19	177	VII.540–78	57
I.11	177	VII.664–85	57
I.12–19	176	VIII.81	49
I.26	177	IX	48
I.29	177	XII.494	50
I.42	49	XIII.749–59	57
I.248	49	XV	50
I.253	49	XVI	48, 51
II.1–2	179	XVI.1	51
II.5–6	179	XVI.9	51
IV.245–7	49	XVI.17–18	51
IV.249	49	XVI.25	51
IV.286–95	53	XVI.34	51
IV.296–466	49	XVI.43	51
IV.332–3	49	XVI.54	51
IV.361	50	XVI.61	51
IV.368	50	XVI.67	51
		XVI.73	51

XIXa	48, 50
XIXa.15	50
XIXa.151	50
XX	48
XXXa	48
XXXIa	48
XXXIb	48
XXXVI.1–35	48
XXXVI.138	49
XXXVI.146	49
XXXVI.231	48
XL	48
LXII.24–46	57
CXI	48

Pap.Graec.Monacum
Inv 216	48

Papyri Herculaneum
1077 18	208

Papyri Oslo
26	104

Papyri Oxyrhynchus
215, lines 4–5	203

Papyri Rylands
601	104

Recueil des Inscriptions concernant les Cultes Isiaques
101/0424	29
111/0102	25
202/0101	26
202/0116	26
202/0117	26
202/0120	26
202/0122	26
202/0123	26
202/0125	26
202/0126	26
202/0127	26
202/0128	26
202/0129	26
202/0130	26
202/0131	26
202/0281	29
202/0421	29
202/0422	29
202/0423	29
202/0426	29
202/0427	29
202/0428	29
202/0433	29
205/0104	25

Sammelbuch griechischer Urkunde aus Ägypten
401	109

Select Papyri
211	120

Supplementum epigraphicum graecum
42.147	25

Survey of Greek Defixiones
1	48
2	48
151	51
152	52
153	52
160	52
152	52

Sylloge Inscriptionum Graecarum
390.27	120

MISCELLANEOUS LITERATURE

Hymn of Shulgi
62–5	109

Qur'ān
19.16	218
19.22	218

www.ingramcontent.com/pod-product-compliance
Lightning Source LLC
Chambersburg PA
CBHW062121300426
44115CB00012BA/1766